The Hamlyn Concise Guide to
AXIS AIRCRAFT OF WORLD WAR II

D0924295

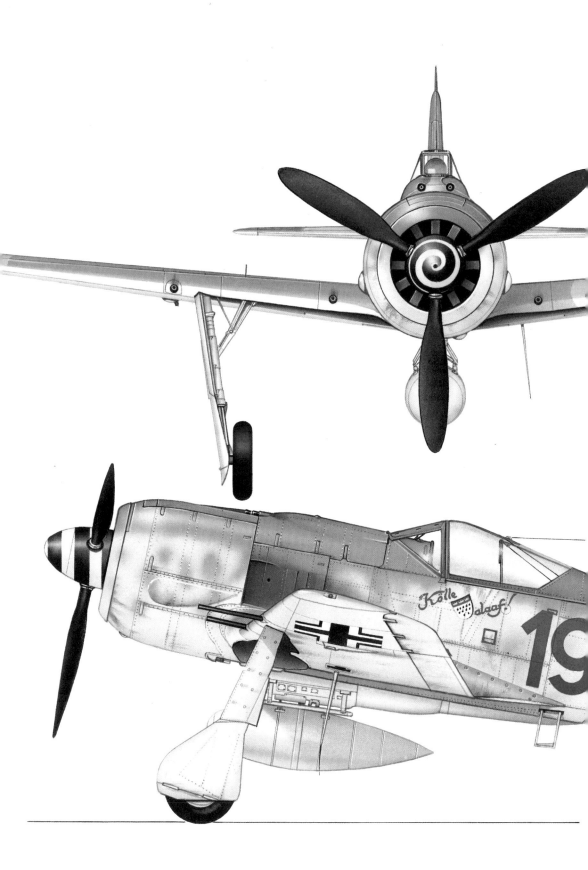

The Hamlyn Concise Guide to
AXIS AIRCRAFT OF WORLD WAR II

David Mondey

Bounty
Books

First published in Great Britain in 1984 by Temple Press

This paperback edition published 2006 by Bounty Books,
a division of Octopus Publishing Group Ltd
2–4 Heron Quays, London E14 4JP

ISBN-13: 978-0-753714-60-7
ISBN-10: 0-753714-60-4

A CIP catalogue record for this book is available
from the British Library

Printed and bound in China

PICTURE ACKNOWLEDGEMENTS

Page 9: US Navy. **29:** John MacClancy Collection. **36:** Imperial War Museum. **38:** Imperial War Museum. **41:** MARS, Lincs. **43:** John MacClancy Collection. **44:** John MacClancy Collection. **75:** John MacClancy Collection. **84:** John MacClancy Collection. **75:** John MacClancy Collection. **84:** John MacClancy Collection. **89:** MARS, Lincs. **90:** Imperial War Museum. **91:** MARS, Lincs. **92:** John MacClancy Collection. **104:** MARS, Lincs. **107:** MARS, Lincs. **112:** John MacClancy Collection. **113:** MARS, Lincs. **116:** John MacClancy Collection. **118:** Imperial War Museum. **119:** John MacClancy Collection. **121:** US Air Force. **122:** John MacClancy Collection. **123:** John MacClancy Collection. **125:** John MacClancy Collection. **136:** US Navy. **154:** Macchi. **155:** Macchi. **157:** Macchi. **158:** Macchi. **164:** John MacClancy Collection. **165:** John MacClancy Collection. **168:** MARS, Lincs. **169:** John MacClancy Collection. **175:** John MacClancy Collection. **176:** MARS, Lincs/MARS, Lincs. **178:** John MacClancy Collection. **185:** US Air Force. **188:** US Air Force. **196:** US Air Force/US Air Force.

CONTENTS

Aichi B7A Ryusei **8**
Aichi D3A **9**
Aichi E13A **10**
Aichi E16A1 Zuiun **11**
Arado Ar 66 **12**
Arado Ar 67 and Ar 68 **12**
Arado Ar 96 **14**
Arado Ar 196 **15**
Arado Ar 197 **17**
Arado Ar 232 **17**
Arado Ar 234 Blitz **18**
Avia B.534 **20**
Blohm and Voss Bv 138 **22**
Blohm and Voss Bv 222 Wiking **24**
Breda Ba.65 **25**
Breda Ba.88 Lince **27**
Bücker Bü 131 Jungmann **28**
Bücker Bü 133 Jungmeister **29**
Bücker Bü 181 Bestmann **29**
CRDA Cant Z.501 Gabbiano **30**
CRDA Cant Z.506 **31**
CRDA Cant Z.1007 **32**
Caproni Ca 100 **34**
Caproni Ca 133 **34**
Caproni Bergamaschi Ca 135 **35**
Caproni Bergamaschi Ca 306/Ca 309 **36**
Caproni Bergamaschi Ca 310 series **37**
DFS 230 **38**
Dornier Do 17/Do 215 **39**
Dornier Do 18 **45**
Dornier Do 24 **46**
Dornier Do 217 **48**
Dornier Do 335 Pfeil **51**
Fiat BR.20 Cicogna **52**
Fiat CR.30 **54**

Fiat CR.42 Falco **56**
Fiat G.50 **59**
Fiat G.55 Centauro **60**
Fiat RS.14 **61**
Fieseler Fi 156 Storch **62**
Focke-Wulf Fw 44 Stieglitz **64**
Focke-Wulf Fw 56 Stösser **65**
Focke-Wulf Fw 189 Uhu **66**
Focke-Wulf Fw 190 **68**
Focke-Wulf Fw 200 Condor **73**
Focke-Wulf Ta 152 **75**
Gotha Go 145 **76**
Gotha Go 242 and 244 **77**
Heinkel He 45 **78**
Heinkel He 46 **79**
Heinkel He 49 and He 51 **80**
Heinkel He 59 **81**
Heinkel He 60 **82**
Heinkel He 72 Kadett **83**
Heinkel He 111 **83**
Heinkel He 115 **90**
Heinkel He 162 Salamander **93**
Heinkel He 177 Greif **95**
Heinkel He 219 Uhu **96**
Henschel Hs 123 **98**
Henschel Hs 126 **99**
Henschel Hs 129 **101**
Junkers Ju 52/3m **103**
Junkers Ju 86 **109**
Junkers Ju 87 **111**
Junkers Ju 88 **118**
Junkers Ju 88 Mistel composites **128**
Junkers Ju 188 **128**
Junkers Ju 290 **130**
Junkers Ju 388 **131**

Junkers W34 **132**
Kawanishi E 7K **133**
Kawanishi H6K **134**
Kawanishi H8K **136**
Kawanishi N1K Kyofu **137**
Kawanishi N1K1-J and N1K2-J Shiden **138**
Kawasaki Ki-10 **140**
Kawasaki Ki-32 **140**
Kawasaki Ki-45 **141**
Kawasaki Ki-48 **143**
Kawasaki Ki-61 Hien **144**
Kawasaki Ki-100 **147**
Kawasaki Ki-102 **148**
Kayaba Ka-1 **149**
Klemm KI 35 **149**
Kyushu K11W Shiragiku **150**
Kyushu Q1W Tokai **151**
Letov S 328 **152**
Macchi MC.200 Saetta **153**
Macchi MC.202 Folgore **155**
Macchi MC.205V Veltro **157**
Meridionali Ro.37bis **159**
Meridionali Ro.43/Ro.44 **159**
Messerschmitt Bf 108 **160**
Messerschmitt Bf 109 **161**
Messerschmitt Bf 110 **174**
Messerschmitt Me 163 Komet **181**
Messerschmitt Me 210/410 **184**
Messerschmitt Me 262 **186**
Messerschmitt Me 321/323 **190**
Mitsubishi A5M **192**
Mitsubishi A6M Zero-Sen **194**
Mitsubishi F1M **198**
Mitsubishi G3M **199**
Mitsubishi G4M **200**

Mitsubishi J2M Raiden **203**
Mitsubishi Ki-15 **205**
Mitsubishi Ki-21 **206**
Mitsubishi Ki-30 **208**
Mitsubishi Ki-46 **209**
Mitsubishi Ki-51 **211**
Mitsubishi Ki-57 **212**
Mitsubishi Ki-67 Hiryu **213**
Nakajima A6M2-N **214**
Nakajima B5N **215**
Nakajima B6N Tenzan **217**
Nakajima C6N Saiun **218**
Nakajima J1N Gekko **219**
Nakajima Ki-27 **220**
Nakajima Ki-43 Hayabusa **222**
Nakajima Ki-44 Shoki **224**
Nakajima Ki-49 Donryu **226**
Nakajima Ki-84 Hayate **228**
Nakajima Ki-115 Tsurugi **230**
Piaggio P.108 **231**
Reggiane Re.2000 series **232**
Repülögpégyàr Levente II **235**
Savoia-Marchetti S.M.79 Sparviero **236**
Savoia-Marchetti S.M.81 Pipistrello **240**
Savoia-Marchetti S.M.82 Canguru **242**
Siebel Fh 104/Si 204 **243**
Tachikawa Ki-36/Ki-55 **245**
Tachikawa Ki-54 **246**
Weiss Wm 21 Sólyom **247**
Yokosuka D4Y Suisei **247**
Yokosuka MXY7 Ohka **250**
Yokosuka P1Y Ginga **251**

Index **252**

Aichi B7A Ryusei

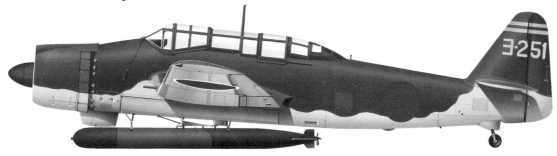

Aichi B7A2 Ryusei of the Yokosuka Kokutai

History and notes

The requirement for a large torpedo/dive-bomber for operation from a new, larger class of aircraft-carrier in 1941 caused the Imperial Japanese navy to draw up the specification of an aircraft to replace the Nakajima B6N and Yokosuka D4Y. As this specification called for an internal bombload of up to 1,102 lb (500 kg), or the carriage of a 1,764-lb (800-kg) torpedo externally, coupled with high maximum speed and long range, a powerful engine was essential. The navy selected what was virtually an experimental powerplant for this task: the Nakajima Homare 11 twin-row radial developing about 1,800 hp (1342 kW).

Aichi began work on this requirement, and its AM-23 prototype flew in mid-1942. This large aircraft, then designated B7A1 Navy Experimental 16-Shi Carrier Attack Bomber, was a mid-wing monoplane of inverted gull-wing configuration, a layout selected so that the main units of the retractable tailwheel landing gear, mounted at the 'elbows' of each wing, would be as short as possible. A section of each outer wing panel folded for carrier stowage. The fuselage and tail unit were conventional, the former providing enclosed accommodation for a crew of two.

As might have been anticipated, the combination of problems from the airframe, coupled with the teething troubles of the new engine, meant that it was almost two years before the type was ordered into production as the B7A2 Navy Carrier Attack Bomber Ryusei (shooting star). Apart from nine prototype B7A1s, only 80 examples were completed by Aichi before its factory was destroyed in the serious earthquake of May 1945: an additional 25 were built by the Naval Air Arsenal at Omura. In addition to these production aircraft, one B7A2 was fitted experimentally with a 2,000-hp (1491-kW) Nakajima Homare 23 radial engine, and it was planned to develop an advanced version, designated B7A3, with the 2,200hp (1641-kW) Mitsubishi MK9A radial, but the disaster of May 1945 brought an end to development plans.

By the time the type entered service, when it was allocated the Allied codename 'Grace', the Japanese navy no longer had any carriers from which the B7A could operate, so the B7A2 saw only limited use from land bases.

Specification
Aichi B7A2

Type: carrier-based torpedo/dive-domber
Powerplant: one 1,825-hp (1361-kW) Nakajima NK9C Homare 12 18-cylinder radial piston engine
Performance: maximum speed at 21,490 ft (6550 m) 351 mph (565 km/h); service ceiling 36,910 ft (11250 m); maximum range 1,889 miles (3040 km)
Weights: empty 8,400 lb (3810 kg); maximum take-off 12,401 lb (5625 kg)
Dimensions: span 47 ft 3 in (14.40 m); length 37 ft 8¼ in (11.49 m); height 13 ft 4½ in (4.075 m); wing area 381.05 sq ft (35.40 m²)
Armament: (late production B7A2) two wing-mounted 20-mm Type 99 Model cannon and one 13-mm (0.51-in) Type 2 machine-gun on trainable mount in aft position, plus either one 1,764-lb (800-kg) torpedo or a similar weight of bombs
Operator: Japanese navy

Given the Allied codename 'Grace', the Aichi B7A Ryusei never reached a carrier due to the length of its development. It was a large aircraft able to carry a 1,764-lb (800-kg) torpedo at a speed of 351 mph (565 km/h). This example is a B7A1, one of a pre-production batch.

Aichi D3A

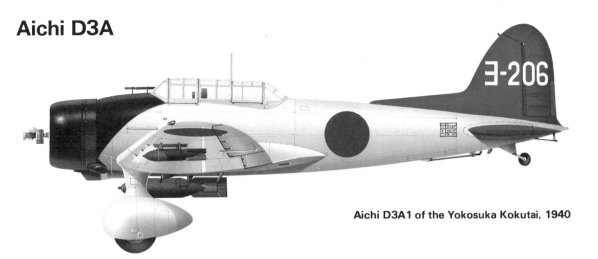

Aichi D3A1 of the Yokosuka Kokutai, 1940

History and notes

Designed to supersede the D1A, the Aichi D3A became far better known than its predecessor. Of low-wing monoplane configuration, the prototype had elliptical wings similar to those of the Heinkel He 70, a conventional tail unit, and a circular-section fuselage; construction was basically all-metal. Non-retractable tailwheel landing gear incorporated main units with large speed fairings, and the prototype's powerplant was the 730-hp (544-kW) Hikari 1 radial that had powered the D1A2. Testing showed that the aircraft was underpowered, had a tendency to snap roll in tight turns, and had ineffective dive brakes. The second prototype incorporated modifications to overcome these shortcomings, including increased wing span, changed outboard wing section leading edges to overcome the roll problem, strengthened dive brakes, and an 840-hp (626-kW) Mitsubishi Kinsei 3 radial engine. In this form the type proved superior to Nakajima's contender for this requirement, and in December 1939 was ordered into production under the designation Navy Type 99 Carrier Bomber Model 11 (Aichi D3A1).

Production aircraft differed from the second proto-type by having a small decrease in wing span, and directional stability was improved by the addition of a long dorsal fin. Power was again increased, with the introduction of a 1,000-hp (746-kW) Mitsubishi Kinsei 43 engine on early production models. In this form the D3A1 completed carrier trials, and entered operational service with the navy in China and Indo-Chia. A total of 129 of these dive-bombers was carried by the task force that launched the attack on Pearl Harbor, and it was a force of D3A1s that sank the British aircraft-carrier HMS *Hermes*, and the cruisers HMS *Cornwall* and HMS *Dorsetshire*, in April 1942.

Identified by the Allies under the codename 'Val', a total of 1,495 D3As of different versions was built. These included the two prototypes, plus six service trials and 470 D3A1 production aircraft. Then followed a single prototype of an improved D3A2 Model 12 which, first flown in June 1942, differed by having a

The Aichi D3A, codenamed 'Val', was the major dive-bomber of the early Japanese campaign, gaining several notable successes including the attack on Pearl Harbor.

Aichi D3A

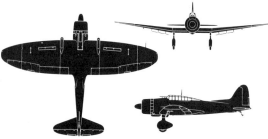

Aichi D3A

modified rear canopy, a 1,300-hp (969-kW) Mitsubishi Kinsei 54 radial engine driving a propeller with spinner, and increased fuel capacity to cater for the more powerful engine. Duly ordered as the D3A2 Model 22, this was the major production version, a total of 1,016 being built by Aichi (815) and Showa (201). With a maximum take-off weight of 8,378 lb (3800 kg), the D3A2 had a maximum speed of 267 mph (430 km/h) at 20,340 ft (6200 m) and service ceiling of 34,450 ft (10500 m). Final variant was the D3A2-K bomber trainer, of which an unspecified number of conversions were made from D3A2s late in the war

after the type had been relegated to second-line duties. Nevertheless, D3As remained in service from beginning to end of the Pacific war, serving finally in *kamikaze* roles.

Specification
Aichi D3A1 (late production)
Type: two-seat carrier- or land-based dive-bomber
Powerplant: one 1,070-hp (798-kW) Mitsubishi Kinsei 44 14-cylinder radial piston engine
Performance: maximum speed at 9,845 ft (3000 m) 239 mph (385 km/h); cruising speed at 9,845 ft (3000 m) 183 mph (295 km/h); service ceiling 30,510 ft (9300 m); range 913 miles (1470 km)
Weights: empty 5,309 lb (2408 kg); maximum take-off 8,047 lb (3650 kg)
Dimensions: span 47 ft 1½ in (14.36 m); length 33 ft 5¼ in (10.19 m); height 12 ft 7½ in (3.85 m); wing area 375.67 sq ft (34,90 m²)
Armament: two 7.7-mm (0.303-in) fixed forward-firing Type 97 machine-guns, 7.7-mm (0.303-in), one Type 92 machine-gun on trainable mount in rear cockpit, plus up to 816 lb (370 kg) of bombs
Operator: Japanese navy

Aichi E13A

History and notes
Developed from the E12A two-seat reconnaissance seaplane, the Aichi E13A was designed to meet an Imperial Japanese Navy requirement for a long-range reconnaissance floatplane to serve as an escort for maritime convoys. The prototype of this three-seat aircraft was completed in the closing months of 1938 as a low-wing monoplane with folding outboard wing panels, conventional tail unit, circular-section fuselage, and twin-float landing gear. Powered by a Mitsubishi Kinsei 43 radial engine, the E13A proved superior to the competing Kawanishi E13K1 during service tests, and was ordered into production as the Navy Type 0 Reconnaissance Seaplane Model 11 (Aichi E13A1). Aichi had built a total of 133 by 1942, when Watanabe

(later Kyushu) became the prime contractor, building 1,237 aircraft; in addition, 48 were built by the Hiro Naval Arsenal to give a total production figure of 1,418 E13A1s. They included an unspecified number of two improved variants introduced in November 1944, comprising the E13A1a which introduced improved float bracing struts, a propeller spinner, and more advanced radio equipment; and the generally similar E13A1b which carried ASV radar.

Identified by the Allies under the codename 'Jake', E13A1s entered service with the navy in late 1941, and flew reconnaissance patrols during the attack on Pearl Harbor. Serving throughout the Pacific war, they were operated from both ships and shore bases for

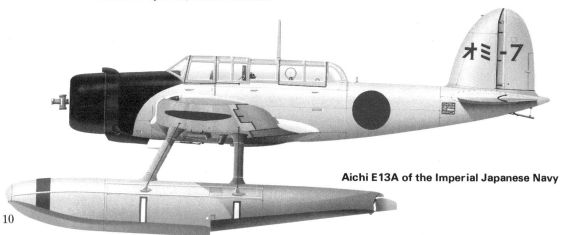

Aichi E13A of the Imperial Japanese Navy

Aichi E13A

Used for all types of maritime patrol operations, the Aichi E13A flew from both land and ship. This is an E13A1b.

roles which included air/sea rescue, long patrol sorties of up to 15 hours, shipping attacks, transport and, in the closing stages of the war, for *kamikaze* operations.

Specification
Aichi E13A1a
Type: long-range reconnaissance floatplane
Powerplant: one 1,080-hp (805-kW) Mitsubishi Kinsei 43 14-cylinder radial piston engine
Performance: maximum speed at 7,150 ft (2180 m) 233 mph (375 km/h); cruising speed at 6,560 ft (2000 m) 137 mph (220 km/h); service ceiling 28,640 ft (8730 m); range 1,299 miles (2090 km)
Weights: empty 5,825 lb (2642 kg); maximum take-off 8,025 lb (3640 kg)
Dimensions: span 47 ft 6¾ in (14.50 m); length 37 ft

0¾ in (11.30 m); height 24 ft 3¼ in (7.40 m); wing area 387.51 sq ft (36.00 m²)
Armament: one 7.7-mm (0.303-in) Type 92 machine-gun on trainable mount in aft position, plus up to 551 lb (250 kg) bombs; Type 99 20-mm cannon could be mounted on a ventral flexible mount for anti-ship strikes
Operator: Japanese navy

Aichi E16A1 Zuiun

History and notes
The design of a twin-float reconnaissance seaplane, to supersede the E13A1 in service, was initiated by Aichi in October 1940. This had the company designation AM-22, and in early 1941 the Imperial Japanese navy drew up a specification based upon this design. The first of three prototypes was flown for the first time during May 1942, but the resolution of stability problems, and of buffeting from the dive brakes occupied 15 months, the navy ordering the E16A1 into production in August 1943 as the Navy Reconnaissance Seaplane Zuiun Model 11.

Of low-wing monoplane configuration, the E16A1 had wings that incorporated trailing-edge flaps, and which could be folded for shipboard stowage. Basic structure was of metal, but the tailplane and wingtips were of wood, and all control surfaces were fabric-covered. The single-step floats each included a controllable rudder to assist in on-water operation, and the forward mounting strut of the floats incorporated by hydraulically-actuated dive brakes to allow the E16A1 to operate as a dive-bomber. Accommodation for the crew of two was provided in tandem cockpits, enclosed by a long transparent canopy. Powerplant of the prototype and of early production Zuiun (auspicious cloud) aircraft consisted of a 1,300-hp (969-kW) Mitsubishi Kinsei 51 radial engine, driving a three-blade propeller. A single prototype of an improved E16A2 was being flight tested at the time of the Japanese surrender, powered by a 1,560-hp (1163-kW) Mitsubishi MK8P Kinsei 62 radial engine.

Production totalled 193 by Aichi and 59 by Nippon. Unfortunately for the navy, by the time the E16A1 entered service the Allies had gained air superiority

and in consequence these aircraft, allocated the Allied codename 'Paul', suffered very heavy losses during 1944. The majority which survived were used for *kamikaze* operations in the Okinawa area.

Specification
Aichi E16A1 (late production)
Type: long-range reconnaissance floatplane
Powerplant: one 1,300-hp (969-kW) Mitsubishi MK8D Kinsei 54 14-cylinder radial piston engine
Performance: maximum speed at 18,045 ft (5500 m) 273 mph (440 km/h); cruising speed at 16,405 ft (5000 m) 208 mph (335 km/h); service ceiling 32,810 ft (10000 m); maximum range, 1,504 miles (2420 km)
Weights: empty 6,493 lb (2945 kg); maximum take-off 10,038 lb (4553 kg)
Dimensions: span 42 ft 0¼ in (12.81 m); length 35 ft 6½ in (10.83 m); height 15 ft 8½ in (4.79 m); wing area 301.40 sq ft (28.00 m²)
Armament: two 20-mm wing-mounted Type 99 Model 2 cannon and one 13-mm (0.51-in) Type 2 machine-gun on flexible mount in aft position, plus one 551-lb (250-kg) bomb on underfuselage mounting
Operator: Japanese navy

The Aichi E16A Zuiun was designed to supersede the E13A, but it never achieved the same success.

11

Arado Ar 66

History and notes

Walter Rethel's last completed design for Arado before his transfer to Messerschmitt was the Arado Ar 66, a two-seat single-bay biplane trainer of mixed construction. The tailplane was mounted on a raised rear fuselage fairing, ahead of the vertical tail surface which comprised a wholly movable rudder, there being no fin. The first prototype, the Ar 66a of 1932, was powered by a 240-hp (179-kW) Argus As 10C inline engine. The second prototype, designated Ar 66b, was generally similar except that it had twin wooden floats, the rudder being extended beyond the bottom of the sternpost and faired into the rear fuselage by the addition of a ventral fin. Ten production Ar 66b aircraft were built subsequently. When Rethel left to join Bayerische Flugzeugwerke, as the Messerschmitt company was then named, Dipl. Ing. Walter Blume assumed responsibility for development of the Ar 66a, which entered series production as the Ar 66c, initial deliveries being made to the Luftwaffe in 1933. The Ar 66c continued to serve with Luftwaffe training schools after the outbreak of World War II, and as late as 1943 it was pressed into service, together with the Gotha Go 145 trainer, to equip the night ground-attack Störk-

ungkampfstaffeln on the Eastern Front, armed with 4- and 9-lb (1.8 and 4-kg) anti-personnel bombs.

Specification
Arado Ar 66c

Type: two-seat trainer
Powerplant: one 240 hp (179 kW) Argus As 10c 8-cylinder inverted Vee piston engine
Performance: maximum speed 130 mph (210 km/h) at sea level; cruising speed 109 mph (175 km/h); service ceiling 14,765 ft (4500 m); range 444 miles (715 km)
Weights: empty 1,996 lb (905 kg); maximum take-off 2,933 lb (1330 kg)
Dimensions: span 32 ft 9¾ in (10.00 m); length 27 ft 2¾ in (8.30 m); height 9 ft 7½ in (2.93 m); wing area 319.0 sq ft (29.64 m²)
Operator: Luftwaffe

Widely used in the pre-war years by civilian and military flying schools, the Arado Ar 66c saw service with the Luftwaffe on the Eastern Front. Note the underwing bomb crutches and unusual tailplane arrangement.

Arado Ar 67 and Ar 68

History and notes

In the closing months of 1933 Arado flew what proved to be the sole example of the Ar 67, a smaller and lighter version of the company's earlier Ar 65; powered by a 640-hp (477-kW) Rolls-Royce Kestrel VI, it had a maximum speed of 211 mph (340 km/h). Like its antecedents, the Ar 67 was of mixed construction and

was, similarly, to have carried two 7.92-mm (0.31-in) machine-guns.

Development was discontinued, however, in favour of the Arado Ar 68 which was the last biplane fighter to enter front-line service with the Luftwaffe. Reaching contemporary standards of aerodynamic efficiency, the aircraft had an oval-section fuselage of steel-tube

Arado Ar 67 and Ar 68

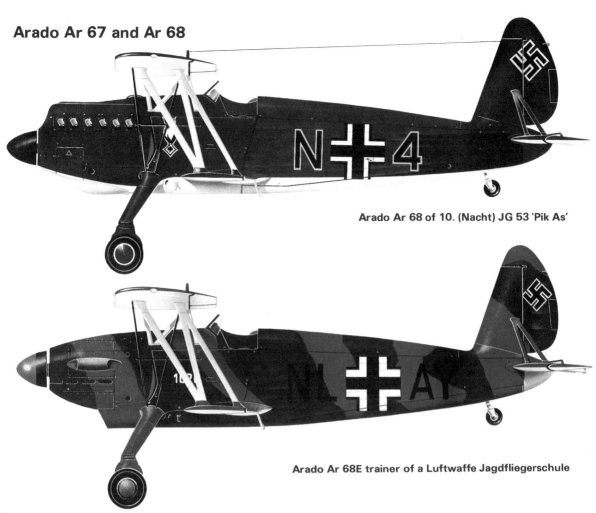

Arado Ar 68 of 10. (Nacht) JG 53 'Pik As'

Arado Ar 68E trainer of a Luftwaffe Jagdfliegerschule

construction, with metal panels covering the rear decking and forward sections, and fixed tailwheel landing gear whose main units incorporated wheel spats. The distinctive fin, which was to be used almost without exception in subsequent single-engined Arado designs, was introduced on the Ar 68.

The prototype Ar 68a flew for the first time in 1934, powered by a BMW VId engine providing a maximum continuous output of 550 hp (410 kW), resulting in disappointing performance. The problem was partially overcome in the Ar 68b second prototype, which was powered by a supercharged 610-hp (455-kW) Junkers Jumo 210 inverted-Vee engine, which both improved forward vision from the cockpit, and provided full power at higher altitudes. Even so, drag from the chin radiator depressed potential performance figures, and a redesigned unit was fitted to the Ar 68c third prototype which, flown in the summer of 1935, was the first to be fitted with the intended armament of two 7.92-mm (0.31-in) MG 17 machine-guns. The fourth and fifth prototypes, designated Ar 68d and Ar 68e, were powered respectively by the BMW VI and Jumo 210 engines, and were regarded as pre-production aircraft. First to enter interim small-scale production was the Ar 68F, powered by a 750-hp (570-kW) BMW VI engine

pending improved supplies of the Jumo 210 engine. As soon as better allocations of the Junkers powerplant were made, production of the Ar 68E began with initial deliveries from the spring of 1937. An improved Ar 68G was planned, but this failed to enter production as the supercharged BMW engine to power it did not

One of the first production Arado Ar 68Es, this aircraft is fitted with a Jumo 210Da engine. Clearly visible is the separation between the forward fuselage light alloy panels and the rear fuselage fabric covering.

Arado Ar 67 and Ar 68

materialise, and the only other variant was the single Ar 68H prototype. This introduced a sliding cockpit canopy, two additional machine-guns, and an 850-hp (634-kW) BMW 132 radial engine. In this form the Ar 68H, first flown in 1937, had a maximum speed some 42 mph (68 km/h) better than that of the Ar 68E, but by then the RLM was convinced that the day of the biplane had ended and Arado was instructed to terminate its development.

Initial deliveries of the Ar 68F were made to the Luftwaffe in the late summer of 1936, commencing with I/JG134 'Horst Wessel'. By the outbreak of World War II, most surviving Ar 68s had been relegated to advanced fighter trainer status with the Jagdflieger-schulen (fighter pilot schools).

Specification
Arado Ar 68E-1
Type: single-seat fighter
Powerplant: one 690-hp (515-kW) Junkers Jumo 210 Da 12-cylinder inverted-Vee piston engine
Performance: maximum speed 190 mph (305 km/h) at sea level; service ceiling 26,575 ft (8100 m); range 258 miles (415 km)
Weights: empty 4,057 lb (1840 kg); maximum take-off 5,457 lb (2475 kg)
Dimensions: span 36 ft 1 in (11.00 m); length 31 ft 2 in (9.50 m); height 10 ft 9 in (3.28 m); wing area 293.86 sq ft (27.30 m²)
Armament: two fixed forward-firing 7.9-mm (0.31-m) MG 17 machine-guns
Operator: Luftwaffe

Arado Ar 96

History and notes
With a total production run of more than 11,500 aircraft by the cessation of hostilities, the Arado Ar 96 was the Luftwaffe's standard advanced trainer, designed by Walter Blume and first flown in 1938. Of all-metal light alloy construction, the prototype was powered by a 240-hp (179-kW) Argus As 10C engine and was fitted with main landing gear which retracted outwards into the wing. In order to widen the track, to make the aircraft easier for student pilots to handle, the legs were repositioned to retract inwards.

Reichsluftfahrtministerium trials were completed successfully and an initial production batch of Ar 96A aircraft was manufactured in 1939, leading to large-scale orders in 1940 for the more powerful Ar 96B which was to become the major production version, with a lengthened fuselage to provide greater fuel capacity for the more powerful engine. It was built in variants that included the unarmed Ar 96B-1 and the Ar 96B-2 which carried either a 7.92-mm (0.31-in) MG 17 machine-gun or a camera gun for gunnery training. An Ar 96C bomb-aiming trainer with a transparent panel in the cockpit floor was evaluated but did not enter production. Manufacture of the Ar 96B was transferred to the Junkers subsidiary Ago Flugzeugwerke at Oschersleben/Bode and then, in mid-1941, to the Czech company Avia, which was joined in the programme by the Prague-based Letov organisation in 1944. Czech production continued until 1948, supplying aircraft to the Czech air force under the designation Avia C.2B.

The Luftwaffe used the Ar 96 for advanced, night and instrument flying training duties with the pilot training schools, fighter training wings, fighter training and replacement units and the officer cadet schools.

The successful Arado Ar 96 design was to play a significant part in the strength and effectiveness of the Luftwaffe, as it was chosen to be their standard advanced trainer. Produced in several variants, the Ar 96 also saw production in Czechoslovakia.

Specification
Arado Ar 96B-2
Type: two-seat advanced trainer
Powerplant: one 465-hp (347-kW) Argus As 410A-1 12-cylinder inverted-Vee piston engine
Performance: maximum speed 205 mph (330 km/h) at sea level; cruising speed 183 mph (295 km/h); service ceiling 23,295 ft (7100 m); range 615 miles (990 km)
Weights: empty 2,854 lb (1295 kg); maximum take-off 3,748 lb (1700 kg)
Dimensions: span 36 ft 1 in (11.00 m); length 29 ft 10¼ in (9.10 m); height 8 ft 6¼ in (2.60 m); wing area 184.07 sq ft (17.10 m²)
Armament: one fixed forward-firing 7.92-mm (0.31-in) MG 17 machine-gun
Operators: Luftwaffe, Hungary, Romania

Arado Ar 196

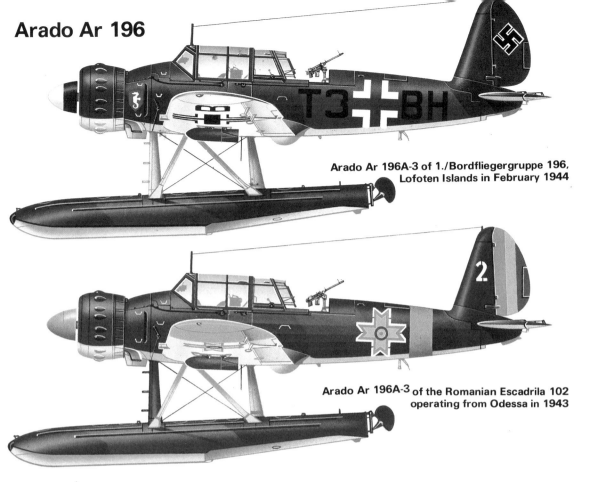

Arado Ar 196A-3 of 1./Bordfliegergruppe 196, Lofoten Islands in February 1944

Arado Ar 196A-3 of the Romanian Escadrila 102 operating from Odessa in 1943

History and notes

In the autumn of 1936 the Reichsluftfahrtministerium's Technische Amt (technical department) issued a specification for a catapult floatplane to replace the Heinkel He 50s then serving with the Bordfliegerstaffeln, the Luftwaffe units responsible for providing the Kriegsmarine with reconnaissance aircraft for its capital ships and other surface vessels. The requirement was for a two-seat single- or twin-float aircraft powered by a single engine in the 800/900-hp (597/671-kW) range and, of the competing proposals, the Focke-Wulf Fw 62 biplane and Arado Ar 196 monoplane were selected for development.

The Ar 196 was of all-metal construction, its rectangular-section steel-tube fuselage frame being faired to an oval section by the use of formers and stringers, with metal skinning forward and fabric covering aft. The wings were metal-skinned two-spar structures, hinged at the trailing edge to fold back along the fuselage sides once the outboard wing-to-float struts had been detached at the float end. Each of the twin floats housed a 66-Imp gal (300-litre) fuel tank.

Evaluation at Erprobungstelle Travemünde in the summer of 1937 was undertaken on two prototypes of each design, but the clear superiority of the more advanced Arado aircraft quickly eliminated the Focke-Wulf contender. Powered by the 880-hp (656-kW)

BMW 132De radial engine, four prototype Ar 196s were ordered, the first two (as tested at Travemünde) with twin floats and designated Ar 196A, the third and fourth in single central/twin outboard stabilising float configuration and identified as Ar 196Bs.

The fourth prototype was the first to be fitted with weapons, carrying two wing-mounted 20-mm MG FF cannon, and a single 7.92-mm (0.31-in) MG 17 machine-gun in the starboard side of the forward fuselage. A fifth prototype, another Ar 196B, had the more powerful 950-hp (708-kW) BMW 132K engine with a three-blade variable-pitch propeller in place of the two-blade two-pitch unit fitted to the first four machines.

Comparative evaluation of the hydrodynamic qualities of the alternative float configurations was conducted by the Aerodynamischen Versuchsanstalt Göttingen, and at Travemünde. Although no distinct advantage could be discerned for either layout, the twin-float version was preferred and 10 pre-production Ar 196A-0 aircraft were ordered.

Total production of the Ar 196 is quoted as 593 aircraft, including those built in 1942-3 by the Société Nationale de Constructions Aéronautiques (SNCA) at St Nazaire, France, and by Fokker in Amsterdam between April and August 1943. First production version was the Ar 196A-1, without cannon generally similar to the Ar 196A-0, which was built in 1939 and

15

Arado Ar 196

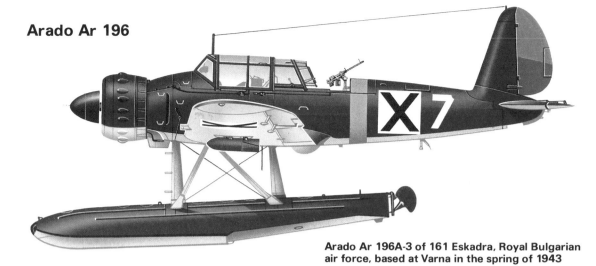

Arado Ar 196A-3 of 161 Eskadra, Royal Bulgarian air force, based at Varna in the spring of 1943

operated from major warships that included the *Admiral Graf Spee*, *Admiral Scheer*, *Deutschland*, *Gneisenau*, *Prinz Eugen* and the *Scharnhorst*. One example operating from the *Admiral Hipper* was captured in Norway, and later evaluated at the Marine Aircraft Experimental Establishment at Helensburgh, Scotland. Sub-variants of the Ar 196A included the coastal patrol Ar 196A-2 which had the full armament of two 20-mm MG FF cannon mounted in the wings and a 7.92-mm (0.31-in) MG 17 machine-gun in the forward fuselage. The generally similar Ar 196A-3, which was also built by Fokker and SNCA, had structural strengthening and introduced additional radio equipment and a three-blade variable-pitch propeller. It was followed by 24 examples of the Ar 196A-4, a catapult version for service with the Bordfliegerstaffeln, and the final production version was the Ar 196A-5 which introduced improved radio equipment and had an MG 81Z installation in the rear cockpit, comprising twin 7.92-mm (0.31-in) MG 81 machine-guns; the last of 91 examples of

this version were built by Fokker during August 1944.

Initial deliveries to the Luftwaffe were to Bordfliegerstaffeln I./196 and 5./196, based at Wilhelmshaven and Kiel-Holtenau, under Kriegsmarine control. The first ship to take its Ar 196A-1 to sea was the pocket battleship *Admiral Graf Spee*, scuttled off Montevideo in December 1939 after being trapped in the estuary of the River Plate by a British cruiser squadron.

The type was used widely for coastal patrol, and a spectacular early success was the capture of the British submarine HMS *Seal* by two Ar 196A-2 floatplanes of 1 Staffel/Küstenfliegergruppe 706, based at Aalborg, Denmark. Damaged by a mine and unable to submerge, the vessel was surrendered after the Arados had attacked with bombs and cannon fire. The Ar 196 served in most major battle zones (the Atlantic, North Sea, Baltic, eastern Mediterranean, Adriatic, Aegean and Black Seas). It also equipped the Bulgarian air force's 161st Coastal Squadron, and the 101st and 102nd Coastal Squadrons of the Romanian air force.

The airscrew spinner on this operational aircraft identifies it as an Arado Ar 196A-4, this version incorporating structural strengthening to enable catapult launching from Kriegsmarine vessels.

Specification
Arado Ar 196A-3

Type: two-seat shipboard and coastal patrol floatplane
Powerplant: one 960 hp (716 kW) BMW 132K 9-cylinder radial piston engine
Performance: maximum speed 193 mph (310 km/h) at 13,125 ft (4000 m); cruising speed 158 mph (255 km/h); service ceiling 22,960 ft (7000 m); range 665 miles (1070 km)
Weights: empty 6,593 lb (2990 kg); maximum take-off 8,225 lb (3730 kg)
Dimensions: span 40 ft 8¼ in (12.40 m); length 36 ft 1 in (11.00 m); height 14 ft 7¼ in (4.45 m); wing area 305.71 sq ft (28.40 m²)
Armament: two fixed forward-firing 20-mm MG FF cannon in wings, one fixed forward-firing 7.92-mm (0.31-in) MG 17 machine-gun in starboard forward fuselage and one trainable 7.92-mm (0.31-in) MG 15 machine-gun in rear cockpit, plus underwing racks for two 110-lb (50-kg) bombs
Operators: Luftwaffe, Bulgaria, Finland, Romania

Arado Ar 197

History and notes

Although German plans for the construction of aircraft-carriers never reached fruition (the *Graf Zeppelin* was launched but never completed), a number of aircraft were developed with carrier operation in mind. One of these was the Arado Ar 197, developed in parallel with the Ar 68H which it closely resembled. The first prototype was powered by a 900-hp (671-kW) Daimler-Benz DB 600A inline engine which turned a three-blade propeller. The second aircraft, with its 815-hp (608-kW) BMW 132J radial engine, was the first navalised example, fitted with catapult spools and arrester hook. Both aircraft flew in the spring of 1937, followed closely by the third prototype, to which was fitted an uprated BMW 132De engine. Evaluation at Erprobungstelle Travemünde was not followed by a production order.

Specification

Type: single-seat naval fighter/light bomber
Powerplant: one 880-hp (656-kW) BMW 132De 9-cylinder radial piston engine
Performance: maximum speed 248 mph (400 km/h) at 8,200 ft (2500 m); cruising speed 220 mph (355 km/h); service ceiling 26,215 ft (7990 m); range 432 miles (695 km)

Considered to be a fully-fledged production prototype, the Arado Ar 197-V3 was fully navalized and armed, but the advances in shipboard fighter monoplane design rendered the design obsolete before production.

Weights: empty 4,057 lb (1840 kg); maximum take-off 5,457 lb (2475 kg)
Dimensions: span 36 ft 1 in (11.00 m); length 30 ft 2¼ in (9.20 m); height 11 ft 9¾ in (3.60 m); wing area 298.71 sq ft (27.75 m²)
Armament: two fixed forward-firing 7.92-mm (0.31-in) MG 17 machine-guns in fuselage and two 20-mm MG FF cannon in upper wing, plus up to four 110-lb (50-kg) bombs on underwing racks
Operator: Luftwaffe (evaluation only)

Arado Ar 232

Arado Ar 232A-0 serving with Transportfliegerstaffel 5 in late 1944

History and notes

In early 1940 work began on the design of a transport aircraft to assist and ultimately replace the venerable and ubiquitous Junkers Ju 52/3m, of which more than 500 had been in service on 1 September 1939, when the German invasion of Poland precipitated World War II. A twin-engine design, the Arado Ar 232 featured a pod and boom fuselage with an hydraulically-operated rear loading door and a novel arrangement of 11 pairs of small wheels used to support the fuselage during loading and unloading operations, the tricycle main landing gear having been partially raised by means of two hydraulic rams.

The first two prototypes, flown in 1941, were powered by two 1,600-hp (1193-kW) BMW 801MA radial engines, but the insatiable demands of the Focke-Wulf Fw 190 production lines necessitated a change of engine for subsequent aircraft. The selection of the lower-powered BMW-Bramo 323R-2 meant that four engines were needed and the third aircraft introduced a 5 ft 7 in (1.70 m) increase in wing centre-section span to accommodate them. This was the first of 20 Ar 232B aircraft, some of which saw service with Luftwaffe units, initially on the Eastern Front and, later in the war, with the 'special missions' Kampfgeschwader 200. A surviving aircraft from 3./KG 200 was flown from Flensburg to the Royal Aircraft Establishment at Farnborough after the capitulation. Others were used during hostilities for experimental purposes, including one with a boundary-layer control system, one with four Gnome-Rhône 14M radial engines, and another with fixed landing gear and skis, for operations in Norway.

Specification

Type: heavy transport
Powerplant: four 1,200-hp (895-kW) BMW-Bramo 323R-2 9-cylinder radial piston engines

Arado Ar 232

Performance: maximum speed 211 mph (340 km/h) at 15,090 ft (4600 m); cruising speed 180 mph (290 km/h) at 6,560 ft (2000 m); service ceiling 26,245 ft (8000 m); range 658 miles (1060 km)
Weights: empty 28,224 lb (12802 kg); maximum take-off 46,595 lb (21135 kg)
Dimensions: span 109 ft 10¾ in (33.50 m); length 77 ft 2 in (23.52 m); height 18 ft 8 in (5.69 m); wing area 1,534.98 sq ft (142.60 m²)

Illustrating to good effect the reason why it was dubbed 'Tausendfüssler' (millipede), the Arado Ar 232V-2 also shows the definitive defensive armament arrangement including a nose machine-gun.

Armament: one 13-mm (0.51-in) MG 131 machine-gun in the nose, one or two similar weapons at the rear of the fuselage pod and one 20-mm MG 151/20 cannon in a power-operated dorsal turret
Operator: Luftwaffe

Arado Ar 234 Blitz

Arado Ar 234B-2 of 9./KG 26 based at Achmer in 1945

History and notes

Just as Messerschmitt's Me 262 was the world's first turbojet fighter, so the Arado Ar 234 Blitz (lightning) was the first jet-powered bomber, although it was designed originally in response to a Reichsluftfahrt-ministerium requirement for a fast reconnaissance aircraft. Work on the Ar 234 began in late 1940 and, early in the following year, Arado's design team, led by Walter Blume and Hans Rebeski, completed a project study designated E.370 which emerged finally in prototype form as the Ar 234 early in 1943. A shoulder-wing design, with its two engines underslung from the wings, the Ar 234 featured a narrow fuselage cross-section, so narrow that it could not accept conventional retractable landing gear. The solution adopted originally was the provision of a jettisonable take-off trolley, and retractable skids on which the aircraft could land.

Delays in development of the Junkers turbojet

engines meant that the first ship set of 004B-0 engines was not delivered to Warnemünde until February 1943, and the waiting prototype airframe was fitted with them so that taxying trials could begin in March. By May two flight-cleared engines had been installed and the aircraft transferred to Rheine airfield, where the maiden flight took place on 15 June. The original take-off technique was to jettison the trolley on reaching a height of 195 ft (60 m), five braking parachutes being deployed to return the equipment safely to the ground for re-use. However, the parachute system proved troublesome, and after the first two trolleys had been destroyed it was decided that the wheels would be released immediately upon take-off.

The trolley-equipped version was designated Ar 234A and the third prototype, which flew on 22 August 1943, was equipped with rocket-assisted take-off gear (RATOG), while the pressurized cockpit boasted an

Arado Ar 234 Blitz

The tailcode '006' identifies this aircraft as the sixth pre-production Arado Ar 234C-3, a multi-purpose four-engined derivative of the basic Ar 234.

ejector seat. The fourth and fifth flew on 15 September and 20 December 1943, respectively. The next to fly was the eighth prototype fitted with four 1,764-lb (800-kg) thrust BMW 003A-1 engines arranged in pairs. The same engines, in four separate nacelles, powered the sixth prototype, flown on 8 April 1944. By then the Junkers 004B engines had been uprated from 1,852-lb (840-kg) to 1,962-lb (890-kg) thrust, and two of these units were installed in the seventh and last of the A-series prototypes which crashed after an engine fire, killing Arado chief test pilot Flugkapitän Selle.

The inability of the Ar 234 to be moved easily before the wheeled trolley had been fitted was clearly unacceptable in an operational environment. Thus, the B-series was evolved, with a slightly widened fuselage to take conventional landing gear, albeit of relatively narrow track. The eighth prototype was the first of the new model and it flew on 10 March 1944. It was followed on 2 April by the tenth machine, which was without cabin pressurization and ejector seat, but fitted with bomb racks beneath the engine nacelles and used to test the BZA (bombenzielanlage für Sturzflug) bomb-aiming computer. Of the remaining B-series prototypes the most important was the thirteenth, with two pairs of BMW 003A-1 engines, and the fifteenth and seventeenth, each with two of the BMW engines, and used as test-beds to hasten the solution of the turbojet's thrust control problems.

Despite their lack of mobility on the ground, in July 1944 the fifth and seventh prototypes were subjected to operational evaluation in the reconnaissance role by 1./ Versuchsverband Oberbefehlshaber der Luftwaffe at Juvincourt, near Reims. Fitted with Walter RATO equipment, they defied interception during numerous sorties over Allied territory and were joined later by some Ar 234B-1s which, in small detachments, equipped experimental reconnaissance units designated Sonderkommandos Götz, Hecht, Sperling and Sommer. Two other units, 1.(F)/33 and 1.(F)/100, were still operational at the war's end. The bomber version first became operational with the Stabstaffel of KG 76, deployed during the Ardennes offensive, but at that stage of the war the number of sorties that could be mounted was limited severely by fuel shortage. Among the most noted bomber operations were attempts to destroy the Ludendorff bridge over the Rhine at Remagen, which was held by US troops. For 10 days from 7 March 1945 almost continuous attacks were made on this target until finally the bridge collapsed, but within two more weeks bomber operations had virtually come to an end for lack of fuel. The Ar 234 was also flown by Kommando Bonow, an experiment night-fighter unit which operated until the end of the war under the control of Luftflotte Reich.

Total construction of the Arado Ar 234 amounted to 274 aircraft, of which 30 were prototypes and 244 production aircraft. This number included 20 Ar 234B-0 pre-production aircraft most of which, without ejection seats or cabin pressurization, were delivered to Rechlin for intensive development flying. They were followed by the first true series versions, the Ar 234B-1 reconnaissance aircraft which could carry two Rb 50/30 or Rb 75/30 cameras, or a combination of an Rb 50/30 and an Rb 20/30, and the Ar 234B-2 bomber which had a maximum bombload of 4,409 lb (2000 kg) carried on ETC 503 bomb racks beneath the engine nacelles. Production of these two versions totalled 210, and experience with these aircraft left little doubt that the basic airframe was capable of using increased power to improve performance, leading to development of the Ar 234C. This resulted in two prototypes being flown, with alternative arrangements of four-engine powerplant in individual and paired nacelles, the latter proving to be the more efficient. The nineteenth prototype served as the first true Arado Ar 234C prototype, having four 1,760-lb (798-kg) thrust BMW 003A-1 Sturm turbojets in paired nacelles beneath each wing. Satisfactory testing of this aircraft led to production of the four-engine Ar 234C-1, which was otherwise similar to the Ar 234B-1 except for having full cabin pressurization and being armed with two rear-firing MG 151/20 20-mm cannon. The similarly

Arado Ar 234 Blitz

powered Ar 234C-2 was planned, corresponding to the Ar 234B-2, and several prototype Ar 234C-3s were built, this was a multi-role version suitable for use in bomber, ground attack and night-fighter roles, but a total of only about 14 Ar 234C-1/-3s was produced. In addition to the multi-purpose Ar 234C-3, planned specialised versions of the Ar 234C included the Ar 234C-3/N two-seat night-fighter, Ar 234C-4 equipped for armed reconnaissance, side-by-side two-seat Ar 234C-5, Ar 234C-6 and Ar 234C-7 bomber, reconnaissance and night fighter aircraft respectively, and the Ar 234C-8 single-seat bomber powered by two 2,381-lb (1080-kg) thrust Jumo 004D engines. Other proposals which failed to materialise were the Ar 234D-1 and Ar 234D-2 reconnaissance and bomber aircraft respectively, which were to have been powered by two 2,865-lb (1300-kg) thrust Heinkel-Hirth HeS 011A turbojets, and a series of Ar 234P advanced night-fighters with BMW, Heinkel-Hirth and Jumo engines.

Specification
Arado Ar 234B-2

Type: twin-turbojet bomber aircraft
Powerplant: two 1,962-lb (890-kg) thrust Junkers Jumo 004B turbojet engines
Performance: maximum speed 460 mph (740 km/h) at 19,685 ft (6000 m); service ceiling 32,810 ft (10000 m); maximum range 1,013 miles (1630 km)
Weights: empty 11,464 lb (5200 kg); maximum take-off 21,715 lb (9850 kg)
Dimensions: span 46 ft 3½ in (14.10 m); length 41 ft 5½ in (12.64 m); height 14 ft 1½ in (4.30 m); wing area 284.18 sq ft (26.40 m²)
Armament: maximum bombload of 4,409 lb (2000 kg) carried on ETC 503 bomb racks beneath the engine nacelles
Operator: Luftwaffe

Avia B.534

Avia B.534-IV of the Slovak air force at Zitomir-Kiev, Ukraine, 1941-2

History and notes

The Avia B.534 was the most important Czech aircraft of the period between the two World Wars, with production totalling 566 — more than that of any other type. It was a classic single-seat fighter biplane, representing the penultimate stage in the evolution of this type, the final stage being provided by biplanes with retractable landing gear, such as the Soviet Polikarpov I-153 and the Grumman fighters for the US Navy.

Designer Frantisek Novotny had re-engined the unsuccessful Avia B.34/2 prototype with a Hispano-Suiza 12Ybrs engine, redesignating it **B.534/1.** This first flew in August 1933, piloted by Václav Koci, and showed great promise. It was an unequal-span staggered single-bay biplane, with splayed N-struts carrying the upper wing centre-section above the fuselage. Wing bracing was by N-struts and there were ailerons on both upper and lower wings. The two-spar riveted

steel wing had fabric covering, while the carefully streamlined fuselage was a riveted and bolted steel-tube structure with detachable metal panels forward and fabric covering aft. The horizontal tailplane was strut-braced and the split-type landing gear, with half-axles hinged beneath the fuselage, was oleo sprung. The second prototype (B.534/2) had an enclosed cockpit, an enlarged rudder and revised landing gear with mainwheel fairings. It established a Czech national speed record on 18 April 1934, reaching 227.26 mph (365.74 km/h).

Development was held up when both prototypes were damaged in crash landings during 1934, but the decision had already been made to order the B.534 for the Czech air arm. The Avia B.534-I, the first production version, followed closely the design of the second prototype. The prototype's metal propeller was replaced by one of wood and, as on the first prototype, the pilot had an open cockpit. The main landing gear units were

Avia B.534

Avia B.534-IV of the 2nd Regiment, Royal Bulgarian air force, 1941⒉

without spats.

Production of the B.534-I totalled 46. Armament comprised twin fuselage-mounted light machine-guns and two more in fairings on the lower wing. Production of the Avia B.534-II series reached 100. This version differed in having all four machine-guns mounted in the fuselage sides, with consequently enlarged fuselage side blister fairings to house them. Underwing racks for light bombs were fitted, since the new fighter was considered suitable also for ground attack. The 46 B.534-III aircraft ordered next had mainwheel fairings, and had the carburettor air intake moved forward under the nose. Six of this version were exported to Greece and 14 to Yugoslavia. The B.534-IV had an aft-sliding cockpit canopy and raised aft fuselage decking. Total Czech orders for this version were 253. The Avia Bk.534 was a cannon-armed version, but otherwise similar to the Series IV aircraft. It was intended that its Hispano-Suiza 12Ycrs engine would have a 20-mm Oerlikon cannon mounted in the Vee of the engine cylinders, with its muzzle in the hollow propeller boss. However, as a result of a shortage of the Oerlikon weapons, many Bk.534s flew with three machine-guns, two mounted in the fuselage sides and one in place of the *moteur canon*. Some B.534-IV and Bk.534 fighters had the standard tail skid replaced by a castoring tailwheel.

At the Zurich International Flying Meet in July 1937, the B.534 demonstrated excellent manoeuvrability and good overall performance, proving itself in competition as the outstanding biplane fighter. In 1935 a 'cleaned up' development was ordered under the designation B.634, basically an aerodynamically refined aircraft powered by an 850-hp (634-kW) Avia-built Hispano-Suiza HS 12Ycrs inline engine. However, the benefits of streamlining and other improvements were offset by an increase in empty weight of some 17 per cent and, as a result, the B.634 did not enter production.

By the time of the Munich crisis in September 1938, B.534s formed the equipment of 21 first-line Czech fighter squadrons. After the occupation of the country by the Germans in March 1939, the puppet Slovak government used some B.534s in the brief border war with Hungary. Three Slovak squadrons subsequently

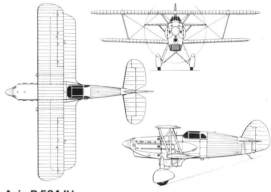

Avia B.534-IV

took part in the invasion of the USSR, along the Ukrainian Front, but by mid-1942 all had been re-equipped and the type was relegated to training. During the winter of 1939-40, Bulgaria received 72 B.534s, which equipped five fighter squadrons. These were retained on Bulgarian territory and their only combat sorties were against Consolidated B-24 Liberator bombers returning from the disastrous 'Tidal Wave' bombing raid on Ploesti oilfields in Romania on 1 August 1943. The B.534s were handicapped by their inadequate performance and soon afterwards were replaced by French-built Dewoitine D.520 monoplanes.

The Luftwaffe used other B.534s and Bk.534s as advanced trainers and as tow-planes for training gliders. Some were fitted with all-round-vision cockpit canopies and others, with arrester hooks, were used for deck landing trials and training in connection with the aircraft-carrier *Graf Zeppelin*, which was launched but never completed.

Finally, three Avias were used by the insurgents at Tri Duby airfield during the Slovak National Rising in the late summer of 1944. Two were lost on the ground during Luftwaffe raids and the third was burned to prevent it from falling into German hands.

The remarkable Avia B.534 is commemorated by a remarkably accurate full-scale replica, completed in 1975, and currently on proud display at the Air Force and Army Museum at Prague-Kbely.

Avia B.534

Avia B.534-IV of 3./JG 71 at Eutingen near Stuttgart, November 1939

Specification
Avia B.534-IV

Type: single-seat fighter

Powerplant: one 850-hp (634-kW) Hispano-Suiza HS 12Ydrs 12-cylinder Vee piston engine

Performance: maximum speed 245 mph (395 km/h) at 12,435 ft (4400 km); cruising speed 214 mph (345 km/h); service ceiling 34,775 ft (10600 m); range 360 miles (580 km)

Weights: empty 3,219 lb (1460 kg); maximum take-off 4,674 lb (2120 kg)

Dimensions: span 30 ft 10 in (9.40 m); length 26 ft 10¾ in (8.20 m); height 10 ft 2 in (3.10 m); wing area 253.61 sq ft (23.56 m²)

Armament: four fixed 7.7-mm (0.303 in) synchronised Model 30 machine-guns in the forward fuselage, plus up to six 44-lb (20-kg) bombs on underwing Pantof racks

Operators: Bulgaria, Croatia, Germany, Hungary and Slovakia

Blohm und Voss Bv 138

Blohm und Voss Bv 138C-1 of 2./KüFlGr 406, Norway, March 1942

History and notes

The first flying-boat design to be built by Hamburger Flugzeugbau GmbH, the aircraft-building subsidiary of Blohm und Voss, under the direction of chief engineer Dr Ing. Richard Vogt, was the Ha 138. Three prototypes of the original twin-engine design were each to have been powered by a different manufacturer's 1,000-hp (746-kW) engine for comparative evaluation, but development delays necessitated redesign to accept three 650-hp (485-kW) Junkers Jumo 205C engines. Almost two years after the completion of the mock-up, the first prototype (Ha 138 V1) took off on its maiden flight, the date being 15 July 1937. A second prototype (Ha 138 V2), with a modified hull design, joined the test programme at the Travemünde centre in November, but the aircraft were quickly proved to be unstable,

both hydrodynamically and aerodynamically. Modifications to the vertical tail surfaces failed to improve the performance adequately and radical redesign was undertaken. The result was the Bv 138A, adopting the designation system of the Blohm und Voss parent company. The hull was much enlarged, its planing surfaces were improved, and the revised tail surfaces were carried by more substantial booms. The prototype was followed by five more pre-series Bv 138A aircraft, preceding the initial production version, the Bv 138A-1 first flown in April 1940, and built to a total of 25 for the reconnaissance units of the Luftwaffe, with which it first saw action during the Norwegian campaign of 1940. Armament of this version comprised one 20-mm cannon in the bow turret, and two 7.92-mm (0.31-in) MG 15 machine guns in open positions located behind

Blohm und Voss Bv 138C-1/U1 of 1.(F)/SAGr 130 operating in the Trondheim area, April 1944

the centre engine nacelle and at the rear of the hull. Structural strengthening of the fourth pre-series aircraft, and the installation of 880-hp (656-kW) Jumo 205D engines and armament comprising one 20-mm MG 151 cannon in the bow turret, a similar weapon in the rear hull position, with provision to carry up to 331 lb (150 kg) of bombs beneath the starboard wing root, resulted in the Bv 138B-0 prototype. This was followed by 19 examples of the production version, designated Bv 138B-1, but the major production version, the Bv 138C-1, resulted from further structural strengthening and the addition of a 13-mm (0.51-in) MG 131 machine-gun in the position behind the centre engine nacelle. Introduced in March 1941, the Bv 138C-1 was built to a total of 227 units before production ended in 1943. Final variant was the mine-sweeping Bv 138 MS with a degaussing loop of dural, field-generating equipment installed and armament deleted, all of them conversions from the Bv 138B-0 pre-production aircraft.

Specification
Bv 138C-1

Type: reconnaissance flying-boat
Powerplant: three 880-hp (656-kW) Junkers Jumo 205D 6-cylinder vertically-opposed inline piston engines
Performance: maximum speed 171 mph (275 km/h) at sea level; cruising speed 146 mph (235 km/h); service ceiling 16,405 ft (5000 m); maximum range 3,107 miles (5000 km)
Weights: empty 17,857 lb (8100 kg); maximum take-off 32,408 lb (14700 kg)
Dimensions: span 88 ft 7 in (27.00 m); length 65 ft 3½ in (19.90 m); height 21 ft 8 in (6.60 m); wing area 1,205.60 sq ft (112.00 m²)
Armament: one 20-mm MG 151 cannon in the bow turret, one similar cannon in the rear hull position and one 13-mm (0.51-in) MG 131 machine-gun in the position at the rear of the centre engine nacelle, plus three 110-lb (50-kg) bombs under starboard wing root, or (Bv 138C-1/U1) six 110-lb (50-kg) bombs or four 331-lb (150-kg) depth-charges
Operator: Luftwaffe

The first Blohm und Voss Bv 138B-0 photographed after conversion from Bv 138A-0 standard, the bow turret being replaced by a shaped metal fairing pending availability of a new turret for the 20-mm MG 151 cannon.

Blohm und Voss Bv 222 Wiking

Blohm und Voss Bv 222A-0 of LTS 222, Petsamo, Finland in March 1943

History and notes

The largest flying-boat to achieve operational status during World War II, the Blohm und Voss Bv 222 was designed originally by Dr Ing. Richard Vogt and Herr R. Schubert (chief of aerodynamics and hydrodynamics), to meet a 1937 Lufthansa requirement for a long-range passenger transport. This was required to operate between Berlin and New York in 20 hours with 16 passengers, or to accommodate up to 24 passengers on shorter routes.

Three aircraft, each powered by six 1,000-hp (746-kW) BMW-Bramo Fafnir 323R radials, were ordered in September 1937, and work on the first began in January 1938. There were a number of notable features incorporated in the design, including an extensive unobstructed floor area, made possible by a beam of almost 10 ft (3.05 m), and an absence of intermediate bulkheads above floor level. The wing incorporated a tubular main spar that served also to contain fuel and oil tanks (a feature of Vogt designs), and the outboard stabilising floats each split into halves to retract sideways into the wing.

This Bv 222V-8, last of the A-series aircraft, had only a brief operational career, falling to RAF Beaufighters over the Mediterranean on 10 December 1942 after less than two months' service.

On 7 September 1940 Flugkapitän Helmut Rodig made the first flight with the prototype, which clearly had military potential. Indeed, soon afterwards it was fitted with enlarged doors for transport duties with the Luftwaffe, undertaking its first sortie on 10 July 1941. After initial service in Norway it was transferred to the Mediterranean theatre, being used to carry supplies for German forces in North Africa.

Armament was introduced with the second and third prototypes, flown on 7 August and 28 November 1941 respectively. The third carried only a 7.92-mm (0.31-in) MG 81 machine-gun in the bow, but the second was fitted additionally with a similar weapon in each of four waist positions and in two upper turrets, plus a pair of 13-mm (0.51-in) MG 131 guns in two gondolas located beneath the centre section. The first prototype was equipped retrospectively with similar bow and waist armament, and with an MG 131 in each of the upper turrets. On 10 May 1942 it became the first Bv 222 to be delivered to Lufttransportstaffel (See) 222. It was joined by the second prototype in August of that year which, following trials at Erprobungsstelle Travemünde, had been provided with a modified planing bottom to the hull to improve its hydrodynamic characteristics. Four or five more prototypes entered service with the Luftwaffe and these, designated Bv 222A, had an interior suitable for the carriage of

Blohm und Voss Bv 222 Wiking

freight or up to 76 equipped troops. A civil version with Junkers Jumo 208 engines was proposed but not built, this having been allocated the designation Bv 222B, but the fourth of the Bv 222As served as prototype for the Bv 222C which introduced Junkers Jumo 207C diesel engines and additional armament. Five Bv 222Cs, basically pre-production aircraft, were completed to production standard and entered service, but plans to build more were prevented by an RLM decision to end the use of diesel engines, which required much maintenance and posed fuel logistics problems.

At the end of 1942, a decision was taken to modify the Bv 222 for a maritime reconnaissance role, for service with a redesignated Aufklärungsstaffel (See) 222 and, later, with 1.(Fern)/See-Aufklärungsgruppe 129 at Biscarosse in France. For this task four of the aircraft already delivered to the Luftwaffe were modified to carry FuG 200 Hohentwiel search radar, plus revised armament which comprised three power-operated dorsal turrets, and two at quarter-span positions above the wings. Examples of the Bv 222C also saw service in Norway. When the war ended, an example captured at Trondheim was flown to RAF Calshot, and then to the Marine Aircraft Experimental

Establishment at Felixstowe for evaluation; it later passed to No.201 Squadron.

Specification
Blohm und Voss Bv 222C

Type: long-range maritime patrol, reconnaissance or transport aircraft
Powerplant: six 1,000-hp (746-kW) Junkers Jumo 207C 6-cylinder vertically-opposed inline diesel engines
Performance: maximum speed 242 mph (390 km/h) at 16,405 ft (5000 m); cruising speed 214 mph (345 km/h) at 18,210 ft (5550 m); service ceiling 23,950 ft (7300 m); range 3,787 miles (6095 km)
Weights: empty 67,572 lb (30650 kg); maximum take-off 108,027 lb (49000 kg)
Dimensions: span 150 ft 11 in (46.00 m); length 121 ft 4¾ in (37.00 m); height 35 ft 9 in (10.90 m); wing area 2,744.89 sq ft (255.00 m²)
Armament: (Bv 222C-09) three 20-mm MG 151 cannon (one each in forward dorsal and two overwing turrets) and five 13-mm (0.51-in) MG 131 machine-guns (one each in bow position and four beam hatches)
Operator: Luftwaffe

Breda Ba.65

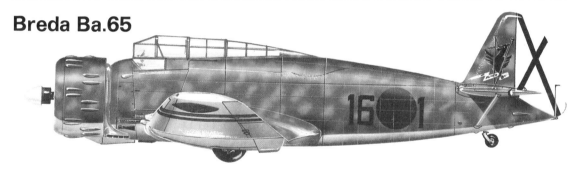

Breda Ba.65 of the Aviazione Legionaria during the Spanish Civil War

History and notes

Intended as an *aeroplano di combattimento*, capable of fulfilling the roles of interceptor fighter, light bomber, or reconnaissance/attack aircraft as required, the prototype Breda Ba.65 (MM 325) made its initial flight in September 1935, piloted by Ambrogio Colombo. It was a cantilever low-wing monoplane with main landing gear units retracting rearwards into underwing fairings. Basic structure of the fuselage and wing was of chrome-molybdenum steel alloy tubing, covered overall with duralumin sheet, except for the trailing edges of the wing, which were fabric-covered. The wing incorporated trailing-edge flaps and Handley Page leading-edge slats. A single fin and rudder tail assembly was strut- and wire-braced, and was of steel construction with light alloy skins.

An initial production order for 81 Ba.65s was placed in 1936, all powered by the French Gnome-Rhône K-14 engine of 700 hp (522 kW) as had been installed in the

prototype. A batch of 13 aircraft from this production series equipped the 65a Squadriglia of the Aviazione Legionaria, the Italian air contingent sent to support the Fascist cause in the Spanish Civil War. The unit took part in operations at Santander in August 1937, then at Teruel, and in the battles for the River Ebro. Like the prototype these were single-seat aircraft, with the pilot's cockpit fully enclosed by a glazed canopy which tapered to the rear.

Experience in Spain indicated that the Ba.65 was suited only to the attack role, and the type served thenceforth with most of the eight *squadriglie* attached to the two Regia Aeronautica assault *stormi* (wings), the 5° and 50°. A second series of 137 aircraft was built by Breda (80) and Caproni-Vizzola (57), before production ended in July 1939. They differed from the first production batch by having Fiat A.80 engines. Six Fiat-powered Ba.65s and four more of the Gnome-Rhône-powered version were sent to the Aviazione Legionaria

Breda Ba.65

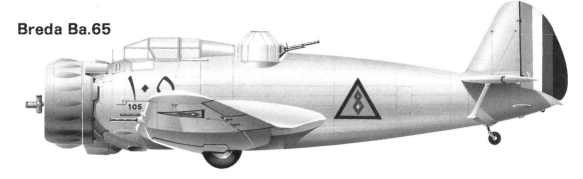

Breda Ba.65 of No. 5 (Fighter) Squadron, Iraq air force

in Spain in 1938.

Following Italy's entry into World War II in June 1940, Ba.65s were involved in the fighting in North Africa against the British. They had a low serviceability rate in desert conditions and put up an unimpressive performance. The last serviceable aircraft was lost during the British offensive in Cyrenaica in February 1941.

A large number of the Ba.65s serving with Italian units were of two-seat configuration, with an observer/gunner in an open cockpit above the trailing edge of the wing. A smaller number of the type had a Breda L type turret, but in either case the observer/gunner operated a single 7.7-mm (0.303-in) machine-gun. While offensive armament could theoretically comprise up to 2,205 lb (1000 kg) of bombs, the load usually carried was up to 661 lb (300 kg) in the fuselage bomb bay or, alternatively, up to 441 lb (200 kg) on underwing racks.

Exports included 25 Fiat-powered Ba.65 two-seaters to Iraq in 1938, two of them dual-control trainers and the remainder with Breda L turrets; 20 Ba.65s with Piaggio P.XI C.40 engines to Chile later in the same year, 17 of them single-seaters and three dual-control trainers; and 10 Fiat-powered two-seaters with Breda

The Breda Ba.65 was obsolete when Italy entered the war and were quickly overcome by British forces in North Africa.

L turrets to Portugal in November 1939. A single Fiat-powered production aircraft was tested with an American Pratt & Whitney R-1830 engine in June 1937 in anticipation of an order from the Chinese Nationalist government, but this failed to materialise. The Iraqi Ba.65s saw limited action against the British during the 1941 insurrection in that country.

Specification
Breda 65/A.80 (single-seat version)
Type: ground-attack aircraft
Powerplant: one 1,000-hp (746-kW) Fiat A.80 RC.41 18-cylinder radial piston engine
Performance: maximum level speed 267 mph (430 km/h); maximum level speed, two-seat version 255 mph (410 km/h); service ceiling 20,670 ft (6300 m); range 342 miles (550 km)
Weights: empty equipped 5,291 lb (2400 kg); maximum take-off 6,504 lb (2950 kg)
Dimensions: span 39 ft 8½ in (12.10 m); length 30 ft 6¼ in (9.30 m); height 10 ft 6 in (3.20 m); wing area 252.96 sq ft (23.50 m²)
Armament: two 12.7-mm (0.5-in) and two 7.7-mm (0.303-in) Breda-SAFAT fixed forward-firing machine-guns in wings, plus up to 661 lb (300 kg) of bombs in fuselage bomb-bay and up to 441 lb (200 kg) of bombs on underwing racks (usually alternatively)
Operators: Regia Aeronautica, Iraq, Portugal, Chile

Breda Ba.88 Lince

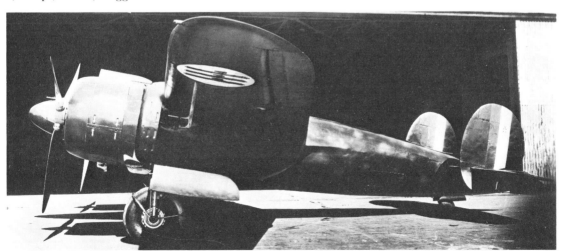

Breda Ba.88 Lince of the 7° Gruppo, 5° Stormo da Combattimento, Regia Aeronautica, based at Castel Benito (Libya) in 1940

History and notes

A propaganda triumph when its appearance was trumpeted by Mussolini's Fascist regime in 1936, the Breda Ba.88 Lince (lynx), designed by Antonio Parano and Giuseppe Panzeri, was a sleek all-metal shoulder-wing monoplane with twin-engine powerplant. The prototype (MM 302), which had a single vertical tail assembly, made its maiden flight during October 1936 flown by Furio Niclot, Breda's chief test pilot. In April 1937 Niclot established two world speed-over-distance records, averaging 321.25 mph (517 km/h) over a 62-mile (100-km) distance and 295.15 mph (475 km/h) over a 621-mile (1000-km) circuit. In December of that year he raised these speeds to 344.24 mph (554 km/h) and 325.6 mph (524 km/h) respectively.

The prototype, which had retractable tailwheel landing gear, and powerplant comprising two 900-hp (671-kW) Gnome-Rhône K-14 radials, was then given a modified tail unit with twin fins and rudders. Regarded as an *aeroplano di combattimento*, suitable for attack, long-range reconnaissance or bombing operations, the Ba.88 then had its military equipment and weapons installed. Immediately, performance and flight character-istics fell off dramatically, but by then production orders were already being executed. The first batch of 80, plus eight dual-control trainers, was built by Breda between May and October 1939. Problems with the prototype led to a number of weight-saving modifications, and more power was provided by the installation of 1,000-hp (746-kW) Piaggio P.XI RC.40 radials.

On 16 June 1940, just after Italy's declaration of war on France and her allies, the Ba.88 had its first taste of action. Twelve aircraft from the Regia Aeronautica's 19° Gruppo Autonomo made bombing and machine-gun attacks on the principal airfields of Corsica; three days later nine Ba.88s made a repeat attack. Analysis of these operations showed that the Ba.88 had only limited value, and any remaining doubts were settled when Ba.88s of the 7° Gruppo Autonomo joined action in Libya against the British. Fitted with sand filters, the engines overheated and failed to deliver their designed power. Attacks on targets at Sidi Barrani had to be aborted in September 1940, the aircraft failing to gain sufficient altitude or maintain formation, and reaching a speed less than half that claimed by the manufacturers.

By mid-November 1940 most surviving Ba.88s had been stripped of useful equipment and were scattered around operational airfields as decoys for attacking British aircraft. During this time, however, further batches of Ba.88s were being delivered, comprising 19 built by Breda and 48 by IMAM (Meridionali). Most went straight to the scrapyard.

Three Ba.88s were modified by the Agusta plant in 1942 to serve as ground-attack aircraft. Wing span was increased by 6 ft 6¾ in (2.00 m) to alleviate wing

A sleek aircraft, the Breda Ba.88 Lince saw most of its service as a decoy on airfields, it being hopelessly outclassed as a bomber at the outbreak of war.

loading problems, their engines were replaced by Fiat A.74s, nose armament was increased to four 12.7-mm (0.5-in) machine-guns, and dive brakes were installed. These Breda Ba.88Ms were delivered to the 103° Gruppo Autonomo Tuffatori (independent dive-bombing group) at Lonate Pozzolo on 7 September 1943. They were flight-tested by Luftwaffe pilots, but that was the last heard of the Breda Ba.88 which represented, perhaps, the most remarkable failure of any operational aircraft to see service in World War II.

Specification

Type: fighter-bomber/reconnaissance aircraft
Powerplant: two 1,000-hp (746-kW) Piaggio P.XI RC.40 14-cylinder radial piston engines
Performance: maximum speed 304 mph (490 km/h);
service ceiling 26,245 ft (8000 m); range 1,019 miles (1640 km)
Weights: empty equipped 10,251 lb (4650 kg); maximum take-off 14,881 lb (6750 kg)
Dimensions: span 51 ft 2¼ in (15.60 m); length 35 ft 4¾ in (10.79 m); height 10 ft 2 in (3.10 m); wing area 358.88 sq ft (33.34 m²)
Armament: three fixed forward-firing 12.7-mm (0.5-in) Breda-SAFAT machine-guns in nose and one 7.7-mm (0.303-in) Breda-SAFAT machine-gun on trainable mounting in rear cockpit, plus up to 2,204 lb (1000 kg) of bombs in fuselage bomb-bay or, alternatively, three 441-lb (200-kg) bombs carried semi-exposed in individual recesses in the fuselage belly
Operators: Italian Regia Aeronautica and Aeronautica Nazionale Repubblicana

Bücker Bü 131 Jungmann

History and notes

The first product of Bücker Flugzeugbau, established at Johannisthal, Germany during 1932, was a two-seat light trainer known as the Bücker Bü 131 Jungmann (youth). Designed by Anders Andersson, the company's Swedish chief engineer, it was a conventional single-bay biplane with fabric-covered wooden wings, a welded steel-tube fuselage that, with the exception of light alloy around the engine and cockpit, was also fabric-covered, and a wire-braced tail unit of similar construction to the fuselage. The tailwheel type landing gear had rather stalky main units, and power for the prototype (D-3150), first flown on 27 April 1934, was provided by an 80-hp (60-kW) Hirth HM 60R inline engine.

The Bü 131A, as the initial production version was designated, proved to be very successful, being manufactured not only for civil flying schools in Germany but also for the Luftwaffe, although production

figures do not appear to have survived. They consisted not only of the initial production Bü 131A, but also an improved production Bü 131B which had a more powerful Hirth HM 504A-2 engine. An experimental Bü 131C was built, powered by a 90-hp (67-kW) Cirrus Minor engine, but following testing this version was not put into production. Bücker exported production aircraft for service in some eight European countries with the largest numbers going to Hungary (100) and Romania (150), and in addition 75 were licence-built in Switzerland. The most extensive licence-construction was in Japan, where 1,037 were built for the Japanese army as the Type 4 Primary Trainer (Ki-86A). This followed the initiation of production on behalf of the Japanese navy for which it was licence-built by Watanabe (later Kyushu) as the Navy Type 2 Primary Trainer Model 11 (K9W1). Production figures for the Japanese navy version differs according to source, varying from 217 to 339, but it seems reasonably certain that more than 200 were used as the navy's standard primary trainer.

Used throughout World War II by the Luftwaffe, the Bü 131 was later displaced by the improved Bücker Bü 181, and many saw service with auxiliary ground-attack squadrons. Carrying 2.2- and 4.4-lb (1- and 2-kg) bombs, they were used by night to maintain nonstop harassment over Soviet lines. Like other classic trainers, many Bü 131s survived the war, and they were even built by Aero in Czechoslovakia during the 1950s under the designation C.4.

First product of Bücker Flugzeugbau, the Bü 131 was a conventional biplane which saw front-line service with a Luftwaffe auxiliary ground-attack squadron on the Eastern Front.

Specification
Bücker Bü 131B

Type: two-seat primary trainer
Powerplant: one 105-hp (78-kW) Hirth HM 504A-2 4-cylinder inverted inline piston engine
Performance: maximum speed at sea level 114 mph (183 km/h); cruising speed 106 mph (170 km/h);

Bücker Bü 131 Jungmann

service ceiling 9,840 ft (3000 m); range 404 miles (650 km)
Weights: empty 860 lb (390 kg); maximum take-off 1,499 lb (680 kg)
Dimensions: span 24 ft 3¼ in (7.40 m); length 21 ft 8 in (6.60 m); height 7 ft 4½ in (2.25 m); wing area 145.32 sq ft (13.50 m²)
Operators: Luftwaffe, Finland, Hungary, Japan, Netherlands, Romania, Spain, Sweden, Switzerland

Bücker Bü 133 Jungmeister

History and notes
Demand for the Bü 131 Jungmann had been such that Bücker's production facilities at Johannisthal were soon overwhelmed. A new factory was established at Rangsdorf and there, where it would be possible to expand production facilities, the company began development of a single-seat advanced trainer based on the Bü 131 design. Generally similar in overall configuration and construction, it differed primarily by being of smaller dimensions, which meant that with a 135-hp (101-kW) Hirth HM 6 inline engine installed the prototype (D-EVEO) had excellent aerobatic performance. Testing by the Luftwaffe resulted in production aircraft being ordered for use in an advanced training role, including the early instruction of fighter pilots, and the initial production examples were designated Bücker Bü 133A and named Jungmeister (young champion); designation of the major production version, which had the more powerful Siemens Sh 14A-4 radial engine, was Bü 133C, but no record appears to have survived of the number of these two versions built for the Luftwaffe. Licence-built aircraft, which had the designation Bü 133B, included about 50 manufactured by Dornier-Werke in Switzerland for the Swiss air force, plus a similar quantity by CASA in Spain.

Specification
Bücker Bü 133C
Type: single-seat advanced trainer
Powerplant: one 160-hp (119-kW) Siemens Sh 14A-4 radial piston engine
Performance: maximum speed at sea level 137 mph (220 km/h); cruising speed 124 mph (200 km/h) service ceiling 14,765 ft (4500 m); range 311 miles (500 km)
Weights: empty 937 lb (425 kg); maximum take-off 1,290 lb (585 kg)

Much of the Luftwaffe's training was done on aircraft of Bücker design, notably the Bü 133 Jungmeister. This was a highly aerobatic single seater, well suited to the rigours of the advanced flying school, such as Jagdfliegerschule 2.

Dimensions: span 21 ft 7¾ in (6.60 m); length 19 ft 8¼ in (6.0 m); height 7 ft 2½ in (2.20 m); wing area 129.17 sq ft (12.0 m²)
Operators: Luftwaffe, Spain, Switzerland

Bücker Bü 181 Bestmann

History and notes
Experience with the Bü 180 showed that even with an engine of small power output the two-seat monoplane could offer quite good performance. With this encouragement the company began the design of a new trainer, one that adopted the constructional techniques used in the Bü 180, but which introduced side-by-side seating in an enclosed cabin to provide ideal conditions for primary training. Identified as the Bücker Bü 181, and later named Bestmann, the new aircraft had wings of wooden basic construction with plywood and fabric covering, a tail unit of similar structure, and a fuselage with steel-tube forward section and a wooden monocoque aft section. Landing gear was of tailwheel type, and

Bücker Bü 181 Bestmann

Photographed at a post-war display of Axis aircraft, the Bücker Bü 181 revealed itself as a highly compact two-seat aircraft. On this example the inside wheel fairings have been removed.

power was provided by a Hirth HM 504 engine. The prototype (D-ERBV) was first flown in early 1939, and following testing by the Luftwaffe, production of the Bü 181A was ordered for service as a standard basic trainer; late production aircraft which incorporated some minor improvements had the changed designation Bü 181D. Details of the number constructed for the Luftwaffe are not known accurately, but it has been estimated that production must have run into many thousands. As the type became available in large numbers it was used also as a communications aircraft and, in small numbers, as a glider tug.

In addition to production by Bücker, 708 were built by Fokker in the Netherlands during the war, and from 1944 to 1946 125 were built in Sweden for the nation's

air force under the designation Sk 25. Wartime production had also started in Czechoslovakia, and continued there by Zlin after the war had ended, this company building the civil Z.281 and Z.381, as well as the military C.6 and C.106 for the Czech air force. Under licence from Czechoslovakia, post-war production was undertaken by Heliopolis Aircraft Works in Egypt, which built a version similar to the Zlin Z.381 for several Arab states, and for the Egyptian air force, unde the name Gomhouria. Many of these latter aircraft remained in service into the 1980s.

Specification
Bücker Bü 181A
Type: two-seat primary trainer
Powerplant: one 105-hp (78-kW) Hirth HM 504 4-cylinder inverted inline piston engine
Performance: maximum speed at sea level 134 mph (215 km/h); cruising speed 121 mph (195 km/h); service ceiling 16,405 ft (5000 m); range 497 miles (800 km)
Weights: empty 1,058 lb (480 kg); maximum take-off 1,653 lb (750 kg)
Dimensions: span 34 ft 9¼ in (10.60 m); length 25 ft 9 in (7.85 m); height 6 ft 8¾ in (2.05 m); wing area 145.32 sq ft (13.50 m²)
Operators: Luftwaffe, Czechoslovakia, Egypt, Sweden, Switzerland

CRDA Cant Z.501 Gabbiano

Cant Z.501 Gabbiano of 2ª Escuadrilla, Grupo 62, Agrupacion Espanola (Spanish Nationalist air force) based in Majorca in 1939

History and notes
In 1931 Cantiere Navale Triestino was reorganised as Cantieri Riuniti dell'Adriatico (CRDA) and Marshal Italo Balbo, then Minister of Aviation in Italy, persuaded Ing. Filippo Zappata to return home from France to become the new company's chief engineer. His first design was the CRDA Cant Z.501 Gabbiano (seagull), a long-range reconnaissance bomber flying-boat of wooden construction, with fabric covering on the upper hull, wing and tail surfaces. Power was supplied by a 900-hp (671-kW) Isotta-Fraschini Asso XI engine, driving a

two-blade wooden or three-blade metal propeller, and its nacelle in the centre section was extended to include a cockpit for the flight engineer, who was responsible also for the operation of a 7.7-mm (0.303-in) machine-gun; two similar weapons were mounted in bow and dorsal positions. Racks were attached to the wing struts, inboard of the floats, and could carry a maximum load of 1,411 lb (640 kg) of bombs.

The prototype made its first flight on 7 February 1934, and in October of that year Cant's chief pilot, Mario Stoppani, flew the aircraft 2,560 miles (4120 km)

CRDA Cant Z.501 Gabbiano

from the company's base at Monfalcone, Trieste to Massawa in Eritrea, distance record for seaplanes. In July 1935, after France had taken the record, Stoppani regained it with a 3,080-mile (4957-km) flight to Berbera in British Somaliland.

The Z.501 entered squadron service with the Regia Aeronautica in 1937, and by the time Italy entered World War II on 10 June 1940 more than 200 formed the equipment of at least 17 squadrons and four flights. The Z.501's operational debut was with a unit of the Aviazione Legionaria, based in Majorca and operating in support of the Nationalist forces in the Spanish Civil War. A small number of Z.501s served with a coastal defence unit of the Romanian air force. A total of 454 was delivered before production ended in 1943.

Specification

Type: reconnaissance bomber flying-boat

Powerplant: one 900-hp (671-kW) Isotta-Fraschini Asso XI 12-cylinder Vee piston engine
Performance: maximum speed 171 mph (275 km/h) at 8,200 ft (2500 m); cruising speed 149 mph (240 km/h) at 6,560 ft (2000 m); cruising range with full payload 621 miles (1000 km); maximum range 1,491 miles (2400 km)
Weights: empty 8,466 lb (3840 kg); maximum take-off 15,510 lb (7035 kg)
Dimensions: span 73 ft 10 in (22.50 m); length 46 ft 11 in (14.30 m); height 14 ft 6 in (4.42 m); wing area 667.38 sq ft (62.00 m²)
Armament: three trainable 7.7-mm (0.303-in) machine-guns, plus up to 1,411 lb (640 kg) of bombs
Operators: Italian Regia Aeronautica, Aeronautica Cobelligerante del Sud, Aeronautica Nazionale Repubblicana, Romania, Spain

CRDA Cant Z.506

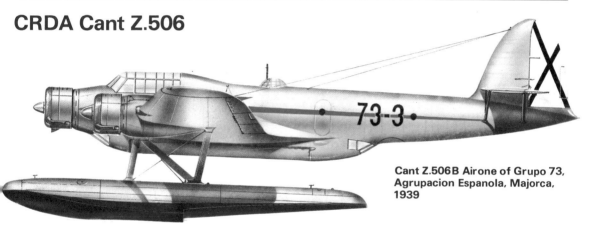

Cant Z.506B Airone of Grupo 73, Agrupacion Espanola, Majorca, 1939

History and notes

In July 1935 there flew the prototype of a large wooden twin-float seaplane, powered by three 840-hp (626-kW) Isotta-Fraschini Asso XI inline engines. This was the CRDA Cant Z.505 which had been designed as a mailplane. On 19 August in the same year, Mario Stoppani conducted the first flight of the slightly smaller and lighter Z.506, a 12/14-passenger transport with three 610-hp (455-kW) Piaggio Stella IX radial engines. The type was put into production in 1936 as the Z.506A, and entered service with the Italian airline Ala Littoria during that year on routes around the Mediterranean. Powered by three 750-hp (559-kW) Alfa Romeo 126 RC.34 radial engines the Z.506A, flown mostly by Mario Stoppani, set several altitude, distance and speed records in 1936-8, including speeds of 191.539 mph (308.25 km/h), 198.7 mph (319.78 km/h) and 200.118 mph (322.06 km/h) over distances of 3,107 miles (5000 km), 1,243 miles (2000 km) and 621 miles (1000 km) respectively. It carried a payload of 4,409 lb (2000 kg) to 25,623 ft (7810 m) and 11,023 lb (5000 kg) to 22,693 ft (6917 m) and later flew 3,345.225 miles

(5383.6 km) over a closed circuit.

A military version, designated Z.506B Airone (heron), was shown at the Milan Aeronautical Exhibition in October 1937. This had a stepped, extensively glazed tandem two-seat cockpit and a ventral gondola which contained the bomb aimer's position and the bomb bay, immediately behind which was a gunner's position. The Z.506B was built at Cant's Monfalcone and Finale Ligure Factories, and by Piaggio under licence. In November 1937 a Z.506B with 750-hp (559-kW) Alfa Romeo 127 RC.55 engines set a load-to-height record of 33,318 ft (10155 m) with a 2,205-lb (1000-kg) payload, and then flew 4,362 miles (7020 km) nonstop from Cadiz to Carevalas. Z.506 variants included an air-sea rescue Z.506S of which at least 20 were produced as conversions from Z.506Bs, and a single Z.506 landplane which was specially prepared with fixed, spatted landing gear for an endurance record attempt by Mario Stoppani; this was at first postponed, then finally cancelled, because of continuing bad weather. In 1936 a heavy bomber prototype, which was essentially a scaled-up version of the Z.506, was built under the designation Z.508. No production version resulted but this aircraft, powered by three 840-hp (627-kW) Isotta-Fraschini Asso XI RC.40 engines, was used to set a number of records, including a speed of 154.26 mph (248.25 km/h) over a 1,234-mile (2000-km) course with an 11,023-lb (5000 kg) payload. Last of this family was the Z.509, a larger and heavier version of the Z.506A of which three were built in 1937 for use on Ala Littoria's transatlantic postal service to South America. This model was powered by three Fiat A.80 RC.41 radial engines, and a new wing of 92 ft 11 in (28.32 m) span and 1,076.43 sq ft (100.00 m²) area was introduced to compensate for increased empty and maximum take-off weights of 22,000 lb (9980 kg) and 35,200 lb (15965 kg) respectively. Production of the Z.506B totalled 324, including two prototypes which were supplied to the Regia Aeronautica and the Regia Marina; the latter service took over 29 aircraft, the balance of a Polish order for 30 which were not delivered as a result of the German invasion. Five were delivered to the Nationalist forces in the Spanish Civil War late in 1938. A number of the Z.506S air-sea rescue aircraft remained in service until 1959.

Specification
Cant Z.506B Airone
Type: reconnaissance/bomber floatplane
Powerplant: three 750-hp (559-kW) Alfa Romeo 126 RC.34 9-cylinder radial piston engines
Performance: maximum speed 227 mph (365 km/h); cruising speed 202 mph (325 km/h); service ceiling 26,245 ft (8000 m); maximum range 1,705 miles (2745 km)
Weights: empty 18,298 lb (8300 kg); maximum take-off 27,117 lb (12300 kg)
Dimensions: span 86 ft 11¼ in (26.50 m); length 63 ft 1¾ in (19.25 m); height 24 ft 3¼ in (7.40 m); wing area 936.49 sq ft (87.00 m²)
Armament: one or two 7.7-mm (0.303-in) machine-guns and one 12.7-mm (0.5-in) machine-gun, plus up to 2,645 lb (1200 kg) of bombs or a torpedo
Operators: Italian Regia Aeronautica, Aeronautica Cobelligerante del Sud, Aeronautica Nazionale Repubblicana, and Luftwaffe

CRDA Cant Z.1007

History and notes
Design studies which culminated in the CRDA Cant Z.1007bis Alcione (kingfisher) began in 1935 and the prototype Z.1007, powered by three 825-hp (615-kW) Isotta-Fraschini Asso XI engines, made its first flight in March 1937. Changes made during initial flight test included the substitution of three-blade Piaggio metal propellers for the original two-blade wooden units, and modifications to the ventral radiators. Annular radiators identified an interim production verison, 34 of which were built. Some were flown by the Regia Aeronautica's 221° Gruppo from 1939 but the aircraft were not used operationally.

In the meantime, Zappata had completed work on a redesigned version powered by three 1,000-hp (746-kW) Piaggio P.XI R2C.40 radials. Early examples had the tailplane mounted lower on the fin than on the prototype, and later aircraft introduced revised horizontal tail surfaces with noticeable dihedral and oval endplate fins and rudders; this change was introduced to improve the field of fire from the dorsal turret. The first aircraft, in fact the thirty-fifth production airframe, was first flown in 1938 as the Z.1007bis, and after a total of eight pre-production examples had been completed for service trials at Guidonia, the type entered quantity production at Cant's Monfalcone factory, and was also built under licence by IMAM at Capodichino, Naples. Defensive armament comprised one Breda M or Caproni-Lanciani Delta E dorsal turret housing a 12.7-mm (0.5-in) Scotti or SAFAT machine-gun, a similar weapon in a ventral position behind the bomb bay, and two 7.7-mm (0.303-in) SAFAT guns in

beam positions. Production of all Z.1007 variants totalled 561, including a small number of the Z.1007ter, which was an improved version of the Z.1007bis with three 1,150-hp (858-kW) Piaggio P.XIX radials and bombload reduced to 2,205lb (1000 kg); maximum speed and range of this version were 311 mph (500 km/h) and 1,398 miles (2250 km) respectively. Final variant of this family had the very different designation Z.1015. Built only as the prototype of a military mailplane, with power provided by three 1,500-hp (1140-kW) Piaggio P.XII RC.35 radials, it had been intended that it would be developed as a bomber. Maximum speed of this prototype was 348 mph (560 km/h).

Specification
Cant Z.1007bis Alcione
Type: medium bomber
Powerplant: three 1,000-hp (746-kW) Piaggio P.XI R2C.40 14-cylinder radial piston engines
Performance: maximum speed 289 mph (465 km/h) at 13,125 ft (4000 m); service ceiling 26,900 ft (8200 m); range 1,087 miles (1750 km) at 236 mph (380 km/h) with maximum internal bombload
Weights: empty 20,712 lb (9395 kg); maximum take-off 30,027 lb (13620 kg)
Dimensions: span 81 ft 4¼ in (24.80 m); length 60 ft 2½ in (18.35 m); height 17 ft 1½ in (5.22 m); wing area 807.32 sq ft (75.00 m²)
Armament: two 12.7-mm (0.5-in) Scotti or SAFAT machine-guns (one each in dorsal and ventral positions) and two beam-mounted 7.7-mm (0.303-in)

CRDA Cant Z.1007

Cant Z.1007bis of 210ª Squadriglia, 50° Gruppo, 16° Stormo, based in Greece in early 1941

Cant Z.1007bis of 230ª Squadriglia, 95° Gruppo, 35° Stormo, Greece, February 1941

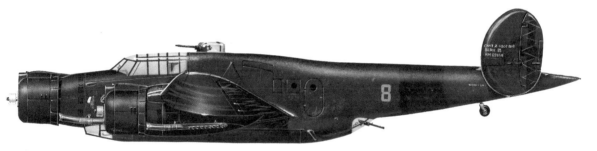

Cant Z.1007bis of the 260ª Squadriglia, 106° Gruppo, 47° Stormo in 1943 with night finish and exhaust shrouds

Cant Z.1007ter of 190ª Squadriglia, 88° Gruppo, 2° Stormo, Co-Belligerent Air Force, based at Lecce-Gelantine, October 1944

SAFAT machine-guns, plus a maximum internal bombload of 2,645 lb (1200 kg) or a maximum external bombload of 2,205 lb (1000 kg)

Operators: Italian Regia Aeronautica, Aeronautica Cobelligerante del Sud and Aeronautica Nazionale Repubblicana, and Luftwaffe

Caproni Ca 100

History and notes

Based on the de Havilland D.H.60 Moth, but incorporating some minor differences in detail design, including an increased-span lower wing, the Caproni Ca 100 was built in some numbers for civil and military use from 1929. Powered initially by the 85-hp (63-kW) de Havilland Gipsy engine, the Ca 100 was fitted also with a variety of engines of different output, including the 90-hp (67-kW) Blackburn Cirrus Minor, the 115-hp (86-kW) Isotta-Fraschini Asso 80R, the 145-hp (108-kW) Colombo S.63 and the 85-hp (63-kW) Fiat A50. A twin-float seaplane version, 30 of which were built by Macchi, was known as the Ca 100 Idro, and in 1934 a light bombing trainer was built, powered by a 130-hp (97-kW) radial engine and able to carry four small bombs. In 1931 a Ca 100 Idro flown by Antonini and Trevisan established a seaplane altitude record of 16,462 ft (5018 m). In 1935 the Peruvian government signed a contract with Caproni which gave the company

Based on the de Havilland Moth, the Caproni Ca 100 was widely used as a basic trainer in both Italy and Bulgaria.

a 10-year monopoly for the manufacture and repair of military aircraft in that country. Several Ca 100s were supplied from Italy, and in May 1937 a factory was opened in Peru, charged with producing 25 Ca 100s within two years but actually building only 12 in that period, at an excessive cost. The type was also manufactured by a Caproni subsidiary in Bulgaria as the KB-1.

Specification

Type: two-seat trainer
Powerplant: one 85-hp (63-kW) de Havilland Gipsy 4-cylinder inline piston engine
Performance: maximum speed 102 mph (165 km/h); cruising speed 87 mph (140 km/h); service ceiling 13,125 ft (4000 m); range 435 miles (700 km)
Weights: empty 882 lb (400 kg); maximum take-off 1,499 lb (680 kg)
Dimensions: span, upper 27 ft 4¾ in (8.35 m) and lower 32 ft 10 in (10.00 m); length 23 ft 11¼ in (7.30 m); height 9 ft 0¼ in (2.75 m); wing area 262.65 sq ft (24.40 m²)
Operators: Regia Aeronautica, Peru, Bulgaria

Caproni Ca 133

History and notes

Designed by Ingeniere Rodolfo Verduzio, the Caproni Ca 133 was an aerodynamically and structurally improved Ca 101. Of welded steel-tube construction with metal and fabric covering, the Ca 133 featured faired engine nacelles with NACA cowlings, main wheel spats, flaps and modified tail surfaces. The civil version accommodating up to 16 passengers, was used by Ala Littoria, and the military version saw wide service with the Regia Aeronautica, particularly in Italian East

Africa. Incorporating two small bomb bays in its structure and armed with four machine-guns it was operated as a bomber under the designation Ca 133. Bomber aircraft deployed as military transports, with an interior fitted out to accommodate 18 fully equipped troops, were redesignated Ca 133T and, similarly, conversions for use in an ambulance role were designated Ca 133S. In 1938 a small number of an improved version of the Ca 133 was introduced under the designation Ca 148, serving initially in East Africa, and some survived to

Caproni Ca 133

fly with the post-war Italian air force. The Ca 148 differed from the earlier aircraft by having the cockpit moved forward by approximately 3 ft (0.91 m), the main cabin door relocated from its original position below the port wing to a point behind the trailing edge, and strengthened landing gear.

Specification
Caproni Ca 133

Type: civil transport and military bomber/transport
Powerplant: three 460-hp (343-kW) Piaggio Stella P.VIII C.16 7-cylinder radial piston engines
Performance: maximum speed 174 mph (280 km/h); cruising speed 143 mph (230 km/h); service ceiling 18,045 ft (5500 m); range 839 miles (1350 km)
Weights: empty 8,818 lb (4000 kg); maximum take-off 14,473 lb (6565 kg)
Dimensions: span 69 ft 8½ in (21.25 m); length 50 ft 4¼ in (15.35 m); height 13 ft 1½ in (4.00 m); wing area 699.68 sq ft (65.00 m²)

Bearing hastily applied markings, this Caproni Ca 133 was flown by the Aeronautica Co-Belligerante del Sud.

Armament: four 7.7-mm (0.303-in) machine-guns in side, dorsal turret and ventral positions, plus up to 1,102 lb (500 kg) of bombs
Operators: Italian Regia Aeronautica, Aeronautica Cobelligerante del Sud and Aeronautica Nazionale Repubblicana, Germany, Spain

Caproni Bergamaschi Ca 135

Caproni Ca 135/P.XI of the 4./III Bombázó Osztály, Magyar Királyi Légierö (Royal Hungarian air force) in southern Russia, 1942

History and notes

A medium bomber designed at Bergamo, the Caproni Bergamaschi Ca 135 was not allocated a type number in the Caproni Bergamaschi Ca 300 series as it was to have been built at Caproni's main Taliedo factory. However, the project was retained at Ponte San Pietro and the prototype, completed in early 1935, was flown for the first time on 1 April. Powered by two 800-hp (597-kW) Isotta Fraschini Asso XI RC radial engines, the Ca 135 was of mixed construction, with a stressed-skin forward fuselage and a wood- and fabric-covered welded steel-tube rear section, the wing being a metal and wood structure with fabric and wood covering. Production Ca 135s had three-blade metal propellers instead of the two-blade wooden propellers of the prototype. Some 14 aircraft, designated Ca 135 Tipo Spagna (Spanish type), were ordered by the Regia Aeronautica in 1936, these having 836-hp (623-kW) Asso XI RC.40 engines, and Breda turrets in nose, dorsal and ventral positions, the dorsal and ventral turrets being retractable.

Maximum take-off weight had risen to 18,497 lb (8390 kg) from the prototype's 16,226 lb (7360 kg), and despite the increased power maximum speed dropped from 248 mph (400 km/h) to 227 mph (365 km/h). To restore overall performance, in 1938 the Tipo Spagna aircraft had Fiat A.80 RC.41 or Piaggio P.XI RC.40 radials installed, each rated at 1,000 hp (746 kW). The Piaggio-engined version was the more successful and, redesignated Ca 135 P.XI, it was given revised engine cowlings, a refined nose section and a Caproni Lanciani dorsal turret. Unsuccessful in a May 1938 Imperial Japanese Army air force competition, in which the Fiat BR.20 was preferred, the Ca 135 P.XI was ordered by the Hungarian air force, which flew about 100 aircraft with the German Luftflotte IV against the Soviets. The last example was retained by Caproni and modified by the incorporation of a dihedral tailplane and 1,400-hp (1044-kW) Alfa Romeo 135 RC.32 Tornado radial engines which increased the maximum speed of this Ca 135bis Alfa to more than 298 mph (480 km/h). Peru also procured the Ca 135, an initial order for six examples with 815-hp (608-kW) Asso XI RC.45 engines being followed by a contract for 32 aircraft designated Ca 135 Tipo Peru (Peruvian type) which had 900-hp (671-kW) Asso XI RC.40 engines in modified cowlings, as well as revised gun positions. Final variant was the single Ca 135 Raid which, built to the order of Brazilian pilot de

Caproni Bergamaschi Ca 135

Of unremarkable design, the Caproni Bergamaschi Ca 135 was another Italian aircraft which was obsolete by the time the war started.

Barros, was powered by 986-hp (736-kW) Isotta-Fraschini Asso engines and provided with additional fuel capacity for extended range. While attempting a flight from Italy to Brazil during 1937, de Barros and the Ca 135 Raid disappeared over North Africa.

Specification
Caproni Ca 135 P.XI
Type: medium bomber
Powerplant: two 1,000-hp (746-kW) Piaggio P.XI

RC.40 14-cylinder radial piston engines
Performance: maximum speed 273 mph (440 km/h) at 15,750 ft (4800 m); cruising speed 217 mph (350 km/h); service ceiling 21,325 ft (6500 m); maximum range 1,243 miles (2000 km)
Weights: empty 13,340 lb (6050 kg); maximum take-off 21,050 lb (9550 kg)
Dimensions: span 61 ft 8 in (18.80 m); length 47 ft 2¾ in (14.40 m); height 11 ft 1¾ in (3.40 m); wing area 645.86 sq ft (60.00 m²)
Armament: three 12.7-mm (0.5-in) machine-guns in nose, dorsal and ventral turrets, plus up to 3,527 lb (1600 kg) of bombs
Operators: Regia Aeronautica, Hungary, Peru

Caproni Bergamaschi Ca 306/Ca 309

History and notes
At the 1935 Milan Exhibition there appeared the prototype of the Caproni Bergamaschi Ca 306 Borea (north wind), a six-passenger low-wing transport with fixed main landing gear faired into the nacelles which housed 185-hp (138-kW) Walter Major engines. Six of these aircraft served ultimately with the Italian airline Ala Littoria, and two more were supplied to the Italian

The Caproni Bergamaschi Ca 309 Ghibli could carry light bombloads, but was also used as reconnaissance and transport aircraft.

colonial government in Libya.

Although built only in small numbers, the Borea was important as the progenitor of a range of light twin-engine aircraft manufactured for a wide variety of roles. The first of these was the aptly-named Ca 309 Ghibli (desert wind), 78 of which were built between the 1936 and 1938 for use in Libya. Production included two civil examples, 165 built for the Regia Aeronautica between 1940 and 1944, and two supplied to Paraguay in 1938. The military versions were used as light transports or reconnaissance bombers with a lengthened glazed nose, bomb racks, cameras, and with armament comprising three 7.7-mm (0.303-in) machine-guns. Another model featured a fixed forward firing 20-mm cannon. Seven squadrons equipped with Ghiblis were operational when Italy entered the war in 1940.

Specification
Caproni Ca 309
Type: general-purpose/light reconnaissance bomber
Powerplant: two 200-hp (149-kW) Alfa Romeo 115-II 6-cylinder inverted inline piston engines

Caproni Bergamaschi Ca 306/Ca 309

Performance: maximum speed 155 mph (250 km/h); cruising speed 130 mph (210 km/h); service ceiling 14,765 ft (4500 m); range 416 miles (670 km)
Weights: empty 3,847 lb (1745 kg); maximum take-off 5,941 lb (2695 kg)
Dimensions: span 53 ft 1¾ in (16.20 m); length 43 ft 7½ in (13.30 m); height 10 ft 8 in (3.25 m); wing area 416.58 sq ft (38.70 m²)
Armament: two 7.7-mm (0.303-in) machine-guns in the wing leading edges and one similar gun flexibly mounted in the nose, plus up to 740 lb (335 kg) of bombs
Operators: Regia Aeronautica, Paraguay

Caproni Bergamaschi Ca 310 series

Caproni Ca 310 Libeccio, one of four delivered to Norway

History and notes

Developed in parallel with the Ghibli, the Caproni Bergamaschi Ca 310 Libeccio (south west wind) was structurally similar to the earlier machine, but was provided with retractable landing gear and powered by two 470-hp (350-kW) Piaggio P.VII C.35 radial engines. The prototype, which was flown for the first time on 20 February 1937, had two 460-hp (343-kW) P.VII C.16 engines. A total of 161 production Ca 310s was delivered to the Regia Aeronautica between 1937 and 1939, including 10 destined originally for Romania. Export deliveries went to Norway (4), Peru (16) and Yugoslavia (12), and this last nation also acquired 12 more under the designation Ca 310bis; this variant, built at Caproni's Taliedo factory, differed primarily by having an unstepped extensively-glazed nose. The designation Ca 310 Idro applied to an experimental civil version with twin floats, but this did not enter production.

The prototype of the Ca 310bis served as a development aircraft for the following Ca 311; the first of 320 built for the Regia Aeronautica was flying on 1 April 1939. As built they were similar to the Ca 310bis, but most were later modified by the introduction of a stepped windscreen, then being redesignated Ca 311M. Defensive armament of this version comprised a Caproni Lanciani turret with a single 7.7-mm (0.303-in) machine-gun, complemented by one machine-gun in the port wing root and another firing aft through a ventral hatch. Yugoslavia ordered 15 Ca 311s, of which five were delivered to the Royal Yugoslav air force in 1941 and 10 to the Croatian air force in 1942. These were followed by the Ca 312, for which the original Ca 310 prototype and one production example served as development aircraft, powered by 650-hp (485-kW) Piaggio P.XVI RC.35 engines with three-blade propellers. The Norwegian

government ordered 15 with the designation Ca 312bis, these having an unstepped, glazed forward fuselage similar to that of the Ca 311, but the German invasion of Norway took place before they could be delivered. The Norwegian aircraft were then diverted for service with the Regia Aeronautica, as were 24 intended originally for the Royal Belgian air force. A modified Ca 310 with two Isotta-Fraschini Asso 120 IRCC 40 engines served as the Ca 313 prototype, first flown on 22 December 1939, but France had already confirmed an order for 200 of these aircraft on 1 October, followed closely by British and Sweden orders for 300 and 64 respectively. However, Italy's entry into the war prevented delivery of any of the British machines and France received only five Ca 313F models, the remainder being diverted to the Regia Aeronautica. Delivery of the first Ca 313S to Sweden was made during November 1940, and a total of 84 had been supplied by early 1941. These received the Swedish designations D 16, S 16, T 16 and Tp 16S, identifying bomber, maritime reconnaissance, torpedo bomber and transport versions respectively. Initial production aircraft were basically Ca 311s with 730-hp (544-kW) Isotta-Fraschini Delta RC.35 I-DS engines, these being identified by the designation Ca 313 R.P.B.1, but a stepped cockpit was a feature of the Ca 313 R.P.B.2, of which 122 were built for the Regia Aeronautica. Ca 313 production totalled 271, this including only a small number of the 905 Ca 313G communications/trainer aircraft ordered for the Luftwaffe, which were not completed because of Caproni's heavy involvement in development and production programmes.

Most extensively built version was the Ca 314, for which the first three production Ca 313 R.P.B.2s, with revised armament, served as prototypes. Variants included the Ca 314A or Ca 314-SC (Scorta), a convoy

Caproni Bergamaschi Ca 310 series

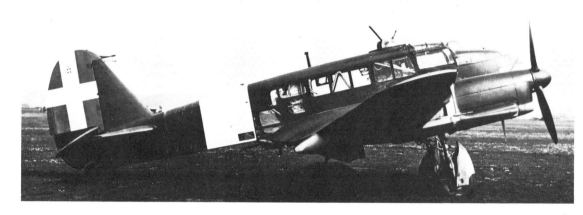

escort/maritime patrol aircraft, the Ca 314B or Ca 314-RA (Ricognizione Aerosiluranti) torpedo-bomber with a 1,894-lb (900 kg) torpedo or a bombload of one 1,102-lb (500-kg) or two 551-lb (250-kg) bombs, and the ground-attack Ca 314C which carried two additional 12.7-mm (0.5-in) Breda-SAFAT machine-guns beneath the wing roots. Production of this version comprised Ca 314A (73), Ca 314B (80) and Ca 314C (134) built at Toliedo, plus 60 Ca 314Cs built at Ponte San Pietro, and a further 60 Ca 314s manufactured by AVIS at Castellamare di Stabia.

Specification
Caproni Ca 314A

Type: convoy escort and maritime patrol aircraft
Powerplant: two 730-hp (544-kW) Isotta-Fraschini Delta RC.35 12-cylinder inverted-Vee piston engines
Performance: maximum speed 245 mph (395 km/h) at 13,125 ft (4000 m); cruising speed 199 mph

The Caproni Bergamaschi Ca 314 was used in a number of roles such as bombing, torpedo bombing, patrol and escort.

(320 km/h) at 13,780 ft (4200 m); service ceiling 21,000 ft (6400 m); maximum range 1,050 miles (1690 km)
Weights: empty 10,053 lb (4560 kg); maximum take-off 14,595 lb (6620 kg)
Dimensions: span 54 ft 7½ in (16.65 m); length 38 ft 8½ in (11.80 m); height 12 ft 1¾ in (3.70 m) wing area 421.96 sq ft (39.20 m²)
Armament: two 12.7-mm (0.5-in) machine-guns in the wing roots and one 7.7-mm (0.303-in) gun in a dorsal turret, plus a bombload of 1,102 lb (500 kg)
Operators: Italian Regia Aeronautica, Aeronautica Cobelligerante del Sud and Aeronautica Nazionale Repubblicana, Croatia, France, Germany, Hungary, Norway, Sweden, Yugoslavia

DFS 230

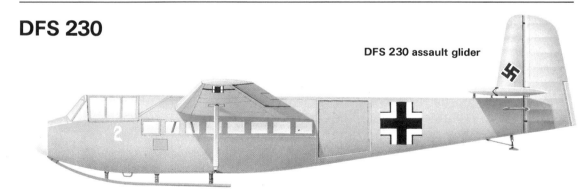

DFS 230 assault glider

History and notes

Following military interest in a research glider being developed by the Deutsches Forschunginstitut für Segelflug (German Gliding Research Institute, or DFS), a contract was awarded for the construction of a prototype. Following successful demonstration during

1937, it was ordered into limited production as the DFS 230A-1. A braced high-wing monoplane of mixed construction, the DFS 230 provided accommodation for a crew of two and eight fully armed troops; towable by a variety of Luftwaffe aircraft, it used jettisonable landing gear for take-off, landing being accomplished

on a central skid mounted beneath the fuselage. The initial production DFS 230A-1 was followed by a dual-control DFS 230A-2, and two basically similar variants that differed only by the incorporation of a braking parachute were built under the respective designations DFS 230B-1 and DFS 230B-2. A solution to the problem of getting down quickly into a confined landing zone was attempted with the DFS 230C-1, which had three braking rockets incorporated into the nose structure, while the DFS 230 V7, enlarged to accommodate 15 fully-equipped troops, served as prototype for the DFS 230F-1 final variant which did not enter production. All of the series built aircraft were manufactured by Gothaer Waggonfabrik AG (Gotha), to a total of 1,022.

The DFS 230 mounted the world's first combat operation by gliderborne troops when the Belgian fort of Eben-Emael was captured on 10 May 1940. DFS 230s were used also in the invasion of Crete, in the

The DFS 230B embodied several modifications, the most noticeable being an external rear fuselage parachute pack to be deployed for rapid diving.

operation for the surprise rescue of Benito Mussolini after he had been imprisoned, and also saw extensive service for supply missions on the Eastern Front.

Specification
Type: assault transport glider
Performance: maximum gliding speed 180 mph (290 km/h); normal towing speed 112 mph (180 km/h)
Weights: empty 1,896 lb (860 kg); maximum take-off 4,630 lb (2100 kg)
Dimensions: span 72 ft 1¼ in (21.98 m); length 36 ft 10½ in (11.24 m); height 9 ft 0 in (2.74 m); wing area 444.56 sq ft (41.30 m²)
Operator: Luftwaffe

Dornier Do 17/Do 215

Dornier Do 17Z-2 of I/KG 2, Tatoi, Greece, May 1941

History and notes
In response to a Lufthansa specification of 1933 for a six-passenger mailplane, Dornier designed a shoulder-wing all-metal monoplane to be powered by two 660-hp (492-kW) BMW VI engines. Three prototypes of this Dornier Do 17 were built in 1934, but although the airline carried out an evaluation programme early in the following year, the aircraft's slim fuselage provided such limited passenger accommodation that all three

were returned to the manufacturer. The design had military potential, however, and a fourth prototype (Do 17 V4) with twin vertical tail surfaces and a shortened fuselage was flown in the summer of 1935. Among development prototypes, the fifth was powered by 860-hp (641-kW) Hispano Suiza 12Ybrs engines, the seventh mounted a 7.92-mm (0.31-in) MG 15 machine-gun in a dorsal blister, and the tenth was fitted with 750-hp (559-kW) BMW VI engines. The initial production

Dornier Do 17/Do 215

Dornier Do 17Z of 9./KG 76 based at Cormeilles-en-Vexin during July 1940

versions were the Do 17E-1 which, developed from the ninth prototype, had a glazed and shortened nose, and carried a 1,102-lb (500-kg) bombload, and the Do 17F-1 reconnaissance aircraft with increased fuel capacity and two cameras. Both of these models made their operational debut with the Legion Condor in Spain during 1937. Their performance was such that they had little difficulty in avoiding contact with the obsolescent aircraft then serving with the Republican air force. Introduced publicly at the 1937 International Military Aircraft Competition held at Dübendorf, near Zürich, the Do 17 V8 prototype (or Do 17M V1) powered by two 1,000-hp (746-kW) Daimler-Benz DB 600A engines soon gained the nickname 'Flying Pencil' because of its slender fuselage. More significantly, it was able to better the performance of international fighters taking part in the contest. Following this demonstration at Dübendorf, Yugoslavia showed interest in the type and the Do 17K was developed for that nation, being similar to the Do 17M but powered by two 980-hp (731-kW) Gnome-Rhône 14N1/2 engines. The type was to be licence-built by Drazavna Fabrika Aviona at Kraljevo, the three versions produced being the Do 17Kb-1 bomber, and the Do 17Ka-2 and Do 17Ka-3 reconnaissance aircraft with secondary bombing and attack capability respectively. Two prototypes of a proposed pathfinder version which did not enter production were built under the designation Do 17L, these being powered by two 900-hp (671-kW) Bramo 323A-1 radial engines because of a shortage of Daimler-Benz DB 600s. The same Bramo powerplant was used for the thirteenth and fourteenth prototypes to develop the airframe/engine combination for the production Do 17M-1, which could carry a 2,205-lb (1000-kg) bombload and was armed with three 7.92-mm (0.31-in) MG machine-guns. A photo-reconnaissance version of the Do 17M entered production under the designation Do 17P, powered by two 875-hp (652-kW) BMW 132N radial engines and carried Rb20/30 and Rb50/30, or Rb 20/8 and Rb50/8 cameras in the Do 17P-1 production series. Two aircraft were built as engine test-beds under the designation Do 17R, one with 950-hp (708-kW) Daimler-Benz DB600Gs, and the other with 1,000-hp (746-kW) Daimler-Benz DB 601As. They were followed by three DB600G-powered high-speed reconnaissance aircraft which had the designation Do 17S-0. Used for test purposes, these had an extensively glazed nose and the airframe incorporated a bulged section in the underside of the forward fuselage,

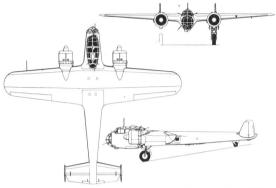

Dornier Do 17Z-2

accommodating a gunner in a prone position to operate an aft-firing MG 15 machine-gun. These experimental reconnaissance machines were followed by a small production batch of 15 pathfinders, comprising three Do 17U-0 and 12 Do 17U-1 aircraft, the five-men crews of which included two radio operators to handle the new and comprehensive communications and navigation radios.

Major production version was the Do 17Z, which appeared in several variants and was built to a total of some 1,700 between 1939-40. They included the Do 17Z-0 which, powered by two 900-hp (671-kW) Bramo 323A-1 engines and armed with three MG 15 machine-guns, was otherwise similar to the Do 17S. The Do 17Z-1 had an additional nose-mounted MG 15 but was underpowered and restricted to a 1,102-lb (500-kg) bombload; this situation was rectified in the Do 17Z-2 which with 1,000-hp (746-kW) Bramo 323P engines could carry a 2,205-lb (1000 kg) bombload and up to eight MG 15 machine guns. Some 22 examples of the Do 17Z-3 reconnaissance aircraft were built, each equipped with Rb50/30 or Rb20/30 cameras, and they were followed by the Do 17Z-4 dual-control conversion trainer. Final bomber variant was the Do 17Z-5 which, generally similar to the Do 17Z-2, differed by having flotation bags in the fuselage and in the rear of the engine nacelles. Do 17 production ended with a single Do 17Z-6 Kauz I (screech owl I) long-range intruder and night-fighter which incorporated a Junkers Ju 88C-2 nose housing a 20-mm MG FF cannon and three MG 15 machine-guns. However, for the nine Do 17Z-10 Kauz II aircraft that followed a new nose was developed which housed four MG FF cannon and four 7.92-mm

Seen on their way to a target in the Low Countries, these two Dornier Do 17Zs of Kampfgeschwader 2 show why the type was known as the 'flying pencil' with its narrow fuselage.

Dornier Do 17/Do 215

Dornier Do 17Z of Kampfgeschwader 2

Dornier Do 17Z-2 of 10.(Kroat)/KG 3 deployed on the central sector of the Eastern Front, December 1941

Dornier Do 17Z-10 Kauz of I/NJG 2 based at Gilze-Rijen in October 1940

(0.31-in) MG 17 machine guns; when deployed as night-fighters they were equipped with Lichtenstein C1 radar and Spanner-II-Anlage infra-red detection apparatus.

Export versions of the Do 17Z were planned under the general designation Do 215, the first to be developed being the Do 215A-1, with 1,075-hp (802-kW) Daimler-Benz DB 601A engines, which was ordered by Sweden in 1939. With the outbreak of World War II the 18 aircraft were embargoed and following conversion to Luftwaffe requirements were delivered for use as four-seat bomber/reconnaissance aircraft under the designations Do 215B-0 and Do 215B-1. Two examples of the Do 215B-3 were delivered to the USSR during 1940, and the Do 215B-4 was a reconnaissance version, similar in configuration to the Do 215B-1, but carrying Rb 20/30 and Rb 50/30 cameras. Final variant was the night-fighter/intruder Do 215B-5 which had an unglazed nose, similar to that of the Do 17Z-10, but housing two 20-mm MG FF cannon and four 7.92-mm (0.31-in) MG machine-guns.

Dornier Do 17s played a significant role in the early phase of World War II, used first on 1 September 1939 when the invasion of Poland began. They played only a small part in the Norwegian campaign, but were used extensively in the invasion of France and the Low Countries, against Allied convoys in the English Channel and targets in England during the Battle of Britain. Deployed in the invasion of Greece, Yugoslavia and the Soviet Union, most had been withdrawn from first-line service by late 1941.

Specification
Dornier Do 17Z-2

Type: four-seat medium bomber
Powerplant: two 1,000-hp (746-kW) Bramo 323P Fafnir 9-cylinder radial piston engines
Performance: maximum speed 255 mph (410 km/h)

Right: The Dornier Do 17Z was employed widely in the assault on Poland as a medium bomber. In this environment, away from effective fighter opposition, the aircraft was able to operate to the full.

Dornier Do 17/Do 215

Dornier Do 215B-5 Kauz III of Stab II/NJG 2, Leeuwarden, summer 1942

at 4,000 ft (1220 m); cruising speed 186 mph (300 km/h) at 13,125 ft (4000 m); service ceiling 26,905 ft (8200 m); range 721 miles (1160 km)
Weights: empty 11,488 lb (5210 kg); maximum take-off 18,940 lb (8590 kg)
Dimensions: span 59 ft 1 in (18.00 m); length 51 ft 10 in (15.80 m); height 14 ft 11 in (4.55 m); wing area 592.0 sq ft (55.00 m²)
Armament: up to seven 7.92-mm (0.31-in) MG 15

machine-guns, plus 2,205 lb (1000 kg) of bombs
Operators: Luftwaffe, Regia Aeronautica, Croatia, Spain, Yugoslavia, Finland

Although fast nearing the end of its operational life, the Dornier Do 17Z was employed in some numbers during the Balkan campaign. This example is seen wearing the distinctive Mediterranean yellow theatre bands.

Dornier Do 18

Dornier Do 18D of FFS (see), summer 1939

Dornier Do 18D of 2./KüFlGr at Kamp/Pomerania, winter 1939-40

History and notes

Successor to the very successful Wal flying-boats, the Dornier Do 18 was developed as a transoceanic mailplane for Lufthansa in 1934. It retained the basic metal hull and stabilising sponsons which had characterised the earlier aircraft, but was aerodynamically more efficient. Powered by two 540-hp (403-kW) Junkers Jumo 5 diesel engines, the Do 18a prototype was first flown on 15 March 1935 and was followed by four of the Do 18E version with improved 600-hp (447-kW) Jumo 205C engines. Lufthansa's sixth aircraft was the sole Do 18F, first flown on 11 June 1937 and which between 27-29 March 1938 established a nonstop straight-line seaplane distance record of 5,214 miles (8391 km) in 43 hours, flying from England to Brazil. It later became the Do 18L when modified by the installation of 880-hp (656-kW) BMW 132N engines, and made its first flight thus powered on 21 November 1939.

The Do 18 was adopted for use with Luftwaffe coastal reconnaissance units, the first military production version being the Do 18D which began to enter service in September 1938. Powered like the Do 18E by Jumo 205C engines, the Do 18D was armed with single 7.92-mm (0.31-in) MG 15 machine-guns in bow and dorsal open positions, and sub-variants introduced in late 1938 were the Do 18D-2 and Do 18D-3 with changes in installed equipment. An improved version of the Do 18D with 880-hp (656-kW) Jumo 205D engines, and armament comprising a 13-mm (0.51-in) MG 131 machine-gun in the bow position and a 20-mm MG 151 cannon in a power-operated dorsal turret, entered service with

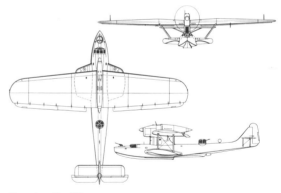

Dornier Do 18

the designation Do 18G-1; subsequently, with the armament removed, a number were converted for air-sea rescue operations, being redesignated Do 18N-1. The designation Do 18H was applied to a small number of aircraft equipped to serve as unarmed dual-control trainers.

A Dornier Do 18 of 2./Küstenfliegergruppe 106 became, on 26 September 1939, the first German aircraft to be brought down by British forces in World War II, being forced down by Lieutenant B.S. McEwen of the Fleet Air Arm's No.803 Squadron, operating from HMS *Ark Royal* in the North Sea. The production of just over 100 Do 18s was completed in 1940 and, following replacement by the Blohm and Voss Bv 138, the type had been relegated to air-sea rescue duties by 1942.

Dornier Do 18

Dornier Do 18G of 6. Seenotstaffel, operating in the central Mediterranean during 1941-2

Specification
Dornier Do 18G-1

Type: four-seat coastal reconnaissance flying-boat
Powerplant: two 880-hp (656-kW) Junkers Jumo 205D 6-cylinder vertically opposed inline diesel engines
Performance: maximum speed 162 mph (260 km/h); cruising speed 137 mph (220 km/h); service ceiling 13,780 ft (4200 m); maximum range 2,175 miles (3500 km)
Weights: empty 12,897 lb (5850 kg); maximum take-off 22,046 lb (10000 kg)
Dimensions: span 77 ft 9 in (23.70 m); length 63 ft 2 in (19.25 m); height 17 ft 6½ in (5.35 m); wing area 1054.89 sq ft (98.00 m²)
Armament: one 13-mm (0.51-in) MG 131 machine-gun in the bow position and one 20-mm MG 151 cannon in the dorsal turret, plus two 110-lb (50-kg) bombs under the starboard wing
Operator: Luftwaffe

Displaying the 'Iron Hand' *Staffel* emblem of 2./KüFlGr 406, this Dornier Do 18D-2 rests on its beaching gear. Visible under the starboard wing are two ETC 50 racks for 110-lb (50-kg) bombs.

Dornier Do 24

History and notes

The Dornier Do 24 originated from a Dutch navy requirement of 1935 for a replacement for the Dornier Wals then being used in the Netherlands East Indies. An all-metal monoplane with a shallow, broad-beamed hull and stabilising sponsons, the Do 24 had a strut-mounted wing which carried three engines. The first two prototypes, for possible German use, were powered by 600-hp (447-kW) Junkers Jumo 205C diesel engines. The third prototype (which was the first to fly, on 3 July 1937) and the fourth were powered by 875-hp (652-kW) Wright R-1820-F52 Cyclones, in order to meet the Dutch desire to use the same engine as those fitted to their Martin 139 bombers; on successful

Dornier Do 24

Dornier Do 24T-1 operated by the Reichsdienst on aeromedical duties

Dornier Do 24T-1 of 8. Seenotstaffel, SBK XII, Black Sea area, 1942

Dornier Do 24T-2 of 7. Seenotstaffel, SBK XI, in the Aegean, 1942

completion of the test programme the rest of the Dutch order were completed at Altenrhein under the designation Do 24K-1. Licence production of a further 48 Do 24K-2 aircraft with 1,000-hp (746-kW) Wright R-1820-G102 engines, was undertaken by Aviolanda in the Netherlands, De Schelde building the wings, but only 25 had been delivered before the German occupation in May 1940. Subsequently, 11 Dutch-built Do 24K-2s with Wright R-1820-G102 engines were transferred to Germany and completed for Luftwaffe use in an air-sea rescue role under the designation Do 24N-1. Evaluation of the Do 24 in this role led to the Dutch line being re-established under control of the German company Weser Flugzeugbau, and production from this source totalled 159 aircraft in three versions, the Do 24T-1, Do 24T-2 and Do 24T-3 which varied slightly in equipment but were all powered by three 1,000-hp (746-kW) BMW-Bramo 323R-2 Fafnir engines. They served

principally with 1. 2. and 3./Seenotgruppe based at Biscarosse, near Bordeaux, and Berre, near Marseilles. An additional 48 Do 24T-1 aircraft were built for the Luftwaffe at the SNCA du Nord plant at Sartrouville in France between 1942 and August 1944, and 40 more were delivered to the French navy after the liberation. Twelve Do 24T-3 aircraft were supplied to Spain, with deliveries starting in June 1944. These were operated, under the designation HR.5, to provide search and rescue cover in the Mediterranean for both Axis and Allied aircrew. Based at Pollensa, Majorca, the type remained in service well into the 1970s and emphasised that aircraft in this category can still provide valuable service. Realising this, Dornier began design in the late 1970s of an amphibian version which incorporates an advanced technology wing developed for the company's Do 228 commuter airliner. Designated Do 24TT and powered by three 1,125-shp (839-kW) Pratt &

Dornier Do 24

Whitney Aircraft of Canada PT6A-45B turboprop engines, the prototype (D-CATD) flew for the first time on 25 April 1983. A variant of the original Do 24 design was a single Do 318 prototype modified in 1944 by Weser with an Arado-designed wing incorporating boundary-layer control to reduce drag. Although tested successfully, the aircraft was scuttled in Lake Constance during 1945.

Specification
Dornier Do 24T

Type: maritime patrol/search and rescue flying-boat
Powerplant: three 1,000-hp (746-kW) BMW-Bramo 323R-2 9-cylinder radial piston engines
Performance: maximum speed 211 mph (340 mk/h) at 9,845 ft (3000 m); cruising speed 183 mph (295 km/h) service ceiling 19,355 ft (5900 m); maximum range

1,802 miles (2900 km)
Weights: empty 20,286 lb (9200 kg); maximum take-off 40,565 lb (18400 kg)
Dimensions: span 88 ft 7 in (27.00 m); length 72 ft 0¼ in (21.95 m); height 18 ft 10¼ in (5.75 m); wing area 1,162.54 sq ft (108.00 m²)
Armament: one 7.92-mm (0.31-in) MG 15 machine-gun in each of the bow and tail positions, and one 20-mm MG 151 cannon in a power-operated dorsal turret
Operators: Luftwaffe, Australia, France, Netherlands, Spain, Sweden

Dornier Do 217

History and notes
Essentially an enlarged Do 17, the Dornier Do 217 was flown as a prototype in August 1938, powered by two 1,075-hp (802-kW) Daimler-Benz DB 601A engines. Although this aircraft crashed a few weeks later, the programme was continued by three prototypes powered by 950-hp (708-kW) Junkers Jumo 211A engines. The last of these (Do 217 V4) carried armament and, to improve directional stability, had enlarged vertical tail surfaces and modified dive brakes, whose four segments when closed formed the tail cone. A further three Jumo-engined aircraft were followed by two with 1,550-hp (1156-kW) BMW 139 radials in an attempt to improve performance, but the more advanced BMW 801 of similar output, introduced in late 1939, was adopted for the production Do 217A reconnaissance aircraft, of which eight were built under the designation Do 217A-0. Carrying two cameras and armed with three 7.92-mm (0.31-in) machine-guns, these entered

service with the Aufklärungsgruppe Oberbefehlshaber der Luftwaffe in 1940. The Do 217A was followed by five examples of a Do 217C bomber version; the first (Do 217C V1) was powered by Jumo 211A engines, but the remainder (Do 217C-0) had DB 601As; all were armed with one 15-mm MG 151 cannon and five 7.92-mm (0.31-in) machine-guns, plus a bombload of 6,614 lb (3000 kg). The first major production version was the Do 217E which appeared in 1940, having a deeper fuselage and an enlarged bomb bay which could accept larger bombs or a torpedo. The initial variant was the Do 217E-1, able to carry a 4,409-lb (2000 kg) bombload and armed with one 15-mm MG 151 cannon and five 7.92-mm (0.31-in) machine-guns, and followed by the Do 217E-2 with revised armament comprising a dorsal turret with a 13-mm (0.51-in) MG 131 machine-gun, a similar gun mounted ventrally, three 7.92-mm (0.31-in) machine-guns in the forward fuselage, and a 15-mm MG 151 cannon in the nose. The 1941 version of this

Dornier Do 217

Dornier Do 217E-2 of 9. KG 2 in 1941

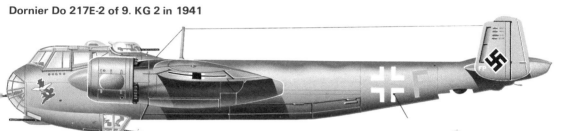

Dornier Do 217E-2 of 6./KG 40 based at Bordeaux—Merignac late in 1942

last aircraft, designated Do 217E-4, was generally similar except that it had BMW 801C engines and introduced cable-cutters in the wing leading edges. The Do 217E-3, developed for anti-shipping operations over the Atlantic, carried additional armour plating to protect the crew, two additional fuel tanks in the bomb bay, and was armed with seven MG 15s supplementing a single 20-mm MG FF cannon in the nose. Series production of this version was finalised by the Do 217E-5, of which about 65 were manufactured, these having underwing racks for the carriage of Henschel Hs 293 missiles. The redesignation Do 217H applied to one high-altitude experimental aircraft developed from a Do 217E and provided with Daimler-Benz DB 601 turbocharged engines. The Do 217E became operational in the reconnaissance role with 3.(F)/11 in the closing months of 1940, and as a bomber with II/KG40 in the spring of 1941.

Starting in 1942, 157 aircraft were built to Do 217J-1 and Do 217J-2 standard, the former being a fighter-bomber with a nose similar to that of the Do 17Z-10 and housing four 7.92-mm (0.31-in) MG 17 machine-guns and four 20-mm MG FF cannon, this armament supplemented by dorsal and ventral positions each with a pair of 13-mm (0.51-in) MG 131 guns. The Do 217J-2 was a night-fighter, with 20-mm MG 151/20 cannon replacing the MG FF weapons of the Do 217J-1 and FuG 212 Lichtenstein C1 radar installed. In the autumn of 1942 Dornier introduced the Do 217K-1 bomber which had a new glazed nose with an unstepped cockpit; the ensuing Do 217K-2 carried two SD 1400 X (Fritz X) missiles beneath the wings and had FuG 203a and FuG 230a guidance equipment installed within the fuselage. It was such a missile launched by a Do 217K-2 of III/KG100 operating from Marseilles that sank the Italian battleship *Roma* when, on 14 September 1943,

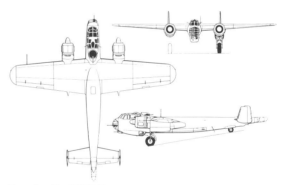

Dornier Do 217E-2

the Italian fleet broke out from La Spezia to join the Allies. Final sub-variant in this Do 217K missile-launching configuration was the Do 217K-3, which could deploy either SD 1400 X or Hs 293 missiles, but this did not represent the last of these advanced weapon-carriers. Under the designation Do 217L two experimental developments of the Do 217K were built and tested, incorporating a revised cockpit and defensive dispositions, and they were followed by the Do 217M-1 which was essentially a Daimler-Benz DB 603A-powered version of the Do 217K-1, and the similar Do 217M-5 with an underfuselage rack for an Hs 293 missile. The Do 217M-3 was a DB 603A-engined equivalent of the Do 217K-3, and the Do 217M-11 an extended-span missile-carrying equivalent of the Do 217K-2.

It seems strange that the last operational variant of this successful bomber was the Do 217N night-fighter, appearing initially as the Do 217N-1 which combined the nose of the Do 217J-2 with the Do 217M airframe; it was soon replaced on the production line by the Do

Dornier Do 217

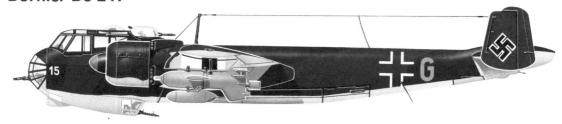

Dornier Do 217E-5 of KG 40 carrying two Henschel Hs 293A stand-off anti-ship guided missiles

217N-2 in which the dorsal turret was deleted, but the limitations of this aircraft in the night-fighter role meant that by October 1943 it had been almost completely replaced by the more effective Messerschmitt Bf 110 or Junkers Ju 88. The remaining variants include the very interesting Do 217P, of which the first Do 217P V1 prototype was flown during June 1942. Developed as a high-altitude reconnaissance aircraft with a pressure cabin, it was powered by two 1,750-hp (1305-kW) DB 603B engines which were boosted by a zation was also a feature of a medium bomber which two-stage supercharger driven by a 1,475-hp (1100-kW) DB 605T engine mounted within the bomb bay. Armament consisted of four MG 81 machine-guns, and one Rb20/30 and two Rb75/30 cameras were installed in the three Do 217P-0 pre-production aircraft. Pressurisation was also a feature of a medium bomber which Dornier had proposed originally in 1939; gaining no interest at that time, the design was resurrected in 1941 under the designation Do 317 and the first of six prototypes, similar to the Do 217M airframe but with revised vertical tail surfaces and power provided by DB 603 engines, was flown in 1943. Pressurization was then, presumably, too complicated or impractical, for the remaining five prototypes were completed without pressurization as Hs 293 missile carriers under the designation Do 217R. Production of all versions of the Do 217 totalled 1,730, and these aircraft were last used in large-scale bombing operations against the UK in early 1944. By the middle of the year the majority remaining in service were missile carriers, and these continued to operate with limited success until the end of the war.

Specification
Dornier Do 217M-1
Type: four-seat medium bomber
Powerplant: two 1,750-hp (1305-kW) Daimler-Benz DB 603A 12-cylinder inverted-Vee piston engines
Performance: maximum speed 348 mph (560 km/h) at 18,700 ft (5700 m); cruising speed 248 mph (400 km/h); service ceiling 31,170 ft (9500 m); maximum range 1,336 miles (2150 km)

The external appearance of the Dornier Do 217 bore much resemblance to the deep-fuselage Do 17, but it was essentially an entirely new aircraft. The bomb bay could be extended to carry a torpedo.

Dornier Do 217

Immediately distinguishable from previous Do 217 models by its completely redesigned forward fuselage, the Dornier Do 217K-1 was primarily a night bomber and anti-shipping aircraft.

Weights: empty 19,489 lb (8840 kg); maximum take-off 36,817 lb (16700 kg)

Dimensions: span 62 ft 4 in (19.00 m); length 55 ft 5¼ in (16.90 m); height 16 ft 4¾ in (5.00 m); wing area 613.54 sq ft (57.00 m²)
Armament: two 13-mm (0.51-in) MG 131 and up to six 7.92-mm (0.31-in) MG 81 machine-guns, plus up to 8,818 lb (4000 kg) of bombs
Operator: Luftwaffe

Dornier Do 335 Pfeil

History and notes

Following feasibility trials with the experimental Göppingen Gö 9 research aircraft, designed by Ulrich Hütter and built by Schempp-Hirth in 1939, the unconventional tandem engine layout patented by Dr Claudius Dornier in 1937 was adopted by the Reichsluftfahrtministerium for a bomber under the project number Do P.231, despite the fact that Dornier's original design proposal was for a fighter! When work was at an advanced stage the project was cancelled, but an emerging need for a high-performance fighter resulted in the reactivation of Dornier's plans for an interceptor. Of all-metal construction and powered by two 1,800-hp (1342-kW) Daimler-Benz DB 603 engines, one buried in the rear fuselage and driving a three-bladed pusher propeller via an extension shaft, the first Dornier Do 335 Pfeil (arrow) prototype made its maiden flight during September 1943. The type was built in a number of versions, albeit in small numbers, beginning with 10 pre-production Do 335A-0 single-seat fighter-bombers built at the Oberpfaffenhofen factory between July and October 1944; they were powered by DB 603A-2 engines, as were production Do 335A-1 fighters. A Do 335A-0 with two Rb 50/30

cameras installed served as the development aircraft for a proposed reconnaissance Do 335A-4. Fourteen prototypes were built, and six more were under construction at the war's end: most served as development aircraft for different variants, the Do 335 V10, for example, becoming the prototype for the two-seat Do 335A-6 night-fighter carrying FuG 220 and FuG 350 radar. Similarly, the Do 335 V11 and Do 335 V12 were used in development of the Do 335A-10 and Do 335A-12 two-seat conversion trainers respectively, having a second cockpit installed above and behind the original crew position. Late in the war efforts were concentrated upon the Do 335B heavy fighter, the Do 335B-1 armed with two 20-mm MG 151/20 cannon, Do 335B-2 with two 30-mm MK 103 cannon, the Do 335B-3 powered by two 2,100-hp (1566-kW) DB 603LA engines, and the Do 335B-4 which was to have a wing of higher aspect ratio. Corresponding night-fighter variants were given the designations Do 335B-5, Do 335B-6, Do 335B-7 and Do 335B-8.

A total of 37 Do 335s was built, including prototypes, and a special operational test unit was established for evaluation of this fighter which, if fully developed, might have earned an accolade for being the fastest

Dornier Do 335 Pfeil

piston engine fighter ever built. It seems likely that the use of the Do 335s by the Erprobungskommando 335 was the nearest that the type came to being used operationally. Three variants of the basic design were projected but failed to materialise: they included a Do 435 two-seat night-fighter, the Do 535 to be developed in conjunction with Heinkel so that the rear piston engine would be replaced by a turbojet of Heinkel design, and a long-range reconnaissance Do 635 which would have united two Do 335 airframes by means of a new wing centre section.

Specification
Dornier Do 335A-1

Type: single-seat fighter-bomber
Powerplant: two 1,750-hp (1305-kW) Daimler-Benz DB 603A-2 12-cylinder inverted-Vee piston engines
Performance: maximum speed 478 mph (770 km/h)

With its tractor and pusher airscrews and cruciform tail arrangement, the Dornier Do 335 was a radical design of World War II. Illustrated is the 7th Do 335A-0, serving with Erprobungskommando 335.

at 21,000 ft (6400 m); cruising speed 426 mph (685 km/h) at 23,295 ft (7100 m); service ceiling 37,400 ft (11400 m); range 857 miles (1380 km)
Weights: empty 16,314 lb (7400 kg); maximum take-off 21,164 lb (9600 kg)
Dimensions: span 45 ft 3¼ in (13.80 m); length 45 ft 5¼ in (13.85 m); height 16 ft 4¾ in (5.00 m); wing area 414.42 sq ft (38.50 m²)
Armament: one 30-mm MK 103 and two 15-mm MG 151 cannon, plus one 1,102-lb (500-kg) or two 551-lb (250-kg) bombs internally and two 551-lb (250-kg) bombs externally
Operator: Luftwaffe

Fiat BR.20 Cicogna

History and notes
Flown for the first time from the Fiat company airfield in Turin by Enrico Rolandi on 10 February 1936, the prototype (MM 274) of the Fiat BR.20 Cicogna (stork) immediately made a favourable impression. Before long this medium bomber was being publicised throughout the aeronautical world by the efficient propaganda machine of Mussolini's Fascist government.

The BR.20 was a cantilever low-wing monoplane, its slab-sided fuselage having a mixed covering of dural sheet and fabric. The wing had sheet metal covering and the fabric-covered tail assembly included twin fins and rudders. The main units of the landing gear retracted rearward into the engine nacelles, leaving the wheels partially exposed, and the fixed tailwheel

had a streamlined protective fairing. The nose included a manually-operated gun turret and below it was a glazed section for the bomb-aimer/navigator. The pilot and co-pilot were seated side-by-side in an enclosed cabin forward of the wing leading edge, the wireless operator's compartment being just forward of the main access door which was on the port side of the fuselage, behind the wing trailing edge. The bomb bay, capable of carrying a weapon load of up to 3,527 lb (1600 kg), was located in the forward fuselage between the pilots' cabin and the wireless operator's compartment. A retractable type DR dorsal turret (replaced by an MI turret from the twenty-first production BR.20 onwards) and a ventral gun position completed the defensive armament.

Fiat Br.20 Cicogna

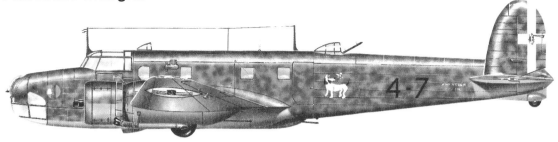

Fiat BR.20M Cicogna of 4ª Squadriglia, 11° Gruppo, 13° Stormo, stationed in Belgium for operations against England in 1940

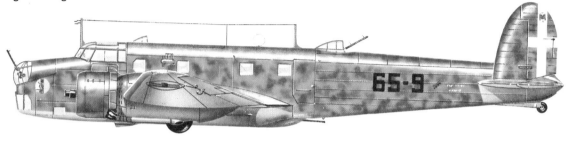

Fiat BR.20 Cicogna of 65ª Squadriglia, 31° Gruppo, 18° Stormo, Catania, Sicily in June 1941

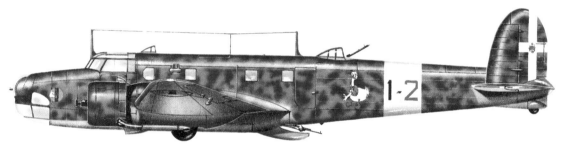

Fiat BR.20M Cicogna of 1ª Squadriglia, 43° Gruppo, 13° Stormo at Bir Dufan, Libya in February 1942

In the spring of 1937 two special BR.20A long-range civil aircraft appeared. They had rounded noses, were stripped of all military equipment and had no break in the fuselage underside as with the bomber. They were built especially to take part in the prestigious Istres-Damascus air race, in which they were able to gain only sixth and seventh places. One other civilianized BR.20 was built, the BR.20L *Santo Francesco*, first flown in early 1939. It had an elongated streamlined nose section and additional fuel tanks, enabling it to make a nonstop flight from Rome to Addis Ababa on 6 March 1939, the three-man crew led by Maner Lualdi achieving an average speed of 251 mph (404 km/h).

The first unit to equip with the BR.20 bomber was the 13° Stormo BT at Lonate Pozzolo, in the autumn of 1936. The original BR.20 remained in production until February 1940, a total of 233 being completed. Of these a single example went to Venezuela and 85 were sold to Japan. The Japanese BR.20s, known as the Type I, were based on the Chinese coastal areas and used to attack inland cities still in Chinese hands. According to

reports the Imperial Japanese Army air force did not find its BR.20s particularly effective and, as soon as the long-awaited Mitsubishi Ki-21 (Type 97 Bomber) was available, surviving Fiats were quickly grounded.

A number of BR.20s operated with the Italian Aviazione Legionaria supporting the Nationalists in Spain. Arriving from the summer of 1937 they took part in day and night raids over the Teruel and Ebro fronts, frequently attacking troop and vehicle concentrations, as well as government-held cities. Nine BR.20s survived to take part in the Nationalist aviation victory parade at Madrid-Barajas on 12 May 1939. When the Italian personnel left for home, the BR.20s were handed over to Spain.

When Italy entered World War II on 10 June 1940, a new version of the basic design, the BR.20M (M for Modificato) had been in production for some six months. It differed from the original BR.20 by having a nose section of entirely new design and smoother outline. In all, 264 examples of the BR.20M were constructed, production ending in the spring of 1942.

53

Fiat BR.20 Cicogna

Fiat BR.20M Cicogna of 56ª Squadriglia, 86° Gruppo, at Castelventrano, April 1942

Regia Aeronautica BR.20s in service in June 1940 totalled 172 with a further 47 in reserve or under repair. The Fiat bombers took part in the brief campaign against France until 23 June 1940 and then 80 factory-fresh BR.20Ms were allocated to the 13° and 43° Stormo and sent to Belgian bases to participate in the Italian effort against the UK as part of the Corpo Aereo Italiano, which supported the Luftwaffe in the later stages of the Battle of Britain. They were involved in day and night raids against the ports of Harwich and Ramsgate and the industrial centre of Ipswich, between October and December 1940, before being withdrawn to Italy.

BR.20s participated subsequently in the campaigns in North Africa, Greece, Yugoslavia and in the attacks against Malta. Some missions were flown in the long-range reconnaissance role and this type of operation became more usual as the war progressed, the BR.20s carrying out many such missions against partisan areas in the Balkans.

At the time of the armistice signed between Italy and the Allies in September 1943, 81 BR.20s were still with first-line operational units in Italy, Yugoslavia, Albania and Greece, but by that time most surviving aircraft were attached to bomber training schools. During the final war years a very few BR.20s remained in flying condition as trainers or transports.

Experimental versions tested included the BR.20C with a powerful 37-mm cannon in the nose section and another BR.20 flown with tricycle landing gear.

Final version to go into production was the BR.20bis, a complete redesign, with a rounded fully glazed nose, more graceful fuselage contours, a retractable tailwheel and pointed vertical tail surfaces. Main improvements, however, were in engine power and defensive armament. Between March and July 1943 15 BR.20bis aircraft

were built, but there is no record of their operational use. Their two 1,250-hp (932-kW) Fiat A.82 RC.42 radial engines gave a maximum speed of 286 mph (460 km/h) and a service ceiling of 30,185 ft (9200 m). Dimensions were slightly increased compared with those of the BR.20M, and maximum take-off weight rose to 25,353 lb (11500 kg). Defensive nose and ventral positions retained single 7.7-mm (0.303-in) machine-guns, there were additional weapons of the same calibre firing through ports on each side of the fuselage and a 12.7-mm (0.5-in) gun mounted in a Breda Type V dorsal turret.

Specification
Fiat BR.20
Type: twin-engine medium bomber
Powerplant: two 1,000-hp (746-kW) Fiat A.80 RC.41 18-cylinder radial piston engines
Performance: maximum speed 268 mph (432 km/h) at 16,405 ft (5000 m); service ceiling 29,530 ft (9000 m); range 1,864 miles (3000 km)
Weights: empty equipped 14,110 lb (6400 kg); maximum take-off 21,826 lb (9900 kg)
Dimensions: span 70 ft 8¾ in (21.56 m); length 52 ft 9¾ in (16.10 m); height 14 ft 1¼ in (4.30 m); wing area 796.5 sq ft (74.00 m²)
Armament: one 12.7-mm (0.5-in) machine-gun and two 7.7-mm (0.303-in) machine-guns (the prototype and first 20 production BR.20s had a DR twin 7.7-mm/ 0.303-in gun dorsal turret in place of a single 12.7-mm/ gun in MI turret on all later BR.20s and BR.20Ms), plus a bombload of up to 3,527 lb (1600 kg)
Operators: Italian Regia Aeronautica, Aeronautica Cobelligerante del Sud and Aeronautica Nazionale Repubblicana, Japan, Spain

Fiat CR.32

History and notes
Not content with the excellent agility displayed by the CR.30 and determined to achieve an overall improvement in performance, Celestion Rosatelli and his design team produced a new fighter closely resembling the CR.30 but somewhat refined and with reduced overall dimensions. Manoeuvrability was enhanced by a judi-

cious redistribution of loading, achieved mainly through relocation of fuel tanks. The resulting Fiat CR.32 prototype (MM 201) took the air for the first time on 28 April 1933. It was an instant success, the first production order being received in March 1934, and the type soon equipped the 1°, 3° and 4° Stormi of the Regia Aeronautica. Series aircraft had variable-pitch propellers

Fiat CR.32

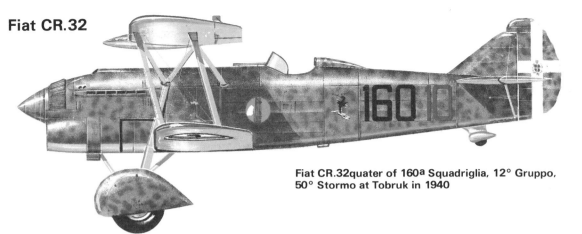

Fiat CR.32quater of 160ª Squadriglia, 12° Gruppo, 50° Stormo at Tobruk in 1940

and could be equipped with a radio transmitter-receiver, panoramic camera or bomb racks. Modified versions for the Regia Aeronautica were built up to 1939, each designed to reduce all-up weight and improve performance. In addition, the CR.32 was demonstrated widely abroad and attracted considerable export orders.

The CR.32 was used extensively in operations supporting the Nationalists in the Spanish Civil War, soon gaining a reputation as one of the outstanding fighter biplanes of all time. At least 380 took part in the air battles fought over Spain, proving formidable adversaries to the Soviet Polikarpov I-15 biplanes and Polikarpov I-16 monoplanes which formed the backbone of the Republican fighter arm.

Like the earlier CR.30, the CR.32s were used for numerous aerobatic displays, many of them in Italy. On the occasion of visits by foreign statesmen the 4° Stormo, based at Rome, invariably put on impressive shows with formations of five or 10 aircraft. During 1936 displays were given in other European capitals and major cities, and in 1937 throughout South America. The team's return to Europe culminated in a brilliant display at Berlin.

The remarkable aerobatic characteristics of the CR.32 and its undoubted success in Spain misled the Italian air ministry, which formed the view that a fighter biplane still had potential as a weapon of war, with the result that the CR.42, developed from the CR.32, was already an outdated concept before the prototype made its first flight.

The CR.32 itself soldiered on into World War II and, when Italy declared war in June 1940, 324 were still in first-line service, although by then hopelessly outclassed. Some were adapted as night-fighters, while those operated by units in Libya were used largely in the ground-attack role against British troops. The greatest wartime successes achieved by CR.32s were in Italian East Africa, aircraft of the 410â and 411â Squadriglie destroying a number of British and South African aircraft before the final Italian surrender.

The Regia Aeronautica received 291 of the original CR.32 version, including prototypes, and the first export customer was China which ordered 16 aircraft in 1933. Armed with twin Vickers machine-guns,

China's CR.32s gave a good account of themselves against the invading Japanese, and were regarded as superior to the Curtiss Hawk biplanes with which most Chinese fighter units were equipped in the period 1934-6. The Hungarian air arm received 76 CR.32s in 1935-6 for use largely as fighter-trainers, but these fired their guns in anger when Hungary moved against the remnants of Czechoslovakia in March 1939, ultimately annexing the territory of Ruthenia. The Hungarians experimented with a CR.32 powered by a 750-hp (559-kW) Gnome-Rhône 14Mars radial engine. The modified aircraft achieved an impressive maximum speed of 261 mph (420 km/h) at 13,125 ft (4000 m), but the Hungarian government's inability to obtain more Gnome-Rhône engines thwarted the plan to re-engine all available CR.32s.

The CR.32bis, which was produced from 1935, differed primarily in its armament, having provision for two forward firing 7.7-mm (0.303-in) SAFAT machine-guns in the lower wings in addition to two fuselage weapons of either 12.7-mm (0.5-in) or 7.7-mm (0.303-in) calibre, but the extra weight of the wing mounted weapons often led to them being discarded. A total of 328 was built, the Regia Aeronautica receiving 283 with the balance of 45 being supplied to Austria, these being ordered in the spring of 1936 to equip Jagdgeschwader II at Wiener Neustadt. In March 1938 the Austrian units were absorbed into Luftwaffe fighter groups, but after a brief period the 36 remaining aircraft were handed over to Hungary. The following CR.32ter, which again differed mainly in armament, had only two SAFAT 12.7-mm (0.5-in) machine-guns. A total of 103 was built, all of them serving in Spain with the Italian Aviazione Legionaria (43) and the Spanish Nationalist air arm (60). Final series version was the CR.32quater, of which 398 were built to bring total production of this fighter to 1,212; it differed by being lighter in weight but had the same armament as the CR.32ter. The Aviazione Legionaria in Spain received 105, 27 were supplied to the Spanish Nationalist air force, Venezuela acquired 10 and a small number, estimated at four, went to Paraguay; the balance was delivered to the Regia Aeronautica. When the Spanish Civil War ended in the spring of 1939, survivors of the CR.32s operated by the Aviazione Legionaria were

Fiat CR.32

handed over to Spain. In addition, Spain had acquired a manufacturing licence in 1938, Hispano Aviacion building 100 machines under the designation HA-132-L Chirri; some of these remained in service as C.1 aerobatic trainers up to 1953.

In attempts to improve performance of the CR.32 a number of experimental prototypes were built, but none gained production status. They included three CR.33s powered by the 700-hp (522-kW) Fiat A.33 RC.35 engine, the first (MM 296) being flown in 1935 and the other two in 1937. Earlier, in 1934, Fiat had flown a CR.40 short-nosed prototype (MM 202) which had been built in parallel with the original CR.32 prototype. It differed by having a gull-wing attached directly to the top of the fuselage and was powered by a 525-hp (391-kW) Bristol Mercury IV engine. It was followed by the CR.40bis (MM 275) which retained the same wing configuration as the CR.40; powered by a 700-hp (522-kW) Fiat A.59R radial engine it had a disappointing maximum speed of only 217 mph (350 km/h). The last of these experimental prototypes was the CR.41 (MM 207), of the same general configuration as the CR.40 it differed in having a 900-hp (671-kW) Gnome-Rhône 14Kfs engine and vertical tail surfaces of increased area to maintain directional stability with the more powerful engine. When tested during 1936-7, the CR.41 demonstrated a maximum speed of 237 mph

Seen in the colours of the Spanish Nationalist air force during the Civil War, the Fiat CR.32 was one of the outstanding aircraft of the 1930s.

(381 km/h), but its development was abandoned in favour of the later CR.42.

Specification
Fiat CR.32

Type: single-seat fighter biplane
Powerplant: one 600-hp (447-kW) Fiat A.30 RA bis 12-cylinder Vee piston engine
Performance: maximum speed 233 mph (375 km/h) at 9,840 ft (3000 m); service ceiling 28,870 ft (8800 m); range 422 miles (680 km)
Weights: empty equipped 2,921 lb (1325 kg); maximum take-off 4,079 lb (1850 kg)
Dimensions: span 31 ft 2 in (9.50 m); length 24 ft 5¼ in (7.45 m); height 8 ft 7½ in (2.63 m); wing area 237.89 sq ft (22.10 m²)
Armament: two fixed forward-firing 7.7-mm (0.303-in) Breda-SAFAT machine-guns
Operators: Italian Regia Aeronautica, Aeronautica Cobelligerante del Sud and Aeronautica Nazionale Repubblicana, China, Hungary, Spain, Paraguay, Venezuela

Fiat CR.42 Falco

History and notes
Developed by Celestino Rosatelli to a requirement of the Italian Air Ministry, the Fiat CR.42 Falco (falcon) resulted from the belief that there was still a role for the highly manoeuvrable fighter biplane. This belief

had been strengthened by the achievements of biplane fighters involved in the air war which had been raging in Spain since 1936. So it was that this new prototype made its maiden flight on 23 May 1938. The CR.42 derived from the earlier CR.32 (retaining its unequal-

Fiat CR.42 Falco of 95ª Squadriglia, 18° Gruppo, 56° Stormo, based at Maldegen, Belgium in 1940 for operations against England

Fiat CR.42 Falco

span wing configuration) and the experimental CR.40 and CR.41 fighters which had introduced a radial engine. The basic structure was of metal, with mixed fabric and light alloy covering, and the wide-track main landing gear units incorporated oleo-pneumatic shock absorbers and had strut and wheel fairings. Power was provided by a Fiat A.74 R1C.38 radial engine in a long-chord cowling.

Following a successful series of test flights by this prototype the Ministero dell'Aeronautica ordered 200 production machines and the first of these series aircraft left the Turin factory during February 1939. Ironically, the tenth production Fiat G.50 low-wing monoplane fighter had left the production line just two months earlier. Final figures for CR.42 production, according to Fiat company records, show a total of 1,781 of all versions including the CR.42 Caccia-Bombardiere (fighter-bomber), which was an early conversion to carry a 441-lb (200-kg) bombload for ground attack. This variant joined operations in North Africa from the spring of 1941, having two underwing racks for 110-lb (50-kg) or 220-lb (100-kg) bombs. Other specialised variants included the CR.42 CN (Caccia-Notturna or night-fighter) which was equipped with exhaust flame dampers, radio and small underwing searchlights.

Belgium ordered 40 CR.42s at the end of 1939, and when the Germans attacked on 10 May 1940 24 of the type had been taken on charge, flying with the 3e and 4e Escadrilles of the Aéronautique Militaire, but most were lost on the ground.

Hungary ordered 68 CR.42s which were delivered during the 1939-40. They participated in the campaign against Yugoslavia and were in action during the invasion of the USSR in the summer of 1941. They were withdrawn from front-line service at the end of 1941.

Neutral Sweden took delivery of the first five of a contract for 72 CR.42s in February 1940, although final deliveries were not made until September 1941. In Flygvapen service the type was designated J 11, and was based at Gothenburg with Flygflottilj 9. A small number of these Swedish aircraft survived until World War II had ended and were modified as target tugs, and several Italian aircraft were converted as two-seat liaison aircraft, with a second cockpit immediately

behind that of the pilot.

When Italy declared war on 10 June 1940, 272 CR.42s were with the fighter *squadriglie*. Aircraft of the 3° Stormo attacked targets in southern France and escorted bombing missions until the armistice with the French was signed on 24 June. CR.42s of the Corpo Aereo Italiano (C.A.I.) operated alongside Luftwaffe units from Belgian bases between September and November 1940. This participation in the Battle of Britain was sporadic and not particularly effective; the 50 CR.42s of the 18° Gruppo which were involved suffered heavy losses and on 3 January 1941 the C.A.I. was recalled to Italy.

The CR.42 then entered action in the Greek campaign, over the Aegean and in Libya. Two fighter *squadriglie* based in Italian East Africa, the 412a and 413a, received their CR.42s in May 1940, but despite the type's robust qualities it was soon apparent that an effective fighter force in that theatre of operations could be maintained only if more fighters could be transferred from Italy. A great airlift over 2,485 miles (4000 km) of enemy territory was organised, and Savoia-Marchetti SM.82 transports flew into East Africa 51 dismantled CR.42s, plus additional engines and spare parts, over a nine-month period from August 1940. The last resistance in this theatre was provided by two surviving CR.42s until the Italians surrendered to the Allies in November 1941.

During early operations over Libya the CR.42s proved themselves effective against both the RAF and ground targets, but as British forces built up the CR.42 was restricted more and more to ground-support activities. In July 1941 the first examples of the CR.42 AS (Africa Settentrionale, or North Africa), optimised

Fiat CR.42 Falco

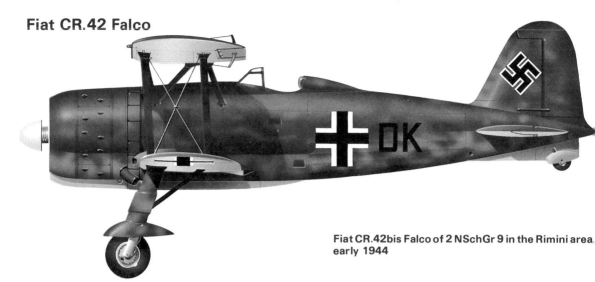

Fiat CR.42bis Falco of 2 NSchGr 9 in the Rimini area early 1944

for the North African theatre, began to arrive in Libya. They had tropical dust filters and were fitted with racks for two 220-lb (100-kg) bombs. From September 1942 losses became very heavy and only 82 CR.42s survived to be evacuated to Italy in January 1943.

However, the type continued to be used operationally in Greece, Albania and Yugoslavia; others were based on Sicily for action against Malta, and in Sicily and on the Italian mainland for use in a fighter role. Despite continuing production only 64 CR.42s remained serviceable at the time of the Italian armistice in September 1943; few were flown by Italian units thereafter. However, small-scale production continued with the CR.42 LW, a night harassment and anti-partisan version produced by Fiat for the Luftwaffe after the Italian aircraft industry in northern Italy had come under German control. Carrying the same bombload as the CR.42 AS, some 150 of these aircraft were used by the Luftwaffe during 1943-4, being flown against the Allies from bases in Austria, Italy and Yugoslavia. The last operations by CR.42s were made in May 1945, but before then two experimental prototypes had been built which did not enter production. They comprised the CR.42 DB flown in March 1941 and powered by a 1,160-hp (865-kW) Daimler-Benz DB 601E engine, giving this aircraft a maximum speed of over 320 mph

(515 km/h), and the ICR.42 developed by Fiat's CMASA subsidiary, basically a CR.42 mounted on twin floats, which was tested in 1940.

Specification
Fiat CR.42

Type: single-seat fighter biplane
Powerplant: one 840-hp (626-kW) Fiat A.74 R1C.38 14-cylinder radial piston engine
Performance: maximum speed 267 mph (420 km/h) at 16,405 ft (5000 m); service ceiling 33,465 ft (10200 m); range 482 miles (775 km)
Weights: empty equipped 3,929 lb (1782 kg); maximum take-off 5,060 lb (2295 kg)
Dimensions: span 31 ft 10 in (9.70 m); length 27 ft 1½ in (8.27 m); height 11 ft 9¼ in (3.59 m); wing area 241.12 sq ft (22.40 m²)
Armament: two fixed forward-firing 12.7-mm (0.5-in) Breda-SAFAT machine-guns
Operators: Italian Regia Aeronautica, Aeronautica Cobelligerante del Sud and Aeronautica Nazionale Repubblicana, Luftwaffe, Belgium, Hungary, Sweden

Until the end of 1942 the Fiat CR.42 Falco was still widely deployed in the fighter role, where it proved no more than adequate.

Fiat G.50

Fiat G.50bis Freccia of 20° Gruppo, 51° Stormo based at Ursel, Belgium in October 1940

History and notes

Design of the Fiat G.50 cantilever low-wing monoplane was begun by Giuseppe Gabrielli in April 1935. After extensive modifications, many ordered by the Italian authorities, the first (MM 334) of two prototypes flew for the first time at Marina di Pisa on 26 February 1937. Test pilot Mario de Briganti reported a tendency to spin and this problem continued even after series production had begun.

The G.50 was an all-metal aircraft, only the movable control surfaces being fabric-covered, with wide-track inward-retracting main landing gear units and a fixed tailwheel; the latter was provided with a streamlined fairing but this was often discarded in service use.

The prototypes and first pre-production batch of 45 G.50 aircraft had a pilot's enclosed cockpit wit a rearward sliding canopy, but later production machines had either an open or partially enclosed cockpit. Apart from the two prototypes, a total of 778 machines was built, 350 being produced by Fiat, which did not start building the type until November 1940, and the balance of 428 by Costruzioni Meccaniche Aeronautiche SA (CMASA), which was a Fiat subsidiary. The initial series-built G.50s were characterised by modified flaps, reshaped vertical tail surfaces and an open cockpit, built by CMASA (206) and Fiat (6), and 45 of the total were exported to Croatia (10) and Finland (35).

Twelve pre-production G.50s formed the Gruppo Sperimentale de Caccia, which operated in Spain with the Italian Aviazione Legionaria for a few weeks before the Republican surrender to General Franco in 1939. When Italy entered World War II, 97 G.50s were in service. They took part in the fighting in southern France in June 1940 and then flew with the Corpo Aereo Italiano (C.A.I.) in Belgium for operations against the UK between September 1940 and January 1941. However, the very limited range of the G.50 reduced it to an almost non-existent role with the C.A.I. Subsequently the G.50-equipped 24° and 154° Gruppi moved to Albania for operations against Greece.

The G.50bis, the first example of which was tested on 9 September 1940, incorporated increased fuel tankage to extend range, redesigned vertical tail surfaces, and had glazed cockpit side panels to protect the pilot from the slipstream. Production totalled 421, 77 of them built by CMASA. The type was used in Croatia, but most G.50bis fighters went to North Africa with the 2° and 155° Gruppi, these aircraft being equipped with carburettor sand filters.

Some G.50s were converted as fighter-bombers with underwing racks for bombs, including anti-personnel bombs, and this version equipped the 50° Stormo in North Africa. The final production variant was the G.50B, a two-seat dual-control fighter-trainer development which had an unusual long glazed canopy, the top section over the rear cockpit being open. The prototype was flown for the first time on 30 April 1940, and CMASA went on to build 100 examples during 1940-3. Single prototypes which did not enter production included the G.50ter powered by a 1,000-hp (746-kW) Fiat A.76 engine which, flown in July 1941, demonstrated a maximum speed of 329 mph (530 km/h), but the G.50V powered by a Daimler-Benz DB 601 engine and flown during the following month attained an astounding 360 mph (580 km/h). Final prototype was the G.50bis A/N, a two-seat fighter-bomber intended for operation from the aircraft carriers *Aquila* and *Sparviero*, conversions from merchant ships which were never completed. Test flown for the first time on 3 October 1942, production G.50bis A/N aircraft would have been armed with four 12.7-mm (0.5-in) machine-guns and carried a 551-lb (250-kg) bomb.

In early 1943 the G.50bis was in use with the 24° Gruppo in Sardinia, the 151° Gruppo in Greece, and the 154° Gruppo in the Aegean; after September 1943 and the armistice between Italy and the Allies, only four G.50s remained in flying condition, used as trainers by the air arm of the Fascist republic still fighting beside Germany.

The Fiat G.50bis, introduced in 1940, was a far cry from the Spitfires and Messerschmitt Bf 109s of the UK and Germany, and the type never proved a success.

Fiat G.50

Apart from the 12 pre-production aircraft flown in Spain and the 10 G.50s supplied to the Croat government, the only aircraft of the type to be exported were 35 G.50s bought by Finland in 1939. They were received too late for the 1939-40 Winter War, but flew with some distinction against the USSR during the Continuation War of 1941-4. Several survived the war, the last example being grounded in 1947.

Specification
Fiat G.50

Type: single-seat fighter monoplane
Powerplant: one 840-hp (626-kW) Fiat A.74 RC.38 14-cylinder radial piston engine
Performance: maximum speed 293 mph (472 km/h); climb to 19,685 ft (6000 m) in 7 minutes 30 seconds; service ceiling 32,265 ft (9835 m); range 416 miles (670 km)
Weights: empty equipped 4,354 lb (1975 kg); maximum take-off 5,324 lb (2415 kg)
Dimensions: span 35 ft 11½ in (10.96 m); length 25 ft 6¾ in (7.79 m); height 9 ft 8½ in (2.96 m); wing area 195.37 sq ft (18.15 m²)
Armament: two fixed forward-firing 12.7-mm (0.5-in) Breda-SAFAT machine-guns
Operators: Italian Regia Aeronautica, Aeronautica Cobelligerante del Sud and Aeronautica Nazionale Repubblicana, Croatia, Finland, Spain

Fiat G.55 Centauro

Fiat G.55/1 Centauro of the Squadriglia Complementare Caccia Montefuscq, based at Caselle in March 1944

History and notes

The Fiat G.55 Centauro (centaur) was an all-metal low-wing monoplane single-seat fighter designed by Giuseppe Gabrielli, and represented a great improvement by comparison with the previous Fiat monoplane fighter to go into production, the G.50. Great care was taken to blend an aerodynamically advanced airframe with a structure which was robust and would lend itself to mass production. Its configuration included fully-retractable landing gear and a raised cockpit providing an excellent view. Fast and manoeuvrable, the type proved popular with its pilots.

The first of three prototypes was flown on 30 April 1942; the third (MM 493) was the only one to carry armament, comprising one engined-mounted cannon and four fuselage-mounted machine-guns. It was evaluated under operational conditions from March 1943, but by then the Italian air ministry had already decided on mass production of the G.55. However, only 16 G.55/0 pre-production and 15 G.55/I initial production aircraft had been delivered to the Regia Aeronautica by September 1943, production thereafter being for the Fascist air arm flying alongside the Luftwaffe. Before wartime production ended 274 more were completed and a further 37 were abandoned at an advanced construction stage.

Before the armistice of September 1943, G.55s had participated in the defence of Rome with the 353 Squadriglia of the Regia Aeronautica. The post-armistice operations were mainly with the Fascist air arm's Squadriglia 'Montefusco', based at Veneria Reale, then with the three *squadriglie* which formed the 2° Gruppo Caccia Terrestre, but losses were heavy, as a result mainly of Allied attacks on the airfields. While the war was still in progress, Fiat flew two prototypes of the G.56, which was developed from the G.55 to accept the more powerful Daimler-Benz DB 603A engine. Built during the spring of 1944 they incorporated minor structural changes and had the fuselage-mounted machine-guns deleted. The first prototype survived the war and was used subsequently by Fiat as a test-bed.

Fiat reinstated the G.55 assembly line after the war, using wartime manufactured assemblies and components to produce the G.55A single-seat fighter/advanced trainer of which the prototype was flown for the first time on 5 September 1946. It differed from the G.55 only in instrumentation and armament; the latter could comprise either two wing-mounted plus two fuselage-mounted 12.7-mm (0.5-in) machine-guns, or two 20-mm wing-mounted Hispano-Suiza cannon plus two fuselage-mounted 12.7-mm (0.5-in) machine-guns. The Italian Aeronautica Militaire procured 19 G.55As and 30 were supplied to Argentina, which returned 17 in 1948 for re-sale to Egypt, these being armed with four 12.7-mm (0.5-in) Breda-SAFAT machine-guns. A two seat advanced trainer variant of the G.55 had been flown in prototype form on 12 February 1946 under the

Fiat G.55 Centauro

designation G.55B. The Italian Aeronautica Militare acquired 10 of these, and 15 were sold to Argentina in 1948.

Specification
Fiat G55/I

Powerplant: one 1,475-hp (1100-kW) Fiat RA 1050 RC.58 Tifone (licence-built DB 605A) 12-cylinder inverted-Vee piston engine
Performance: maximum speed 391 mph (630 km/h); climb to 19,685 ft (6000 m) in 7 minutes 12 seconds; service ceiling 41,665 ft (12700 m); range 746 miles (1200 km)
Weights: empty equipped 5,798 lb (2630 kg); maximum take-off 8,197 lb (3718 kg)

An immeasurable improvement over the G.50, the G.55 Centauro featured a licence-built DB 605A engine, which gave the type a top speed of 391 mph (630 km/h).

Dimensions: span 38 ft 10½ in (11.85 m); length 30 ft 9 in (9.37 m); height 10 ft 3¼ in (3.13 m); wing area 227.23 sq ft (21.11 m²)
Armament: one 20-mm Mauser MG 151/20 engine-mounted cannon, two similar wing-mounted cannon, and two fuselage-mounted 12.7-mm (0.5-in) Breda-SAFAT machine-guns, plus provision for two 353-lb (160-kg) bombs on underwing racks
Operators: Italian Regia Aeronautica and Aeronautica Nazionale Repubblicana, Argentina, Egypt

---

Fiat RS.14

History and notes

Designed at the CMASA works at Marina di Pisa by Manlio Stiavelli, the Fiat RS.14 (Ricognizione Stiavelli) was a long-range maritime reconnaissance floatplane.

The first of two prototypes (MM 380) made its maiden flight during May 1939, a four/five-seat all-metal cantilever low/mid-wing monoplane powered by two Fiat A.74 RC.38 radial engines. The fuselage had an almost perfect streamlined finish, terminating in a cantilever tail unit incorporating a tall fin and rudder, and was mounted on large twin floats with struts that were smoothly faired to cause a minimum of drag. These features were retained in the 186 series aircraft built by CMASA between May 1941 and September 1943.

The amply glazed, pointed nose section housed the observer/bomb-aimer, who also operated an AGR 90 camera in the rear fuselage. The cabin housed the pilot and co-pilot side-by-side, with the wireless operator's

Endowed with a very good range, the Fiat RS.14 flew anti-submarine patrols from a number of bases round the Italian coast, Sicily and Sardinia.

compartment immediately behind them. In a bombing role the RS.14 could carry a long ventral gondola to accommodate various combinations of anti-submarine bombs up to a maximum 882 lb (400 kg).

The RS.14 formed the equipment of a number of *squadriglie da ricognizione strategica marittima* (maritime strategic reconnaissance squadrons) located at bases round the Italian coast and in Sicily and Sardinia. They performed useful convoy escort work and covered enormous distances on anti-submarine patrols. A small number survived after the September 1943 armistice with the Italian Co-Belligerent Air Force. After the war surviving machines were used on liaison routes between the Italian mainland and outlying points in the Mediterranean, carrying a maximum of four passengers.

A development of the basic design was the AS.14 (Assalto Stiavelli), a twin-engine landplane with retractable landing gear. Intended for ground-attack, it was to be armed with a 37-mm cannon and two 12.7-mm (0.5-in) machine-guns in the nose and two similar weapons firing from a ventral position. The heavy armament and armour protection which was to be installed would nevertheless allow for a level speed of 273 mph (440 km/h). The prototype was first flown on 11 August 1943, but no production was undertaken.

Specification
Fiat RS. 14

Type: long-range maritime reconnaissance floatplane
Powerplant: two 840-hp (626-kW) Fiat A.74 RC.38 14-cylinder radial piston engines
Performance: maximum speed 242 mph (390 km/h) at 13,125 ft (4000 m); service ceiling 20,670 ft (6300 m); range 1,553 miles (2500 km)
Weights: empty equipped 12,059 lb (5470 kg); maximum take-off 18,673 lb (8470 kg)
Dimensions: span 64 ft 1¼ in (19.54 m); length 46 ft 3¼ in (14.10 m); height 18 ft 5¾ in (5.63 m); wing area 538.21 sq ft (50.00 m²)
Armament: one 12.7-mm (0.5-in) and two 7.7-mm (0.303-in) machine-guns, plus up to 882 lb (400 kg) of bombs
Operators: Italian Regia Aeronautica, Aeronautica Cobelligerante del Sud and Aeronautica Nazionale Repubblicana

Fieseler Fi 156 Storch

History and notes
Best-known of all the Fieseler designs because of its extensive use during World War II, the Fieseler Fi 156 Storch (stork) was a remarkable STOL (short take-off and landing) aircraft that was first flown nearly 50 years ago, during the early months of 1936. A braced high-wing monoplane of mixed construction, with a conventional braced tail unit and fixed tailskid landing gear with long-stroke main units, the Fi 156 was powered by an Argus inverted-Vee piston engine, and its extensively glazed cabin provided an excellent view for its three-man crew. As with the Fi 97, the key to the success of this aircraft was its wing incorporating the company's high-lift devices, comprising in the initial production series a fixed slot extending over the entire span of the wing leading edge, with slotted ailerons and slotted camber-changing flaps occupying the entire trailing edge. Flight testing of the first three prototypes (Fi 156 V1, V2 and V3) showed that the capability of this aircraft more than exceeded its STOL expectations, for with little more than a light breeze blowing it needed a take-off run of only about 200 ft (60 m) and could land in about one-third of that distance.

Built to complete against fixed-wing submissions from Messerschmitt and Siebel and an autogyro from Focke-Wulf, the three prototypes were followed by the

With its high-lift wing devices and stalky under-carriage for high vertical descent rates, the Fieseler Fi 156C-1 equipped the majority of Luftwaffe *Gruppen* as a liaison aircraft.

Fieseler Fi 156 Storch

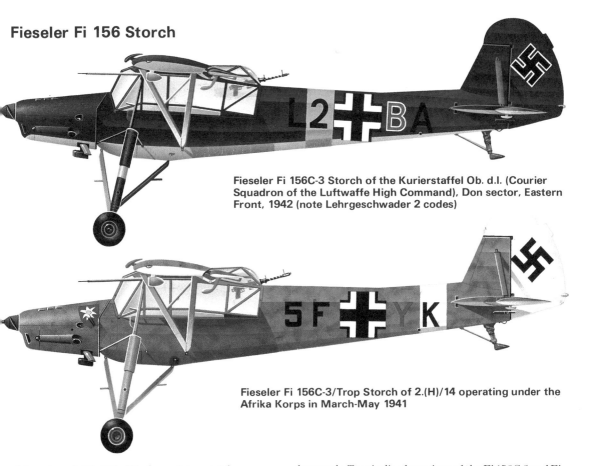

Fieseler Fi 156C-3 Storch of the Kurierstaffel Ob. d.l. (Courier Squadron of the Luftwaffe High Command), Don sector, Eastern Front, 1942 (note Lehrgeschwader 2 codes)

Fieseler Fi 156C-3/Trop Storch of 2.(H)/14 operating under the Afrika Korps in March-May 1941

ski-equipped Fi 156 V4 for winter trials, a pre-production Fi 156 V5 and, in early 1937, by 10 Fi 156A-0 aircraft for service evaluation. One of these was demonstrated publicly for the first time at an international flying meeting at the end of July 1937, by which time the general-purpose Fi 156A-1 was in production. Service tests confirmed that Germany's armed forces had acquired a 'go-anywhere' aircraft, and for the remainder of World War II the Storch was found virtually everywhere German forces operated, production of all variants totalling 2,549 aircraft. In view of this number it is not surprising that there were several variants, the first being the projected but not built Fi 156B with movable leading-edge slots. The major production version was the C-series, the initial pre-production Fi 156C-0 being a development of the Fi 156A-1 and introducing raised rear-cabin glazing to allow for installation of a rear-firing 7.92-mm (0.31-in) machine-gun. The designation Fi 156C-1 applied to a variant intended to be deployed in liaison and staff transport roles, and the Fi 156C-2 was basically a two-crew reconnaissance version carrying a single camera; some late examples of the Fi 156C-2 were, however, equipped to carry one stretcher for casualty evacuation. The Fi 156C-3 was the first to be equipped for multi-purpose use, the majority of the type being powered by the improved Argus As 10P engines, this engine being standard in the generally similar Fi 156C-5 which had provision to carry an underfuselage camera or drop tank. Tropicalised versions of the Fi 156C-3 and Fi 156C-5, incorporating engine dust/sand filters, were built under the respective designations Fi 156C-3/Trop and Fi 156C-5/Trop. The final production variant was an improved casualty evacuation aircraft with an enlarged loading/unloading hatch for a single stretcher. Pre-production Fi 156D-0 aircraft were powered by the Argus As 10C engine, but production Fi 156D-1s had the Argus As 10P engine as standard. Ten unusual pre-production aircraft were built under the designation Fi 156E-0, intended for operation from rough terrain; the standard landing gear was replaced by main units that each incorporated two wheels in tandem, the wheels of each unit being linked by pneumatic rubber track. Final wartime variant was the Fi 256, a larger capacity five-seat civil version, of which only two examples were built at the Morane-Saulnier factory in Puteaux, France, during 1943-4.

Because of their capability, Fi 156s were used in some remarkable exploits. Best known are the rescue of Benito Mussolini from imprisonment in a hotel amid the Apennine mountains, on 12 September 1943, and the flight made by Hanna Reitsch into the ruins of Berlin on 26 April 1945, carrying General Ritter von Greim to be appointed by Adolf Hitler as his new commander of the Luftwaffe.

During the war the Fi 156 had been built for the Luftwaffe by Morane-Saulnier in France and by Mraz in Czechoslovakia. These two companies continued

Fieseler Fi 156 Storch

production after the war, Morane-Saulnier producing
M.S.500, M.S.501 and M.S.502 variants and Mraz the
K-65 Cap.

Specification
Fieseler Fi 156C-2

Type: two-seat army co-operation/reconnaissance
aircraft
Powerplant: one 240-hp (179-kW) Argus As 10C-3 8-
cylinder inverted-Vee piston engine
Performance: maximum speed 109 mph (175 km/h)
at sea level; economical cruising speed 81 mph
(130 km/h); service ceiling 15,090 ft (4600 m); range
239 miles (385 km)
Weights: empty 2,050 lb (930 kg); maximum take-off
2,921 lb (1325 kg)
Dimensions: span 46 ft 9 in (14.25 m); length 32 ft
5¾ in (9.90 m); height 10 ft 0 in (3.05 m); wing area
279.87 sq ft (26.00 m²)
Armament: one rear-firing 7.92-mm (0.31-in) machine

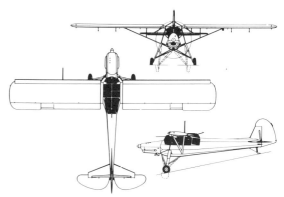

Fieseler Fi 156C Storch

gun on trainable mount
Operators: Luftwaffe, Bulgaria, Croatia, Finland,
Hungary, Italy, Romania, Slovakia, Spain, Sweden,
Switzerland, UK, USA and USSR

Focke-Wulf Fw 44 Stieglitz

History and notes

Second only to the Fw 190 fighter as the most prolific
Focke-Wulf design, the Focke-Wulf A 44 (Fw 44)
Stieglitz (goldfinch) trainer appeared in 1932, the
prototype making its first flight in the late summer of
that year in the hands of Gerd Achgelis. Powered by a
140-hp (104-kW) Siemens Sh 14a radial, the aircraft
was a single-bay biplane with a fabric-covered welded
steel-tube fuselage and wooden wings with fabric and
plywood covering. In its original form it had a number
of unacceptable flight characteristics, but these were
eradicated following an extensive test programme
undertaken by Kurt Tank, who had joined the company
in November 1931 from BFW, and headed the design
and flight test department of Focke-Wulf when
Heinrich Focke became preoccupied with his rotary-
wing activities. The initial examples were followed by
two Fw 44B/E prototypes powered by the 135-hp

**The Focke-Wulf Fw 44 Stieglitz was one of the
major Luftwaffe trainers of the war, proving
extremely aerobatic in the right hands.**

(101-kW) Argus As 8 inline engine, and following satisfactory testing small numbers were delivered to the
Luftwaffe. Major productions variants were the
generally similar Fw 44C, Fw 44D and Fw 44F, which
differed from each other by minor equipment changes.
All three were powered by the Siemens Sh 14a
engine, as was the final production Fw 44J.

The Stieglitz became an outstanding aerobatic
mount, particularly in the hands of Achgelis, Emil
Kropf and Ernst Udet, and it won export orders from
Bolivia, Chile, China, Czechoslovakia, Finland, Romania,
Switzerland and Turkey; licence production was undertaken in Argentina, Austria, Brazil, Bulgaria and
Sweden. The Stieglitz was also built in substantial
numbers for the Luftwaffe, serving as a trainer until
the end of World War II and was used also by the pre-
war Deutsche Verkehrsfliegerschule and the Deutsche
Luftsportverband.

Specification
Focke-Wulf Fw 44C

Type: two-seat trainer
Powerplant: one 150-hp (112-kW) Siemens Sh 14a 7-
cylinder radial piston engine
Performance: maximum speed 115 mph (185 km/h);
cruising speed 107 mph (172 km/h); service ceiling
12,795 ft (3900 m); range 419 miles (675 km)
Weights: empty 1,157 lb (525 kg); maximum take-off
1,985 lb (900 kg)
Dimensions: span 29 ft 6½ in (9.00 m); length 23 ft
11½ in (7.30 m); height 8 ft 10¼ in (2.70 m); wing
area 215.29 sq ft (20.00 m²)
Operators: Luftwaffe, Bulgaria, China, Finland,
Romania, Slovakia, Turkey

Focke-Wulf Fw 56 Stösser

History and notes

The first Focke-Wulf design for which Kurt Tank had responsibility from its beginning, the Focke-Wulf Fw 56 Stösser (falcon) was evolved to meet a Reichsluftfahrtministerium specification for an advanced trainer powered by the Argus As 10C engine. Tank's design incorporated a steel-tube fuselage with metal panels forward and fabric covering aft, and a wing of wooden construction with plywood covering back to the rear spar and fabric to the trailing edge. The first Fw 56a prototype was flown in November 1933 and, after initial testing had revealed landing gear deficiencies, the Fw 56 V2 second machine had new main landing gear units. It also featured an all-metal wing and was without the original faired headrest behind the cockpit. The Fw 56 V3 third aircraft, flown in February 1934, introduced further-modified landing gear and had a wooden wing similar to that of the first. Three pre-production aircraft were completed in 1934 under the designation Fw 56A-0, these incorporating minor wing and engine cowling modifications. The first two carried a pair of 7.92-mm (0.31-in) MG 17 machine-guns in the upper fuselage decking and had a rack to carry three 22-lb (10-kg) practice bombs, but the third had only a single MG 17 gun.

The Stösser was evaluated competitively at Rechlin in the summer of 1935 and was selected, in preference to the Arado Ar 76 and Heinkel He 74, for use as a Luftwaffe advanced trainer. It also played a part in the development of Ernst Udet's ideas on the techniques of dive-bombing, later used so effectively by Junkers Ju 87 Stuka units. In late 1936 Udet flew the second prototype at Berlin-Johannisthal, and at his instigation it was fitted with a bomb rack beneath each wing, each carrying three 2.2-lb (1-kg) smoke bombs. It was flown to great effect by Flugkapitän Wolfgang Stein and substantial orders were placed for the production Fw 56A-1 to equip the fighter and dive-bomber pilot schools of the Luftwaffe. Austria and Hungary also ordered the Stösser, and a small number was delivered to civil pilots, including Gerd Achgelis. Total production was approximately 1,000 aircraft.

Specification
Focke-Wulf Fw 56A-1

Type: single-seat advanced trainer
Powerplant: one 240-hp (179-kW) Argus As 10C 8-cylinder inverted-Vee piston engine
Performance: maximum speed 173 mph (278 km/h) at sea level; service ceiling 20,340 ft (6200 m); range 249 miles (400 km)
Weights: empty 1,532 lb (695 kg); maximum take-off 2,194 lb (995 kg)
Dimensions: span 34 ft 5½ in (10.50 m); length 25 ft 3 in (7.70 m); height 11 ft 7¾ in (3.55 m); wing area 150.7 sq ft (14.00 m²)
Armament: two 7.92-mm (0.31-in) MG 17 machine-guns
Operators: Luftwaffe, Hungary

The Fw 56 Stösser was used by both fighter and dive bomber training schools, its high performance suiting it to both roles.

Focke-Wulf Fw 189 Uhu

History and notes

In February 1937 a Reichsluftfahrtministerium specification for a short-range reconnaissance aircraft was issued to Arado, Hamburger Flugzeugbau and Focke-Wulf. Kurt Tank responded with the Focke-Wulf with Fw 189 Uhu (eagle owl), an all metal stressed-skin low-wing monoplane that had an extensively glazed fuselage pod, and twin booms carrying the tail surfaces. The mainwheels retracted to the rear, into the booms. The crew nacelle provided accommodation for pilot, navigator/radio operator and engineer/gunner, and power for the prototype was supplied by two 430-hp (321-kW) Argus As 410 engines. Construction of this aircraft began in April 1937 and designer Tank performed the first flight in July 1938. The Fw 189 V2 second prototype, flown in August, was armed with one 7.92-mm (0.31-in) MG 15 machine-gun in each of nose, dorsal and rear positions, two fixed MG 17 weapons in the wing roots, and four underwing racks each carrying a 110-lb (50-kg) bomb. A third, unarmed, prototype was flown in September, this Fw 189 V3's engines driving Argus-designed air-pressure-actuated variable-pitch propellers.

The award of a development contract was followed by the first flight of a fourth prototype, forerunner of the production Fw 189A, which was powered by two Argus As 410A-1 engines and armed with only two MG 15 machine-guns. The fifth prototype was representative of the proposed Fw 189B dual-control trainer, its redesigned fuselage nacelle having a stepped cockpit and much reduced glazing. It was the dual-control trainer which gained the first order in the summer of 1939, for three Fw 189B-0 pre-series and 10 Fw 189B-1 production five-seat crew trainers. These preceded the Fw 189A into manufacture and service, some being used as conversion trainers by 9.(H)/LG 2 during the spring and summer of 1940. In a similar manner the construction of 10 Fw 189A-0 pre-production aircraft began in 1940, some of them being delivered to 9.(H)/LG 2 for operational trials, and being followed by the initial production Fw 189A-1 which was armed similarly to the Fw 189 V2 prototype, except that the MG 15 was deleted from the nose position and an Rb

20/30 or Rb 50/30 camera was carried. Further developments of this version included the Fw 189A-1/Trop which carried desert survival equipment, and the Fw 189A-1/U2 and Fw 189A-1/U3 which were equipped as personal transports for the use of Generalfeldmarschall Kesselring and General Jeschonnek respectively. The remaining Fw 189A variants included the Fw 189A-2 introduced in 1942, which had the flexibly-mounted MG 15 machine-guns replaced by twin 7.92-mm (0.31-in) MG 81Zs; the Fw 189A-3 two-seat dual-control trainer which was built in limited numbers; and introduced in late 1942, the light ground-attack Fw 189A-4 which was armed with two 20-mm MG 151/20 cannon and two 7.92-mm (0.31-in) machine-guns in the wing roots, and had armour protection for the underside of the fuselage, engines and fuel tanks. Unbuilt projects included the close-support Fw 189C and the Fw 189D twin-float trainer; the seventh prototype, which had been intended to serve as the development aircraft for this last variant, was completed instead as an Fw 189B-0. The use of alternative powerplant was planned for the Fw 189E, a French-built Fw 189A-1 airframe being modified by the installation of two 700-hp (522-kW) Gnome-Rhône 14M radial engines, but when this prototype crashed while being flown to Germany for evaluation, further development was abandoned. Final production version was the Fw 189F-1, basically an Fw 189A-2 re-engined with two 580hp (433-kW) Argus As 411MA-1 engines; a similarly-powered Fw 189F-2 introducing electrically-actuated landing gear and increased armour and fuel capacity was planned, but none had been built when production ended in 1944. Total production of the Fw 189 then amounted to 864 aircraft including prototypes, built not only by Heinkel but also by Aero in Prague from 1940 to 1943, and by SNCASO at Bordeaux-Mérignac until 1944.

Fw 189s were supplied in small numbers to the Slovakian and Hungarian air forces operating on the Eastern Front, in which theatre the type was deployed most extensively by the Luftwaffe, but at least one *Staffel* used the type operationally in North Africa.

Specification
Focke-Wulf Fw 189A-1

Type: two-seat short-range reconnaissance aircraft
Powerplant: two 465-hp (347-kW) Argus As 410A-1 12-cylinder inverted Vee piston engines
Performance: maximum speed 208 mph (335 km/h); cruising speed 196 mph (315 km/h); service ceiling 22,965 ft (7000 m); range 416 miles (670 km)
Weights: empty 6,185 lb (2805 kg); maximum take-off 8,708 lb (3950 kg)
Dimensions: span 60 ft 4½ in (18.40 m); length 39 ft 5½ in (12.03 m); height 10 ft 2 in (3.10 m); wing area 409.04 sq ft (38.00 m²)
Armament: two trainable 7.92-mm (0.31-in) MG 15 machine-guns and two fixed 7.92-mm (0.31-in) MG 17 machine-guns, plus four 110-lb (50-kg) bombs
Operators: Luftwaffe, Hungary, Slovakia

The Luftwaffe's 'eye in the sky', the Fw 189 Uhu was mainly used on the Eastern Front where it flew over the Soviet ground formations, providing valuable information for Wehrmacht commanders.

Focke-Wulf Fw 189 Uhu

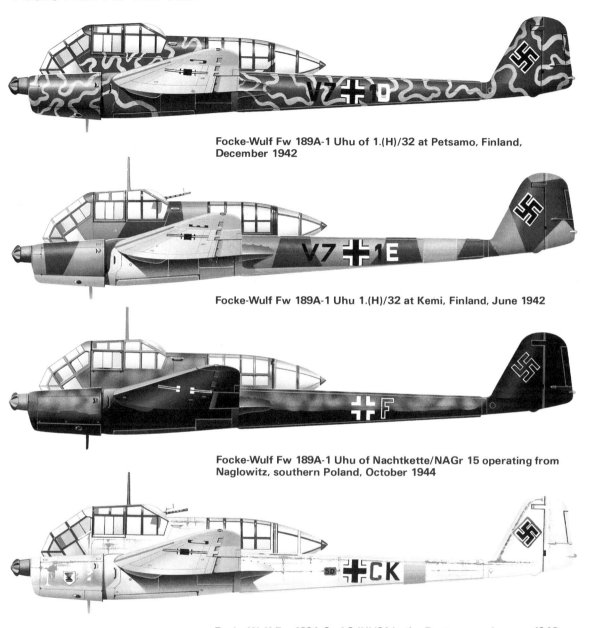

Focke-Wulf Fw 189A-1 Uhu of 1.(H)/32 at Petsamo, Finland, December 1942

Focke-Wulf Fw 189A-1 Uhu 1.(H)/32 at Kemi, Finland, June 1942

Focke-Wulf Fw 189A-1 Uhu of Nachtkette/NAGr 15 operating from Naglowitz, southern Poland, October 1944

Focke-Wulf Fw 189A-2 of 2.(H)/31 in the Rostov area January 1943

Focke-Wulf Fw 189A-2 of Hungarian 3/1 Short-Range Reconnaissance Squadron at Zamocz, Poland, March 1944

Focke-Wulf Fw 190

History and notes

Acknowledged generally by pilots to be a superior aircraft to the Luftwaffe's other main World War II fighter, the Messerschmitt Bf 109, the Focke-Wulf Fw 190 was developed under a contract placed by the Reichsluftfahrtministerium in the autumn of 1937. Kurt Tank submitted two proposals, one powered by a liquid-cooled Daimler-Benz DB 601 and the other by the then-new air-cooled BMW 139 radial. The radial was selected and detail design work began in the summer of 1938 under the leadership of OberIng R. Blaser. A cantilever low-wing monoplane of stressed-skin construction, the prototype Fw 190 V1 was rolled out in May 1939 and the first flight took place on 1 June 1939 at Bremen in the hands of Flugkapitän Hans Sander. A second aircraft, the Fw 190 V2, flew in October 1939, armed with two 13-mm (0.51-in) MG 131 and two 7.92-mm (0.31-in) MG 17 machine-guns. Both machines were fitted with large ducted spinners to reduce drag, but overheating problems were experienced and an NACA cowling was substituted. Before the first prototype had flown, however, a decision had been taken to replace the BMW 139 by the more powerful but longer and heavier BMW 801. This necessitated a number of major changes, including structural strengthening and relocation of the cockpit farther aft: the latter change solved a centre of gravity problem and, as a bonus, that of pilot discomfort from fumes and overheating of the cockpit, caused by proximity of the engine with the BMW 139 installation. The third and fourth prototypes were abandoned, and the Fw 190 V5 with the new engine was completed in early 1940. Later in the year the aircraft was fitted with a wing of increased span, 3 ft 3½ in (1.00 m) greater than the original 31 ft 2 in (9.50 m), and although some 6 mph (10 km) slower, this Fw 190 V5g was more manoeuvrable and superior in climb performance to the short-span version now designated Fw 190 V5k. Of a pre-production batch of 30 Fw 190A-0 aircraft, the first nine had the original wing, the remainder being of greater span. During February 1941 the first of these aircraft were delivered to Erprobungskommando 190 at Rechlin-Rogenthin for service evaluation, and in

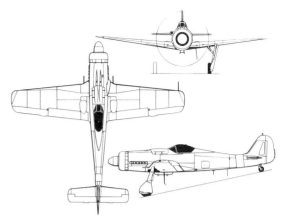

Focke-Wulf Fw 190D-9

March Jagdgeschwader 26 began to prepare for the new fighter's introduction into Luftwaffe service. Initial production version was the Fw 190A-1 with long-span wings, powered by the 1,660-hp (1238-kW) BMW 801C-1 radial, equipped with FuG 7a radio, and armed with four 7.92-mm (0.31-in) MG 17 machine-guns. It was this version which, flown by 6./JG 26, first clashed with RAF Supermarine Spitfires on 27 September 1941, leaving little doubt that the armament of four MG 17s was quite inadequate. This deficiency was dealt with first in the Fw 190A-2 which, powered by an improved BMW 801C-2 engine, had two MG 17s mounted above the engine and two 20-mm FF cannon in the wing roots, armament which was often augmented by two MG 17s in the outer wing panels. The ensuing Fw 190A-3, which introduced the 1,800-hp (1342-kW) BMW 801Dg engine, had the MG FF cannon moved to the outer wing panels, being replaced in the wing root positions by faster-firing MG 151s. Sub-variants included the Fw 190A-3/U1 and Fw 190A-3/U3 close-support and Fw 190A-3/U4 reconnaissance aircraft, these conversions usually involving removal of the outboard MG FF cannon and the addition of ETC 500 bomb racks or Rb 12 cameras.

In the summer of 1942 deliveries of the Fw 190A-4 began, introducing MW-50 water-methanol injection to boost the output of its BMW 801D-2 engine to 2,100 hp (1566 kW) for short periods and raising its maximum speed to 416 mph (670 km/h) at 21,000 ft (6400 m). The generally similar Fw 190A-4/Trop introduced tropical filters to protect the engine when deployed in the Mediterranean theatre and was equipped to carry a 551-lb 250-kg bomb beneath the fuselage, but the MW-50 water-methanol system was deleted from the Fw 190A-4/R6 which could carry two underwing 210-mm (8.27-in) WGr.21 rocket tubes. The Fw 190A-4/U8, which had its fixed armament reduced to the two MG 151 cannon but could mount a 1,102-lb (500-kg) bomb beneath the fuselage, was able to gain increased range from the carriage of a 66-Imp gal (300-litre) drop tank beneath each wing. All of the versions mentioned so far

A Focke-Wulf 190A-3 converted to carry four SC 50 bombs (110-lb/50-kg) by means of attaching a ETC-250 bomb rack to the centreline. Fighter-bomber versions were widely used.

Focke-Wulf Fw 190

Focke-Wulf Fw 190A-3 of EJG 1, Bad Aibling, May 1945

Focke-Wulf Fw 190A-5/U8 of I/SKG 10 based at Poix, France in 1943

Focke-Wulf Fw 190A-5 of II/JG 54 'Grunherz' at Petsen, Estonia, 1944

Focke-Wulf Fw 190A-6/R11 of 1./NG 10 At Werneuchen, summer 1944, equipped with Neptun radar

Focke-Wulf Fw 190A-8 of III/JG 11 at Gross-Ostheim, December 1944

Focke-Wulf Fw 190

An early production Fw 190D-9, showing the cooling gills open just aft of the spinner. This was the major version of the 'long nose' Fw 190, known as the 'Dora-9'.

had a tendency for the engine to overheat, this being overcome in the Fw 190A-5 which had a new mounting for the engine, positioning it some 6 in (15 cm) farther forward. Introduced in early 1943, this version was built in many sub-variants, including the Fw 190A-5/U2 which, armed by two MG 151/20 cannon and an underfuselage ETC 501 bomb rack, and able to carry 66-Imp gal (300-litre) underwing drop tanks, was equipped with flame-damping equipment so that it could be deployed for night operations. The similar Fw 190A-5/U3 could carry a 1,102-lb (500-kg) bomb beneath the fuselage and a 254-lb (115-kg) bomb under each wing; but the Fw 190A-5/U4 was equipped with two Rb 12 cameras for deployment in a reconnaissance role. Fighter-bomber versions included the Fw 190A-5/U6 and the long-range Fw 190A-5/U8, and the Fw 190A-5/U11 close-support aircraft carried a 30-mm MK 103 cannon beneath each wing. The heavily armed Fw 190A-5/U12 carried fixed armament of two MG 151/20 cannon and two MG 17 machine-guns, supplemented by two WB 151A pods which each contained a pair of MG 151/20s. The Fw 190A-5/U14 and Fw 190A-5/U15 were both torpedo-bomber variants, able to carry an LT F5b and LT 950 torpedo respectively, and a 30-mm MK 108 cannon mounted in the outboard wing position was standard for the Fw 190A-5/U16.

In June 1943 a new major version was introduced, the Fw 190A-6 derived from the experimental Fw 190A-5/U10 incorporated a redesigned lighter-weight wing that could accommodate four 20-mm MG 151/20 cannon and was the forerunner of the Fw 190A-6/R1 with six 20-mm MG 151/20 cannon, the Fw 190A-6/R2 with two 30-mm MK 108 cannon mounted one in each outboard wing position, the Fw 190A-6/R3 which added an MK 103 cannon beneath each wing, and the Fw 190A-6/R6 which was the final A-6 variant, carrying a 210-mm (8.27-in) WGr.21 rocket tube under each wing. This led to a version similar to the Fw 190A-6 in which the engine-mounted 7.92-mm (0.31-in) MG 17 machine-guns were replaced by two 13-mm (0.51-in) MG 131s and this, designated Fw 190A-7, was introduced in December 1943 but only built in small num-

bers. However, it was followed by the extensively-built Fw 190A-8 which had internal fuel capacity increased by 25.3 Imp gal (115 litres) and manufactured initially in variants similar to those of the Fw 190A-6. Also produced was the Fw 190A-8/R7 with armour protection for the cockpit, but versions for new roles included the Fw 190A-8/R11 all-weather fighter with a heated canopy and PKS 12 radio navigation equipment; the Fw 190A-8/U1 two-seat conversion trainer, first flown on 23 January 1944; and the Fw 190A-8/U3 which was the director component of the Fw 190/Ta 154 Mistel composite aircraft.

Experience with the Fw 190As had shown them to be very effective when combat took place at altitudes below 22,965 ft (7000 m), but above that height the output of the BMW 801 powerplant began to drop off. Development was initiated to overcome this deficiency, beginning with the modification of three Fw 190A-1s, the first of them designated Fw 190B-0; this was given a wing of increased area and a pressurized cockpit, and its BMW 801D-2 engine was provided with a GM-1 power boost system. The other two, designated Fw 190B-2 and Fw 190B-3, were similar but had a standard wing and carried armament comprising two MG 17 machine-guns and two MG 151/20 cannon. Further development was then concentrated on the Fw 190C, a small number being built with 1,750-hp (1305-kW) Daimler-Benz DB 603 engines with Hirth 9-2281 turbochargers in large ventral fairings, which gave rise to the nickname Kanguruh. Extensive testing proved the turbochargers to be unreliable, leading to this programme being abandoned in favour of the Fw 190D, and in late 1943 several Fw 190A-7s were modified by the installation of Junkers Jumo 213A inline engines to serve as Fw 190D-0 prototypes,. The use of this engine necessitated the inclusion of a 1 ft 7¾ in (0.50 m) rear fuselage plug to compensate for a 2 ft 0 in (0.60 m) lengthening of the nose, and the fin was increased in area for the same reason. Thus was derived the Fw 190D-9 production version, known popularly as the 'long-nose 190' or 'Dora 9', which was armed with two wing-mounted MG 151/20 cannon and two MG 131 guns above its engine, and had an MW 50 water-methanol injection system to boost the emergency power output to 2,240 hp (1670 kW). A 66-Imp gal (300-litre) drop tank or a 551-lb (250-kg) bomb could be carried on each underwing rack, and later aircraft were equipped with bubble canopies as introduced earlier on the Fw 190F. Two Fw 190D-9 airframes were converted to Fw 190D-10 standard for evaluation purposes by installing the Jumo 213C engine; this allowed a 30-mm cannon to fire through the propeller shaft and spinner, replacing the two MG 131 machine-guns, but no production resulted. This was the fate also of the ensuing Fw 190D-11, of which seven prototypes were built with Jumo 213F engines, two MG 151/20 cannon in the wing roots, and two MK 108s in the outer wing panels. Final variants included the Fw 190D-12, which was essentially a ground-attack aircraft with

Focke-Wulf Fw 190

Focke-Wulf Fw 190A-9 of I/JG 6 at Delmenhorst, winter 1944-5

Focke-Wulf Fw 190A-8 of Stab/JG 2 'Richthofen' at Merzhausen, December 1944

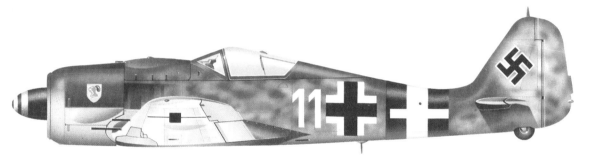

Focke-Wulf Fw 190A-8 of II/JG 4 at Babenhausen, winter 1944-5

Focke-Wulf Fw 190D-9 of 10./JG 54, January 1945

Focke-Wulf Fw 190D-9 of Stab/JG 4 based at Babenhausen in early 1945

Focke-Wulf Fw 190

additional armour protection for the engine, and armed with two MG 151/20s in the wings and a single MK 108 cannon firing through the spinner; and the generally similar Fw 190D-13 which had the MK 108 replaced by an MG 151/20. The development and production of a proposed fighter/reconnaissance aircraft designated Fw 190E was abandoned.

Introduction into service of the Fw 190D-9 provided a fighter aircraft that was regarded by many pilots as being superior to any other in Luftwaffe service, but by the time that it was in large-scale use, in early 1945, the optimum deployment of these superb aircraft was already being limited by the serious shortage of aviation fuel. However, the Fw 190D had been preceded into service by the Fw 190F-1, a specialised ground-attack version which was introduced in early 1943; generally similar to the Fw 190A-4, it differed by having additional armour protection for the cockpit and powerplant, the outboard 20-mm cannon deleted, and an ETC 501 bomb rack installed beneath the fuselage. Similarly, the Fw 190F-2 was related to the Fw 190A-5 but introduced a bubble canopy, and the Fw 190F-3 corresponding to the Fw 190A-6 could carry a 66-Imp gal (300-litre) drop tank or a 551-lb (250-kg) bomb beneath the fuselage and, in the Fw 190F-3/R1 and Fw 190F-3/R3 versions, four ETC 50 underwing bomb racks or two similarly-located 30-mm MK 103 cannon. The Fw 190F-8 was based on the Fw 190A-8, with two engine-mounted 13-mm (0.51-in) MG 131 machine-guns and four ETC 50 bomb racks, and the Fw 190F-8/U2 and Fw 190F-8/U3 were fitted with the TSA bomb sight for anti-shipping strikes with, respectively, a 1,543-lb (700-kg) BT 700 or a 3,086-lb (1400-kg) BT 1400 weapon. The Fw 190F-9, introduced in mid-1944 and representing the last of the F-series, was an alternative version of the Fw 190F-8 powered

by the BMW 801 TS/TH engine. Alphabetically the last of the Fw 190s, and a specialised ground attack version like the F-series which it preceded into service, the Fw 190G-1 fighter-bomber was derived from the Fw 190A-5, but carried a 3,968-lb (1800-kg) bomb which necessitated the introduction of strengthened landing gear; wing-mounted armament was reduced to two MG 151/20 cannon, and the Junkers-designed wing racks accommodated two 66-Imp gal (300-litre) drop tanks. The Fw 190G-2 and Fw 190G-3 were basically the same, but were equipped with Messerschmitt and Focke-Wulf wing racks respectively. Final production variant of all was the Fw 190G-8 which incorporated the modifications introduced on the Fw 190A-8 and was powered by the 1,800-hp (1342-kW) BMW 801D-2 engine.

No accurate production figures appear to exist for the Fw 190, but it is estimated that more than 19,500 were built by Focke-Wulf at Tutow/Mecklenburg, Marienburg, Cottbus, Sorau/Silesia, Newbrandenburg and Schwerin, and by Ago at Oschersleben, Arado at Brandenburg and Warnemunde, Fieseler at Kassel, Dornier at Wismar, and by Weserflugzeugbau. Without doubt the most advanced fighter aircraft operated by any nation at the time of its introduction into service in the autumn of 1941, continuing development and refinement enabled the Fw 190 to hold its own until Germany surrendered to the Allies in May 1945.

A specialist ground attack version of the Fw 190 was the Fw 190G-2. This example carries a SC 500 bomb (1,102-lb/500-kg) on a ETC-501 rack and two 66-gal (300-litre) tanks under the wings for extra range.

Focke-Wulf Fw 190

Focke-Wulf Fw 190F-8 of SchG 4 based at Koln, January 1945

Specification
Focke-Wulf Fw 190D-9

Type: single-seat fighter/fighter-bomber
Powerplant: one 1,776-mph (1324-kW) Junkers Jumo
213A-1 12-cylinder inverted-Vee piston engine
Performance: maximum speed 426 mph (685 km/h)
at 21,655 ft (6600 m); climb to 19,685 ft (6000 m) in 7
minutes 6 seconds; service ceiling 39,370 ft (12000 m);
range 519 miles (835 km)

Weights: empty 7,694 lb (3490 kg); maximum take-off
10,670 lb (4840 kg)
Dimensions: span 34 ft 5½ in (10.50 m); length 33 ft
5½ in (10.20 m); height 11 ft 0 in (3.35 m); wing area
196.99 sq ft (18.30 m²)
Armament: two 0.51-in (13-mm) MG 131 machine-
guns and two 20-mm MG 151 cannon, plus one 1,102-lb
(500-kg) SC500 bomb
Operators: Luftwaffe, Hungary, Turkey

Focke-Wulf Fw 200 Condor

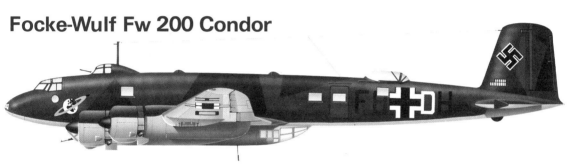

Focke-Wulf Fw 200C Condor of 1./KG 40, based at Bordeaux-Merignac in late 1940

History and notes

Kurt Tank's ideas for a new transport aircraft for
Deutsche Lufthansa were submitted to directors of the
airline on 16 July 1936, with a promise that the first
examples would fly within a year. In fact, the Focke-
Wulf Fw 200 V1, the first of three prototypes, on which
work had started in the autumn of 1936, flew on 27 July
1937, which was still a very creditable performance.
An all-metal low-wing monoplane, the Fw 200 was
powered initially by four 875-hp (652-kW) Pratt &
Whitney Hornet radial engines and was designed to
provide accommodation for up to 26 passengers in two
cabins. Two further prototypes, the second of which
became Adolf Hitler's personal transport, were each
powered by four 720-hp (537-kW) BMW 132G-1 radials.
The second prototype and four examples of the initial
production Fw 200A Condor were delivered to Lufthansa,
two Fw 200As to DDL Danish Air Lines and two to
Lufthansa's Brazilian associate Syndicato Condor.

The prototype, redesignated Fw 200S-1 and named
Brandenburg, made a number of record flights in the
latter half of 1938, beginning on 10 August when
Lufthansa's Alfred Henke flew nonstop from Berlin to

New York in a time of 24 hours 56 minutes, returning
on 13 August in 19 hours 55 minutes. Departing on 28
November the Fw 200S-1 set a 46 hour 18 minute
record for the journey from Berlin (via Basra, Karachi
and Hanoi) to Tokyo. Further aircraft were supplied to
Lufthansa before the outbreak of World War II and on
14 April 1945 a survivor flew the airline's last scheduled
service before the cessation of hostilities, from Bar-
celona to Berlin.

The prototype's flight to Tokyo had resulted in an
order for five Fw 200B airliners from Dai Nippon KK
and a single maritime reconnaissance aircraft for the
Japanese navy. However, none of these Condors were
supplied to Japan, but three of the airliners were
completed under the designation Fw 200-B2 and
delivered instead to Lufthansa, powered by 830-hp
(619-kW) BMW 132H radial engines. Lufthansa also
received a single Fw 200B-1 which had four 850-hp
(634-kW) BMW 132DC Radials. The requirement of
the Japanese navy for a long-range reconnaissance
aircraft had led to construction of the Fw 200 V10
military prototype, which had increased fuel capacity
and armament comprising a 7.92-mm (0.31-in) MG 15

Focke-Wulf Fw 200 Condor

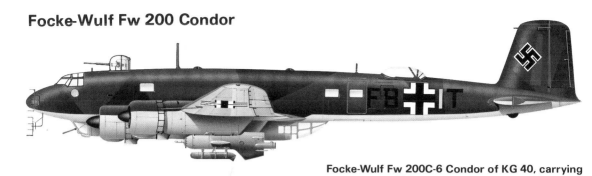

Focke-Wulf Fw 200C-6 Condor of KG 40, carrying Henschel Hs 293A anti-ship missiles, in 1943

machine-gun in a dorsal turret and fore- and aft-firing MG 15s in a ventral gondola. There was at first virtually no interest in this version of the Condor, but when just before the outbreak of World War II the Luftwaffe decided to establish a long-range anti-shipping unit the Fw 200 V10 was evaluated and a batch of 10 pre-production Fw 200C-0 aircraft with structural strengthening was delivered in September 1939. The first four were unarmed and these, together with Lufthansa's four Fw 200Bs, were used to equip KGrzbV 105 at Kiel-Holtenau in April 1940. The other six Fw 200C-0s were armed with one 7.92-mm (0.31-in) MG 15 machine-gun in each of forward and aft dorsal turrets, with a third weapon firing through a ventral hatch. Operated initially by Oberstleutnant Edgar Petersen's Fernaufklärungstaffel (later 1./KG 40), the unit's first operational sortie was flown on 8 April 1940.

The initial production reconnaissance version was the Fw 200C-1, armed with one 20-mm MG FF cannon in the nose, one MG 15 in a ventral gondola and similar single weapons in forward and rear dorsal positions; offensive armament also included four 551-lb (250-kg) bombs on underwing racks. The Fw 200C-2 was generally similar, differing by having the rear of the outboard engine nacelles cut away and provided with streamlined bomb racks, but the structural weakness for military use of these two early versions led to the improved Fw 200C-3 introduced in 1941. In addition to strengthening of the structure, more powerful Bramo 323R-2 radial engines were introduced, and armament changes accounted for sub-variants that included the Fw 200C-3/U1 with a 15-mm MG 151 cannon in a power-operated forward turret, and the nose-mounted MG FF cannon being replaced by an MG 151/20 of the same calibre. The Fw 200C-3/U2 had the MG 151/20 cannon deleted to allow installation of a Lofte 7D bomb sight; the Fw 200C-3/U3 carried an MG 131 machine-gun in each of the front and rear dorsal positions; and the final Fw 200C-3/U4 variant accommodated an extra gunner and there were two additional beam-mounted MG 131s. Despite the structural improvement introduced in the Fw 200C-3 the weakness problem was never completely resolved, and throughout its operational career many Fw 200s became major casualties when they broke their back on landing. In early 1942 production of the Fw 200C-4 was initiated; essentially similar to the Fw 200C-3, this version carried FuG Rostock search radar (later FuG 200

Focke-Wulf Fw 200C-8/U10 Condor

Hohentwiel equipment) and was armed with an MG 151 cannon in the forward dorsal turret, an MG 151/20 in the nose of the ventral gondola, unless a Lofte 7D bomb sight was required when it was replaced by an MG 131 machine-gun, and MG 15s at the other stations. Single examples of Fw 200C-4/U1 and Fw 200C-4/U2 high-speed transports were also built, the former being allocated for the use of Heinrich Himmler and equipped with an armour plate seat for his protection. To provide greater offensive capability, under the designation Fw 200C-6 a number of Fw 200C-3/U1 and Fw 200C-3/U2 aircraft were modified to serve as interim missile-carriers. Each equipped with two under-wing Henschel Hs 293A rocket-propelled guided bombs and with FuG 203b Kehl missile control equipment, this version entered service with III/KG 40 in November 1943. A definitive version of the Fw 200C-6 was built in small numbers and these Fw 200C-8 aircraft, which added Hohentwiel search radar to their onboard equipment, were the final production version. No accurate production records appear to exist and it is believed that approximately 280 Condors were built, but despite their small numbers these aircraft were the scourge of Allied shipping before the introduction of measures to attack them effectively.

Specification
Focke-Wulf Fw 200C-3/U4

Type: long-range reconnaissance bomber
Powerplant: four 1,200-hp (895-kW) Bramo 323R 9-cylinder radial piston engines

Focke-Wulf Fw 200 Condor

Performance: maximum speed 224 mph (360 km/h); cruising speed 208 mph (335 km/h); service ceiling 19,685 ft (6000 m); range 2,212 miles (3560 km); endurance 14 hours

Weights: empty 37,490 lb (17005 kg); maximum take-off 50,057 lb (24520 kg)

Dimensions: span 107 ft 9¼ in (32.85 m); length 76 ft 11¼ in (23.45 m); height 20 ft 8 in (6.30 m); wing area 1,290.10 sq ft (119.85 m²)

The premier long range maritime patrol aircraft in the Luftwaffe, the Focke-Wulf Fw 200 Condor was also used on the Eastern Front on transport duties.

Armament: four 13-mm (0.51-in) MG 131 machine-guns in dorsal and beam positions, and one MG 131 or one 20-mm MG 151 in a ventral gondola, plus four 551-lb (250 kg) bombs

Operator: Luftwaffe

Focke-Wulf Ta 152

History and notes

Further improvements to the Fw 190D series airframe to provide even better performance at high altitude led to the introduction of the Focke-Wulf Ta 152 and Ta 153. The latter was built only as a development proto-type, powered by a Daimler Benz DB603 engine, and introduced an entirely new high aspect ratio wing of increased span, together with revision of the fuselage structure, tail surfaces and internal systems. It was abandoned to avoid disruption of existing production facilities for the Fw 190.

The Ta 152 as conceived originally was structurally closer to the Fw 190D, except that the flap and landing gear systems were hydraulically and not electrically actuated. In the autumn of 1944 a prototype appeared with a Junkers Jumo 213E engine and high aspect ratio long-span wings, and although it crashed on 8

October its replacement in the Ta 152H test programme had the Jumo engine but standard Fw 190 wings. The first of 20 pre-production Ta 152H-0 aircraft flew in October 1944 and these, built at Focke-Wulf's Cottbus factory, were mostly rebuilt from Fw 190A-1 airframes and powered by the Jumo 213E engine with an MW-50 water-methanol injection system. Service trials were undertaken by Erprobungskommando 152 at Rechlin before the type's operational debut with JG 301. This unit was tasked with the protection of bases used by the Messerschmitt Me 262 jet fighter, which was particularly vulnerable to attack during take-off and landing. The only production version was the Ta 152H-1 which, armed with one engine-mounted 30-mm MK 108 cannon and two 20-mm MG 151/20 cannon in the wing roots, began to leave the Cottbus lines in November 1944. The second planned production version

Focke-Wulf Ta 152

Clearly visible in this photograph is the extended wingspan of the Focke-Wulf Ta 152H (*Hühenjagen*, or altitude fighter). This, the third Ta 152H-0, was later shipped to the United States for testing.

was the Ta 152C, the first 2,100-hp (1566-kW) Daimler-Benz DB 603LA-engined development prototype being flown for the first time on 19 November 1944. The extra length of this engine required a compensating rear fuselage plug and enlarged tail surfaces, and wing span was increased to 36 ft 1 in (11.00 m). Production sub-variants would have differed mainly in armament, the Ta 152C-1 and Ta 152C-2 (the latter with improved radio) with an engine-mounted 30-mm MK 108 and four 20-mm MG 151/20 cannon, but the Ta 152C-3 would have had the MK 108 replaced by an MK 103. Final

planned production version was the photo-reconnaissance Ta 152E with Jumo 213E engine, to be built with a standard wing as the Ta 152E-1 or in a high-altitude variant with the H-series wing under the designation Ta 152E, but only a single prototype was completed. Only about 190 Ta 152H-1s were produced, and total production including pre-production aircraft and prototypes is estimated at about 220.

Specification
Focke-Wulf Ta 152H-1
Type: high-altitude fighter
Powerplant: one 1,750-hp (1305-kW) Junkers Jumo 213E 12-cylinder inverted-Vee piston engine
Performance: maximum speed 472 mph (760 km/h) at 41,010 ft (12500 m) with MW-50 water-methanol fuel injection and GM-1 power boost; initial climb rate 3,445 ft (1050 m) per minute with MW-50; service ceiling 48,555 ft (14800 m); range 746 miles (1200 km)
Weights: empty 8,643 lb (3920 kg); maximum take-off 10,472 lb (4750 kg)
Dimensions: span 47 ft 6¾ in (14.50 m); length 35 ft 5½ in (10.80 m); height 13 ft 1½ in (4.00 m); wing area 252.96 sq ft (23.50 m²)
Armament: one 30-mm MK 108 and two 20-mm MG 151/20 cannon
Operator: Luftwaffe

Gotha Go 145

History and notes
The Gotha company, having been closed down in 1919 under the terms of the Versailles Treaty, was re-formed on 2 October 1933. Its first product was the Gotha Go 145 trainer, a single-bay biplane of wooden construction with fabric covering, powered by an Argus As 10C engine. The prototype was first flown in February 1934 and following successful test and evaluation the initial production version entered service with the Luftwaffe during the following year under the designation Go 145A. An improved Go 145B was also

introduced in 1935, differing by having an enclosed cockpit and landing gear spats, and the final production variant was the Go 145C gunnery trainer carrying a single 7.92-mm (0.31-in) machine-gun in the rear cockpit.

Although used originally as a pilot training aircraft, the Go 145 served extensively with the *Störkamptfstaffeln* which were set up in December 1942, when the Luftwaffe decided to emulate use by the Soviet Union of the Polikarpov Po-2 as a 'nuisance raider' during the hours of darkness. In October 1943 these units were redesignated *Nachtschlachtgruppen* and they remained operational on the Eastern Front until the end of the war. Rather more than 9,500 Go 145s were built in Germany by Ago, BFW, Focke-Wulf and Gotha, and the type was licence-built in Spain and Turkey. The Spanish version was built by Construcciones Aeronauticas SA under the designation CASA 1145-L, and the type was operated by the Spanish air force for some years after World War II.

As well as being a basic trainer, the Gotha Go 145 was used as a 'nuisance raider', especially on the Eastern Front. This involved nightly attacks over Soviet lines with small bombloads.

Specification
Gotha Go 145B
Type: two-seat basic trainer
Powerplant: one 240-hp (179-kW) Argus As 10C inverted-Vee piston engine
Performance: maximum speed 132 mph (212 km/h)

Gotha Go 145

at sea level; cruising speed 112 mph (180 km/h); service ceiling 12,140 ft (3700 m); range 391 miles (630 km)
Weights: empty 1,940 lb (880 kg); maximum take-off 3,043 lb (1380 kg)

Dimensions: span 29 ft 6¼ in (9.00 m); length 28 ft 6½ in (8.70 m); height 9 ft 6 in (2.90 m); wing area 234.12 sq ft (21.75 m²)
Operators: Luftwaffe, Slovakia, Spain, Turkey

Gotha Go 242 and 244

Gotha Go 244B of 4./KGrzbV 106 early in 1943

History and notes

The work of Dipl. Ing. Albert Kalkert, the Gotha Go 242 assault glider was developed with the approval of the Reichsluftfahrtministerium since it offered almost three times the troop-carrying capacity of the DFS 230 then in use. The wings were constructed of wood with plywood and fabric covering, with twin booms extending aft from the wing structure to carry twin fins and rudders united by a wide span tailplane and elevator. The central fuselage pod was of tubular steel construction with fabric covering, mounting beneath it a twin-wheel jettisonable dolly for take-off, and a semi-retractable nose skid and two fixed skids for landing. The fuselage pod accommodated a crew of two, seated side-by-side, and up to 21 fully-equipped troops or an equivalent weight in military loads, such as a Kubelwagen utility vehicle, loaded through the hinged rear fuselage. Two prototypes were flown in 1941 and production followed without delay, permitting entry into service during 1942. The type's operational debut was made in the Aegean and Mediterranean theatres, Go 242 units being based in Greece, North Africa and Sicily. Heinkel He 111 tugs were employed usually, and the Go 242 had provisions for the installation of a variety of RATO (rocket-assisted take-off) propulsion units, typically four Rheinmetall-Borsig RI-502 solid fuel rockets, each developing 1,102-lb (500-kg) thrust. The initial production Go 242A-1 differed from the prototypes by introducing strengthened tailbooms of deeper cross-section and, although essentially a cargo glider, could be armed with up to four 7.92-mm (0.31-in) MG 15 machine-guns; the ensuing Go 242A-2 was generally similar except that it was equipped for troop carrying and had additional doors in the hinged tail section. In 1942 improved versions were introduced beginning with two cargo-carrying variants, the Go 242B-1 with fixed tricycle landing gear and the later Go 242B-2 with revised landing gear which incorporated a semi-retrac-

table nosewheel and main units with oleo-pneumatic shock struts. Corresponding troop transport versions, which differed by having additional drop doors in the tail of the fuselage pod, had the respective designations Go 242B-3 and Go 242B-4. Production of all versions of the Go 242 totalled 1,528, this number including also a Go 242B-5 training variant which, generally similar to the Go 242B-2, was equipped with dual controls. Several other variants of the Go 242 were projected, but only one was built in small numbers. This was the Go 242C-1 developed specially for an attack on the British fleet in Scapa Flow, which had a planing bottom incorporating flotation bags and underwing stabilising floats so that it could land on water. Like the Go 242A-1 it had a jettisonable two-wheel dolly for take-off, and the plan was that these gliders would each carry a small assault boat and its crew. Although a few were delivered to 6./KG 200, the planned assault on Scapa Flow was never mounted.

After the fall of France Gnome-Rhône 14M radial engines became available to Germany in large numbers, and the Go 242 was modified to serve as a twin-engine transport, each of the twin booms being extended forward of the leading edge of the wing to mount one of these powerplants. A total of 133 conversions was made from the five Go 242B variants, and these were designated correspondingly Go 244B-1 to Go 244B-5. Initial deliveries were made in March 1942, to KgrzbV 104 and KgrzbV 106 based in Greece and Crete respectively, but these aircraft proved to be relatively easy targets for Allied fighters and by November 1942 all had been withdrawn from operational deployment and transferred to schools used to train airborne troops. Although the majority of Go 244s were powered by Gnome-Rhône 14M radial engines, some had the 660-hp (492-kW) BMW 132Z or the captured Russian Shvetsov M-25A of 750 hp (559 kW).

Specification
Gotha Go 244B-2

Type: assault cargo/troop transport
Powerplant: two 700-hp (522-kW) Gnome-Rhône 14M
14-cylinder radial piston engines
Performance: maximum speed 180 mph (290 km/h);
service ceiling 24,605 ft (7500 m); range 373 miles
(600 km)
Weights: empty 11,243 lb (5100 kg); maximum take-
off 17,196 lb (7800 kg)

The Gotha Go 242B was a troop glider, featuring
rear clamshell doors which enabled a *Kübelwagen*
to be carried. He 111s were the usual tugs.

Dimensions: span 80 ft 4½ in (24.50 m); length 51 ft
10 in (15.80 m); height 15 ft 5 in (4.70 m); wing area
693.22 sq ft (64.40 m²)
Armament: four 7.92-mm (0.31-in) MG 15 machine-
guns (optional)
Operator: Luftwaffe

Heinkel He 45

History and notes
Designed as a general-purpose military aircraft of
mixed construction, the Heinkel He 45 single-bay
biplane appeared in 1932. The prototype He 45a,
powered by a BMW VI 73Z engine, was unarmed and
the second prototype, the He 45b, was similar but
fitted with a four-blade propeller. The He 45c was the
first to carry armament, which comprised one fixed
forward-firing 7.92-mm (0.31-in) MG 17 machine-gun
and a flexible rear-firing MG 15 of similar calibre. The
type saw limited operational service with reconnaissance
units but its principal use was as a trainer in various
roles. The initial He 45A-1 trainers and He 45A-2
reconnaissance aircraft were followed into production
by the improved He 45B-1 reconnaissance aircraft with
one 7.92-mm (0.31-in) machine-gun, and the He 45B-2
bomber with a 220-lb (100-kg) bombload. The major
production version was the He 45C, generally similar
to the He 45c third prototype, but differing by having
ailerons only on the lower wings; the He 45D was
marginally improved. Because production capacity at
Heinkel's Warnemünde factory was very limited, the
He 45 was built also by Focke-Wulf (219), BMW (156)
and Gotha (68), with Heinkel manufacturing the balance
of 69 aircraft. This last number included three development aircraft with the 880-hp (656-kW) Daimler-Benz
DB 600 inline engine, and one with a 600-hp (447-kW)

A tough if uninspiring aircraft to fly, the Heinkel
He 45 was first manufactured in substantial numbers
in the He 45C form, one of the latter being illustrated.

BMW 116 radial. In addition to the He 45s built for the
Luftwaffe, a small number was used by the Nationalist
forces during the Spanish Civil War and, in addition,
Heinkel built a small number of reconnaissance aircraft
for China under the designation He 61. This was
essentially an He 45 airframe powered by a 660-hp
(492-kW) BMW VI engine. At the outbreak of World
War II only about 20 remained in first-line service with
the Luftwaffe, and these were then very quickly
transferred for use in a training role.

Specification
Heinkel He 45C

Type: two-seat reconnaissance and training aircraft
Powerplant: one 750-hp (559-kW) BMW VI 7,3Z 12-
cylinder Vee piston engine

Heinkel He 45

Performance: maximum speed 180 mph (290 km/h) at sea level; cruising speed 137 mph (220 km/h); service ceiling 18,045 ft (5500 m); range 746 miles (1200 km)
Weights: empty 4,642 lb (2105 kg); maximum take-off 6,053 lb (2745 kg)

Dimensions: span 37 ft 8¾ in (11.50 m); length 32 ft 9¾ in (10.00 m); height 11 ft 9¾ in (3.60 m); wing area 372.44 sq ft (34.60 m²)
Armament: one fixed forward-firing 7.92-mm (0.31-in) MG 17 machine-gun
Operators: Luftwaffe, Bulgaria, China, Hungary

Heinkel He 46

History and notes

The emerging Luftwaffe's need for an army co-operation and reconnaissance aircraft was met in 1931 by the Heinkel He 46, flown originally in He 46a prototype form as an unequal-span single-bay biplane. Small as the lower wing was, it reduced the field of view available to the observer and it was soon removed, necessitating an increase of 8ft 2½ in (2.50 m) in the span of the upper parasol wing. Power was supplied by a licence-built 450-hp (336-kW) Bristol Jupiter engine, also fitted originally to the He 46b second prototype which flew in 1932. The second aircraft was later re-engined with the Siemens SAM 22B radial, which was adopted as powerplant for the production versions, beginning with the He 46C-1 which was based on the He 46c third development aircraft. A total of 478 aircraft of all versions was built by Heinkel at Warnemünde (200), and by Fieseler (12), Gotha (24), MIAG at Leipzig (83) and by Siebel (159), all of them built between 1933 and 1936. The initial production He 46C-1 could carry a camera, or up to 20 22-lb (10-kg) bombs stored vertically beneath the rear cockpit; 20 of this version were sent to Spain in September 1938 for use by the Nationalist forces, and 18 generally-similar He 46C-2 aircraft were built for Bulgaria, these differing by introducing NACA-type engine cowlings. Minor improvements were incorporated in six He 46D-0 pre-production aircraft, and the addition of NACA cowlings resulted in the production He 46E built in He 46E-1, He 46E-2 and He 46E-3 versions, but because of engine serviceability problems these variants were often flown without the cowlings; a small number of he 46E-2s was supplied to Hungary. The designation He 46F was allocated to an experimental aircraft which combined an He 46C airframe with a 560-hp (418-kW) Armstrong Siddeley Panther engine complete with cowling. Successful testing of this aircraft resulted in the production of 14 similarly-powered He 46F-1 and He 46F-2 unarmed observer training aircraft.

An Heinkel He 46C operated by Aufklärungsgruppe (H) 112, with the rear seated observer preparing his Zeiss camera equipment. Note the large-diameter wooden airscrew (12 ft 1¾ in/3.70 m).

Heinkel He 46

The Luftwaffe's reconnaissance squadrons had been equipped with the He 46 by 1936, and although replaced progressively by the Henschel Hs 126 from 1938, the He 46 remained in service in a utility and training role and, from 1943, entered its final operational period with the Störkampfstaffeln (later Nachtschlacht-gruppen).

Specification
Heinkel He 46C-1
Type: two-seat reconnaissance/army co-operation aircraft
Powerplant: one 650-hp (485-kW) Siemens SAM 22B 9-cylinder radial piston engine
Performance: maximum speed 155 mph (250 km/h); cruising speed 130 mph (210 km/h); service ceiling 19,685 ft (6000 m); range 621 miles (1000 km)
Weights: empty 3,892 lb (1765 kg); maximum take-off 5,071 lb (2300 kg)
Dimensions: span 45 ft 11 in (14.00 m); length 31 ft 2 in (9.50 m); height 11 ft 4 in (3.45 m); wing area 346.61 sq ft (32.20 m²)
Armament: one 7.92-mm (0.31-in) MG 15 machine-gun and 20 22-lb (10-kg) bombs
Operators: Luftwaffe, Bulgaria, France, Hungary, Spain

Heinkel He 49 and He 51

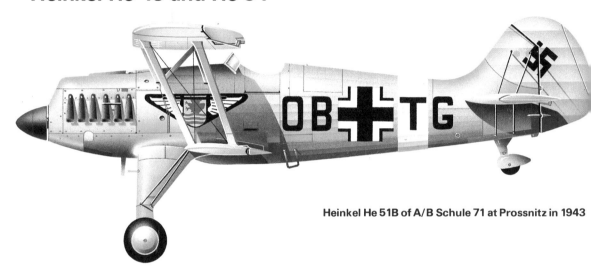

Heinkel He 51B of A/B Schule 71 at Prossnitz in 1943

History and notes
When the Heinkel He 49a single-seat biplane made its first flight in November 1932 it was ostensibly a civilian advanced trainer. However, its BMW VI engine gave it a top speed of almost 199 mph (320 km/h), which was in keeping with its true role as the forerunner of the first fighter to serve with the Luftwaffe upon its official formation in April 1935. Two more prototypes were built, the He 49b flown in February 1933 with a fuselage lengthened by 1 ft 3¾ in (0.40 m), and the He 49c with faired landing gear. The type was ordered as the He 51, the initial He 51A-0 pre-production example being flown for the first time in May 1933; eight more were built to this standard and were unarmed. Of all-metal construction, with fabric covering, the He 51 was a single-bay biplane, armed with two 7.92-mm (0.31-in) MG 17 machine-guns mounted above the engine. Deliveries of the initial He 51A-1 production version began in July 1934, and in April 1935 some of them equipped the Luftwaffe's first fighter unit, the Jagdgeschwader 'Richthofen'. In January 1936 the He 51B was introduced on the production line, a structurally strengthened version, of which 12 pre-production aircraft were built initially under the designation He 51B-0, then being followed by 12 generally similar He 51B-1 aircraft. An He 51A-1 converted to have float landing gear was the forerunner of 38 He 51B-2 floatplane fighters with twin aluminium floats and equipped for catapult launching from Kriegsmarine cruisers and other large warships; racks were sometimes fitted to carry up to six 22-lb (10-kg) bombs. An experimental high-altitude version of the basic He 51B, with increased-span two-bay wings, was completed under the designation He 51B-3. Following testing of this aircraft two additional prototypes were built for high-altitude tests under the designations He 52B and He 52D, but no production resulted. Final version was the C-series, the He 51C-1 intended primarily for export to the Spanish Nationalists being equipped as standard with racks for six 22-lb (10-kg) bombs. A total of 79 was shipped to Spain, 51 being used by the Nationalist air force and the balance going to the Legion Condor. Subsequently, a small number of the generally similar He 51C-2, which differed by having

Heinkel He 49 and He 51

Heinkel He 51B serving with A/B schule 123 at Agram (Zagreb) in 1942

improved radio equipment, was supplied to the Luftwaffe. Total production of all versions reached 700, built by Heinkel, and by Arado, Erla Maschinenwerk and Fieseler. Some He 51s remained in first-line service with the Luftwaffe until 1938, then being relegated to the training role, in which capacity they were used for much of World War II.

Specification
Heinkel He 51B-1
Type: single-seat fighter
Powerplant: one 750-hp (559-kW) BMW VI 7,3Z 12-cylinder inverted-Vee piston engine
Performance: maximum speed 205 mph (330 km/h) at sea level; cruising speed 174 mph (280 km/h) at sea level; service ceiling 25,260 ft (7700 m); range 354 miles (570 km)
Weights: empty 3,219 lb (1460 kg); maximum take-off 4,178 lb (1895 kg)
Dimensions: span 36 ft 1 in (11.00 m); length 27 ft 6¾ in (8.40 m); height 10 ft 6 in (3.20 m); wing area 292.79 sq ft (27.20 m²)
Armament: two 7.92-mm (0.31-in) MG 17 machine-guns
Operators: Luftwaffe, Spain

Heinkel He 59

Heinkel He 59D of Seenotzentrale Ägaisches Meer, used for air-sea rescue duties in the Aegean during 1941

History and notes
Designed by Reinhold Mewes in 1930 as a reconnaissance bomber, the Heinkel He 59 twin-engine biplane was first flown in September 1931, the aircraft involved being the He 59b second prototype which was fitted with faired, wheeled landing gear. The first prototype, the He 59a flown in January 1932, had the wheel gear replaced by twin single-step floats, and all subsequent production aircraft were completed in marine configuration. The He 59 was of mixed construction, with a welded steel-tube fuselage and wooden wings, the airframe being fabric-covered. In early 1932 a small batch of He 59A evaluation aircraft was built, these aircraft being generally similar to the He 59a prototype, and these were followed by a pre-production run of 16 He 59B-1 aircraft which differed by having minor equipment changes and the installation of a 7.92-mm (0.31-in) MG 15 machine-gun in the nose. Heinkel and

Heinkel He 59

A Heinkel He 59B-2 'Zapatones' (big shoes) operated by 3./KüFlGr 106 photographed at List in 1936. This aircraft has the bomb aimer's glazed panels and forward gunner nose section.

Arado then initiated production of the He 59B-2 which introduced an all-metal nose with glazed panels for the bomb-aimer, plus a glazed ventral position housing an MG 15 gun to supplement those in nose and dorsal positions. It was this version that was first to see operational use, being used by the Legion Condor in Spain for night bombing, or for anti-shipping patrols when the nose machine-gun was replaced by a 20-mm MG FF cannon. It was followed by the He 59B-3 which, intended specifically for the reconnaissance role, had its armament reduced to two MG 15 machine-guns, and introduced fuselage fuel tanks to supplement that contained as standard in the floats. By 1938 the He 59Bs were approaching obsolescence for operational use, and the Walter Bachmann Flugzeugbau at Ribnitz

began a series of more specialised conversions of these aircraft. They resulted in the He 59C-1, a stripped-down version for long-range reconnaissance or training use, the He 59C-2 equipped to carry six inflatable dinghies, medical supplies and an external folding ladder for use in air-sea rescue, and the He 59D-1 which combined the roles of the He 59C aircraft. A torpedo-bombing trainer was then developed under the designation He 59E-1, its general configuration being similar to that of the He 59C-1, and the He 59E-2 long-range reconnaissance trainer carried three cameras. Final variant was the He 59N navigation trainer, produced as conversions of the He 59D-1, which carried full defensive armament and advanced radio equipment.

With the outbreak of World War II the majority of the He 59s were deployed as multi-role trainers, but some of the reconnaissance versions continued in use during the early months of the war and a few were used in mine-laying operations.

Specification
Heinkel He 59B-2

Type: coastal reconnaissance floatplane
Powerplant: two 660-hp (492-kW) BMW VI 6,0ZU 12-cylinder Vee piston engines
Performance: maximum speed 137 mph (220 km/h) at sea level; cruising speed 133 mph (215 km/h); ceiling 11,480 ft (3500 m); range 1,087 miles (1750 km)
Weights: empty 13,702 lb (6215 kg); maximum take-off 19,482 lb (9000 kg)
Dimensions: span 77 ft 9 in (23.70 m); length 57 ft 1 in (17.40 m); height 23 ft 3½ in (7.10 m); wing area 1,650.16 sq ft (153.30 m²)
Armament: three 7.92-mm (0.31-in) MG 15 machine-guns in nose, dorsal and ventral positions, plus a bombload of 2,205 lb (1000 kg), or one torpedo
Operators: Luftwaffe, Spain

Heinkel He 60

History and notes
Like the He 59, the Heinkel He 60 was designed by Reinhold Mewes and was a twin-float single-bay biplane of mixed construction, developed for catapult operations from the larger German warships. The He 60a prototype was flown in early 1933; its powerplant was a 660-hp (492-kW) BMW VI engine which provided insufficient power and which was replaced in the He 60b second machine by a 750-hp (559-kW) version of the same engine. This installation provided only marginally improved performance and was not adopted for subsequent aircraft. The He 60c third prototype was the first to be equipped for catapult launching, and was used for shipboard trials which established the type's suitability for its intended role. Fourteen pre-production He 60A unarmed trainers were built, and these entered service with Kriegsmarine

training units during the summer of 1933. They were followed by the initial production version, the He 60B, which had provision for the installation of a 7.92-mm (0.31-in) machine-gun on a trainable mount in the rear cockpit. In an attempt to improve performance one production aircraft was used for development under the designation 60B-3, this having a 900-hp (671-kW) Daimler-Benz DB 600 engine, but problems with the supply of DB 600 engines resulted in no further production of this version. Consequently, all of the generally similar He 60C production aircraft, introduced from 1934 and differing only in detail improvements, were powered by the BMW VI engine. He 60B and He 60C versions served aboard German battle-ships and cruisers, and with four coastal reconnaissance wings, and the type was first tested operationally during the Spanish Civil War. Although withdrawn

Heinkel He 60

from front-line duties in northern Europe fairly early in World War II, then being relegated to training duties under the designation He 60D, the He 60 remained in service as a maritime reconnaissance aircraft with units based in Greece and Crete.

Specification
Heinkel He 60B
Type: shipboard reconnaissance aircraft/trainer
Powerplant: one 660-hp (492-kW) BMW VI 12-cylinder Vee piston engine
Performance: maximum speed 149 mph (240 km/h) at sea level; cruising speed 134 mph (215 km/h); service ceiling 16,405 ft (5000 m); range 590 miles (950 km)
Weights: empty 6,009 lb (2725 kg); maximum take-off 7,552 lb (3425 kg)
Dimensions: span 44 ft 3½ in (13.50 m); length 37 ft 8¾ in (12.50 m); height 17 ft 4½ in (5.30 m); wing area 604.95 sq ft (56.20 m²)

A standard production Heinkel He 60C-1 photographed while being winched down into the sea. Visible in the rear cockpit is the 7.9-mm MG 15 machine-gun.

Armament: one 7.92-mm (0.31-in) MG 15 machine-gun on trainable mount in rear cockpit
Operators: Luftwaffe, Spain

Heinkel He 72 Kadett

History and notes
Designed in 1933 to meet an official requirement for an elementary trainer, the Heinkel He 72 Kadett was a single-bay biplane of metal basic construction with fabric covering, and powered initially by a 140-hp (104-kW) Argus As 8B inline engine. The type duly entered production under the designation He 72A, early construction retaining the Argus As 8B engine as used in the prototype, but late examples having the 150-hp (112-kW) Argus As 8R. Major production version, however, was the He 72B-1 powered by the Siemens Sh14A radial engine, and 30 generally similar He 72B-3 aircraft were built for civil use and for these, marketed under the name Edelkadett, an optional luggage locker could be provided behind the rear cockpit. A twin-float seaplane version was planned under the designation He 72BW but did not progress beyond the prototype stage, this same fate being shared by the He 172 prototype of 1934, which had its Siemens Sh 14A engine enclosed by a NACA cowling.

The Kadett was used initially to equip a number of the National Socialist Flying Corps training schools before formation of the Luftwaffe, then becoming a standard pilot trainer. Consequently, the He 72B was probably built in some quantity, but no production details appear to have survived.

The Heinkel Kadett was one of several single-bay biplanes that became standard Luftwaffe trainers.

Specification
Heinkel He 72B
Type: two-seat primary trainer
Powerplant: one 160-hp (119-kW) Siemens Sh 14A 7-cylinder radial piston engine
Performance: maximum speed 115 mph (185 km/h); cruising speed 106 mph (170 km/h); service ceiling 11,485 ft (3500 m); range 295 miles (475 km)
Weights: empty 1,191 lb (540 kg); maximum take-off 1,907 lb (865 kg)
Dimensions: span 29 ft 6¼ in (9.00 m); length 24 ft 7¼ in (7.50 m); height 8 ft 10¼ in (2.70 m); wing area 222.82 sq ft (20.70 m²)
Operators: Luftwaffe, Slovakia

Heinkel He 111

History and notes
Although the Heinkel He 111 was designed ostensibly as a civil airliner for Lufthansa, its military potential was of a far greater importance. The first prototype of Siegfried and Walter Günter's enlarged, twin-engine development of the remarkable He 70 was fitted with a

Heinkel He 111

glazed nose when flown at Rostock-Marienehe on 24 February 1935, in the hands of Flugkapitän Gerhard Nitschke. An all-metal cantilever low-wing monoplane, it was powered by two 660-hp (492-kW) BMW VI 6,0Z engines and was followed by two further prototypes, each with shorter-span wings than those fitted on the first prototype. The third aircraft became the true bomber prototype and the second, which flew on 12 March 1935, was a civil version with a mail compartment in the nose and two passenger cabins, with seats for four and six passengers. After tests at Staaken this prototype eventually joined the Lufthansa fleet, although much of the development work on the civil version was carried out by the fourth prototype, the first to be revealed to the public and demonstrated at Berlin's Tempelhof Airport on 10 January 1936. Lufthansa received six He 111C 10-seat airliners during 1936, and these first entered service on the Berlin—Hannover—

Two ground crew prepare a Heinkel He 111 for a mission in 1940. The He 111 carried the brunt of the bombing operations in this year, to Holland, Belgium, France and finally Britain.

Amsterdam, Berlin—Nuremberg—Munich and Berlin—Dortmund—Cologne routes. Lufthansa received subsequently a number of He 111G-3 transports with 880-hp (656-kW) BMW 132Dc engines and, later, a further generally similar batch under the alternative designation He 111L.

Development of the military counterpart continued with the manufacture of 10 He 111A-0 pre-production aircraft, based on the third prototype, but with a longer nose and armed by three MG 15 machine-guns in nose, dorsal and ventral positions. Two were used for operational trials at Rechlin but poor handling, power deficiencies and inadequate performance resulted

Heinkel He 111

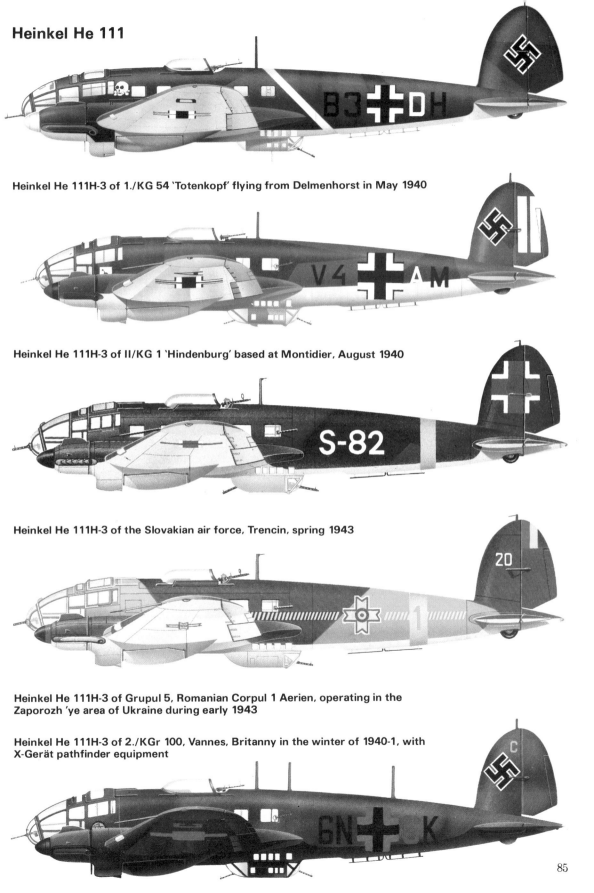

Heinkel He 111H-3 of 1./KG 54 'Totenkopf' flying from Delmenhorst in May 1940

Heinkel He 111H-3 of II/KG 1 'Hindenburg' based at Montidier, August 1940

Heinkel He 111H-3 of the Slovakian air force, Trencin, spring 1943

Heinkel He 111H-3 of Grupul 5, Romanian Corpul 1 Aerien, operating in the Zaporozh 'ye area of Ukraine during early 1943

Heinkel He 111H-3 of 2./KGr 100, Vannes, Britanny in the winter of 1940-1, with X-Gerät pathfinder equipment

Heinkel He 111

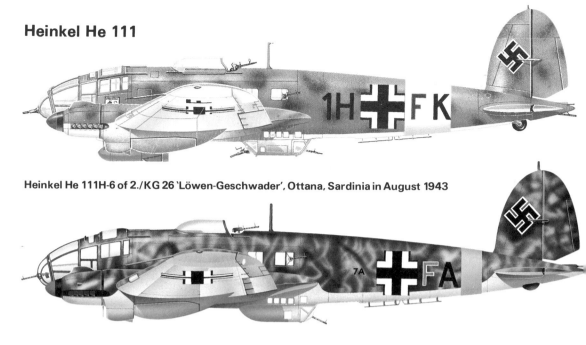

Heinkel He 111H-6 of 2./KG 26 'Löwen-Geschwader', Ottana, Sardinia in August 1943

Heinkel He 111H-6 of Gefechtsverband Kuhlmey at Immola, Finland, July 1944

in rejection, and all 10 were later sold to China. The solution was the installation of two 1,000-hp (746-kW) Daimler-Benz DB 600A engines, first fitted to the fifth (B-series) prototype which flew in early 1936 as the forerunner of the first production versions built at Marienehe from the autumn of 1936. These comprised the He 111B-1 powered by the 880-hp (656-kW) DB600, followed by the He 111B-2 with 950-hp (708-kW) DB 600CG engines. The improvement in the performance of these aircraft resulted in the Reichsluftfahrtministerium placing such large orders that it was necessary to build a new He 111 construction facility at Oranienburg, near Berlin, this being completed in 1937.

The B-series was followed by the He 111D-1 with improved DB 600Ga engines, but the urgent need to divert DB 600 powerplant for fighter production meant that this version was built in only small numbers. This brought introduction of the 1,000-hp (746-kW) Junkers Jumo 211A-1, installed initially in an He 111D-0 airframe to serve as the prototype of the He 111E-0 pre-production series. In the initial production He 111E-1 bomber of February 1938 the bombload was increased to 3,748 lb (1700 kg), but the He 111E-3 had another increase to 4,409 lb (2000 kg), and the ensuing He 111E-4 could carry 2,205 lb (1000 kg) of this total on underfuselage racks; final sub-variant of the E-series, the He 111E-5 introduced an additional 183.7 Imp gal (835 litres) of auxiliary fuel carried within the fuselage. The next version into production was the He 111G which first introduced a new wing of simplified construction with straight, instead of curved taper. This was used first in the He 111G-3 civil transport built for Lufthansa, and there was some delay before it was approved by the RLM. Then followed the He 111G-1, basically similar to C-series aircraft but for the addition of the new wing, and the He 111G-4 which

was powered by the 900-hp (671-kW) DB 600G engine; four He 111G-5 aircraft supplied to Turkey had Daimler-Benz 600Ga engines. Next came, unsequentially, the similar He 111F-1 powered by Jumo 211A-3 engines of which 24 were supplied to Turkey, and 40 virtually identical aircraft were built for the Luftwaffe in 1938 under the designation He 111F-4.

Developed in parallel were the H-series and P-series, the latter introducing in 1939 a major fuselage redesign which replaced the stepped cockpit by an extensively-glazed cockpit and nose section and, at the same time, moved the nose gun position to starboard to improve the pilot's view. The pre-production He 111P-0 also introduced a revised ventral gondola, with the gunner in a prone position, and was powered by two 1,150-hp (858-kW) DB 601 Aa engines. Relatively few He 111Ps were built before this version was superseded by the H-series, the He 111P-1 which was virtually identical to the pre-production aircraft being delivered first in the autumn of 1939; the He 111P-2 differed only by having changes in radio equipment, and the He 111P-3 was a dual-control trainer. Heavier armour protection and up to six MG 15 machine-guns were introduced in the five-crew He 111P-4 which, in addition to carrying 2,205 lb (1000 kg) of bombs internally had ETC 500 racks beneath the fuselage for a similar external load; the He 111P-6 had all-internal stowage for 4,409 lb (2000 kg) of bombs, and later P-series conversions, for use as glider tugs with 1,175-hp (876-kW) DB 601N engines installed, were redesignated He 111P-2/R2.

The major production version, built in a large number of variants, was the H-series, the He 111H-0 and He 111H-1 pre-production/production batches being basically the same as He 111P-2s except for the installation of 1,010-hp (753-kW) Jumo 211A engines.

Heinkel He 111

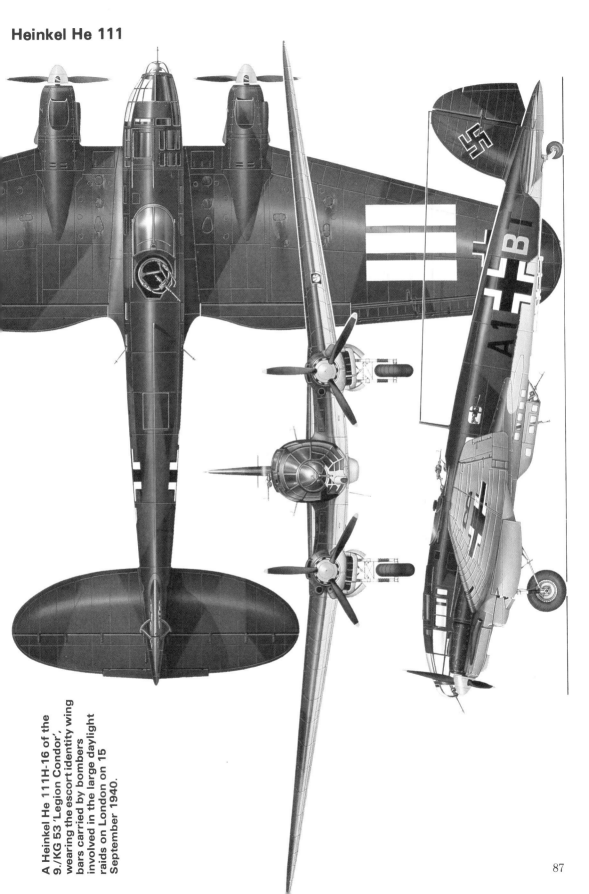

A Heinkel He 111H-16 of the 9./KG 53 'Legion Condor', wearing the escort identity wing bars carried by bombers involved in the large daylight raids on London on 15 September 1940.

Heinkel He 111

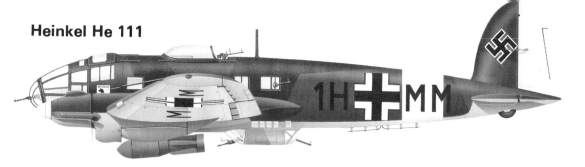

Heinkel He 111H-6 of KG 2 carrying bomb externally

The He 111H-2 which became available in the autumn of 1939 had Jumo 211A-3 engines and carried two additional MG 15 machine-guns, one in the nose and one in the ventral gondola, and the He 111H-3 introduced armour protection and armament comprising a 20-mm MG FF cannon and an MG 15 in the ventral gondola, two MG 15s in the nose, one dorsally mounted, and similar weapons in beam positions. The He 111H-4 introduced Jumo 211D-1 engines and was equipped with two external racks to carry a 3,968-lb (1800 kg) bombload that could include two 1,686-lb (765-kg) differed only by having increased fuel capacity. When He 111H-3 and He 111H-5 aircraft were later fitted with a nose-mounted device to fend off balloon cables they were both redesignated He 111H-8, and subsequent re-conversion for use as glider tugs was made under the designation He 111H-8/R2. Junkers Jumo 211F-1 engines with variable-pitch propellers, and a fixed MG 17 machine-gun mounted in the tail, identified the He 111H-6; and the He 111H-10 was developed and built in small numbers especially for the night bombing offensive against the UK, these being equipped with Kute-Nase balloon cable-cutters in the wing leading edges and additional armour protection. Armament changes and a fully-enclosed dorsal position accommodating an MG 131 machine-gun identified the He 111H-11, in which the nose position carried a 20-mm MG FF cannon and the ventral MG 15 was replaced by a twin-barrel MG 81Z; when the beam guns were later replaced by MG 81Zs these aircraft were redesignated He 111H-11/R1, and changed their designation yet again to become He 111H-11/R2 when adapted to tow Gotha Go 242 gliders. The He 111H-12 and He 111H-15 were both built in small numbers, without the ventral gondola, to serve as missile launchers for Henschel and Blohm und Voss weapons respectively. The first of the pathfinder versions had the designation He 111H-14, and when converted later to serve as a glider tug was redesignated He 111H-14/R2.

Built in large numbers, following introduction in the autumn of 1942, the He 111H-16 was generally similar to the He 111H-11, but equipped to carry a bombload of up to 7,165 lb (3250 kg), although this necessitated the use of R-Geräte rocket-assisted take-off equipment; it was built in sub-variants that included the He 111H-16/R1 which had a revolving dorsal turret with an MG 131 machine-gun, He 111H-16/R2 equipped for rigid-bar towing of gliders, and the He 111H-16/R3 which

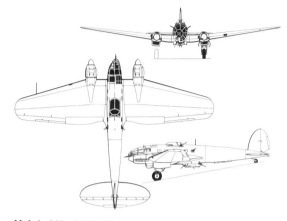

Heinkel He 111H-16

carried additional radio equipment for use as a path-finder. The ensuing He 111H-18 was also a pathfinder, with exhaust flame dampers to make it suitable for night operations, followed by the He 111H-20 built in sub-variants that included the He 111H-20/R1 carrying 16 paratroops, He 111H-20/R2 night bomber/glider tug, He 111H-20/R3 night bomber with heavier armour protection and improved radio, and the virtually identical He 111H-20/R4 with GM-1 power boosting equipment for the powerplant; when a 1,750-hp (1305-kW) Jumo 213E-1 engine with two-stage superchargers was installed in He 111H-20/R3 aircraft they were redesignated He 111H-21. The He 111H-22 was equipped to carry a Fieseler Fi 103 (V-1) missile beneath each wing, and the final H-series variant was the He 111H-23 paratroop transport with 1,776-hp (1324-kW) Jumo 213A-1 engines.

Produced in parallel with the F-series, the He 111J-0 and He 111J-1 were intended as torpedo-bombers and powered by 950-hp (708-kW) DB 600CG engines, but the He 111J-1 production aircraft, of which about 88 were built, were equipped as bombers. A single prototype was built of a proposed high-altitude bomber under the designation He 111R, powered by two 1,810-hp (1350-kW) DB 603U engines, but no production aircraft resulted. Final, and certainly the most unusual version, was the He 111Z (Zwilling, or twin), designed to tow the Messerschmitt Me 321 Gigant transport glider. It comprised two 111H-6 airframes joined by a new wing centre-section which mounted a fifth Jumo 211F-2 engine. Two prototypes and 10 He 111Z-1

Heinkel He 111

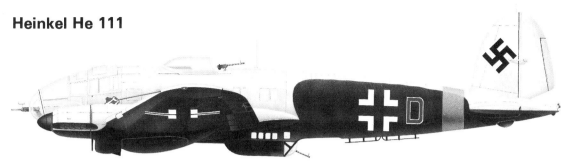

Heinkel He 111H-8/R2 of Schleppgruppe (towing wing) 4 based at Pskov-South in early 1942

production aircraft were built during the winter of 1941-2.

First deliveries to an operational squadron were made late in 1936, to 1./KG 154 at Fassberg, and in February 1937 30 He 111B-1s were sent to the Legion Condor bomber unit K/88 in Spain, following operational trials in which four of the pre-production He 111B-0s were flown by a flight of VB 88. The He 111 bore the brunt of the Luftwaffe's bombing effort in early World War II: Poland in the autumn of 1939, Norway and Denmark in April 1940, France and the Low Countries in May and against British targets during the Battle of Britain. Large-scale introduction of the Junkers Ju 88, and the He 111's vulnerability to British fighters, resulted in the Heinkel bomber being transferred to night operations and to a variety of specialised roles, as a missile-carrier, torpedo-bomber, pathfinder and glider-tug. Transport duties were also undertaken, including operations to supply the beleaguered German army at Stalingrad between November 1942 and February

1943, and by the end of the war He 111s were virtually flown only in the transport role. Production of more than 7,000 German-built aircraft for the Luftwaffe was completed in the autumn of 1944. In addition to those manufactured in Heinkel factories at Marienehe and Oranienburg, He 111s were built by Norddeutsche Dornierwerke in Wismar, by Allgemeine Transport-gesellschaft in Leipzig, Arado in Babelsberg and Brandenburg/Havel and at other centres. Some 236 He 111Hs were built by CASA in Spain during and after the war as the CASA 2.111, approximately 130 with Jumo 211F-2 engines and the rest with Rolls-Royce Merlin 500-29s; some were converted later for transport and training duties.

Ground staff pull a bomb trolley to a Heinkel He 111 which has already started its engines prior to a sortie. Large bombs were carried externally on the He 111, using a rack underneath the bomb bay.

Heinkel He 111

Specification
Heinkel He 111H-16

Type: medium bomber
Powerplant: two 1,350-hp (1007-kW) Junkers Jumo 211F-2 12-cylinder inverted-Vee piston engines
Performance: maximum speed 227 mph (365 km/h) at sea level; service ceiling 21,980 ft (6700 m); range 1,212 miles (1950 km)
Weights: empty 19,136 lb (8680 kg); maximum take-off 30,865 lb (14000 kg)
Dimensions: span 74 ft 1¾ in (22.60 m); length 53 ft 9½ in (16.40 m); height 13 ft 1¼ in (4.00 m); wing area 931.11 sq ft (86.50 m²)
Armament: one 20-mm MG FF cannon, one 13-mm (0.51-in) MG 131 machine-gun and three 7.92-mm (0.31-in) MG 81Z machine-guns, plus a normal internal bombload of 2,205 lb (1000 kg)
Operators: Luftwaffe, China, Hungary, Romania, Spain, Turkey

A formation of He 111s on their way to a target in Britain in late 1940. Such formations were a familiar sight to Londoners during this time, the He 111 being the major type in these raids.

Heinkel He 115

History and notes

Developed as a replacement for the He 59, the Heinkel He 115 was first flown as a prototype in 1936, powered by two 960-hp (716-kW) BMW 132K radial engines, and armed with a 7.92-mm (0.31-in) MG 15 machine-gun in the observer's position aft of the cockpit and another in the angular glazed nose. Both weapons were later removed and the positions faired over to streamline the aircraft for a series of speed record attempts starting on 30 March 1938: eight records were set with various payloads up to 4,409lb (2000 kg) over 1,000-km (621-mile) and 2,000-km (1,243-mile) courses at an average speed of just under 205 mph (330 km/h). The generally similar second prototype was followed by a third which introduced the 'glasshouse' cockpit canopy which became a feature of production aircraft. The fourth machine was the production prototype, with the bracing wires between floats and fuselage replaced by additional struts, followed by 10 pre-production He 115A-0 aircraft, armed with a single 7.92-mm (0.31-in) MG 15 machine-gun, built during 1937.

Successful service evaluation led to the initial production version for the Luftwaffe, the He 115A-1, which re-introduced the nose-mounted MG 15 machine-gun of the first prototype. In addition to being built in small numbers for the Luftwaffe, generally similar aircraft were also supplied to Norway and Sweden under the designation He 115A-2. A modified bomb bay and improved radio equipment were introduced in the He 115A-3, the first major production version for the

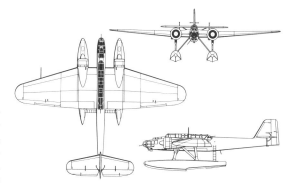

Heinkel He 115B-1

Luftwaffe, which used the type widely in its coastal reconnaissance squadrons. In 1939 production was initiated of the He 115B-1, which had much greater fuel capacity to provide a range increase of more than 65 per cent by comparison with A-series aircraft; it was complemented by the He 115B-2 which had reinforced floats to permit operation from snow- and ice-covered surfaces. The B-series aircraft could trade their increased range for a bombload comprising 1,102-lb (500-kg) of bombs and a 2,205-lb (1000-kg) magnetic mine, and soon after the outbreak of World War II these aircraft were deployed to drop parachute mines in British waters. In 1940 Heinkel flew the improved He 115C-0,

Right: Showing the distinctive Heinkel planform of the wings, derived from the earlier He 70 fast mailplane, this He 115 taxis to take-off position.

which entered service during 1941 under the designation He 115C-1. It carried as additional armament a 20-mm MG 151 cannon beneath the glazed nose, and sometimes an MG 17 machine-gun in each wing root, and had provision for the installation of extra fuel tanks in the bomb bay at the expense of a reduced bombload.

Sub-variants of the C-series included the He 115C-2 with reinforced floats, the He 115C-3 and He 115C-4 which were specialised minelaying and torpedo-carrying versions respectively, the last having armament reduced to a single rear-firing MG 15 machine-gun. An improved version was planned with the more powerful 1,600-hp (1193-kW) BMW 801C radial engines as the He 115D-0, which as a conversion from an He 115A-1 airframe, but when development of this engine was abandoned no further examples were built, and the production line was closed down in 1941 after the completion of all outstanding orders for He 115Cs.

The He 115 was without doubt the most effective of the Luftwaffe's attack and reconnaissance floatplanes, and continuing operational success resulted in the production line being re-opened in 1943 for series construction of an improved He 115E-1. Generally similar to C-series aircraft, it was armed with two 7.92-mm (0.31-in) MG 81 machine-guns in each of the nose and rear positions, augmented in some cases by an MG 151/20 cannon mounted beneath the nose. When production finally ended a total of approximately 500 He 115s of all versions had been built.

Four He 115s were operated by the Royal Air Force, their source being one He 115A-2 which was flown to the UK in April when Norway was invaded, and three more, together with a Luftwaffe He 115B-1 captured by the Norwegians, which set out for Sullom Voe in Shetland two months later. One He 115A-2 ran out of fuel en route and had to be sunk, but the others were flown at the Marine Aircraft Experimental Establishment at Helensburgh, and subsequently by BOAC, three being modified for clandestine operations to Norway and in the Mediterranean.

Specification
Heinkel He 115B-1

Type: coastal reconnaissance floatplane
Powerplant: two 865-hp (645-kW) BMW 132N 9-cylinder radial piston engines
Performance: maximum speed 220 mph (355 km/h) at 11,155 ft (3400 m); cruising speed 183 mph (295 km/h); service ceiling 18,045 ft (5500 m); maximum range 2,082 miles (3350 km)

With flaps partially deployed, this He 115 shows the entry ladder reaching from the rear of the float to the rear cockpit.

Heinkel He 115

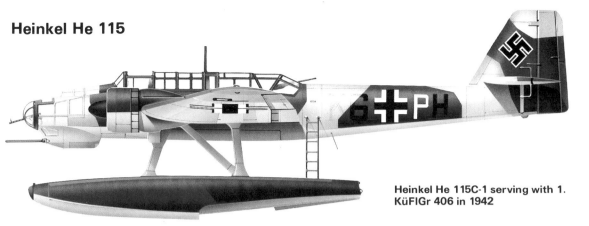

Heinkel He 115C-1 serving with 1.
KüFlGr 406 in 1942

Weights: empty 11,684 lb (5300 kg); maximum take-off 22,928 lb (10400 kg)
Dimensions: span 72 ft 2 in (22.00 m); length 56 ft 9 in (17.30 m); height 21 ft 8 in (6.60 m); wing area 941.87 sq ft (87.50 m²)

Armament: one fixed forward-firing and one rear-firing 7.92-mm (0.31-in) machine-gun, plus a maximum bombload of 2,756 lb (1250 kg)
Operators: Luftwaffe, Finland, Norway, Sweden, UK

Heinkel He 162 Salamander

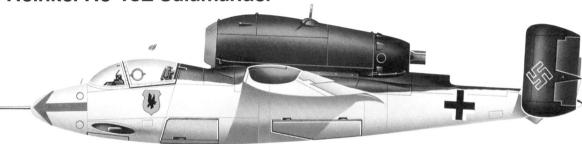

Heinkel He 162A Salamander

History and notes

In 1944 Germany's increasingly desperate situation and the need to reduce the effectiveness of Allied bombing attacks on the country's industrial capacity led to concentration of production and development resources on fighters, including the Heinkel He 162 jet-propelled interceptor. Pilots were to be drawn largely from the Hitler Youth and the initial production rate was to be 1,000 aircraft per month, rising quickly to no less than 4,000 per month from the Heinkel Rostock-Marienehe plant (1,000), Junkers factory at Bernburg (1,000) and the Mittelwerke GmbH works at Nordhausen (2,000). Extensive component sub-contracting was to be employed and underground assembly facilities used.

The specification was issued on 14 September 1944 and the aircraft was to be ready for mass production by 1 January 1945. It had to use the minimum of strategic materials and require non-specialist labour in its manufacture. It also had to weigh less than 4,409 lb (2000 kg), be able to take off in no more than 1,640 ft (500 m) and carry two 30-mm cannon. The result was an aircraft with a one-piece wing of wooden construction, a semi-monocoque fuselage of duralumin with a plywood nose and nosewheel doors. In addition to the 153-Imp gal (695 litre) fuel tank behind the cockpit, the wing was sealed between main and auxiliary spars to provide an integral tank with 39.6-Imp gal (180-litre) capacity. This supplied a 1,764-lb (800-kg) thrust BMW 190-003E-1 turbojet mounted on top of the fuselage, simplifying installation and avoiding problems with intake and tailpipe ducting.

The ambitious programme that had been drawn up required detail design to be complete by 30 October 1944 and the prototype to have flown by 10 December! In fact, the mock-up was shown to Reichsluftfahrt-ministerium representatives at Vienna-Schwechat on 23 September, drawings were released to the factory on 29 October and the prototype, in the hands of chief test pilot Flugkapitän Peter, flew on 6 December. During the 20-minute flight, Peter achieved a speed of 522 mph (840 km/h) and climbed to 19,685 ft (6000 m), but defective bonding resulted in the loss of a landing gear door in flight. On 10 December, before assembled military and government personnel, the starboard wing leading edge was torn off during a low-level, high-speed pass and Peter was killed in the resulting crash.

Despite this setback the second prototype flew on 22

Heinkel He 162 Salamander

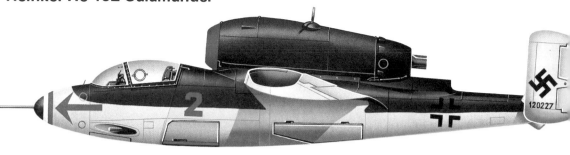

Heinkel He 162A-2 of II/JG 1 captured by the Allies at Leck in 1945

December and further development aircraft joined the test programme, revealing some aerodynamic problems. The third and fourth prototypes, both flown on 16 January 1945, were accordingly fitted with wingtip extensions with marked anhedral, the vertical tail surfaces were increased in area and the nose was weighted to bring the centre of gravity forward. The armament installation, of two 30-mm MK 108 cannon, proved to be too heavy for the relatively lightly-built airframe and 20-mm MK 151/20 weapons were substituted. The 10 prototypes built by Heinkel at Vienna-Schwechat were also designated He 162A-0 as preproduction aircraft, and the few He 162A-1 production airframes were followed by the most extensively built He 162A-2. This introduced a number of aerodynamic changes, including increased incidence at the wing root and the fitting of spoilers at the same location.

First deliveries were made to Erprobungskommando 162 at Rechlin in January 1945, for operational evaluation and service trials. 1./JG 1 began training on the He 162 at Parchim in February 1945, moving to Ludwiglust on 8 April and to Leck in Schleswig-Holstein on 14 April. Here, on 3 May, it was joined by 11./JG 1 which had been forced to flee from Warnemünde by the Soviet advance. Next day personnel and some 50 aircraft were amalgamated into one Gruppe of three squadrons but British forces occupied the airfield on 8 May and

accepted the unit's surrender. A total of 116 He 162s was built, and more than 800 were in various stages of assembly when the underground production centres were overrun.

Specification
Heinkel He 162A-2

Type: single-seat fighter
Powerplant: one 1,764-lb (800-kg) thrust BMW 003A-1 turbojet
Performance: maximum speed 522 mph (840 km/h) at 19,685 ft (6000 m); initial climb rate 1,950 ft (595 m) per minute; service ceiling 39,500 ft (12040 m); endurance 57 minutes at 35,990 ft (10970 m); range 410 miles (660 km) at 35,990 ft (10970 m)
Weights: empty 4,520 lb (2050 kg); maximum take-off 5,941 lb (2695 kg)
Dimensions: span 23 ft 7½ in (7.20 m); length 29 ft 8¼ in (9.05 m); height 8 ft 4½ in (2.55 m); wing area 120.56 sq ft (11.20 m²)
Armament: two 20-mm MG 151/20 cannon
Operator: Luftwaffe

An unusual design, the Heinkel He 162 was a hasty and slightly foolhardy answer to Germany's air defence problems, attempting to provide a fighter at the smallest cost and quickest time.

Heinkel He 177 Greif

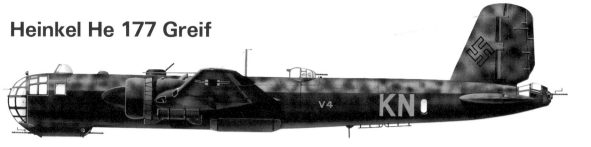

Heinkel He 177A-5 of II/KG 1 based at Prowehren in East Prussia during 1944

History and notes

In the spring of 1938, Heinkel received from the Reichsluftfahrtministerium a development contract for its P.1041 project, evolved in response to an official specification for a long-range bomber. Although almost 1,200 examples of the resulting Heinkel He 177 Greif (griffon) were built, the type never fulfilled its potential and, indeed, earned itself the nickname of the 'Flaming Coffin'. This was, perhaps, a little unfair, although the Daimler-Benz DB 606 engines were prone to overheating and a number of inflight engine fires occurred. Heinkel's designer, Siegfried Günter, required two 2,000-hp (1491-kW) engines to power his brainchild, but a suitable power unit in this class was not then available and two Daimler-Benz DB 601 engines were coupled together to produce the 2,600-hp (1939-kW) DB 606. Another novel feature of the He 177 was the main landing gear, comprising twin main legs on each side, which retracted sideways into the wing, inboard and outboard of each engine nacelle.

The first prototype flew on 19 November 1939 at Rostock-Marienehe, in the hands of Dipl. Ing. Francke of Erprobungsstelle E-2 at Rechlin. This first flight was cut short when the engine temperatures rose rapidly and vibration was experienced; the tail surfaces were also judged to be inadequate, and these were increased in area following the crash of the second prototype, which disintegrated when flutter was experienced during diving trials. This trouble also claimed the fourth prototype. The fifth prototype was the first to be armed (four MG 15 machine-guns singly mounted in nose, dorsal, ventral and tail positions), and was the first to suffer an engine fire and be lost. Three more prototypes were built, the first two with modified nose sections which mounted two MG FF cannon and an MG 131 machine-gun and following further testing 35 He 177A-0 pre-production aircraft were built, 15 at Rostock, 15 at Oranienburg and five by Arado at Warnemünde. These were used for development trials and the conversion training of crews for the initial production He 177A-1, which was introduced in March 1942. Arado built a total of 130 in four sub-variants, each with minor armament variations, under the designations He 177A-1/R1 to He 177A-1/R4.

A number of early production He 177A-1s were delivered in July 1942 for operational trials with 1./KG 40 at Bordeaux-Mérignac, but structural weaknesses in the wing necessitated substantial redesign, and the first of the modified He 177A-3s to see service with the Luftwaffe were delivered during the closing months of

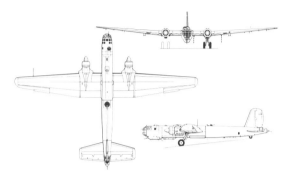

Heinkel He 177A-5/R6

1942. A total of 170 of the A-3 series was built at Oranienburg, the first 15 being designated He 177A-3/R1 and retaining the DB 606A/B engines. The remainder of the batch were powered by DB 610 engines, and included the He 177A-3/R2 with improved armament, the He 177A-3/R3 carrying three Henschel Hs 293 missiles and the He 177A-3/R4 having a gondola containing the FuG 203 missile-control equipment. The introduction of a 75-mm (2.95-in) cannon in a ventral gondola identified the He 177A-3/R5, and three He 177A-3/R7 aircraft were built and equipped to carry two torpedoes. Final production version was the He 177A-5 featuring a strengthened wing to allow for the carriage of heavier underwing loads, deletion of the Fowler flaps, and the introduction of shortened main landing gear legs. It was produced initially in He 177A-5/R1 to He 177A-5/R4 sub-variants with minor armament changes, followed by the He 177A-5/R5 which mounted a remotely controlled barbette to the rear of the bomb bay and the generally similar He 177A-5/R6 in which two forward bomb bays were deleted. The He 177A-5/R7 introduced a pressurized cockpit, while the He 177A-5/R8 was equipped with barbettes in chin and rear positions. Most interesting were five He 177A-5 aircraft converted to carry revised offensive armament, the bomb bay area being used to mount an array of 33 rocket tubes, these weapons being fired upwards at a forward angle of 60°. Delivered in June 1944, and known as the He 177 Zerstörer (destroyer), they were flown initially by Erprobungskommando 25 at Tarnewitz, but it seems unlikely that they were used operationally.

Six He 177A-6/R1 aircraft were built as development machines for a proposed He 177A-6 production version, including armour protection for the crew compartment and fuel tanks, and extra armament; and the He

Heinkel He 177 Greif

A Heinkel He 177A-3/R2 runs its engines prior to flight. The aircraft was deceptive: what appeared to be twin engines actually housed four, two coupled in each nacelle.

177 V22 served as prototype for the He 177A-6/R2, this variant having a new forward fuselage and defensive armament of two 20-mm MG 151/20 cannon, plus four MG 81 and three MG 131 machine-guns. The final variant resulted from the conversion of six He 177A-5 airframes to incorporate a 118 ft 1½ in (36.00 m) span wing which had been designed for the planned He 177A-7 high-altitude bomber, but these were flown with four DB 610 engines, instead of the intended 3,600-hp (2685-kW) DB 613s produced by the coupling of two DB 603Gs.

During the first half of 1944 French- and German-based He 177s took part in Operation 'Steinbock', an offensive against British targets, making their attacks in a high-speed shallow dive from altitude. This enabled them to penetrate the defences without difficulty, but did little for bombing accuracy. The type also saw service on the Eastern Front, but Germany's critical fuel supply and the concentration of fighter production and operations led to virtual withdrawal of the He 177 by the end of 1944. One of these aircraft which was particularly noteworthy was modified extensively at Letov in Prague during 1943-4 to provide an enlarged bomb bay to accommodate the planned German atomic bomb; it was never completed.

Specification
Heinkel He 177A-5/R2
Type: heavy bomber and missile-carrier
Powerplant: two 2,950-hp (2200-kW) Daimler-Benz DB 610A/B engines, each comprising two 12-cylinder inverted-Vee DB 605 engines close-coupled
Performance: maximum speed 304 mph (490 km/h) at 19,685 ft (6000 m); cruising speed 258 mph (415 km/h); ceiling 26,245 ft (8000 m); range 3,417 miles (5500 km) with two Hs 293 missiles
Weights: empty 37,038 lb (16800 kg); maximum take-off 68,343 lb (31000 kg)
Dimensions: span 103 ft 1¾ in (31.44 m); length 66 ft 11¼ in (20.40 m); height 20 ft 11¾ in (6.39 m); wing area 1,097.95 sq ft (102.00 m²)
Armament: three 7.92-mm (0.31-in) MG 81 and three 13-mm (0.51-in) MG 131 machine-guns, and two 20-mm MG 151/20 cannon, plus 2,205 lb (1000 kg) of bombs internally and two Henschel Hs 293 missiles under the wings
Operator: Luftwaffe

Heinkel He 219 Uhu

History and notes
Potentially one of the Luftwaffe's most effective night-fighters, the Heinkel He 219 Uhu (owl) was another aircraft which suffered from misjudgements by senior members of the government and the Luftwaffe high command (principally, in this case, Generalfeldmarschall Erhard Milch, Inspector General of the Luftwaffe). Although the aircraft had proved itself a match for British bombers, including the de Havilland Mosquito, Milch succeeded in having the programme abandoned in favour of the Junkers Ju 388J and the Focke-Wulf Ta 154. Despite this, some aircraft were produced after the official cessation and production totalled 288 including prototypes.

The Reichsluftfahrtministerium had been lukewarm about the project from the beginning, Heinkel's private venture P.1060 fighter-bomber proposal receiving little encouragement until 1941 when it was seen to have potential as a night-fighter. The all-metal shoulder-wing monoplane that finally emerged incorporated a number of noteworthy features. The pilot and navigator, seated back-to-back, enjoyed excellent visibility from the cockpit in the extreme nose, well forward of the guns so that the pilot's eyes were not affected by their flashes. The crew were also provided with ejector seats, the He 219 being the world's first operational aircraft to be so equipped, and it was also the first aircraft with tricycle landing gear to achieve opera-

Heinkel He 219 Uhu

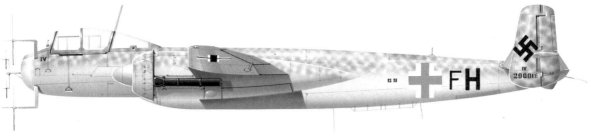

Heinkel He 219A Uhu of 1./NG 1, Munster-Handorf, autumn 1944

tional status with the Luftwaffe.

The first prototype was flown on 15 November 1942, powered by two 1,750-hp (1305-kW) Daimler-Benz DB 603A engines, and in December armament trials were undertaken at Peenemünde. Armed originally with two 20-mm MG 151 cannon in a ventral tray and a trainable 13-mm (0.51-in) MG 131 machine-gun in the rear cockpit, in February 1943 the aircraft was fitted with four 30-mm MK 108 cannon in place of the MG 151s. The second prototype, flown in December 1942 and carrying four MG 151s in the ventral tray with a similar weapon in each wing root, acquitted itself well against a Ju 188S and a Dornier 217 so that the 'off the drawing board' order for 100 aircraft, placed in August 1942, was increased to 300. Further prototypes (including the fourth which carried FuG 220 Lichtenstein SN-2 radar) were flown in the development programme while production got under way at Rostock, Vienna-Schwechat and the Polish factories at Mielec and Buczin. From April 1943 a small number of He 219A-0 pre-production aircraft flew with 1./NJG 11 at Venlo in the Netherlands, and on the night of 11 June 1943 Major Werner Streib shot down five Avro Lancasters in a single sortie. The first six operational sorties flown by the unit resulted in claims for 20 RAF aircraft, including six Mosquitoes. Despite the cancellation of the project in May 1944, production deliveries of a number of versions were made, principally to 1./NJG 1 and NJGr10.

The He 219A-1 reconnaissance bomber having been abandoned at the project stage, the first production version was the He 219A-2/R1 night-fighter, armed as standard with two MK 108 cannon in the ventral tray and two MG 151/20s in the wing roots. A *schräge Musik* installation of two MK 108 cannon behind the cockpit, firing obliquely upward and forward, was introduced retrospectively to this version. However, the first major production version was the He 219A-5 series, the initial He 219A-5/R1 being similar to the He 219A-2/R1, but with an 86-Imp gal (390-litre) fuel tank added at the rear of each engine nacelle to provide a 400-mile (645-km) increase in range. Other sub-variants included the He 219A-5/R2 with 1,800-hp (1342-kW) DB 603E engines, the He 219A-5/R3 with 1,800-hp (1342-kW) DB 603Aa engines, and the more altered DB 603E-powered He 219A-5/R4 which accommodated a third crew member and had a stepped cockpit, with a 13-mm (0.51-in) MG 131 machine-gun on a trainable

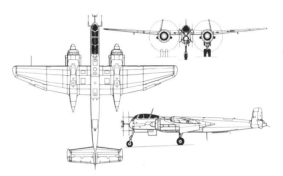

Heinkel He 219A-5/R1

mounting. The need to find a counter to the RAF's Mosquitoes brought development of the He 219A-6 which was introduced in 1944, this being basically a stripped-down conversion of the He 219A-2/R1, powered by 1,750-hp (1305-kW) DB 603L engines and armed with four 20-mm MG 151/20 cannon; a generally similar variant armed with only two MG 151 cannon was built later under the designation He 219B-2. Final production version was the He 219A-7 series which introduced larger, improved supercharger intakes for its DB 603G engines; otherwise similar to the He 219A-5, the sub-variants all carried the then-standard *Schräge Musik* installation of two MK 108 cannon plus, in the He 219A-7/R1, two more MK 108s in the wing-roots and two MG 151s and two MK 103s in the ventral tray. The He 219A-7/R2 had MK 108s in place of the ventral MK 103s; the He 219A-7/R3 had wing-root MK 108s replaced by MG 151s; and the He 219A-7/R4, which was equipped with tail warning radar, carried only four MG 151s. Six He 219A-7/R5 aircraft were powered by 1,900-hp (1417-kW) Junkers Jumo 213E engines, but were otherwise similar to the He 219A-7/R3. A single He 219A-7/R6 was powered by two 2,500-hp (1864-kW) Jumo 222A/B engines, and the single three-crew He 219B-1 which had been intended to use the same powerplant was, in fact, flown with DB 603Aa engines.

Specification
Heinkel He 219A-7/R1
Type: two-seat night-fighter
Powerplant: two 1,900-hp (1417-kW) Daimler-Benz DB 603G 12-cylinder inverted-Vee piston engines
Performance: maximum speed 416 mph (670 km/h);

Heinkel He 219 Uhu

cruising speed 391 mph (630 km/h); service ceiling 40,025 ft (12200 m); range 1,243 miles (2000 km)
Weights: empty 24,692 lb (11200 kg); maximum take-off 33,730 lb (15300 kg)
Dimensions: span 60 ft 8¼ in (18.50 m); length 50 ft 11¾ in (15.54 m); height 13 ft 5½ in (4.10 m); wing area 479.01 sq ft (44.50 m²)

The Heinkel 219 underwent several design modifications in its early development. This He 219V-3 has enlarged vertical tail surfaces to help eradicate stability problems.

Armament: four 30-mm MK 108, two 20-mm MG 151/20 and two 30-mm MK 103 cannon
Operator: Luftwaffe

Henschel Hs 123

Henschel Hs 123A of 5.(Schlacht)/LG 2, St Trond, Belgium, May 1940

History and notes

Designed to an official requirement for a dive-bomber, issued in 1933, the Henschel Hs 123 single-bay sesquiplane was of all-metal construction, with fabric covering used only for the rear portions of the wings and the control surfaces. Powered by a 650-hp (485-kW) BMW 132A-3 radial engine, the prototype flew in 1938 and quickly established its superiority over the rival Fieseler Fi 98. The third prototype was the first to be armed, carrying two fixed forward-firing 7.92-mm (0.31-in) MG 17 machine-guns in the fuselage top decking. The first three aircraft were flown to Rechlin for testing in August 1935, in the course of which activity two of them were destroyed when their wings

came off in dives. A fourth prototype tested successfully the structural changes introduced to overcome this problem and initial production orders were placed for the Hs 123A-1, which retained the blistered cowling of the second and third prototypes, rather than the NACA cowling of the first. Power was provided by the BMW 132Dc radial engine and, in addition to the two fixed MG 17 machine-guns, a mounting for a 551-lb (250-kg) bomb or an external fuel tank was included beneath the fuselage, and four 110-lb (50-kg) bombs could be carried on underwing racks. The Hs 123 was built at Henschel's Schönefeld and Johannisthal factories in Berlin, but although the company built two prototypes of an improved Hs 123B version with the 960-hp (716-

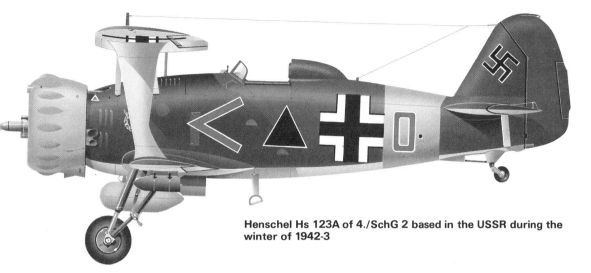

Henschel Hs 123A of 4./SchG 2 based in the USSR during the winter of 1942-3

kW) BMW 132K engine, the second having two additional MG 17 machine-guns and an enclosed cockpit, the Luftwaffe expressed its satisfaction with the Junkers Ju 87 and production ended. The Hs 123A first entered service with 1./StG 162 in the autumn of 1936, although its career as a front-line dive-bomber was short-lived because the Junkers Ju 87A Stuka began to replace it in 1937. Five Hs 123As were supplied to the Legion Condor in Spain in December 1936; the type also saw operational service as a close support aircraft in Poland during the closing months of 1939 and in the campaigns in France and Belgium during the spring of 1940. It was withdrawn finally in 1944.

Specification
Henschel Hs 123A-1

Type: dive-bomber/close-support aircraft (1-seat)
Powerplant: one 880-hp (656-kW) BMW 132Dc 9-cylinder radial piston engine
Performance: maximum speed 211 mph (340 km/h) at 3,935 ft (1200 m); cruising speed 196 mph (315 km/h) at 6560 ft (2000 m); ceiling 29,530 ft (9000 m); range 531 miles (855 km)
Weights: empty 3,307 lb (1500 kg); maximum take-off

A Henschel Hs 123A-1 of II(Schlacht)/LG 2, this unit undertook the first ground support mission of World War II. Note the fuel tank on the underfuselage bomb crutches.

4,884 lb (2215 kg)
Dimensions: span, upper 34 ft 5½ in (10.50 m) and lower 26 ft 3 in (8.00 m); length 27 ft 4 in (8.33 m); height 10 ft 6 in (3.20 m); wing area 267.49 sq ft (24.85 m²)
Armament: two fixed forward-firing 7.92-mm (0.31-in) MG 17 machine-guns, plus provision for 992 lb (450 kg) of bombs
Operator: Luftwaffe

Henschel Hs 126

History and notes
In 1935 Henschel developed the parasol-wing Henschel Hs 122 short-range reconnaissance aircraft as a replacement for the Heinkel He 45 and He 46, but although a few of the 660-hp (492-kW) Siemens SAM 22B-engined aircraft were built, the Hs 122 was not adopted for Luftwaffe use. From it, however, Henschel's chief designer Friedrich Nicolaus derived the Hs 126 which incorporated a new wing, cantilever main landing gear

Intended for battlefield reconnaissance, the Henschel Hs 126 had good short and rough field performance, making it extremely versatile in its given role.

and a canopy over the pilot's cockpit, the observer's position being left open. The prototype, in fact, was converted from an Hs 122A airframe and flown in the

Henschel Hs 126

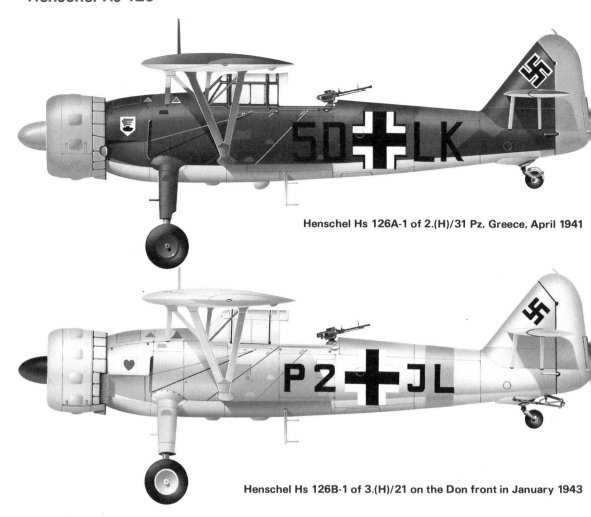

Henschel Hs 126A-1 of 2.(H)/31 Pz, Greece, April 1941

Henschel Hs 126B-1 of 3.(H)/21 on the Don front in January 1943

autumn of 1936, powered by a 610-hp (455-kW) Junkers Jumo 210 engine. It was followed by two further development aircraft, both powered by the 830-hp (619-kW) Bramo Fafnir 323A-1 radial engine; the first was equipped with an engine supercharger and enlarged vertical tail surfaces, while the second had modified main landing gear legs. During 1937 Henschel built 10 pre-production Hs 126A-0 aircraft based on the third prototype, and some were used for operational evaluation by the Luftwaffe's Lehrgruppe reconnaissance unit in the spring of 1938. Initial production version was the Hs 126A-1, generally similar to the pre-production aircraft but powered by the 880-hp (656-kW) BMW 132Dc radial engine. Armament comprised one forward-firing 7.92-mm (0.31-in) MG 17 machine-gun, plus one similar weapon on a trainable mounting in the rear cockpit, and five 22-lb (10-kg) bombs or a single 110-lb (50-kg) bomb could be carried on an underfuselage rack. A hand-held Rb 12.5/9x7 camera in the rear cockpit was supplemented by a Zeiss instrument in a rear-fuselage bay. Six of this version were used by the Legion Condor in Spain during 1938, being transferred

later to the Spanish air force, and 16 were delivered to the Greek air force. An improved but similar He 126B-1 was introduced during the summer of 1939, this incorporating FuG 17 radio equipment and either the Bramo 323A-1 or 900-hp (671-kW) 323A-2.

Production aircraft were built in Berlin, at Schönefeld and Johannisthal, from 1938 and entered operational service first with AufklGr. 35. By the outbreak of World War II the re-equipment of He 45- and He 46-equipped reconnaissance units with the Hs 126 was well under way. The type was withdrawn progressively from front-line service during 1942 on replacement by the Focke-Wulf Fw 189. Just over 600 aircraft were built.

Specification
Henschel Hs 126B-1
Type: two-seat short-range reconnaissance aircraft
Powerplant: one 850-hp (634-kW) Bramo 323A-1 9-cylinder radial piston engine
Performance: maximum speed 193 mph (310 km/h) at sea level; service ceiling 27,230 ft (8300 m);

Henschel Hs 126

Henschel Hs 126B-1 of 2./NAGr 12, operating from Graz in Arpil 1945

maximum range 447 miles (720 km)
Weights: empty 4,476 lb (2030 kg); maximum take-off 6,813 lb (3090 kg)
Dimensions: span 47 ft 6¾ in (14.50 m); length 35 ft 7¼ in (10.85 m); height 12 ft 3½ in (3.75 m); wing area 340.15 sq ft (31.60 m²)
Armament: two 7.92-mm (0.31-in) MG 17 machine-guns, plus one 110-lb (50-kg) or five 22-lb (10-kg) bombs
Operators: Luftwaffe, Greece, Spain

Henschel Hs 129

Henschel Hs 129B-1 of 8./SchG 2 operating from Tunis-El Alouina in February 1943

History and notes

Henschel was one of four companies (the others being Focke-Wulf, Gotha and Hamburger Flugzeugbau) to which, in April 1937, the Reichsluftfahrtministerium issued a specification for a twin-engine ground-attack aircraft. It was required to carry at least two 20-mm MG FF cannon and to have extensive armour plating protection for crew and engines. The two designs for which development contracts were awarded on 1 October 1937 were the Focke-Wulf Fw 189C and Henschel Hs 129. The latter was another Friedrich Nicolaus design with a light alloy stressed-skin fuselage of triangular section. It contained a small cockpit with a restricted view, necessitating the removal of some instruments to the inboard sides of the engine cowlings. The windscreen was made of 75-mm (2.95-in) armoured glass and the nose section was manufactured from armour plating. Nose armament comprised two 20-mm MG FF cannon and two 7.92-mm (0.31-in) MG 17

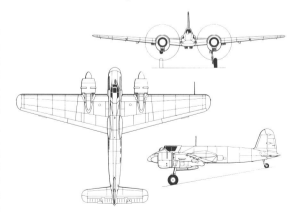

Henschel Hs 129B-1/R4

machine-guns. The prototype flew in the spring of 1939, powered by two 465-hp (347-kW) Argus As 410

Henschel Hs 129

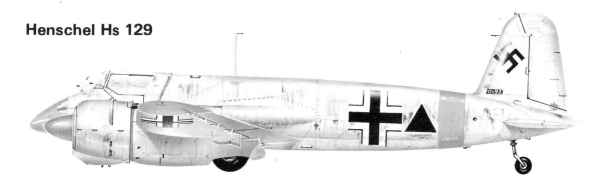

Henschel Hs 129B-1 of 8./SchG 1 in the USSR, February 1943

Henschel Hs 129B-1 of 8./SchG 1 operating over the Kursk salient in the summer of 1943

engines, and two further prototypes were flown competitively against the modified Fw 189 development aircraft for the Fw 189C. Although the Henschel aircraft was considered to be underpowered and sluggish, and to have too small a cockpit, the company was awarded a contract for eight pre-production Hs 129A-0 aircraft, and these were issued initially to 5 (Schlacht)./LG 2 in 1940, but transferred to 4./SG 101 at Paris-Orly in 1941, with the exception of two which were converted at Schönefeld to accept Gnome-Rhône 14M 4/5 radial engines. It was with this powerplant that 10 Hs 129B-0 development aircraft were delivered from December 1941; improvements included a revised cockpit canopy and the introduction of electrically-actuated trim tabs, and armament comprised two 20-mm MG 151/20 cannon and two 7.92-mm (0.31-in) MG 17 machine-guns. The production Hs 192B-1 series went into service first with 4./SchG 1 at Lippstadt in April 1942 and also became operational on the Eastern

The Henschel Hs 129 proved of great value as a 'tank-buster' on the Eastern Front, but only relatively small numbers were built.

Front, where the type was to be used most widely, although it served also in North Africa, Italy, and in France after the D-Day landings. Sub-variants of the Hs 129B-1 series included the Hs 129B-1/R1 with additional offensive armament in the form of two 110-lb (50-kg) bombs or 96 anti-personnel bombs; the Hs 129B-1/R2 with a 30-mm MK 101 cannon beneath the fuselage; the Hs 129B-1/R3 with four extra MG 17 machine-guns; the Hs 129B-1/R4 with an ability to carry one 551-lb (250-kg) bomb instead of the Hs 129B-1/R1's bombload; and the Hs 129B-1/R5 which incorporated an Rb 50/30 camera installation for reconnaissance duties.

By the end of 1942 the growing capability of Soviet tank battalions made it essential to develop a version of the Hs 129 with greater fire-power, leading to the Hs 129B-2 series which was introduced into service in the early part of 1943. They included the Hs 129B-2/R1 which carried two 20-mm MG 151/20 cannon and two 13-mm (0.51-in) machine-guns; the generally similar Hs 129B-2/R2 introduced an additional 30-mm MK 103 cannon beneath the fuselage; the Hs 129B-2/R3 had the two MG 13s deleted but was equipped with a 37-mm BK 3,7 gun; and the Hs 129B-2/R4 carried a 75-mm (2.95-in) PaK 40 gun in an underfuselage pod. Final production variant was the Hs 129B-3 of which approximately 25 were built and which, developed from the Hs 129B-2/R4, substituted an electro-pneumatically operated 75-mm BK 7,5 gun for the PaK 40. The lethal capability of the Hs 129B-2/R2 was amply demonstrated in the summer of 1943 during Operation 'Citadel', the German offensive which was intended to regain for them the

Henschel Hs 129

Henschel Hs 129B-2/R2 of IV (Pz)/SG 9 at Czernovitz in March 1944

initiative on the Eastern Front after the defeat at Stalingrad. During this operation some 37,421 sorties were flown, at the end of which the Luftwaffe claimed the destruction of 1,100 tanks. However accurate these figures, not all of those destroyed could be credited to Hs 129s, but there is little doubt that the 879 of these aircraft that were built (including prototypes) played a significant role on the Eastern Front.

Specification
Henschel Hs 129B-1/R2
Type: single-seat ground-attack aircraft
Powerplant: two 700-hp (522-kW) Gnome-Rhône 14M

4/5 14-cylinder radial piston engines
Performance: maximum speed 253 mph (407 km/h) at 12,565 ft (3830 m); service ceiling 29,525 ft (9000 m); range 348 miles (560 km)
Weights: empty 8,400 lb (3810 kg); maximum take-off 11,266 lb (5110 kg)
Dimensions: span 46 ft 7 in (14.20 m); length 31 ft 11¾ in (9.75 m); height 10 ft 8 in (3.25 m); wing area 312.16 sq ft (29.00 m²)
Armament: two 20-mm MG 151/20 cannon, two 7.92-mm (0.31-in) MG 17 machine-guns and one 30-mm MK 101 cannon
Operators: Luftwaffe, Romania

Junkers Ju 52/3m

History and notes
When in 1915 Junkers flew the world's first all-metal aeroplane, the J 1, the company could not have visualised the growth of a whole line of aircraft using the corrugated skin which was to become a trademark, culminating in the Junkers Ju 52 series.

The Ju 52 started life as a single-engine aircraft, and the first Ju 52ba prototype flew on 13 October 1930 powered by an 800-hp (597-kW) Junkers L.88 engine. Extensive flight testing was carried out before the prototype was re-engined with a 755-hp (563-kW) BMW VIIau engine, in which form it was redesignated Ju 52be. The second prototype was tested with several engines, including the 755-hp (563-kW) BMW VII (Ju 52de), the 750-hp (559-kW) Armstrong Siddeley Leopard radial (Ju 52di) and finally the 750-hp (559-kW) Junkers Jumo 204 diesel (Ju 52do).

Production deliveries began with the third aircraft, but only six single-engine Ju 52s were built before the company decided to evaluate a three-engine configuration. The airframe of what would have been the seventh Ju 52 was converted to take three 550-hp (410-kW) Pratt & Whitney Hornet radials, becoming designated Ju 52/3mce. When flown in April 1931 it was such a success that the single-engine version was discontinued. The first customer was Lloyd Aereo Boliviano which received a total of seven Ju 52/3mde aircraft beginning in 1932.

Like its predecessor, the Ju 52/3m could operate

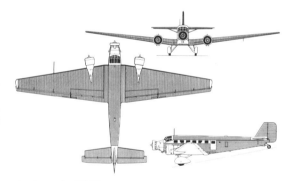

Junkers Ju 52/3mge

also on skis or floats, and orders were placed by Sweden's AB Aerotransport and Finland's Aero O/Y for floatplane versions. Wheel landing gear was fitted to the otherwise similar Ju 52/3mce aircraft ordered by Deutsche Lufthansa for delivery from the spring of 1932, and it was with this airline that the type began to make a name for itself. Contemporary Lufthansa records quote the price as Reichsmarks 275,000, and with 15-17 passengers on board the Junkers had a cruising speed of 132 mph (212 km/h). Large fixed flaps running the whole length of the wing trailing edge cut the landing speed to 59 mph (95 km/h), enabling the Ju 52/3m to use small airfields, a factor particularly useful to airlines operating in South America. An oxygen supply system was monitored by the radio operator

'Tante Ju' became the maid of all work for the Luftwaffe in all theatres. This aircraft is seen over a Channel port.

and could be switched on at passengers' request. Production of the Ju 52/3m built up quickly, and by the end of 1935 97 were in service with a number of airlines, including 51 with Lufthansa.

Meanwhile, the military potential of the type was being examined by the clandestine Luftwaffe, who considered ordering it as a stop-gap until Dornier Do 11 bombers were delivered. Problems with the latter could not be satisfactorily overcome, however, so orders were placed for Ju 52/3mge aircraft, and later for improved Ju 52/3mg3e machines with 725-hp (541-kW) BMW 132A-3 engines and other improvements. Bomb-release mechanism was installed in three bomb bays, such an arrangement being necessary because the wing centre-section and main spars did not permit a single bay. It was also necessary to develop vertical bomb storage magazines since space between the spars did not allow horizontal stowage. A fairing containing a bomb-aiming device, fuse-setting mechanism

and release lever was fitted below the fuselage, and hinged to the fairing was a retractable 'dustbin' installation for a machine-gun, which could be winched up into the fuselage for take-off and landing. The military model also had two additional fuel tanks in the wings, plus an improved fuel-jettison system; when experience proved that the latter was never used it was later removed.

The Ju 52/3m had its first taste of military action when 20 Luftwaffe aircraft were flown to Seville in 1936 to support the Nationalist forces in the Spanish Civil War. They were used in a ferrying role, bringing back 10,000 Moorish troops from Morocco to Spain. At the end of the year a special air force, the Legion Condor, was formed, comprising Luftwaffe personnel

Junkers Ju 52/3m

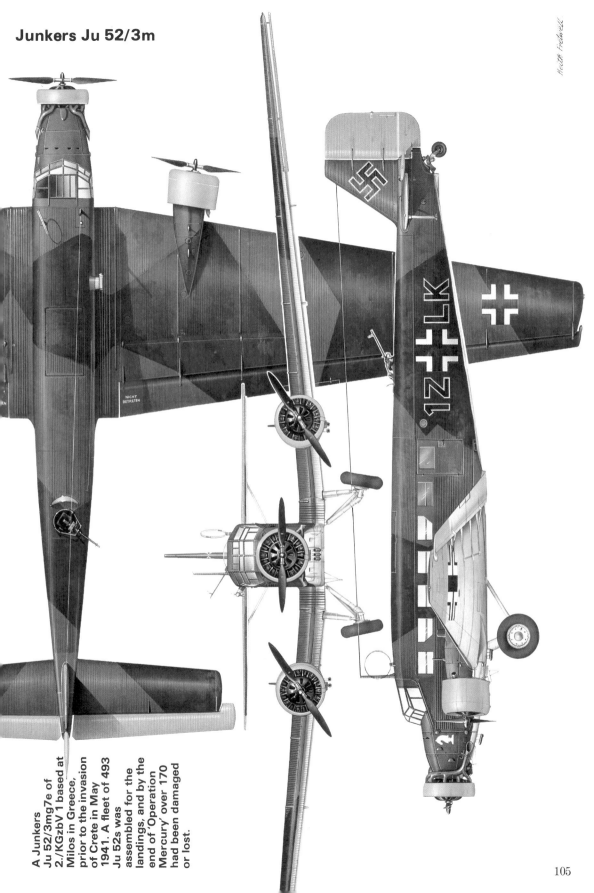

A Junkers
Ju 52/3mg7e of
2./KGzbV 1 based at
Milos in Greece,
prior to the invasion
of Crete in May
1941. A fleet of 493
Ju 52s was
assembled for the
landings, and by the
end of 'Operation
Mercury' over 170
had been damaged
or lost.

Junkers Ju 52/3m

Junkers Ju 52/3mg4e of Stab IV/KGzbv 1, Crete, 1941

and aircraft operating in Spanish Nationalist uniforms and markings. The Ju 52s were employed as bombers until replaced a year later by Do 17s and He 111s. Their final operation was flown in March 1939, and the Ju 52 had flown throughout the Civil War, amassing some 13,000 operational hours and dropping more than 6,000 tons of bombs. Only eight were lost, five being shot down and the others destroyed on the ground. The type had proved its reliability in action and was blooded for the greater conflict about to begin.

Meanwhile, Ju 52/3ms were continuing in production for civil airlines, with whom the type remained in service until after the end of World War II. More than 230 were registered to Lufthansa, although some were no doubt passed on to other customers, including the Luftwaffe. In the period 1934-5, 450 were delivered to the Luftwaffe, and in 1939 that force received 593. It is of interest to note that three Ju 52/3mg4e aircraft were delivered to the Swiss air force for transport work, and two of these were still on active strength in 1983, with the third preserved for a museum.

With the outbreak of World War II in 1939, the Luftwaffe took over 59 of Lufthansa's fleet of Ju 52/3ms and the type was used extensively in airborne assault operations and supply missions. As German troops moved across Europe, overrunning Denmark, Norway, Belgium, the Netherlands and France, the Ju 52/3m was seen in ever increasing numbers in supply and paratrooping roles. At the beginning of the Norwegian operation 571 Ju 52/3m transports were available in addition to other types, being used on 9 April 1940 in the Luftwaffe's first major airborne operation.

After Norway had been occupied, a second major airborne assault began against the Low Countries, on 10 May 1940. Once again the Ju 52/3m was in the thick of operations, with 430 aircraft, but this time much stiffer opposition was encountered and almost 40 per cent of the transports were lost. A total of 162 Ju 52/3m transports was shot down, although some of these were repaired later as German land forces moved forward and captured the battle zones.

With the greater percentage of the west coast of Europe in Axis hands the British stepped up their offensive against German shipping, many mines being laid in coastal waters at the entrance to estuaries and rivers along much of the occupied coast. In a bid to help counter this a number of minesweeping groups were formed with specially adapted **Ju 52/3m(MS)** aircraft. These had large dural rings fitted beneath the fuselage and braced below the engines, the hoops energized by an auxiliary motor in the fuselage to deal with magnetic mines. Other Ju 52/3m aircraft each carried a container with small explosive charges to detonate other types of mines. It was the practice to fly in groups of three aircraft at about 124 mph (200 km/h), with the altitude some 130 ft (40 m) above the estimated level of the mine. There were probably few volunteers for this hazardous task!

Nine subsequent military versions with progressive improvements included the Ju 52/3mg4e with internal equipment changes and a tailwheel replacing the tailskid, which was followed by the considerably improved Ju 52/3mg5e that introduced 830-hp (619-kW) BMW 132T engines, exhaust heat for de-icing, interchangeable wheel, float or ski landing gear and more advanced radio equipment. The similar Ju 52/3mg6e had wheeled landing gear as standard, and simplified radio, the Ju 52/3mg7e added an autopilot and a large loading hatch plus, in the similar Ju 52/3mg8e, an additional cabin roof hatch. Late-production examples of this last aircraft introduced improved BMW 132Z engines. In early production form the Ju 52/3mg9e was almost identical, but late construction had strengthened landing gear and glider towing equipment as standard, as did the Ju 52/3mg10e which differed only by being capable of float operations. Penultimate variant was the Ju 52/3mg12e which introduced BMW 132L powerplant, some of these production aircraft being completed to airline standards and supplied to Lufthansa under the designation Ju 52/3m12. Final version was the Ju 52/3mg14e, similar to late production examples of the Ju 52/3mg9e, but with improved armour protection for the pilot and heavier defensive armament.

The virtual failure of the Italian campaign against Greece and Yugoslavia, together with the build-up of British forces on Crete, made it necessary for Germany to take action in the Balkans, and on 20 May 1941

Right: The Ju 52 was widely used in the desert. Here, a group of Ju 52s airlift supplies to a Bf 110 operating far out in the sands.

Junkers Ju 52/3m

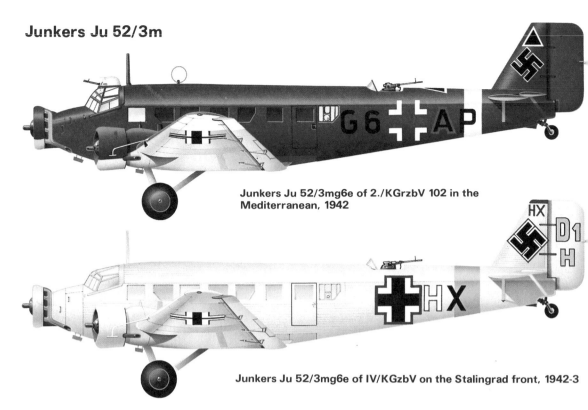

Junkers Ju 52/3mg6e of 2./KGrzbV 102 in the Mediterranean, 1942

Junkers Ju 52/3mg6e of IV/KGzbV on the Stalingrad front, 1942-3

Operation 'Mercury' began. It was the Luftwaffe's greatest airborne assault and involved the landing of 22,750 men and their supplies on Crete. Of these, 10,000 were parachuted in, 750 were carried in 80 DFS 230 gliders, 5,000 were landed by Ju 52/3m, and 7,000 were seaborne. The attack took place in two waves, and 493 Ju 52/3m transports were used. Stiff resistance was encountered from Allied troops that included Australians and New Zealanders, and although the Luftwaffe had complete air superiority the German losses were heavy, with 4,500 men lost and 271 Ju 52/3m transports destroyed or seriously damaged; this was the last mission on which German paratroops were employed in large numbers in the airborne role.

The Ju 52/3m force also received severe mauling at the hands of the RAF during 1942-3 when it attempted to relieve German forces operating in North Africa, the biggest single loss occurring on 18 April 1943 when 52 Junkers from about 100 were shot down near Cape Bon. Ju 52/3m aircraft were also operating on the Eastern Front in the USSR and suffering heavy losses; in 1941 these exceeded production, with 451 being delivered and more than 500 lost. This high casualty rate demanded action, and a new production line was laid down at the Amiot factory at Colombes, with arrangements being made with a number of sub-contractors in the Paris area. The first French-assembled aircraft was accepted in June 1942; 40 more were delivered in the next six months, and 321 in the following year.

When German forces were surrounded at Stalingrad in 1942-3, an attempt was made to fly in supplies, but the Luftwaffe lost 490 transports, of which 266 were Ju 52/3m transports. Assembly of the Ju 52/3m was arranged with PIRT in Budapest from German-supplied components, and the first of 26 was completed in January 1944. The Luftwaffe received four and the balance went to the Hungarian air force.

Production of the Ju 52/3m ended in Germany in mid-1944, and while figures vary it seems likely that the total number built in Germany and France from 1932 until 1944 was 4,845. Post-war, the French built more than 400 for Air France and their air force, by which the type was designated AAC.1. CASA built 170 in Spain for the air force under the designation CASA 352, and it is largely these aircraft, surplus to Spanish military requirements, that have begun to appear in museums and private collections.

Brief mention must be made of developments of the basic Junkers three-motor concept. First was the Ju 252, flown in prototype form in October 1941 with three Jumo 211F engines and stressed-skin construction replacing the corrugated metal, so long a Junkers feature. Shortage of raw materials meant that the new pressurized transport had a very low priority, and Junkers was asked to look at a redesign using more wood in the construction and substituting 1,000-hp (746-kW) BMW-Bramo 323R radial engines. In the event only 15, including four prototypes, were built.

The redesign was undertaken, and the resulting Ju 352 (not to be confused with the CASA-built Ju 52/3m designated CASA 352) flew on 1 October 1943. It was considered to be a major improvement on the old Ju 52/3m and was ordered into production with a first pre-production batch of 10 following two prototypes. A hydraulically-operated loading ramp beneath the rear

Junkers Ju 52/3m

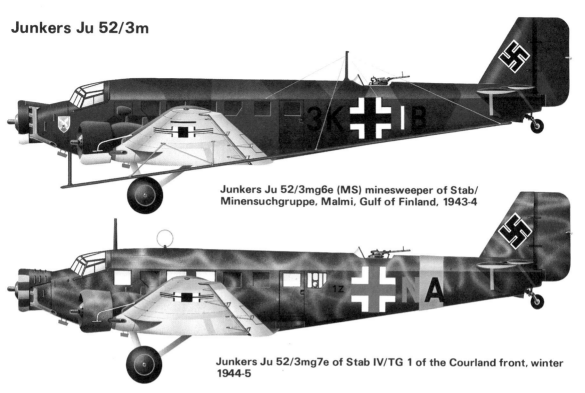

Junkers Ju 52/3mg6e (MS) minesweeper of Stab/
Minensuchgruppe, Malmi, Gulf of Finland, 1943-4

Junkers Ju 52/3mg7e of Stab IV/TG 1 of the Courland front, winter
1944-5

fuselage raised it off the ground sufficiently for
vehicles to be loaded, and reversible pitch propellers
reduced the landing run by up to 60 per cent.

Full production was ordered, but by mid-1944 the
war situation for Germany was worsening rapidly and
transport aircraft production ceased. In addition to the
two prototypes and 10 pre-production Ju 352s, 33 Ju
352A-1 transports were built. Probably the last survivors
were one presented by the Czech air force to the Soviet
air force in 1946, and an example flown to RAF
Farnborough for evaluation.

Specification
Junkers Ju 52/3mg3e
Type: medium bomber and troop transport

Powerplant: three 725-hp (541-kW) BMW 132A-3 9-
cylinder radial piston engines
Performance: maximum speed 171 mph (275 km/h)
at 2,955 ft (900 m); economical cruising speed 130
mph (210 km/h); service ceiling 19,360 ft (5900 m);
range with auxiliary tanks 808 miles (1300 km)
Weights: empty 12,610 lb (5720 kg); maximum take-
off 23,149 lb (10500 kg)
Dimensions: span 95 ft 11½ in (29.25 m); length 62 ft
0 in (18.90 m); height 18 ft 2½ in (5.55 m); wing area
1,189.45 sq ft (110.50m²)
Armament: single 7.92-mm (0.31-in) MG 15 machine-
guns in open dorsal position and in retractable
ventral position, plus up to 1,102 lb (500 kg) of bombs
Operators: Luftwaffe, Bulgaria, Croatia, Hungary,
Portugal, Romania, Slovakia, Spain, Switzerland

Junkers Ju 86

History and notes
It would be fair to say that the Junkers Ju 86 was
already obsolescent at the beginning of World War II,
and was accepted rather grudgingly by the Luftwaffe,
which preferred the Heinkel He 111. It is all the more
surprising, therefore, that within two years the type
was operating in the reconnaissance role at higher
altitudes than other Luftwaffe aircraft could reach.

Like the contemporary He 111, the Ju 86 was
developed as an airliner and bomber, and five prototypes
of each were ordered in 1934. The Junkers aircraft flew
five months later, four months ahead of its competitor,
and had been designed around the new Junkers Jumo

205 diesel engine.

Initial flight trials were disappointing, handling in
particular being poor, and during subsequent modifications (which may have improved but not eradicated
the problems) gun positions were installed. The third
prototype was completed as a bomber and flew in
January 1935, four months before the second prototype
which was built as a commercial aircraft with 10
passenger seats. The fourth prototype, destined to
become the first definitive Ju 86B airliner, flew in May
1935, followed three months later by the fifth prototype,
the production prototype for the Ju 86A bomber.

Production at Junker's Dessau factory began on

Junkers Ju 86

Junkers Ju 86E-2 of the C-schule for bomber training

both versions in late 1935 with an initial batch of 13 Ju 86A-0 and seven Ju 86B-0 pre-production aircraft, the first deliveries being made in February 1936. Bombers carried a crew of four and had a defensive armament of three machine-guns. The first export delivery was of a Ju 86B-0 to Swissair in April 1936 for night mail service, and the balance of six of these pre-production aircraft went to Lufthansa. In February 1937 a second aircraft went to Swissair under the export designation Ju 86Z-1, but when re-engined subsequently with BMW 132Dc radials it was redesignated Ju 86Z-2. Lufthansa also received an additional six aircraft in 1937 and these, powered by Jumo 205C diesel engines, had the designation Ju 86C-1.

Junkers had received some export orders for military models with alternative powerplants. Sweden acquired three Ju 86K-1 aircraft with 875-hp (652-kW) Pratt & Whitney Hornet radial engines, and subsequently 16 more were built under licence by SAAB in Sweden and powered by either Swedish- or Polish-built Bristol Pegasus engines, both variants having the designation Ju 86K-13. Other versions of the Ju 86K were sold to Chile, Hungary and Portugal and these (with Gnome-Rhône, Bristol Pegasus III or Swedish-built Pegasus XII engines) had the respective designations Ju 86K-9, Ju 86K-4 and Ju 86K-5. Hungary later assembled 66 more aircraft under licence, powered by licence-built Gnome-Rhône radials, and these had the designation Ju 86K-2.

Meanwhile, modifications to the military models resulted in the Jumo 205C-engined Ju 86D-1, five of which served with the Legion Condor during the Spanish Civil War, but the diesel engines were not standing up well to combat conditions and the aircraft had proved markedly inferior to the He 111. Disenchantment with the Ju 86D and the very poor serviceability of its engines led the Luftwaffe to make savage and sudden cuts in the Junkers programme and the diesel engines were dropped. Instead, the 810-hp (604-kW) BMW 132F radial was installed, resulting in the designation Ju 86E-1, this type being followed by the Ju 86E-2 with uprated 865-hp (645-kW) BMW 132Ns. Performance showed little improvement but reliability was greatly improved.

In 1938, in an attempt to improve pilot visibility, Junkers redesigned the entire nose section, bringing the pilot farther forward and shortening and lowering the nose to provide a fully glazed enclosure of more streamlined contours. The revisions were included on the final 40 production Ju 86E-2s under the designation Ju 86G-1, and manufacture of the Ju 86 ceased in 1938 with a total of about 390 aircraft (excluding licence-manufacture).

Withdrawal of the type from Luftwaffe front-line service began in late 1938, but at various times during World War II it was found necessary to recall groups from training establishments, for instance in the relief of Stalingrad, but casualties were heavy. In spite of its unsuitability for front-line service, the Ju 86 still had one useful (and unique) role to fill for the Luftwaffe.

Junkers had been experimenting for some time with a high-altitude version of the Jumo diesel engine, together with pressure cabin design, and in September 1939 submitted proposals for a high-altitude reconnaissance version of the Ju 86. The go-ahead was given, and two Ju 86D airframes were converted, gun positions faired over (since no fighter would be able to reach the aircraft at its operational altitude) and a two-seat pressure cabin was fitted. The prototypes flew in February and March 1940 as Ju 86P aircraft, and reached altitudes of more than 32,810 ft (10000 m). A third prototype with wing span increased by 10 ft 2 in (3.10 m) reached 39,700 ft (12100 m), and the success of the trials earned an order for the conversion of 40 Ju 86Ds to Ju 86Ps. Two models were built, the Ju 86P-1 bomber with a load of 2,205 lb (1000 kg) and the Ju 86P-2 reconnaissance aircraft with three cameras.

One of the prototypes flew a reconnaissance mission over the UK at 41,010 ft (12,500 m) in the summer of 1940 and was undetected, and this was followed by other production models both over the UK and USSR. While standard Allied fighters were unable to reach them the Ju 86Ps remained unscathed, but in August 1942 a stripped-down Spitfire Mk V caught a Ju 86P at 37,000 ft (11275 m) over Egypt and after a chase to 42,000 ft (12800 m) shot it down.

In an effort to gain more altitude a higher aspect ratio wing was designed, increasing the span to 104 ft 11¾ in (32.00 m), and uprated Jumo engines with four-blade propellers were installed. Two versions were again built, the Ju 86R-1 reconnaissance aircraft and the Ju 86R-2 bomber, each comprising conversions of the respective Ju 86P types. Only a few aircraft reached service, but during tests an altitude of 47,250 ft (14400 m) was reached. Further development of the Ju 86R-3 with 1,500-hp (1119-kW) supercharged Jumo 208s and designed to reach 52,500 ft (16000 m), and of a proposed Ju 186, with four Jumo 208s or two Jumo 218s

Junkers Ju 86

Junkers Ju 86K-2 of the Hungarian 4th Bomber Regiment operating in the Soviet Union during 1942

(which were coupled Jumo 208s) was abandoned.

Probably the last surviving Ju 86s were those with the Swedish air force which completed their service as transports in 1956; one is preserved in the Swedish air force museum.

Specification
Junkers Ju 86D-1

Type: four-seat medium bomber
Powerplant: two 600-hp (447-kW) Junkers Jumo 205C-4 diesel engines
Performance: maximum speed 202 mph (325 km/h) at 9,840 ft (3000 m); cruising speed 177 mph (285 km/h) at 11,480 ft (3500 m); service ceiling 19,360 ft (5900 m); maximum range 932 miles (1500 km)

Weights: empty 11,354 lb (5150 kg); maximum take-off 18,078 lb (8200 kg)
Dimensions: span 73 ft 9¾ in (22.50 m); length 58 ft 7½ in (17.87 M); height 16 ft 7¼ in (5.06 m); wing area 882.67 sq ft (82.00 m²)
Armament: single 7.92-mm (0.31-in) machine-guns in nose, dorsal and ventral positions, plus a bombload of up to 1,764 lb (800 kg) carried internally
Operators: Luftwaffe, Chile, Hungary, Manchukuo, Portugal, South Africa, Sweden

A Ju 86G-1 in pre-war three-tone splinter camouflage. This was a version of the Ju 86E-2, and had been largely supplanted at the outbreak of war. These continued service as a trainer.

Junkers Ju 87

History and notes

The reputation of the Junkers Ju 87 as a weapon of war was made in the early days of World War II, when this dive-bomber was used in the Polish campaign, following up its success there with operations across Europe. The Stuka, as it became known universally (from Sturzkampfflugzeug, or dive-bomber), was considered by the Luftwaffe to be virtually invincible, but this was true only after air superiority had been gained. During the Battle of Britain in 1940 the RAF rapidly disproved the myth and the Stukas were so severely mauled that they were eventually withdrawn from operations over western Europe.

Junkers began construction of three prototypes of

the Ju 87 in 1934, and a specification was issued around it. Ironically, in view of later events, the first aircraft was powered by a 640-hp (477-kW) Rolls-Royce Kestrel engine. Square twin fins and rudders proved too weak and during dive testing in 1935 they collapsed and the aircraft crashed.

The second prototype had a redesigned single fin and rudder and a 610-hp (455-kW) Junkers Jumo 210A engine. It was soon joined by a third prototype with further modifications, and official evaluation took place in 1936 against three competitive aircraft, the Arado Ar 81, Hamburger Ha 137 and Heinkel He 118. Orders were placed with Junkers and Heinkel for 10 aircraft each, the other two types being eliminated.

Junkers Ju 87

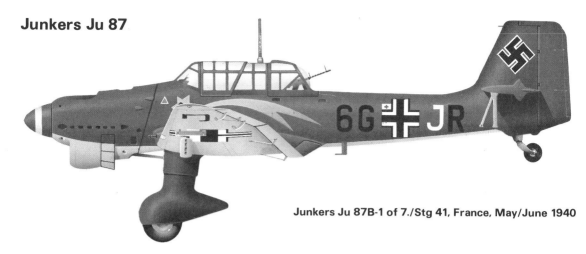

Junkers Ju 87B-1 of 7./Stg 41, France, May/June 1940

The pre-production batch of Ju 87A-0 aircraft had 640-hp (477-kW) Jumo 210Ca engines and changes to facilitate production, these being followed by Ju 87A-1 initial production aircraft which began to replace Hs 123 biplanes in the spring of 1937, and three aircraft were tested under operational conditions by the Condor Legion during the Spanish Civil War.

The Ju 87A-2 was the next production model, with a 680-hp (507-kW) Jumo 210Da engine with supercharger, but this remained in production and service for only about six months before a major redesign was undertaken with the seventh prototype and Ju 87B-0 pre-production series. The new model was the Ju 87B-1 with considerably more power, its Jumo 211Da giving 1,200 hp (895 kW), while the fuselage and landing gear were completely redesigned. Large, streamlined spats replaced the earlier model's trousered main landing gear units and the fin and rudder were enlarged. Again tested in Spain, the new variant proved its abilities, and the production rate was stepped up by mid-1939 to 60 per month; as a result, on the outbreak of World War II the Luftwaffe had 336 Ju 87B-1s on strength.

The Ju 87B-2 which followed had a number of detailed improvements and was built in several variants including ski-equipped versions and, at the other

Although quickly obsolete as a weapon due to its vulnerability in the face of effective fighter opposition, the Junkers Ju 87 was a terrifying war machine, bringing death from the skies and signalling its arrival with a screaming siren.

Three Ju 87s set out on a mission during the Blitzkrieg on Poland. It was in this campaign that the aircraft established its fearsome reputation.

Junkers Ju 87

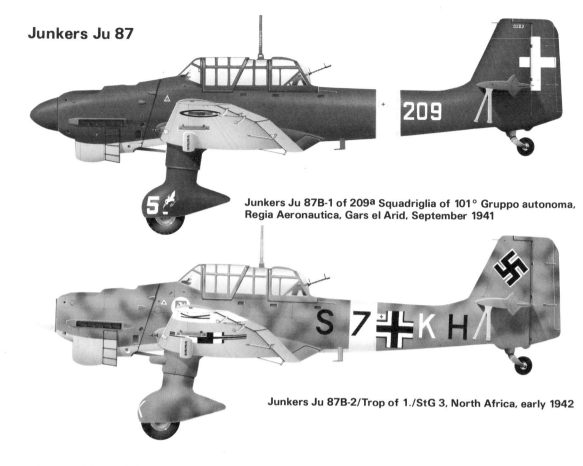

Junkers Ju 87B-1 of 209ª Squadriglia of 101° Gruppo autonoma, Regia Aeronautica, Gars el Arid, September 1941

Junkers Ju 87B-2/Trop of 1./StG 3, North Africa, early 1942

extreme, with tropical operation kit as the Ju 87B-2/Trop. Italy received a number of Ju 87B-2s and named the type Picchiatello, while others went to Axis countries, including Bulgaria, Hungary and Romania. A long-range anti-shipping version of the Ju 87B series appeared as the Ju 87R type, variants from Ju 87R-1 to Ju 87R-4 all having detail differences but a common armament (one 551-lb/250-kg bomb) and provision for underwing drop tanks. A pre-production batch (Ju 87C-0) of a navalised version, the Ju 87C-1, was built for operation from the aircraft-carrier *Graf Zeppelin*, but the ship was not completed and the aircraft were converted back to Ju 87B standard.

Although the Stukas had suffered mightily at the hands of the RAF, the Luftwaffe had no immediate replacement available and development continued, the next production model being the Ju 87D-1 with the new 1,410-hp (1051-kW) Jumo 211J-1 engine. Considerable changes were made in the aircraft's appearance and armour was increased, probably the most popular improvement! Production of this version began in 1941 and deliveries during that year totalled 476, with 917 in 1942. The type was deployed extensively in the Middle East and on the Eastern Front, and in the former area was even used as a glider tug under the designation Ju 87D-2. The Ju 87D-3 had extra armour protection for the ground-attack role, and an odd experimental version of the Ju 87D-3 had a pod above each wing, both capable of carrying two persons and intended to

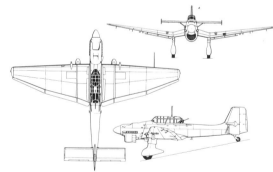

Junkers Ju 87B-2

be used to drop agents behind enemy lines. The pods were designed to be released in a shallow dive and to descend by parachute, but the point of this is obscure and it is not known if flight trials and release ever took place. The designation Ju 87D-4 applied to a torpedo-bomber version. The Ju 87D-5 had the outer wing panels extended to give a span of 49 ft 2½ in (15.00 m), the increase being necessary to cope with the heavier loads that were being carried. Dive brakes were omitted as the variant was intended only for ground-attack.

The Ju 87s in use on the Eastern Front were, by 1943, being severely mauled by the Red Air Force during daytime operations. A night assault version,

Junkers Ju 87

Junkers Ju 87

Junkers Ju 87B-2 of Stab II/StG 1 on the Eastern Front, late 1941

also without dive brakes, was developed as the Ju 87D-7 with flame-damped exhausts, two wing-mounted 20-mm MG 151/20 cannon and night-flying equipment. The Ju 87D-8 final production version was a similar but simplified aircraft. A final operational version should be mentioned, the Ju 87G-1, which was a conversion of the Ju 87D-5 for tank-busting operations with a 37-mm cannon beneath each wing. For a while this version enjoyed considerable success on the Eastern Front, but when Soviet fighters could be spared for deployment against the type its low speed and poor manoeuvrability with the heavy cannon made it extremely vulnerable. The Ju 87H series were trainers, produced by conversion

of Ju 87D airframes.

The final production figure for all models of the Ju 87 was in excess of 5,700; most of these were built after 1940, when the RAF had already shown the type to be very vulnerable without adequate fighter cover. It can only be assumed that the type continued in production for so long because no suitable replacement was forthcoming.

A line-up of the Ju 87Bs of StG 2 'Immelmann' in the Mediterranean theatre in 1941. The type was still widely used, but the days of glory of 1939 were long gone.

Junkers Ju 87

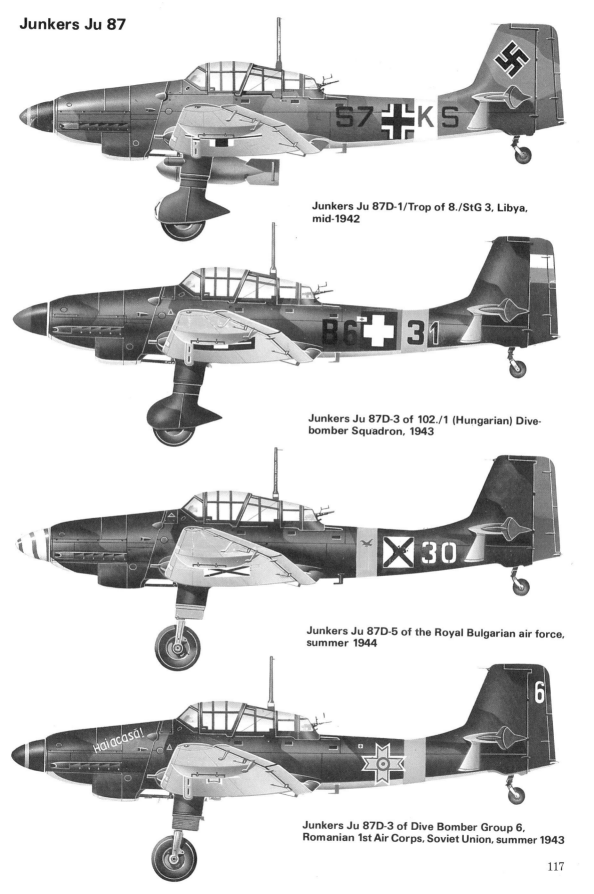

Junkers Ju 87D-1/Trop of 8./StG 3, Libya, mid-1942

Junkers Ju 87D-3 of 102./1 (Hungarian) Dive-bomber Squadron, 1943

Junkers Ju 87D-5 of the Royal Bulgarian air force, summer 1944

Junkers Ju 87D-3 of Dive Bomber Group 6, Romanian 1st Air Corps, Soviet Union, summer 1943

117

Junkers Ju 87

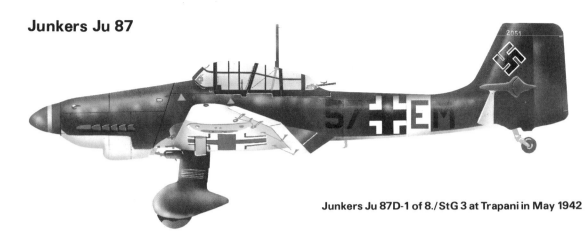

Junkers Ju 87D-1 of 8./StG 3 at Trapani in May 1942

Specification
Junkers Ju 87D-1

Type: two-seat dive-bomber/assault aircraft
Powerplant: one 1,400-hp (1044-kW) Junkers Jumo
211J-1 12-cylinder inverted-Vee piston engine
Performance: maximum speed 255 mph (410 km/h)
at 12,600 ft (3840 m); cruising speed 199 mph (320
km/h) at 16,700 ft (5090 m); service ceiling 23,915 ft
(7290 m); maximum range 954 miles (1535 km)
Weights: empty equipped 8,598 lb (3900 kg);
maximum take-off 14,550 lb (6600 kg)
Dimensions: span 45 ft 3½ in (13.80 m); length 37 ft

8¾ in (11.50 m); height 12 ft 9½ in (3.90 m); wing
area 343.38 sq ft (31.90 m²)
Armament: two 7.92-mm (0.31-in) forward-firing MG
17 machine-guns in wings and twin 7.92-mm (0.31-in)
MG 81Z machine-guns in rear cockpit, plus a
maximum bombload of one 3,968-lb (1800-kg) bomb
beneath fuselage, or various alternative loads
beneath fuselage and wings, including anti-personnel
bombs
Operators: Luftwaffe, Bulgaria, Croatia, Hungary,
Italy, Romania

Junkers Ju 88

History and notes

Unarguably the most versatile German warplane of
World War II, the Junkers Ju 88 remained in production
right through the war in developed forms. It originated
in a 1935 specification for a three-seat high-speed

bomber to be capable of more than 298 mph (480
km/h); Henschel and Messerschmitt tendered initially

**A Junkers Ju 88A runs up with the crew entry
hatch under the cockpit still open.**

Junkers Ju 88

Junkers Ju 88A-1 of I/KG 51 'Edelweiss' based at Melum-Villaroche in the autumn of 1940

to the same specification but later withdrew.

The prototype Ju 88 flew on 21 December 1936 with two 1,000-hp (746-kW) Daimler-Benz DB 600Ae inline engines with annular radiators, giving them the appearance of radials; the use of these radiators was to continue throughout the development of the aircraft. Further prototypes followed, the third having 1,000-hp (746-kW) Junkers Jumo engines and this, during evaluation, reached 323 mph (520 km/h). The high

The Ju 88 proved itself to be the most versatile Axis aircraft of the war, able to operate in virtually any role, from fighter to level bomber.

performance of the Ju 88 encouraged record-breaking flights, and in March 1939 the fifth prototype set a 1,000-km (621-mile) closed-circuit record of 321.25 mph (517 km/h) carrying a 4,409-lb (2000-kg) payload. A total of 10 prototypes was completed and the first of the pre-production batch of Ju 88A-0 bombers flew in early 1939. Production aircraft were designated Ju 88A-1 and began to enter service in September 1939.

Early teething troubles were gradually ironed out and sub-variants began to appear, including the Ju 88A-2 with jettisonable rocket packs for assisting take-off in overload conditions, the Ju 88A-3 dual-control trainer and the Ju 88A-4, the first considerably

Junkers Ju 88

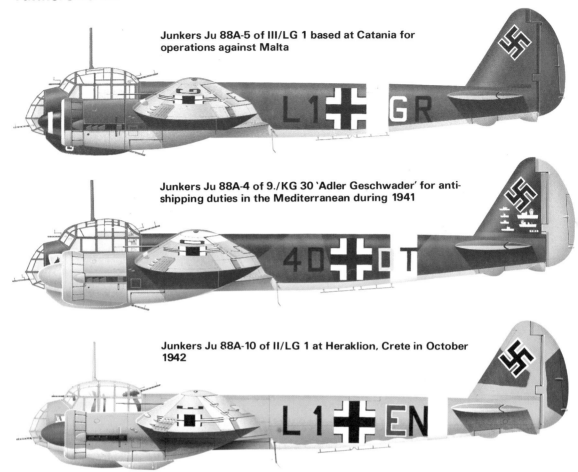

Junkers Ju 88A-5 of III/LG 1 based at Catania for
operations against Malta

Junkers Ju 88A-4 of 9./KG 30 'Adler Geschwader' for anti-
shipping duties in the Mediterranean during 1941

Junkers Ju 88A-10 of II/LG 1 at Heraklion, Crete in October
1942

modified development. Designed around the new and
more powerful Jumo 211J engine, the Ju 88A-4 had
increased span and was strengthened to take greater
loads.

Because of problems with the new engine the Ju
88A-4 was overtaken by the Ju 88A-5, which featured
the new wing but retained the former engines.
During the Battle of Britain many Ju 88A-5s were
fitted with balloon-cable fenders and cutters to combat
the UK's balloon barrage, and in this form they
became Ju 88A-6 aircraft. Some Ju 88A-5s, converted
to dual-control trainers, were designated Ju 88A-7.

By the time definitive Ju 88A-4s began to enter
service, lessons learned in the Battle of Britain had
dictated heavier armament and better protection for
the crew. Several different armament layouts were
used, but a typical installation was a single 7.92-mm
(0.31-in) MG 81 machine-gun on the right side of the
nose and operated by the pilot, and two 7.92-mm (0.31-
in) MG 81s or one 13-mm (0.51-in) MG 131 machine-gun
firing forward through the transparent nose panels,
operated by the bomb aimer. The same option was
available in the ventral gondola beneath the nose,
firing aft, while two other MG 81s were in the rear of

the cockpit canopy. Some 4,409 lb (2000 kg) of the
bombload was carried beneath the wings, both inboard
and outboard of the engines, while the internal bomb
bay held another 1,102 lb (500 kg).

Sub-variants of the basic Ju 88A extended up to the
Ju 88A-17; space considerations preclude detailed
mention of all these, but the Ju 88A-12 and Ju 88A-16
were trainers; the Ju 88A-8 and Ju 88A-14 had cable
cutters; the Ju 88A-11 was a tropical variant; and the
Ju 88A-17 was the Ju 88A-4 adapted to carry two 1,686-
lb (765-kg) torpedoes. The Ju 88A-15 with enlarged
bomb bay could carry 6,614 lb (3000 kg) of bombs.

By the end of 1942 the Luftwaffe had taken delivery
of more than 8,000 Ju 88's. While the Ju 88A was in
quantity production, Junkers was developing the Ju
88B, the prototype of which flew in 1940 with two
1,600-hp (1193-kW) BMW 801MA radial engines. Main
change in appearance was to the forward fuselage,
which was enlarged and extensively glazed, and there
was a marginal increase in performance over the Ju
88A, though this was not sufficient to warrant a change
in the production lines, and only 10 pre-production
aircraft were built.

It was inevitable that the Ju 88's basic design

Junkers Ju 88

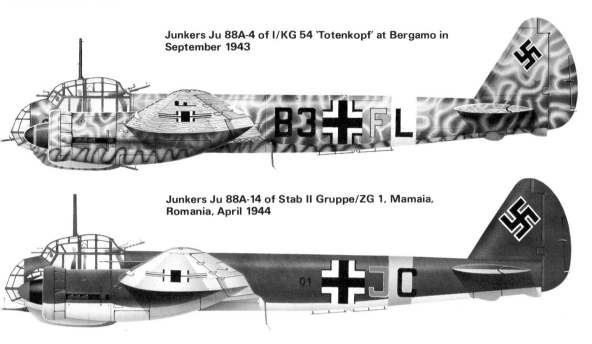

Junkers Ju 88A-4 of I/KG 54 'Totenkopf' at Bergamo in September 1943

Junkers Ju 88A-14 of Stab II Gruppe/ZG 1, Mamaia, Romania, April 1944

would also be adapted to the fighter role, although initially the need for bombers dictated a low priority for fighter versions. However, the second preproduction Ju 88A was adapted in mid-1939 to have a solid nose with three 7.92-mm (0.31-in) MG 17 machine-guns and one 20-mm FF/M cannon firing forward. Single 7.92-mm (0.31-in) MG 15 machine-guns were mounted in dorsal and ventral positions firing aft.

The fighter version would have become the Ju 88C-1, with an additional forward-firing 20-mm cannon, but plans to use 1,600-hp (1193-kW) BMW 801 engines had to be dropped since these were required for the Focke-Wulf Fw 190. However, many Ju 88A-1s were converted on the production line as Ju 88C-2 fighters. Around 130 were built, and these operated as night-fighters in 1940-1; they also carried out night intruder patrols over British bomber bases.

The first Ju 88 fighter to be built from scratch was the Ju 88C-4, which had the longer span wing of the Ju 88A-4 and 1,340-hp (999-kW) Jumo 211J engines. Attempts to provide more power by the use of 1,700-hp (1268-kW) BMW 801D radial engines produced the Ju 88C-3, of which only one was built, and the Ju 88C-5; a pre-production batch of 10 was built before the lack of BMW engines again killed the idea.

The Ju 88C-6 which followed after less than 100 Ju 88C-4s was basically a more heavily armoured day fighter and went into large-scale production; it was a sub-variant of this type, the Ju 88C-6b, which became the first radar-equipped Ju 88 night-fighter, with nose-

In the desert, the Ju 88 was used as both level bomber and dive bomber. Many met their fate at the hands of British and US fighters.

A Ju 88A-5 prepares to take-off carrying a pair of
SC 250 551-lb 250-kg bombs underneath the wings
inboard of the engine nacelles. The aircraft's
structure was able to absorb massive combat
damage as well as vastly differing weapon loads.

Junkers Ju 88

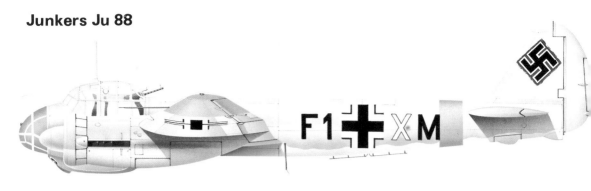

Junkers Ju 88C-6 of 4./KG 76 at Taganrog, Ukraine, late 1942 with simulated glazed nose to fool fighters

Junkers Ju 88S-1 of I/KG 66, Dedelsdorf, 1944-5

mounted Lichtenstein radar. It was to turn the tide appreciably against the RAF bombers, for on five operations between 21 January and 30 March 1944 342 bombers were destroyed out of 3,759 dispatched.

Alphabetically out of sequence was the Ju 88R-1, which had the same airframe and armament as the Ju 88C-6b but used BMW 801MA radial engines, the supply position on these having eased. The Ju 88R-2 was similar, but with BMW 801D engines.

Long-range reconnaissance versions of the Ju 88 were developed as Ju 88D aircraft; they were based on the Ju 88A-4, and almost 1,500 were built between 1941 and 1944 to see action on all fronts. The variants from Ju 88D-1 to Ju 88D-5 differed in engine and detail.

In an effort to improve stability of the Ju 88 a new, tall, square-cut fin and rudder was fitted to a Ju 88R-2, the new variant becoming, in its production form, the Ju 88G-1. The twin nose cannon were removed, but the aircraft carried Lichtenstein nose radar, with Flensburg aerials on the wings that enabled it to home in on RAF bombers using tail-warning radar emission.

The Ju 88G-1 had BMW 801D engines and developed into a number of sub-types; the Ju 88G-4 was the first to use the Me 110's *schräge Musik* installation of two MG 151 cannon which fired forwards and upwards. Main differences among the various sub-types were in the types of radar and armament fitted, although the later variants from Ju 88G-6c reverted to Jumo engines. The last production model of the series was the Ju 88G-7c.

Development of the basic Ju 88D reconnaissance aircraft resulted in the Ju 88H series, the prototype of which combined the wings and BMW engines of a Ju 88G-1 with the fuselage and tail of a Ju 88D-1. 'Plugs' were inserted in the fuselage fore and aft of the wing, increasing its length by 10 ft 8 in (3.25 m) to 57 ft 10¾ in (17.65 m). With the additional fuel tanks that could now be carried the Ju 88H had a range of 3,200 miles (5150 km).

Ten Ju 88H-1 reconnaissance aircraft and 10 Ju 88H-2 long-range fighters were built, the latter with six forward-firing 20-mm MG 151 cannon in place of the Ju 88H-1's cameras and radar. Despite being built in such small numbers, these types saw action over the Atlantic.

As Ju 87s were converted for tank-busting missions, so were a number of Ju 88s as the Ju 88P series. In 1942 a Ju 88A-4 airframe became the prototype, and was tested with a 75-mm (2.95-in) KwK 39 cannon mounted in a larger underbelly fairing. A small batch was ordered as the Ju 88P-1 with 75-mm (2.95-in) PaK 40 cannon, a 7.92-mm (0.31-in) MG 81 forward-firing machine-gun being used by the pilot for aiming the cannon. The usual ventral and dorsal rear-firing machine-guns were carried for defence. Other sub-variants with different forward-firing cannon were the Ju 88P-2 and Ju 88P-3 (two 37-mm BK cannon) and the Ju 88P-4 (one 50-mm BK5 cannon). Thirty-two of this final variant were delivered.

Performance of the Ju 88 bombers by 1942 was such that they were becoming progressively unable to

Junkers Ju 88

Another shot of a Ju 88A-5 with mounted bombs shows the neatly streamlined engine nacelles and the two cockpit mounted machine-guns, one rearward and one forward-firing.

Junkers Ju 88

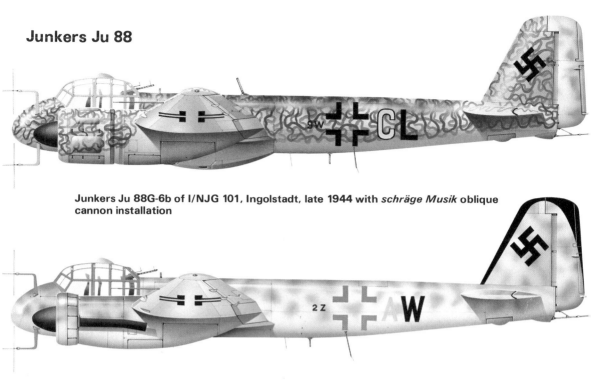

Junkers Ju 88G-6b of I/NJG 101, Ingolstadt, late 1944 with *schräge Musik* oblique cannon installation

Junkers Ju 88G-7a of IV/NJG 6, Schwäbisch Hall, 1944-5 with fin painted to represent Ju 88C

escape from enemy fighters, and in order to improve their chances the Ju 88S series was developed. Two BMW 801D 1,700-hp (1268-kW) radial engines were married to the Ju 88A-4 airframe for the prototype Ju 88S, which reached a speed of 332 mph (535 km/h). A pre-production series was ordered, followed in 1943 by production Ju 88S-1 aircraft with BMW 801G-2 engines which, with power boosting, gave 1,730-hp (1290-kW) at 5,005 ft (1525 m). To save weight, armament was reduced to a single rear-firing 13-mm (0.51-in) MG 131 machine-gun and a maximum speed (with nitrous oxide injection) of 379 mph (610 km/h) was reached at 26,245 ft (8000 m). Two more sub-variants were built, the Ju 88S-2 and Ju 88S-3, the latter having Jumo 213A engines which, with injection, gave 2,125 hp (1585 kW) and a speed of 382 mph (615 km/h) at 27,885 ft (8500 m). Only a few Ju 88S aircraft were built, with production beginning in 1944, and a high-speed photo-reconnaissance version, the Ju 88T, was also built in small numbers. Total Ju 88 production reached almost 15,000 in nine years.

Specification
Junkers Ju 88A-4

Type: four-seat bomber/dive-bomber
Powerplant: two 1,350-hp (1007-kW) Junkers Jumo 211J-1 12-cylinder inverted-Vee piston engines
Performance: maximum speed 292 mph (470 km/h) at 17,390 ft (5300 m); maximum cruising speed 248 mph (400 km/h) at 16,405 ft (5000 m); service ceiling 26,900 ft (8200 m); maximum range 1,696 miles (2730 km)

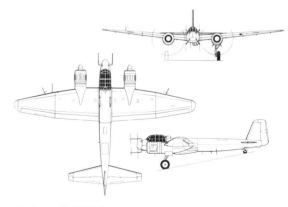

Junkers Ju 88G-1

Weights: empty equipped 21,737 lb (9860 kg); maximum take-off 30,865 lb (14000 kg)
Dimensions: span 65 ft 7½ in (20.00 m); length 47 ft 2¾ in (14.40 m); height 15 ft 11 in (4.85 m); wing area 586.6 sq ft (54.50m²)
Armament: one forward-firing 7.92-mm (0.31-in) MG 81 machine-gun, plus one forward-firing 13-mm (0.51-in) MG 131 or two 7.92-mm (0.31-in) MG 81 machine-guns, two similar guns in rear of cockpit firing aft and two firing aft below the fuselage, plus up to 4,409 lb (2000 kg) of bombs carried internally and externally
Operators: Luftwaffe, Finland, France, Hungary, Italy, Romania

Junkers Ju 88

landed accidentally at RAF Woodbridge in July 1944, so bringing the secrets of its SN-2 and FuG 227 Flensburg radar to the Allies.

Junkers Ju 88 Mistel composites

History and notes

In May 1916 a Bristol Scout was carried to a height of 1,000 ft (305 m) on the centre-section of a Porte Baby flying-boat, to test the feasibility of carrying a fighter to within firing range of the German Zeppelins which were carrying out raids on England.

Twenty-two years later Short Brothers flew their Mayo composite, the lower component being a four-engine flying-boat which was used to carry a heavily laden four-engine seaplane aloft with a greater load than the seaplane could have lifted off the water, thereby increasing the seaplane's range.

In 1943 the wheel turned full circle, with the possibility of pick-a-back aircraft for military purposes revived in Germany following experiments with light aircraft mounted above gliders. The proposal was that time-expired Junkers Ju 88 airframes be converted to pilotless missiles by the installation of a warhead packed with explosives. One of these would then be flown to within range of a target, controlled by the pilot of a single-engine fighter which was mounted on struts above the bomber's centre section. The fighter would release the Ju 88 and then guide it to the target.

The first conversion combined a Ju 88A-4 and a Messerschmitt Bf 109F, and this proved sufficiently successful for Junkers to be contracted to convert 15 Ju 88A airframes to Mistel (mistletoe) configuration, as it was called, presumably to imply its parasitic connection; the programme was codenamed 'Beethoven'.

An initial batch of trainers was converted, using Bf 109F-4s as the upper component. The lower component was stripped of nonessential equipment but retained a two-crew layout for training. The nose section could be completely removed by quick-release bolts and an 8,378-lb (3800 kg) warhead attached.

Operational flying began in mid-1944 when four Allied ships were attacked at night, all being hit but not sunk. Encouraged by these results, the Luftwaffe ordered a further 75 Ju 88G-1 fighters to be converted, this time with Focke-Wulf Fw 190A-6 or Fw 190F-8 fighters as the upper components of what became the Mistel 2 composite. Unfortunately, the combination of the Ju 88G with full fuel load and warhead, plus the Fw 190, meant that the lower component was considerably overloaded and burst tyres caused a number of take-off accidents.

Several combinations of Mistel were used, and this is a Ju 88G-1 used for Mistel training. The usual fighter was the Fw 190, but Bf 109s were also used.

Plans for a night attack on the British Fleet in Scapa Flow by 60 Mistel combinations, in December 1944, were thwarted by bad weather. The aircraft were unable to leave their Danish bases, perhaps fortunately for the Luftwaffe, since the combination was not only capable of only 236 mph (380 km/h) but also ungainly, and the group might well have been decimated by British night-fighters.

The next assault was to be against Soviet arms factories, with a planned date during March 1945. A total of 125 Misteln was then on order, of which 100 were required for this operation, which had to be cancelled when advancing Soviet troops occupied the airfields which were to have been used.

Sporadic attacks were made against bridges on the Eastern and Western Fronts, but heavy losses were suffered by the Misteln. Development continued, however, including the use of new Ju 88G-10 and Ju 88H-4 airframes on the production line. The Ju 88G-10s were twinned with Fw 190A-8s with overwing long-range tanks as Mistel 3C aircraft, while the Ju 88H-4/Fw 190A-8 composite became the Mistel 3B. A different role was served by a modified Mistel 3B where the lower component with a crew of three became an ultra long-range pathfinder, carrying its own Fw 190A-8 escort as the upper component, for launch only in emergency.

One of the last Mistel combinations tested consisted of a Ta 152H/Ju 88G-7 which flew in the last few weeks of the war. Total Mistel production has been estimated at around 250. Detailed performance specifications for Misteln are not known, but reference may be made to individual type specifications of aircraft used.

Junkers Ju 188

History and notes

A successor to the Junkers Ju 88 was at an advanced stage of design at the outbreak of World War II, but by late 1942 it had become obvious that the new bomber, the Ju 288, would be late entering service and a stop-gap design was required to bring the series up to date.

Junkers had been working as a private venture on an improved Ju 88, and the first interim result of this was the prototype Ju 88B which featured a completely new forward fuselage; 10 pre-production aircraft were built, and these paved the way to the Junkers Ju 188 which featured the new nose; pointed-tip wings with an increase of 6 ft 6¾ in (2.00 m) in span; a new tail unit with the tall, square fin and rudder as used on the Ju 88G; and a streamlined dorsal turret.

The first prototype Ju 188 flew in the spring of 1942

Junkers Ju 188

Junkers Ju 188D-2 of 1./FAGr 124 at Kirkenes, Norway

with BMW 801MA radial engines, and was followed by the second prototype in January 1943. The performance warranted production orders, but it was stipulated that the design must be such that either BMW 801 or Jumo 213 engines could be fitted without modifications to the airframe, so that if one type of engine became unavailable it would not affect production. Deliveries of Ju 188E-1 aircraft with 1,600-hp (1193-kW) BMW 801ML engines began in February 1943, and 283 had entered service by the end of the year. Further lines were opened at the beginning of 1944 by ATG, Leipzig and Siebel/Halle. Designation of the first model with the Jumo 213A-1 was Ju 188A-2, and with water-methanol injection its engines were boosted from 1,776 hp (1324 kW) to 2,240 hp (1670 kW) for take-off. The Ju 188A-3 was a minor variant, with nose radar and the ability to carry two torpedoes beneath the wing.

Two reconnaissance versions followed, the Ju 188D-1 and Ju 188D-2, with crew reduced from four to three, the forward-firing 20-mm cannon deleted and with extra fuel tanks fitted to give a range of 2,110 miles (3395 km). The type of cameras carried depended on mission, and the Ju 188D-2 was equipped with nose radar, being intended mainly for over-sea operations.

The Ju 188E variants were for the most part similar to the Ju 188Ds except that they had BMW 801 engines; the Ju 188E-1's 1,600-hp (1193-kW) engines soon gave way to uprated 1,700-hp (1268-kW) BMW 801Ds, while the Ju 188E-2 was the BMW-powered equivalent of the Ju 188A-3 torpedo-bomber. Similar reconnaissance equivalents were the Ju 188F-1 and Ju 188F-2 (Ju 188D-1 and Ju 188D-2). The Ju 188G and Ju 188H models with manned rear turrets did not reach flight-test stage, but three Ju 188R night-fighters were built in 1944. The variant did not go into production, however, since it was unable to offer much improvement over the Ju 88G.

High-altitude models proposed originally as the Ju 188J (fighter), Ju 188K (bomber) and Ju 188L (reconnaissance) went ahead, but the types were later redesignated Ju 388J, Ju 388K and Ju 388L. Simpler versions of these (for high-altitude intruder and reconnaissance work, with no defensive armament) became the Ju 188S and Ju 188T. With Jumo 213E-1 engines with water-methanol injection giving 2,168 hp (1617

A Junkers Ju 188E-1 shows the extremely pointed wings of this Ju 88 development. Several flew bombing missions over Britain.

Junkers Ju 188

Kw) at take-off and 1,690 hp (1260 kW) at 31,400 ft (9570 m), the Ju 188T could reach 435 mph (700 km/h) at 37,730 ft (11500 m). Operating at this altitude, the Ju 188S could carry only 1,764 lb (800 kg) of bombs.

Total production of all Ju 188 variants reached 1,076, of which more than half were reconnaissance variants. Probably the most unusual operator was France's Aéronavale, which ordered 12 Ju 188Es just after the war. These were built at Toulouse by SNCASE, from German components, and were used for test purposes.

Specification
Junkers Ju 188E-1
Type: four-seat medium bomber
Powerplant: two 1,700-hp (1268-kW) BMW 801D-2 14-cylinder radial piston engines
Performance: maximum speed 311 mph (500 km/h) at 19,685 ft (6000 m); cruising speed 233 mph (375 km/h) at 16,405 ft (5000 m); service ceiling 30,660 ft (9345 m); range 1,209 miles (1945 km)
Weights: empty equipped 21,737 lb (9860 kg); maximum take-off 31,989 lb (14510 kg)
Dimensions: span 72 ft 2 in (22.00 m); length 49 ft 0½ in (14.95 m); height 14 ft 7 in (4.44 m); wing area 602.80 sq ft (56.00 m²)

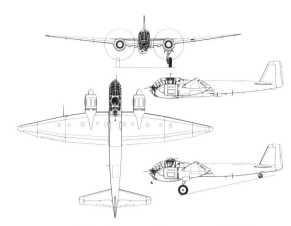

Junkers Ju 188E-1 (upper side view: Ju 188E-2)

Armament: one forward-firing 20-mm MG 151 cannon in nose, a single 13-mm (0.51-in) MG 131 machine-gun each in dorsal turret and rear of cockpit canopy, and one 7.92-mm (0.31-in) MG 81 machine-gun in lower front fuselage firing aft, plus a maximum bombload of 6,614 lb (3000 kg)
Operator: Luftwaffe

Junkers Ju 290

History and notes
The concept of the heavy bomber found few advocates in the Luftwaffe, and those companies who did succeed in pressing their claims for consideration usually failed in execution, witness the unsuccessful He 177. The Junkers Ju 290 was another example of such an aircraft, and its development came through the Ju 89 bomber of 1936 and the succeeding Ju 90 transport.

Three prototypes of the four-engine Ju 89 were under construction in 1936, but the programme was cancelled in the following year after the first prototype had flown. In the hopes of saving something from this work, Junkers obtained permission to use major components of the third prototype for a transport version which became the Ju 90, and attempts were made to interest Deutsche Lufthansa in the project.

The airline eventually began to take notice after the Ju 90 prototype flew on 28 August 1937. Three more prototypes followed, then a batch of 10 Ju 90B-1 aircraft fitted out as 38/40-seat airliners, and despite the loss of the first two prototypes in crashes Lufthansa placed an order for eight with 880-hp (656-kW) BMW 132H radial engines. The remaining two were ordered by South African Airways with Pratt & Whitney SC3-G Twin Wasp engines as Ju 90Z-2 transports, but were never delivered.

Because the big aircraft was underpowered, redesign was undertaken for installation of the new BMW 139

This Junkers Ju 290A-3 long-range maritime patrol aircraft was converted from a transport version before delivery to the Luftwaffe.

Junkers Ju 290

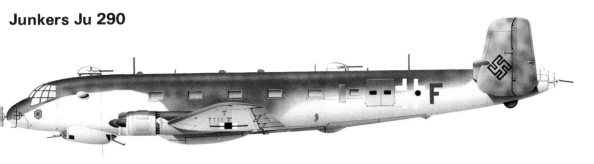

Junkers Ju 290 of FAGr 5 operating from Mont de Marsan in France during 1944

radial engines, on the assumption that these would soon be available. On the outbreak of war, the Luftwaffe took over Lufthansa's Ju 90B-1s for transport work, but the fourth prototype was re-engined with BMW 801MAs since the BMW 139 had been abandoned. The original Ju 90S designation for this model was changed to Ju 290; various changes were incorporated, including fuselage, wing and tail modifications, and from this point consideration was given to the use of the Ju 290 for maritime reconnaissance.

Two pre-production Ju 290A-0 aircraft with 1,600-hp (1193-kW) BMW 801L engines were followed by five Ju 290A-1 armed transports. Two were used in the attempted relief in Stalingrad, but one crashed on take-off with wounded troops aboard. The Ju 290A-2 was the maritime-reconnaissance armed version, and the first three aircraft were delivered in the summer of 1943, being followed by three Ju 290A-3 machines with new Focke-Wulf turrets and two Ju 290A-3s with 1,700-hp (1268-kW) BMW 801D engines.

Next variant, the Ju 290A-4, of which five were built, differed only in armament, while the 11 Ju 290A-5 aircraft which followed had heavier armament, more effective armour in the cockpit, improved protection for the fuel tanks and better lateral gun positions. A single Ju 290A-6 was used as a transport, ending its days in Spain, but the Ju 290A-7 was designated as a reconnaissance bomber; it was comparatively heavily armed and could carry missiles beneath the wings. Although 25 were begun only a few were completed and they did not enter service. Minor changes were made in the Ju 290A-8 to be built at the same time, but only two of these were completed. One survived the war to be scrapped in Czechoslovakia in 1956. Three Ju 290A-9 aircraft were completed as maritime reconnaissance machines, with increased fuel capacity for long-range work.

The Ju 290B-1 was the last version to be built, only one prototype of this long-range, high-altitude heavy bomber flying in 1944. A number of later variants were proposed but production of the Ju 290 ended in the autumn of 1944 for lack of suitable materials.

The ultimate development was the Ju 390, powered by six 1,700-hp (1268-kW) BMW 801D engines; it was a scaled-up Ju 290 with a span of 181 ft 7¼ in (55.35 m), length of 110 ft 2¾ in (33.60 m) and wing area of 2,841.77 sq ft (264.00 m²); two prototypes were built, both of which were flown in 1943. The second, on a test flight, flew from an airfield near Bordeaux to within about 12 miles (19 km) of the US coast north of New York before returning, proof that the specification for a bomber capable of attacking New York from European bases might well be met, but the scheme did not proceed any further.

Specification
Junkers Ju 290A-7

Type: long-range maritime reconnaissance bomber
Powerplant: four 1,700-hp (1268-kW) BMW 801D 14-cylinder radial piston engines
Performance: maximum speed 273 mph (440 km/h) at 19,030 ft (5800 m); cruising speed 220 mph (355 km/h); service ceiling 19,685 ft (6000 m); range 3,784 miles (6090 km)
Weights: empty 72,764 lb (33005 kg); maximum take-off 101,413 lb (46000 kg)
Dimensions: span 137 ft 9½ in (42.00 m); length 95 ft 7¾ in (29.15 m); height 22 ft 4¾ in (6.83 m); wing area 2,191.60 sq ft (203.60 m²)
Armament: one 20-mm MG 151 cannon in each of two dorsal turrets, one MG 151 in tail position, one MG 151 in glazed nose and one MG 151 in nose position in ventral gondola, two 20-mm MG 151 cannon in lateral positions, and one 13-mm (0.51-in) MG 131 machine-gun in rear of ventral gondola, plus a bombload of up to 6,614 lb (3000 kg) or three Henschel Hs 293, 294 or FX-1400 Fritz-X missiles
Operator: Luftwaffe

Junkers Ju 388

History and notes

The failure of the Junkers Ju 288 series and the programme's cancellation in mid-1943 spawned yet another variant of the ubiquitous Ju 88 airframe. The Ju 288 had been Junkers' response to a specification issued in July 1939 for a pressurized bomber of advanced design with a maximum speed in excess of 400 mph (645 km/h) and an ability to carry 1,102 lb (500

Junkers Ju 388

kg) of bombs over 3,355 miles (5400 km). Apart from a forward fuselage similar to that of the Ju 188, the new aircraft bore no resemblance to its predecessors, and had twin fins and rudders.

The whole story of the Ju 288 was one of technical problems on the one hand and continual requests for redesign on the other. As an example, the original wing span was to have been 51 ft 6 in (15.70 m), yet the final variant had been stretched to 74 ft 4 in (22.65 m)! A total of 22 prototypes of various versions was flown, of which 17 crashed during flight test, but the reasons for final cancellation of the programme were shortages of raw materials and a reluctance to affect other production programmes by initiating a new one at a critical time in the war.

Against this unfortunate background, it was extremely urgent to fill the gap left by the abandoned Ju 288. Fortunately, Junkers had carried on development of high-altitude models of the Ju 188 and three of these, originally designated Ju 188J, Ju 188K and Ju 188L, became the Ju 388J (all-weather fighter), Ju 388K (bomber) and Ju 388L (photo-reconnaissance) models. Although all were intended originally to have Jumo 213E engines, supplies of these were unreliable since they were in great demand, and the three models thus used the turbo-supercharged BMW 801TJ radial.

Since high-altitude reconnaissance was the biggest priority, the first prototype of the new series was a Ju 388L, converted from a Ju 188T, while the following pre-production batch was converted from Ju 88S airframes, the first of them being handed over to the Luftwaffe in August 1944. Construction of Ju 388Ls

A photographic reconnaissance development of the Junkers Ju 88, the Ju 388L-0 was only built in small numbers. This example was unusual in having three-blade propellors.

totalled 47 by the time production was halted in December 1944 when photo-reconnaissance aircraft were, it was decided, no longer a priority. The Ju 388J fighter was even less fortunate, only three prototypes being completed, and 10 pre-production Ju 388K-0 bombers plus five Ju 388K-1 production models had been completed before the axe fell on this, the final development of the Ju 88.

Specification
Junkers Ju 388L-1

Type: three-seat photographic reconnaissance aircraft
Powerplant: two 1,890-hp (1409-kW) BMW 801TJ 14-cylinder radial piston engines
Performance: maximum speed 382 mph (615 km/h) at 40,305 ft (12285 m) or 407 mph (655 km/h) at 29,790 ft (9080 m) with water-methanol boost; service ceiling 44,095 ft (13440 m); maximum range with external tanks 2,159 miles (3475 km)
Weights: empty 22,601 lb (10252 kg); maximum take-off 32,353 lb (14675 kg)
Dimensions: span 72 ft 2 in (22.00 m); length 49 ft 10½ in (15.20 m); height 14 ft 3¼ in (4.35 m); wing area 602.80 sq ft (56.00 m²)
Armament: one remotely-controlled FA15 tail barbette with two 13-mm (0.51-in) MG 131 machine-guns
Operator: Luftwaffe

Junkers W34

History and notes
Built as a single-engine commercial transport in 1926, the Junkers W34 saw considerable service with the

Luftwaffe from its formation until the end of World War II. Derived from the basic F13 of 1919, the W34 could be powered by a variety of engines from 280 hp

Junkers W34

(209 kW) upwards, but the examples in Lufwaffe service were mainly the W34hi with a BMW 132A radial engine, or the W34hau with a 650-hp (485-kW) Bramo 322 driving a four-blade propeller.

W34s were used as navigation trainers and light transports and normally seated six people; their corrugated construction made them particularly hardy and was, of course, almost a trademark of Junkers transports of the 1920s and 30s.

Specification
Junkers W34hi

Type: navigation trainer and light transport
Powerplant: one 660-hp (492-kW) BMW 132A 9-cylinder radial
Performance: maximum speed 165 mph (265 km/h); cruising speed 146 mph (235 km/h); service ceiling 20,670 ft (6300 m); range 559 miles (900 km)
Weights: empty 3,748 lb (1700 kg); maximum take-off

The Junkers W34 was employed by the Luftwaffe as a navigation trainer as well as for general communications and transport duties.

7,056 lb (3200 kg)
Dimensions: span 58 ft 2¾ in (17.75 m); length 33 ft 8¼ in (10.27 m); height 11 ft 7 in (3.53 m); wing area 462.86 sq ft (43.00 m²)
Operators: Luftwaffe, Croatia, Finland, Romania, Slovakia

Kawanishi E7K

History and notes

In March 1932 Aichi and Kawanishi began the competitive design of a new three-seat long-range reconnaissance floatplane. This was required by the Imperial Japanese Navy air force as a replacement for the Navy Type 90-3 Reconnaissance Seaplane which, built as the Kawanishi E5K, had proved to be disappointing in service use. A fabric-covered equal-span single-bay biplane of conventional design and construction, the Kawanishi E7K1 was carried on large strut-mounted twin floats, accommodated a crew of three in tandem open cockpits, and was powered by a 620-hp (462-kW) Hiro Type 91 'arrow' engine. First flown on 6 February 1933, the prototype passed its manufacturer's tests satisfactorily and in late May 1933 was handed over to the Japanese navy for service trials in competition with the AB-6 developed by Aichi to meet the same requirement. Navy evaluation left little doubt that Kawanishi's new floatplane was the better of the two, but no production order was forthcoming until after the receipt of a second prototype in late 1933. Some six months later, during May 1934, the E7K1 was ordered into production and given the designation Navy Type 94 Reconnaissance Seaplane. When it began to enter service in early 1935, the E7K1 very soon gained a good reputation for ease of handling, both on the water and in the air, but performance of the Hiro engine, derived from a French Lorraine powerplant, was disappointing. As a result, late production aircraft had a more powerful (750-hp/559-kW) version of the Hiro Type 91 installed, but this proved no more reliable and with E7K1 production then totalling 183 (57 built by Nippon) Kawanishi began to look at alternatives.

During 1938 the company built a prototype E7K2 which was generally similar to the earlier production aircraft, but with the unreliable Hiro engine replaced by a Mitsubishi Zuisei (holy star) 11 radial engine. Flown for the first time during August 1938, this was ordered into production by the navy some three months later under the designation Navy Type 94 Reconnaissance Seaplane Model 2; at the same time the E7K1 version was retrospectively redesignated as the Navy Type 94 Reconnaissance Seaplane Model 1. Production of the E7K2 totalled about 350 aircraft, some 60 built by Nippon, and the E7K as a type saw extensive use for both beach- and ship-based operations from 1935 until the beginning of the Pacific war. By that time the E7K1s had been relegated to second-line duties, but the radial engined higher-performance (some 23 mph/37 km/h faster) E7K2s remained in first-line roles until early 1943. These included anti-submarine patrol and inshore convoy escort, tasks for which they had never been intended, and many were still in use in liaison and training roles when the war ended. One more job remained, for like many obsolete types the E7Ks were pressed into service during the

By the time the Pacific war started, the E7K1s had been relegated to training duties, but the radial-engined E7K2s flew on until early 1942.

Kawanishi E7K

late stages of the war to take part in desperate *kamikaze* attacks. When, in the second half of 1942, codenames began to be allocated to Japanese aircraft to provide a simple and easily pronounceable means of referring to a type, the E7K2 became known as 'Alf', male Christian names being allocated to aircraft that were deployed basically as fighters or reconnaissance seaplanes.

Specification
Kawanishi E7K2

Type: three-seat reconnaissance seaplane
Powerplant: one 870-hp (649-kW) Mitsubishi Zuisei 11 14-cylinder radial piston engine

Performance: maximum speed 171 mph (275 km/h) at 6,560 ft (2000 m); cruising speed 115 mph (185 km/h) at 3,280 ft (1000 m); service ceiling 23,165 ft (7060 m); endurance 11 hours 15 minutes
Weights: empty 4,630 lb (2100 kg); maximum take-off 7,275 lb (3300 kg)
Dimensions: span 45 ft 11¼ in (14.00 m); length 34 ft 5½ in (10.50 m); height 15 ft 11 in (4.85 m); wing area 469.32 sq ft (43.60 m²)
Armament: three 7.7-mm (0.303-in) machine-guns (one forward-firing and two in rear cockpit on trainable mountings, one firing upward and one downward), plus up to 265 lb (120 kg) of bombs on underwing racks.
Operator: Japanese Navy

Kawanishi H6K

History and notes
The air arm of the Imperial Japanese Navy had gained its first experience of large flying-boats from the Kawanishi H3K2, or Navy Type 90-11 Flying-Boat. This had its beginnings in the British Short Brothers K.F.1 prototype designed for the Japanese navy which, after a first flight on 10 October 1930, was soon sent to Japan where it served as a pattern for four H3K2s, built by Kawanishi under the supervision of a British technical team. This emphasises how, in its early involvement in aviation, the Japanese industry was dependent upon copying the designs of foreign manufacturers. From their study of these designs and the constructional techniques adopted, Japan's young engineers gained valuable experience in a comparatively short time. By the early and mid-1930s they had acquired sufficient knowledge to start the design and development of a number of first-class aircraft.

When, in 1933, the navy considered the moment had come to acquire a larger and more efficient flying-boat, Kawanishi was given a specification against which it was required to submit proposals for two alternative designs with three and four engines, identified as the Type Q and R respectively. Unfortunately the proposals were not satisfactory, and in early 1934 the navy issued a revised and more demanding specification, which called for a cruising speed of 137 mph (220 km/h) combined with a range of approximately 2,795 miles (4500 km). This performance (if achieved) would better that of the Sikorsky S-42 flying-boat which had made some important pioneering flights. Kawanishi's re-appraisal of the requirement resulted in a new design, identified initially as the Type S and the work of a team headed by Yoshio Hashiguchi and Shizuo Kikahura, who had both had an opportunity of studying flying-boat design at Short Brothers in the UK.

Required to fulfil the roles of bombing, reconnaissance and transport, the prototype had a slender and graceful two-step full above which was mounted a parasol wing, the wing having a stabilising float strutted and braced beneath its undersurface just outboard of midspan, and mounting at its leading edge four 840-hp (626-kW) Nakajima Hikari (splendour) 2 radial engines. The tail unit, strut-mounted high on the rear fuselage, comprised a monoplane

The Kawanishi H6K was one of the best flying-boats of the war, proving extremely seaworthy. As the war stepped up, the H6K could no longer operate in a bomber role and switched to transport.

Kawanishi H6K

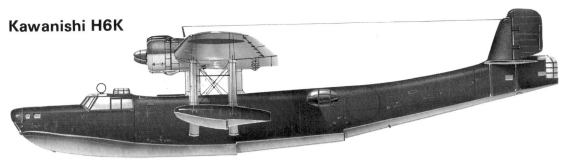

Kawanishi H6K5 of the Imperial Japanese navy

tailplane and twin fins and rudders, and for normal operations use the hull provided accommodation for a crew of nine. First flown on 14 July 1936, the H6K1 prototype in early tests showed a need of hull modification to improve water handling, and the more extended manufacturer's tests and service trials that followed this work revealed the type to be satisfactory but underpowered. Three more prototypes were ordered, all with Hikari 2 engines originally, but the first, third and fourth of the prototypes were each given four 1,000 hp (746-kW) Mitsubishi Kinsei (golden star) 43 radial engines before they entered service in January 1938 under the designation Navy Type 97 Flying-Boat Model 1. Simultaneously, the type was ordered into production and eventually a total of 215 of all versions was built, the initial H6K2 production model being generally similar to the re-engined prototypes except for minor equipment changes. Armament comprised three 7.7-mm (0.303-in) machine-guns on trainable mounts in bow, power-operated dorsal turret and non-powered tail turret, and up to 2,205 lb (1000 kg) of bombs could be carried. Two generally similar aircraft which were equipped to serve specifically as VIP transports had the designation H6K3.

The major production version was the H6K4 which had greater fuel capacity and improved defensive armament comprising four 7.7-mm (0.303-in) machine-guns in bow, two side blisters and open dorsal position, plus one 20-mm cannon in a tail turret; its powerplant was unchanged initially, but from August 1941 the Kinsei 43 engines were replaced by 1,070-hp (798-kW) Kinsei 46s. Final armed military production version was the H6K5 which, generally similar to the H6K4, deleted the open bow gun position and introduced a turret with a single 7.7-mm (0.303-in) machine-gun immediately to the rear of the flight deck, and performance was improved by the installation of uprated Kinsei 51 or 53 engines. In 1939 two H6K2s had been modified to serve as prototypes for an unarmed version for use as a military staff transport and for operation on the long over-water routes of Greater Japan Air Lines. Following successful testing the company began production of the H6K2-L, based on the early H6K4 with Kinsei 43 engines, and equipped to accommodate 18 passengers. Sixteen of this version, plus two similar aircraft converted from H6K4s, were supplied to Greater Japan Air Lines, being followed by 20 H6K4-L unarmed transports for the Japanese navy; these later aircraft

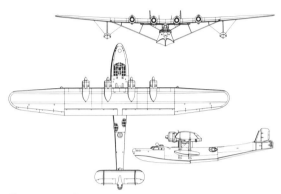

Kawanishi H6K5

differed by being based on the H6K4, with Kinsei 46 engines, and were provided with additional cabin windows.

The H6K saw early operational service during the Sino-Japanese War, but was used extensively with the outbreak of the Pacific war, the armed versions receiving the Allied codename 'Mavis' in 1942, by which time the increasing capability of fighter aircraft ranged against the type was such that it could no longer be deployed in a bomber role. Instead the type found increasing reconnaissance/transport use in areas where comparatively little fighter opposition could be expected, many remaining in service until the end of the war. The unarmed transport versions were given the Allied codename 'Tillie.'

Specification
Kawanishi H6K5

Type: long-range maritime reconnaissance/bomber flying-boat
Powerplant: four 1,300-hp (969-kW) Mitsubishi Kinsei 51 or 53 14-cylinder radial piston engines
Performance: maximum speed 239 mph (385 km/h) at 19,685 ft (6000 m); cruising speed 161 mph (260 km/h) at 13,125 ft (4000 m); service ceiling 31,365 ft (9560 m); maximum range 4,210 miles (6775 km)
Weights: empty 27,293 lb (12380 kg); maximum take-off 50,706 lb (23000 kg)
Dimensions: span 131 ft 2¾ in (40.00 m); length 84 ft 1 in (25.63 m); height 20 ft 6¾ in (6.27 m); wing area 1,829.92 sq ft (170.00 m²)
Armament: see text
Operator: Japanese Navy

Kawanishi H8K

History and notes

Soon after the first three Kawanishi H6K2s entered service in January 1938, the Imperial Japanese Navy issued a development contract to the company for a new large flying-boat to serve as a replacement for that aircraft, appreciating that it would be two or three years before a prototype would emerge. The estimate was fairly accurate, the Kawanishi H8K1 prototype making a first flight on the last day of December 1940, and while like its predecessor it was powered by four engines, in other respects it differed considerably. The high-set cantilever monoplane wing tapered in both chord and thickness from wing root to wingtip and served also to mount strutted and braced underwing stabilising floats at about two-thirds span. The hull was more conventional, losing the graceful lines of the H6K, and mounted at its rear a tail unit with single fin and rudder. Power for the three prototypes and early production aircraft was provided by four Misubishi MK4A Kasei (Mars) 11 radial engines mounted in nacelles at the wing leading edge. Accommodation was provided for a crew of 10, and defensive armament comprised five 20-mm cannon in port and starboard blisters and in nose, dorsal and tail turrets, supplemented by three 7.7-mm (0.303-in) machine-guns in two side hatches and a ventral position. Comprehensive armour protection was provided and the bulk fuel tanks within the hull were partially self-sealing and incorporated a carbon dioxide fire-extinguishing system.

The H8K was, therefore, an advanced aircraft, and designed to a specification that called for performance superior to that of the Short Sunderland. Not surprisingly, Kawanishi was greatly disappointed with early tests which showed that the first of the H8K1 prototypes was dangerously unstable on the water. Modifications were begun immediately to rectify this situation, including an increase in hull depth of 1 ft 9¾ in (0.55 m). New tests showed considerable improvement, but the second and third prototypes introduced the deeper hull and additional less major hull modifications, as well as an enlarged vertical tail fin. Service trials conducted with the modified flying-boats showed acceptable water performance, still not as good as that of the H6K, but they demonstrated such marked improvement in flight characteristics that the navy had no hesitation in ordering the type into production in late 1941 under the designation Navy Type 2 Flying-Boat, which acquired subsequently the Allied codename 'Emily'. The type remained in operational use until the end of the war, by which time construction of all versions totalled 167.

The initial H8K1 production version (16 built), which was the same as the second and third prototypes, was soon superseded by the major series version, the H8K2 (112 built) which introduced more powerful Mitsubishi MK4Q engines, a revised tail unit, more extensive armament and ASV radar. After being used for service trials, the original H8K1 prototype was given Mitsubishi MK4Q engines and converted for use in a transport role, then being redesignated H8K1-L; it was later developed as a production transport accommodating 29 to 64 passengers according to role, being powered by the MK4Q engines and having armament reduced to one 20-mm cannon and one 13-mm (0.51-in) machine-gun. Ordered into production as the Navy Type 2 Transport Flying-Boat Seiku (clear sky), the variant was built to the extent of 36 aircraft. Two early production examples were used as development aircraft for an improved version with retractable wingtip floats and a retractable dorsal turret, being redesignated H8K3; they were later tested with 1,825-hp (1361-kW) Mitsubishi MK4T-B Kasei 25b engines under the changed designation H8K4, but no production aircraft were built.

167 Kawanishi H8Ks of all types were built, and they saw service from March 1942 onwards as long-range bombers, patrol aircraft and transports.

Kawanishi H8K

Early production aircraft entered service in 1942, the type's operational debut being made on the night of 4-5 March 1942 when two aircraft based at Watje Atoll in the Marshall Islands, some 2,300 miles (3700 km) east of Pearl Harbor, were despatched to make a bombing attack on Oahu Island. This operation involved refuelling from a submarine at French Frigate Shoals, and it seemed unjust that such an ambitious piece of planning was frustrated by heavy cloud cover over the target area. Nevertheless, H8Ks proved highly effective, and the type was deployed on bombing, reconnaissance and transport missions, its heavy defensive armament making it a formidable adversary.

Specification
Kawanishi H8K2

Type: long-range bomber/reconnaissance flying-boat
Powerplant: four 1,850-hp (1380-kW) Mitsubishi MK4Q Kasei 22 14-cylinder radial piston engines
Performance: maximum speed 289 mph (465 km/h) at 16,405 ft (5000 m); cruising speed 183 mph (295 km/h) at 13,125 ft (4000 m); service ceiling 27,740 ft (8760 m); maximum range 4,443 miles (7150 km)
Weights: empty 40,520 lb (18,380 kg); maximum overload take-off 71,650 lb (32500 kg)
Dimensions: span 124 ft 8 in (38.00 m); length 92 ft 3½ in (28.13 m); height 30 ft 0¼ in (9.15 m); wing area 1,722.28 sq ft (160.00 m²)
Armament: five 20-mm cannon in bow, dorsal, tail and two beam positions, and four 7.7-mm (0.303-in) machine-guns in cockpit, ventral and two beam positions, plus up to 4,409 lb (2000 kg) of bombs or depth charges, or two 1,764-lb (800-kg) torpedoes
Operator: Japanese Navy

Kawanishi N1K Kyofu

History and notes
Foreseeing that close air support might well be needed during amphibious landings in areas where there was no adjacent airfield for land-based fighters, the Imperial Japanese Navy initiated in 1940 the development of a series of floatplane fighters. In September 1940 Kawanishi was instructed to design a single-seat floatplane specifically for this purpose, the company's design team producing the Kawanishi N1K1, a comparatively heavy mid-wing monoplane of all metal construction. A single central float was complemented by strut-mounted stabilising floats mounted near the wingtips, the tail unit was conventional, and power was provided by a

Mitsubishi Kasei 14 radial engine, driving originally contra-rotating propellers to offset the on-water torque effect of this powerful engine. However, flight testing of the first of eight prototype/service-test aircraft, flown on 6 May 1942, ran into problems with the gearbox for the contra-rotating propeller, with the result that testing continued with a conventional

The Kawanishi N1K Kyofu was designed as a float-plane fighter. Known by the Allies as 'Rex', the aircraft saw little service and it accomplished only minor success, being too slow to take on the fast American bombers.

Kawanishi N1K Kyofu

engine/single-propeller powerplant. This proved that the on-water torque problems were tricky, but not too difficult, leading to the decision to retain this simpler arrangement for production aircraft.

Satisfactory service trials resulted in the N1K1 being ordered into production as the Navy Fighter Seaplane Kyofu (mighty wind), the first of these entering service during early 1943. By then, however, the war situation was beginning to change, the Japanese moving from offensive to defensive operations and, as a result, the raison d'être for the N1K1 no longer applied. Production ended in early 1944 after a total of 97 aircraft, including prototypes/service test aircraft, had been built, and a planned N1K2 with a more powerful Mitsubishi MK4R Kasei 23 engine failed to materialise. Nevertheless, the production aircraft that had been completed continued in service, deployed in a defensive role, and these acquired the Allied codename 'Rex'.

Specification
Kawanishi N1K1 (late production)
Type: single-seat floatplane fighter
Powerplant: one 1,530-hp (1141-kW) Mitsubishi MK4E Kasei 15 14-cylinder radial piston engine
Performance: maximum speed 304 mph (490 km/h) at 18,700 ft (5700 m); cruising speed 230 mph (370 km/h) 6,560 ft (2000 m); service ceiling 34,645 ft (10560 m); maximum range 1,034 miles (1665 km)
Weights: empty 6,063 lb (2750 kg); maximum take-off 8,179 lb (3710 kg)
Dimensions: span 39 ft 4½ in (12.00 m); length 34 ft 9¼ in (10.60 m); height 15 ft 7 in (4.75 m); wing area 252.96 sq ft (23.50 m²)
Armament: two fuselage-mounted 7.7-mm (0.303-in) machine-guns and two wing-mounted 20-mm cannon, plus two 66-lb (30-kg) bombs carried on underwing racks
Operator: Japanese Navy

Kawanishi N1K1-J and N1K2-J Shiden

History and notes
In November 1942, only three months after the N1K1 Kyofu had flown for the first time, Kawanishi began development as a private venture of a land-based version of the same aircraft under the designation Kawanishi N1K1-J. The airframe of this prototype was basically of the same construction as that of its floatplane predecessor, but the float landing gear gave place to tailwheel landing gear with retractable main units. To achieve exceptional performance it was planned to use as powerplant the newly-developed Nakajima NK9H Homare (honour) 21 radial engine, but proper use of the full power of this unit required a propeller of large diameter. This, in turn, brought problems in design of the main landing gear legs, one that was solved by the introduction of telescopic units which contracted as the leg was folded inward into the undersurface of the wing/wing root; conversely, the telescopic portion extended after the leg had been lowered. First flown in early 1943, the N1K1-J prototype demonstrated excellent performance coupled with superb manoeuvrability, this capability being offset somewhat by unreliability of the 1,820-hp (1357-kW) Homare 11 engine and the rather complex landing gear, both plagued with problems that at first proved difficult to resolve. However, by July 1943 four prototypes had been completed and were tested by the Imperial Japanese Navy, leading to instructions for Kawanishi to concentrate on development of this aircraft. By the end of the year the situation had improved somewhat, and the navy authorised large-scale production under the official designation Navy Interceptor Fighter Shiden (violet lightning), this being allocated subsequently the Allied codename 'George'.

The initial production N1K1-J, powered by Homare

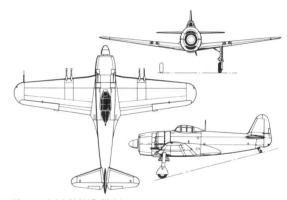

Kawanishi N1K2 Shiden

21 engines and with armament comprising two 7.7-mm (0.303-in) machine-guns and four wing-mounted 20-mm cannon, began to enter service in early 1944; the type proved to be full of troubles on the ground, but handled so well in the air that it was considered by Allied pilots to be a formidable adversary. A total of 1,007 was built by Kawanishi at Himeji and Nauro, in variants which included the N1K1-Ja with revised armament comprising only the four wing-mounted cannon; the N1K1-Jb which had the same armament, but with a modified wing so that the cannon could be mounted within the wing structure, plus underwing racks to carry two 551-lb (250-kg) bombs and, in some late series aircraft, an underfuselage pannier to carry six air-to-ground rockets; and the N1K1-Jc fighter-bomber which retained the wing-mounted cannon and had underwing racks to carry four 551-lb (250-kg) bombs.

Nevertheless, there was no doubt that the N1K1-J had been pushed into service very rapidly and operational

Kawanishi N1K1-J and N1K2-J Shiden

Kawanishi N1K2-J Shiden of the 343rd Kokutai

use highlighted the shortcomings, inadequate wheel brakes proving to be a particularly hazardous problem. It was decided in mid-1943 to review the design of the aircraft, leading to a number of changes including a change from mid-wing to low-wing configuration. This, in turn, made it possible to dispense with the complicated main landing gear units that had caused many problems, the legs being replaced by standard-length units. The fuselage was lengthened, the vertical tail surfaces were redesigned, and the aircraft's construction was simplified to the extent that the numbers of components were reduced by more than a third. However, no change was made in powerplant for, despite its unreliability, the Homare engine was powerful and readily available.

The resulting N1K2-J prototype was flown for the first time on 31 December 1943 and was ordered into production immediately by the Japanese navy as the Navy Interceptor Fighter Shiden KAI. Its manufacture was bedevilled by the speed with which it was required and the constant introduction of modifications, the continuing unreliability of the Homare engine and, in the later stages of the war, by the effects of US bombing on the supply of components. Despite this, the type continued to give a good account of itself, being particularly active in the regions of Formosa, Honshu, Okinawa and the Philippines before, in the final months of the war, being used also in a *kamikaze* role. The production N1K2-J, which had the same armament as the N1K1-Jb, was built to a total of 423,

401 of them by Kawanishi at Himeji and Nauro; this number included eight prototypes and an unknown but small number of N1K2-K two-seat trainers armed with four 20-mm cannon. The balance of 22 was built by other Japanese manufacturers. Further attempts to improve the capability of this fighter were frustrated by events, but development prototypes included two N1K3-J aircraft, with the engine moved forward 6 in (15.2 cm) to enhance longitudinal stability and armed with four wing-mounted 20-mm cannon plus two 13.2-mm (0.52-in) machine-guns; two similarly-armed N1K4-J prototypes each with an improved 2,000-hp (1491-kW) NK9H-S Homare 23 engine; plus a carrier-based variant of the N1K4-J which had the designation N1K4-A. Destroyed while under construction was the single prototype of the N1K5-J; this would have had the same armament as the N1K3-J and a 2,200-hp (1641-kW) Mitsubishi MK9A radial engine. The designation N1K3-A was allocated to a proposed carrier-based version of the N1K3-J, but no examples were built.

Specification
Kawanishi N1K2-J
Type: single-seat land-based interceptor fighter
Powerplant: one 1,900-hp (1484-kW) Nakajima NK9H Homare 21 18-cylinder radial piston engine

Under the designation Kawanishi N1K1-J, the Shiden was a land-based derivative of the N1K Kyofu but was only marginally more successful.

Kawanishi N1K1-J and N1K2-J Shiden

Performance: maximum speed 370 mph (595 km/h) at 18,370 ft (5600 m); cruising speed 230 mph (370 km/h) at 9,845 ft (3000 m); service ceiling 35,300 ft (10760 m); maximum range with drop tank 1,451 miles (2335 km)
Weights: empty 5,858 lb (2657 kg) maximum take-off 10,714 lb (4860 kg)

Dimensions: span 39 ft 4½ in (12.00 m); length 30 ft 8 in (9.35 m); height 13 ft 0 in (3.96 m); wing area 252.96 sq ft (23.50 m²)
Armament: four wing-mounted 20-mm Type 99 Model 2 cannon, plus two 551-lb (250-kg) bombs on underwing racks
Operator: Japanese Navy

Kawasaki Ki-10

History and notes
The Kawasaki Aircraft Engineering Company, an aircraft division formed by Kawasaki Heavy Engineering Company in 1918, became engaged in Japanese military aviation from that time. Like other Japanese companies involved in the aircraft industry, it gained most of its initial experience from the study of foreign designs and construction, building aircraft of Dornier and Salmson design and benefiting, between 1923 and 1933, from an association with German designer Dr Richard Vogt. Thus, the company had gained considerable expertise when the Kawasaki Ki-10 was designed and developed to meet an Imperial Japanese Army requirement of September 1934 for a high-performance biplane fighter. An unequal-span single-bay biplane of very clean design, it had a conventional tail unit and fixed tailskid landing gear, and accommodated its pilot in an open cockpit. Power for the Ki-10 prototypes was provided by an 850-hp (634-kW) Kawasaki Ha-9-IIa Vee liquid-cooled engine, and every effort was made to produce an aerodynamically clean installation. This was of great importance to Kawasaki in this particular instance, for the company's competitor for this contract was Nakajima, which had been instructed to produce an aircraft of monoplane configuration. The result was that when the prototype was flown for the first time during March 1935, very careful note was made of its performance, and development and refinement was continuous to raise the standard of performance to the highest possible level before army service trials began. An identical second prototype joined the test programme in April 1935, with third and fourth prototypes introducing progressive refinements, and late in the year Kawasaki's Ki-10-I was ordered into production with the official designation Army Type 95 Fighter Model 1.

The Ki-10 was soon regarded as the peak of biplane development in Japan, highlighted by the large number (588) built before production ended in December 1938. In addition to the initial series Ki-10-I (300 built), an improved Ki-10-II entered production from mid-1937 following the testing of a prototype which introduced increased wing span and a lengthened fuselage to improve stability; a total of 280 was built under the official designation Army Type 95 Fighter Model 2. Development continued with the Ki-10-I KAI prototype which introduced redesigned landing gear, a repositioned and improved radiator replacing the large drag-inducing version of earlier aircraft, and aerodynamically improved engine cowlings. Testing showed a worthwhile increase in performance, leading to two Ki-10-II KAI prototypes with the 850-hp (634-kW) Kawasaki Ha-9-IIb engine and combining the features of the Ki-10-I KAI and the production Ki-10-II. Although these last prototypes had a maximum speed of 277 mph (445 km/h), it was decided that the biplane fighter had passed the peak of its capability and no production aircraft resulted. Nevertheless the Japanese army's Ki-10s saw extensive use in operations against the Chinese in China and Manchuria, but most had been relegated to second-line roles by the time of the Pacific war. However, in the early stages the type was encountered occasionally, and the Allied codename 'Perry' was allocated.

Specification
Kawasaki Ki-10-II
Type: single-seat fighter
Powerplant: one 850-hp (634-kW) Kawasaki Ha-9-IIa 12-cylinder Vee piston engine
Performance: maximum speed 248 mph (400 km/h) at 9,845 ft (3000 m); climb to 16,405 ft (5000 m) in 5 minutes; service ceiling 37,730 ft (11500 m); range 684 miles (1100 km)
Weights: empty 2,998 lb (1360 kg); maximum take-off 3,836 lb (1740 kg)
Dimensions: span 32 ft 9¾ in (10.00 m); length 24 ft 9¼ in (7.55 m); height 9 ft 10 in (3.00 m); wing area 247.58 sq ft (23.00 m²)
Armament: two fixed forward-firing 7.7-mm (0.303-in) machine-guns
Operator: Japanese Army

Kawasaki Ki-32

History and notes
In competition with Mitsubishi, Kawasaki began in May 1936 the design of a light bomber to replace in service the Kawasaki Ki-3 which, designated officially

Kawasaki Ki-32

as the Army Type 93 Single-engined Bomber, was considered to be obsolescent. The new Kawasaki Ki-32 design was a cantilever mid-wing monoplane with a conventional tail unit and fixed tailwheel landing gear, the main units having fairings and large streamlined spats for the wheels. The pilot and bomb-aimer/radio operator were seated in tandem beneath a long 'greenhouse' canopy, and power was provided by a Kawasaki Ha-9-II engine. In March 1937 the first of eight prototypes were flown, only to run into problems with the engine installation and particularly with overheating of the liquid-cooled engine. Resolution of these faults was protracted, with a result that the competing Mitsubishi Ki-30 was ordered into production, for in July 1937 Japan had become involved in a full-scale war with China. However, so urgent was the need for all available air power that 12 months later the Ki-32 also entered production with the official designation Army Type 98 Single-engined Light Bomber.

Used extensively during the Sino-Japanese War and proving, because of very good handling characteristics, to be superior in some respects to the Mitsubishi Ki-30, the Ki-32 was ultimately built in larger numbers, a total of 854 being produced. The type remained in first-line service at the beginning of the Pacific war, being

The Kawasaki Ki-32 was largely obsolete at the outbreak of war, but a few were used as trainers.

used in initial operations before being relegated to a secondary role, and was allocated the Allied codename 'Mary'.

Specification
Type: two-seat light bomber
Powerplant: ore 850-hp (634-kW) Kawasaki Ha-9-IIb 12-cylinder Vee piston engine
Performance: maximum speed 261 mph (423 km/h) at 12,925 ft (3940 m); cruising speed 186 mph (300 km/h); service ceiling 29,265 ft (8920 m); maximum range 1,218 miles (1960 km)
Weights: empty 5,181 lb (2350 kg); maximum take-off 8,289 lb (3760 kg)
Dimensions: span 49 ft 2½ in (15.00 m); length 38 ft 2½ in (11.65 m); height 9 ft 6 in (2.90 m); wing area 365.98 sq ft (34.00 m²)
Armament: two 7.7-mm (0.303-in) machine-guns, one forward-firing and one on trainable mount, plus a bombload of 661 to 992 lb (300 to 450 kg) according to mission range
Operator: Japanese Army

Kawasaki Ki-45 Toryu

History and notes
In early 1937 Kawasaki was instructed by the Imperial Japanese Army to initiate the design and development of a twin-engine fighter that would be suitable for long-range operations over the Pacific. The concept derived from army interest in developments taking place in other countries, and particularly in the Messerschmitt Bf 110 which was in an early stage of flight testing in Germany. Kawasaki's original design to meet this requirement had the company designation Ki-38, but army evaluation of a mock-up in late 1937 required so

many changes that a complete redesign was started. Consequently, it was not until January 1939 that the first Kawasaki Ki-45 Toryu (dragon killer) prototype was flown, a cantilever mid-wing monoplane with retractable tailwheel landing gear. A slender fuselage provided enclosed accommodation for two in tandem, and mounted a conventional tail unit. Powerplant comprised two of the Nakajima Ha-20B radial, a new engine then under development, mounted at the wing leading edge in extended nacelles which served also to house the main gear units when retracted. It was these

Kawasaki Ki-45 Toryu

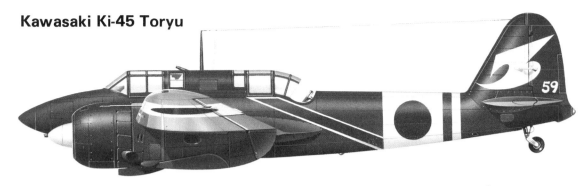

Kawasaki Ki-45 KAIc Toryu of the 1st Chutai, 53rd Sentai, based at Matsudo, Chiba prefecture in early 1945

two items that provided the major initial problems, the landing gear proving unreliable until provided with electrical actuation, and the engine failing to deliver its planned rated power of 820 hp (611 kW). The engine power-output problem proved more difficult to resolve and, finally, it was decided to substitute the 1,000-hp (746-kW) Nakajima Ha-25, the first of the resulting Ki-45-I prototypes flying in July 1940. Further problems followed with this engine installation, taking considerable time to resolve, and it was not until September 1941 that the Ki-45 KAI entered production under the official designation Army Type 2 Two-seat Fighter Model A Toryu (company designation Ki-45 KAIa), armament of this initial series version comprising one forward-firing 20-mm cannon, two 12.7-mm (0.5-in) machine-guns in the nose, and a 7.92-mm (0.31-in) machine-gun on a flexible mount in the rear cockpit; there was also provision to carry two drop tanks or two 551-lb (250-kg) bombs on underwing racks. The type entered service in August 1942 but was first used in combat during October 1942, soon being allocated the Allied codename 'Nick'. The Ki-45 KAIa was to be joined by a new version developed especially for the ground-attack/anti-shipping role, the Ki-45 KAIb built at Akashi and Gifu; early production examples had the Ha-25 engines, but later aircraft had the more developed Mitsubishi Ha 102. Standard armament comprised one 20-mm cannon in the nose, a foward-firing 37-mm cannon in the fuselage, and one rear-firing 7.92-mm (0.31-in) machine-gun, plus the underwing provision for drop tanks or bombs; a number of alternative weapon installations were tried experimentally, including the use of a 75-mm (2.95-in) cannon for attacks on shipping. A specialised anti-shipping version was produced subsequently, the Ki-45 KAId with Ha-102 engines, standard underwing provisions, and armament as for the Ki-45 KAIb except that two 20-mm cannon were mounted in the nose.

The Ki-45 KAIa was, for its day, heavily armed and proved effective against the USAF's Consolidated B-24 Liberators and, when these bombers were used more extensively for night operations, the Ki-45 was adapted to attack them. Thus the night-fighting capability of the type was discovered, leading to development of the Ki-45 KAIc night-fighter, which proved to be one of the most successful Japanese aircraft in this category; a total of 477 was built. Powered by Mitsubishi Ha-102

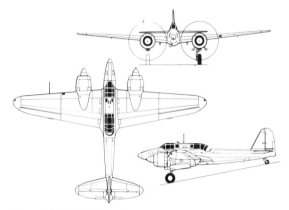

Kawasaki Ki-45 KAIc Toryu

engines, it had no armament installed in the nose as it was intended that this should house AI (air interception) radar, but development of this important aid to the night fighter was not ready in time; armament therefore comprised as standard one forward-firing 37-mm cannon, two obliquely-mounted upward-firing 20-mm cannon, one in each side of the fuselage, and one 7.92-mm (0.31-in) aft-firing machine-gun.

Ki-45 Toryus remained in service until the end of the Pacific war, production totalling 1,701 including prototypes, being used for the defence of Tokyo, and in the Manchuria, Burma and Sumatra areas of operation. A Ki-45-II with two 1,500-hp (1119-kW) Mitsubishi Ha-112-II radial engines was planned, but was developed instead as a single-seat fighter under the designation Kawasaki Ki-96, but this project did not progress beyond the prototype stage. One additional role was pioneered by the Ki-45 when, on 27 May 1944, four of these aircraft became the first to launch *kamikaze* attacks, directed against Allied shipping operating off the coast of New Guinea.

Specification
Kawasaki Ki-45-KAIc

Type: two-seat night-fighter
Powerplant: two 1,080-hp (805-kW) Mitsubishi Ha-102 14-cylinder radial piston engines
Performance: maximum speed 339 mph (545 km/h) at 22,965 ft (7000 m); climb to 16,405 ft (5000 m) in 6 minutes 7 seconds; service ceiling 32,810 ft (10000 m);

Kawasaki Ki-45 Toryu

range 1,243 miles (2000 km)
Weights: empty 8,818 lb (4000 kg); maximum take-off 12,125 lb (5500 kg)
Dimensions: span 49 ft 4½ in (15.05 m); length 36 ft 1 in (11.00 m); height 12 ft 1½ in (3.70 m); wing area 344.46 sq ft (32.00 m²)
Armament: cannon and machine-guns as listed in

The Ki-45 Toryu was a successful heavy fighter employed with great success against the Consolidated B-24 Liberator, especially at night.

text; all versions had provision for two drop tanks or two 551-lb (250-kg) bombs on underwing racks
Operator: Japanese Army

Kawasaki Ki-48

History and notes

Imperial Japanese Army aircraft confronted by the Soviet-built Tupolev SB-2 bomber, providing support for the Chinese during 1937, were somewhat shattered by its capability, its maximum speed being such that Japanese army fighter aircraft were virtually unable to intercept except when a standing patrol found itself in a position to launch a surprise attack. Almost at once the army instructed Kawasaki to begin the design of a twin-engine light bomber of even better capability, specifying a maximum speed of about 301 mph (485 km/h). Work on what was to become known as the Kawasaki Ki-48 began in January 1938, the result being a cantilever mid-wing monoplane with conventional tail unit, retractable tailwheel landing gear and, in the type's prototype form, two 950-hp (708-kW) Nakajima Ha-25 radial engines mounted in nacelles at the wing leading edges. The fuselage provided accommodation for a crew of four (the bombardier, navigator and radio-operator each doubling as gunners) and also incorporated an internal bomb bay.

Involvement in the Ki-45 programme delayed the maiden flight of the first of four Ki-48 prototypes until July 1939, but tail flutter problems then caused further delay until the introduction of modifications. Service testing resulted in unqualified approval of the type, which was ordered into production in late 1939 under the official designation Army Type 99 Twin-engined Light Bomber Model 1A (company designation Ki-48-Ia). Armament of this version comprised three 7.7-mm (0.303-in) machine-guns on flexible mounts in nose, dorsal and ventral positions, plus up to 882 lb (400 kg) of bombs, this being unchanged in the improved Ki-48-

Ib that followed the Ki-48-Ia into production, and differed by introducing minor equipment changes and detail refinements; manufacture of these two initial versions had totalled 557 when production ended in June 1942.

Ki-48s entered service in the summer of 1940, becoming operational in China during the autumn of that year. In China their speed gave the Ki-48's almost complete immunity from enemy defences, but their deployment against Allied aircraft at the beginning of the Pacific war revealed that their superior performance was illusory. Codename 'Lily' by the Allies, this initial production version had a number of deficiencies for the different kind of operations then required, and it was fortunate for the Japanese army that an improved version was already under development. This had the company designation Ki-48-II and differed from the earlier model by introducing a slightly lengthened fuselage, protected fuel tanks, armour protection for the crew, increased bombload and more powerful Nakajima Ha-115 engines, an advanced version of the

This picture of a Kawasaki Ki-48-Ia shows its similarity in concept to the Tupolev SB-2, the type which spurred its development.

Kawasaki Ki-48

Ha-25 which incorporated a two-stage supercharger. The first of three prototypes was completed in February 1942, and in the spring of that year the type entered production as the Army Type 99 Twin-engined Light Bomber Model 2A (company designation Ki-48-IIa). It was built also as the Ki-48-IIb which, generally similar to the Ki-48-IIa, was intended for use in a dive-bombing role, and so incorporated dive brakes in the undersurface of each outer wing panel. Final production variant was the Ki-48-IIc, also basically the same as the Ki-48-IIa, but with improved armament. A total of 1,408 Ki-48-IIs of all versions was built, to bring overall production to 1,977 including prototypes.

Unfortunately for the Japanese army, when the Ki-48-II was introduced into operational service its speed was still too low and its defensive armament inadequate to provide a reasonable chance of survival against Allied fighter aircraft. Attempts to increase armament merely upped the overall weight and speed suffered proportionately: it was clear by the summer of 1944 that the day of the Ki-48 had passed, and in October it was declared obsolescent. The majority ended their days in *kamikaze* attacks, but some examples were used as test-beds for the experimental Ne-0 turbojet engine and Kawasaki's Igo-1B radio-guided bomb.

Specification
Kawasaki Ki-48-IIb

Type: four-seat light/dive-bomber
Powerplant: two 1,150-hp (858-kW) Nakajima Ha-115 14-cylinder radial piston engines
Performance: maximum speed 314 mph (505 km/h) at 18,375 ft (5600 m); service ceiling 33,135 ft (10100 m); maximum range 1,491 miles (2400 km)
Weights: empty 10,031 lb (4550 kg); maximum take-off 14,881 lb (6750 kg)
Dimensions: span 57 ft 3 in (17.45 m); length 41 ft 10 in (12.75 m); height 12 ft 5½ in (3.80 m); wing area 430.57 sq ft (40.00 m²)
Armament: three 7.7-mm (0.303-in) machine-guns on trainable mounts in nose, dorsal and ventral positions, plus up to 1,764 lb (800 kg) of bombs
Operator: Japanese Army

Kawasaki Ki-61 Hien

History and notes
The overall similarity between the Kawasaki Ki-61 single-seat fighter and the Messerschmitt Bf 109 led to an Allied belief that the Japanese aircraft was, in fact, a licence-built version of Messerschmitt's famous fighter. There was, however, no truth in this suggestion, but the Ki-61 was powered by a licence-built version of the Daimler-Benz DB 601A, Kawasaki's first example of this engine, designated Ha-40, being completed in mid-1941. Anticipated availability of this engine had led to Kawasaki receiving instructions to proceed with the development of two different fighter aircraft round this powerplant; but the first of these, the Ki-60, proved disappointing when tested and its development was abandoned. Efforts were then concentrated on the Kawasaki Ki-61, the first of 12 prototypes being flown during December 1941. Early tests were highly satisfactory, and when an initial production example was flown by the Imperial Japanese Army in mock combat against a captured example of the USAAF's Curtiss P-40E and an imported Messerschmitt Bf 109E, the Ki-61 was found to be so superior in overall performance that the army had no hesitation in accepting the type for service under the official designation Army Type 3 Fighter Model 1.

More than 30 production examples of the Ki-61-I were completed by the end of 1942. The type was a cantilever low-wing monoplane with a conventional tail unit, retractable tailwheel landing gear, single-seat accommodation beneath a transparent canopy, and power was provided by the 1,175-hp (876-kW) Kawasaki Ha-40 engine. When the Ki-61-I began to

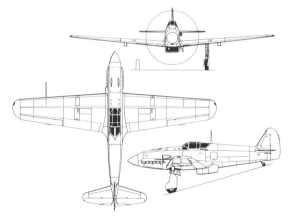

Kawasaki Ki-61-I

enter combat operations from New Guinea in April 1943 the type was quickly found to be an outstanding aircraft, well able to hold its own against Allied fighters. As production began to build up the Ki-61 appeared in all theatres where the Japanese army was operating, soon receiving the Allied codename 'Tony'.

The initial Ki-61-I was armed with two fuselage-mounted 7.7-mm (0.303-in) machine-guns and two wing-mounted 12.7-mm (0.5-in) guns, but sub-variants included the Ki-61-Ia with the wing-mounted machine-guns replaced by two imported 20-mm Mauser MG 151 cannon, and the Ki-61-Ib that had four machine-guns all of 12.7-mm (0.5-in) calibre. Unfortunately, despite its capability in the air the Ki-61-I was not an easy aircraft to maintain, and there were considerable problems

Kawasaki Ki-61 Hien

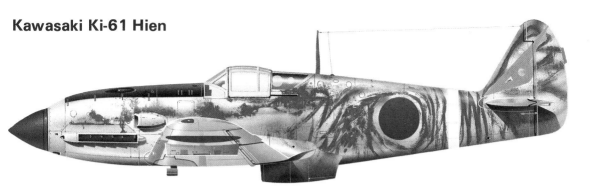

Kawasaki Ki-61-I-KAIc of the 3rd Chutai, 19th Sentai, Okinawa, 1944-5

Kawasaki Ki-61-I-KAIc of the HQ Chutai, 244th Sentai, Chofu, Tokyo, 1944-5

Kawasaki Ki-61-I-KAIc of the 23rd Independent Chutai, Yontan, Okinawa, April 1945

Kawasaki Ki-61-I-KAIc of the 1st Chutai, 244th
Sentai, Chofu, Tokyo, 1944-5

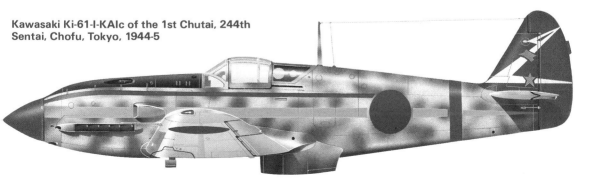

Kawasaki Ki-61 Hien

with the Ha-40 engine. An improved Ki-61-Ic appeared in early 1944, its structure being simplified and strengthened and incorporating a detachable rear fuselage and a non-retractable tailwheel to ease maintenance problems. The engine shortcomings were less easy to resolve, the major problem resulting from main bearing failures, and when no remedial action proved effective a dwindling supply of Ha-40s began to reduce the number of machines coming off the line, their number including some Ki-61-Id aircraft which substituted two 30-mm Ho-105 cannon for the 20-mm weapons of the Ki-61-Ic. Production ended finally in January 1945 after 2,666 (including prototypes) had been built.

The development of an improved version of the Ki-61 had started in the autumn of 1942 with eight Ki-61-II prototypes which introduced a wing of greater area and a new cockpit canopy to enhance the field of view. Increased power was provided by the 1,500-hp (1119-kW) Kawasaki Ha-140 engine, a development of the Ha-40, but this proved even more unreliable than its predecessor. Early flight tests, beginning in August 1943, were a nightmare; not only was the engine temperamental, but the new wing suffered structural failure. To resolve the airframe problems 30 Ki-61-II KAI prototypes and pre-production aircraft were built with a reversion to the proven wing of the Ki-61-I, and to compensate for the longer engine the fuselage was lengthened by 8½ in (21.6 cm) and the vertical tail surfaces were increased in area. Production was initiated and two versions were built, the initial production Ki-61-IIa with armament comprising two fuselage-mounted 12.7-mm (0.5-in) machine-guns and two wing-mounted 20-mm Ho-5 cannon, and the Ki-61-IIb with an armament of four 20-mm Ho-5 cannon. However, there proved to be no real solution to the shortcomings of the Ha-140 engine, and production of the Ki-61-II was con-

Powered by a licence-built DB 601A engine, the Ki-61 bore a resemblance to the Messerschmitt Bf 109, but could not emulate its success.

sequently decimated. Between January 1944 and January 1945, when engine production was brought to an end by a USAF attack on the Akashi engine factory, only 99 aircraft had been delivered. This total included a single Ki-61-III prototype of a proposed version with a cut-down rear fuselage to allow the installation of a bubble canopy with all-round view, this being a conversion of one of the Ki-61-IIs. Kawasaki was left with 275 completed airframes awaiting engines, undoubtedly a bitter pill to swallow, for if the company's Ha-140 engine had developed anywhere near its rated power the Ki-61-II would have proved a very capable high-altitude fighter.

Specification
Kawasaki Ki-61-Ic

Powerplant: one 1,175-hp (876-kW) Kawasaki Ha-40 12-cylinder inverted-Vee piston engine
Performance: maximum speed 348 mph (560 km/h) at 16,405 ft (5000 m); service ceiling 32,810 ft (10000 m); maximum range 1,181 miles (1900 km)
Weights: empty 5,798 lb (2630 kg); maximum take-off 7,650 lb (3470 kg)
Dimensions: span 39 ft 4¼ in (12.00 m); length 29 ft 4¼ in (8.95 m); height 12 ft 1¾ in (3.70 m); wing area 215.29 sq ft (20.00 m²)
Armament: two fuselage-mounted 12.7-mm (0.5-in) machine-guns and two wing-mounted 20-mm Ho-5 cannon of Japanese design and manufacture; all versions had provision for underwing drop tanks, but Ki-61-Ic and all Ki-61-IIs could carry two 551-lb (250-kg) bombs in place of drop tanks
Operator: Japanese Army

Kawasaki Ki-100

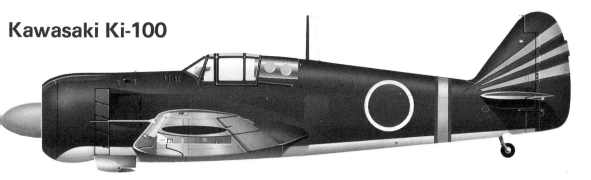

Kawasaki Ki-100-Ia of the 3rd Chutai, 18th Sentai operating from Kashiwa in the spring of 1945

Kawasaki Ki-100-Ib of the 3rd Chutai, 59th Sentai

History and notes

The Kawasaki Ki-61-II with the company's Ha-140 engine was seen as an interim high-altitude interceptor to tackle the USAF's Boeing B-29s at their cruising altitude of some 30,000 ft (9145 m). However, development of the Ha-140 as a reliable powerplant was terminated finally when the Akashi factory where the engine was built was destroyed during an air raid. With the requirement becoming daily more urgent, Kawasaki was instructed to convert the 275 Ki-61-II airframes gathering dust in the Kagamigahara factory with alternative powerplant. No other inline engine was available and adaptation of the slender fuselage of the Ki-61 to allow installation of a large-diameter radial engine at first appeared impractical. However, Kawasaki's design team converted three airframes to serve as prototypes, installing a Mitsubishi Ha-112-II engine which had the same power output as the unreliable Ha-140. When the first of these was flown, on 1 February 1945, Kawasaki discovered that it had a first-class fighter, one that some commentators have described as Japan's premier fighter aircraft of the Pacific war. By the end of May 1945 all of the remaining 272 Ki-61 airframes had been converted to the new configuration, entering service as the Army Type 5 Fighter Model 1A, which was identified by the company as the Kawasaki Ki-100-Ia.

With the Ki-100 proving such a success, it was decided to initiate production of this aircraft, the resulting Ki-100-Ib differing only by having the cut-down rear fuselage and all-round-view canopy that had been designed for the proposed Ki-61-III. A total of 99 of this version was built before production was brought

to an end by the growing weight of USAAF air attacks. A more effective version had been planned, to be powered by the Mitsubishi Ha-112-IIru engine which incorporated a turbocharger to improve high-altitude performance, but only three of these Ki-100-II prototypes had been built and flown by the end of the war.

Specification
Kawasaki Ki-100-Ia/b

Type: single-seat interceptor fighter
Powerplant: one 1,500-hp (1119-kW) Mitsubishi Ha-112-II 14-cylinder radial piston engine
Performance: maximum speed 367 mph (590 km/h) at 32,810 ft (10000 m); climb to 32,810 ft (10000 m) in 20 minutes; cruising speed 217 mph (350 km/h); service ceiling 35,005 ft (10670 m); range 1,243 miles (2000 km)

By fitting a radial engine into the Ki-61 airframe, Kawasaki produced one of the finest Japanese aircraft of the war.

Kawasaki Ki-100

Weights: 5,952 lb (2700 kg); maximum take-off 8,091 lb (3670 kg)
Dimensions: span 39 ft 4½ in (12.00 m); length 28 ft 10½ in (8.80 m); height 12 ft 3½ in (3.75 m); wing area 215.29 sq ft (20.00 m²)

Armament: two fuselage-mounted 12.7-mm (0.5-in) machine-guns and two wing-mounted 20-mm Ho-5 cannon, plus two drop tanks or two 551-lb (250-kg) bombs
Operator: Japanese Army

Kawasaki Ki-102

History and notes
Derived from the Ki-96 twin-engine single-seat fighter, development of which was abandoned after three prototypes had been completed, the Kawasaki Ki-102 was intended as a two-seat attack fighter for primary deployment in the close-support role. Some assemblies of the Ki-96 prototypes were incorporated into the three Ki-102 prototypes, the first of which was completed in March 1944. A cantilever mid-wing monoplane with a conventional tail unit, retractable tailwheel landing gear and two Mitsubishi Ha-112-II radial engines, the Ki-102 accommodated its two-man crew in separate enclosed cockpits in tandem. Completion of the prototypes was followed by the construction of 20 pre-production aircraft and in October 1944 the type was ordered into production under the official designation Army Type 4 Assault Plane (Kawasaki designation Ki-102b) and production was to total 215 aircraft. With the Imperial Japanese Army still anxious to procure a twin-engine high-altitude fighter, Kawasaki modified six of the pre-production Ki-102s to serve as prototypes of such an interceptor under the designation Ki-102a. This differed from the attack fighter by having improved two-seat accommodation, a revised tail unit and Mitsubishi Ha-112-IIru engines with turbochargers. Successful testing of this version in mid-1944 resulted in a high-priority production order, but problems with the turbocharged engine resulted in only about 15 being delivered to the army before the war ended. The design had also been revised to produce a night-fighter version under the designation Ki-102c, but there was only time to complete two examples. These had increased wing span, a lengthened fuselage, redesigned tail surfaces, primitive AI radar, and armament comprising two 30-mm Ho-105 cannon in the underfuselage and two 20-mm Ho-5 cannon mounted obliquely in the fuselage to fire forward and upward. Ki-102b aircraft, which were allocated the Allied codename 'Randy', saw comparatively little service, some being used in action over Okinawa, but the majority were held in reserve in Japan.

Specification
Kawasaki Ki-102b
Type: twin-engine ground-attack aircraft
Powerplant: two 1,500-hp (1119-kW) Mitsubishi Ha-112-II 14-cylinder radial piston engines
Performance: maximum speed 360 mph (580 km/h) at 19,685 ft (6000 m); service ceiling 36,090 ft (11000 m); range 1,243 miles (2000 km)
Weights: empty 10,913 lb (4950 kg); maximum take-off 16,094 lb (7300 kg)
Dimensions: span 51 ft 1 in (15.57 m); length 37 ft 6¾ in (11.45 m); height 12 ft 1¾ in (3.70 m); wing area 365.98 sq ft (34.00 m²)
Armament: one 57-mm Ho-401 cannon in the nose, two 20-mm Ho-5 cannon in the underfuselage, and one 12.7-mm (0.5-in) machine-gun on a flexible mounting in the rear cockpit, plus two 44-Imp gal (200-litre) drop tanks or two 551-lb (250-kg) bombs carried on underwing racks
Operator: Japanese Army

The Kawasaki Ki-102 was designed as an assault aircraft, and as such carried a 57-mm cannon under the nose. It saw only limited service, the majority of aircraft being held back in Japan.

Kayaba Ka-1

History and notes

The Imperial Japanese Army became interested during the late 1930s in autogyro developments taking place in the USA and, believing that such an aircraft might be developed for use as an artillery spotter, imported from America in 1939 a Kellett KD-1A. However, soon after this aircraft had arrived in Japan it was irreparably damaged during a flight test and the army arranged for the wreck to be transferred to the Kayaba Industrial Company, which had been carrying out research into the autogyro configuration. Shortly afterwards Kayaba was requested to proceed with design and development of a two-seat autogyro based on the Kellett. The resulting Kayaba Ka-1 prototype comprised a fuselage with two separate open cockpits in tandem, a tail unit incorporating a tailplane with twin inverted fins, fixed tailwheel landing gear, and an Argus As 10c engine mounted conventionally in the nose of the fuselage to drive a two-blade tractor propeller; the pylon for the three-blade unpowered rotor was incorporated in the fuselage structure, mounted just forward of the front cockpit.

First flown on 26 May 1941, the Ka-1 proved successful in early flight testing, and the type was ordered into production to serve in the originally intended role as a spotter-plane for artillery units. At the same time Japanese shipping losses were beginning to rise and it was suggested that the very short take-off run required by such aircraft would make them suitable for operation from the light escort carrier *Akitsu Maru*. A few production Ka-1s were modified for this role and equipped to carry two 132-lb (60-kg) depth charges, but because of their limited payload capability these had to be flown as single-seaters. Operating for some time off Japanese coastal waters they were the world's first operational armed rotary-wing aircraft, with production of both versions totalling approximately 240. This number included one Ka-1 KAI which was tested with rockets attached to the rotor tips in an attempt to improve payload capability, and a single aircraft that was evaluated with a 240-hp (179-kW) Jacobs L-4MA-7 7-cylinder radial engine, allocated the designation Ka-2.

Specification
Kayaba Ka-1
Type: rotary-wing spotter/liaison/patrol aircraft
Powerplant: one 240-hp (179-kW) licence-built Argus As 10c 8-cylinder inverted Vee piston engine
Performance: maximum speed 102 mph (165 km/h); cruising speed 71 mph (115 km/h); service ceiling 11,485 ft (3500 m); range 174 miles (280 km)
Weights: empty 1,709 lb (775 kg); maximum take-off 2,579 lb (1170 kg)
Dimensions: rotor diameter 40 ft 0¼ in (12.20 m); length 30 ft 2¼ in (9.20 m); rotor disc area 1,258.34 sq ft (116.90 m²)
Armament: two 132-lb (60-kg) depth charges
Operator: Japanese Army

Klemm Kl 35

History and notes

The first product of Klemm Leichtflugzeugbau GmbH after its formation in 1926 was the L 25 two-seater, some 600 of which were built with a variety of engines. Designed primarily for the civil market, the Klemm Kl 35a prototype was flown in 1935 and, like the L 25, was an open-cockpit two-seater monoplane of wooden construction, with an inverted gull wing and powered by a Hirth HM 60R engine. The Kl 35b second

A pretty aircraft, the Klemm Kl35 was used by the Luftwaffe as a primary trainer.

149

Klemm K1 35

prototype was followed by the initial production version, the Kl 35B built between 1935 and 1938 and powered by the 105-hp (78-kW) Hirth HM 504A-2 engine. A floatplane version was introduced in 1938 under the designation KI 35BW, and was provided with optional wood or metal floats. One was used to set a number of world class records, both solo and two-up, with solo altitude and speed over 100 km (161 miles) records accredited at 21,814 ft (6649 m) and 142.1 mph (228.7 km/h) respectively.

Luftwaffe use was primarily of the KI 35D version, which deleted the wheel spats of earlier versions and introduced strengthened landing gear suitable for use with wheels, skis or floats. The type was operated as a primary trainer by Luftwaffe pilot training schools throughout World War II. The KI 35 was also exported to Czechoslovakia, Hungary, Romania and Sweden, the air force of the last country operating the type under the designation SK 15.

Specification
Klemm KI 35D
Powerplant: one 80-hp (60-kW) Hirth HM 60R 4-cylinder inverted inline piston engine
Performance: maximum speed 132 mph (212 km/h) at sea level; cruising speed 118 mph (190 km/h); service ceiling 14,270 ft (4350 m); range 413 miles (665 km)
Weights: empty 1,014 lb (460 kg); maximum take-off 1,654 lb (750 kg)
Dimensions: span 34 ft 1½ in (10.40 m); length 24 ft 7¼ in (7.50 m); height 6 ft 8¾ in (2.05 m); wing area 163.62 sq ft (15.20 m²)
Operators: Luftwaffe, Hungary, Sweden, UK

Kyushu K11W Shiragiku

History and notes
The Watanabe Ironworks Company was responsible for the design of a crew trainer to meet the requirements of the Imperial Japanese Navy, but by the time that the trainer was ordered into production this manufacturer had been reorganised as the Kyushu Aeroplane Company, explaining the designation of this aircraft as the Kyushu K11W. A mid-wing cantilever monoplane with retractable tailwheel landing gear, the K11W had a deep-section fuselage to provide the requisite accommodation for a complete bomber crew and an instructor. This was arranged with the pilot and radio/operator gunner in a canopied cockpit above the wing, and with the instructor, bomb-aimer and navigator in a cabin below the wing. Power was provided by a Hitachi

GK2B Amakaze (heavenly wing) radial engine.

The K11W1 prototype was first flown during November 1942, its early testing and service trials being completed quite quickly because only minor faults were found. Ordered into production as the Navy Operations Trainer Shiragiku (white chrysanthemum), the first examples began to enter service in the summer of 1943, these carrying a rear-firing 7.7-mm (0.303-in) machine-gun and two 66-lb (30-kg) bombs for armament training. Used extensively by the navy, almost 800 had been built by August 1945, this total including a small

Bearing the markings carried by Japanese aircraft after the surrender, this K11W Shiragiku shows the deep fuselage necessary for a bomber crew trainer.

Kyushu K11W Shiragiku

number of an alternative version of all-wood construction which, designated K11W2, was built to fulfil ASW and transport roles. Like many Japanese aircraft, K11Ws were pressed into service as *kamikaze* attacks during the final stages of the Pacific war.

Specification
Kyushu K11W1
Type: bomber crew trainer
Powerplant: one 515-hp (384-kW) Hitachi GK2B Amakaze 21 9-cylinder radial piston engine
Performance: maximum speed 143 mph (230 km/h)

at 5,580 ft (1700 m); cruising speed 109 mph (175 km/h) at 3,280 ft (1000 m); service ceiling 18,400 ft (5620 m); range 1,094 miles (1760 km)
Weight: empty 3,697 lb (1677 kg); maximum take-off 6,173 lb (2800 kg)
Dimensions: span 49 ft 1¾ in (14.98 m); length 33 ft 7¼ in (10.24 m); height 12 ft 10¾ in (3.93 m); wing area 328.31 sq ft (30.50 m²)
Armament: one rear-firing 7.7-mm (0.303-in) machine-gun, plus two 66-lb (30-kg) bombs when required for training purposes
Operator: Japanese Navy

Kyushu Q1W Tokai

History and notes
The growing numbers and capability of Allied submarines operating in Japanese home waters induced the Imperial Japanese Navy to initiate the development of specialised ASW aircraft to combat this menace to the nation's offshore shipping. Issued in 1942, the specification emphasised that long-range capability and early availability were of primary importance. The Kyushu Q1W to this requirement, designed by Watanabe, was a cantilever mid/low-wing monoplane of all-metal construction with retractable tailwheel landing gear, powered by two Hitachi GK2C Amakaze 31 radial engines mounted in nacelles at the wing leading edges. The fuselage provided accommodation for a crew of three in an enclosed cabin, and considerable pains had been taken to ensure that all three members of the crew were assured of a maximum field of view. To ease the task of locating enemy submarines it was planned that the Q1W would be equipped with a new search radar, but delay in its development resulted in the installation of an earlier, less effective type, supplemented by MAD (magnetic anomaly detection) gear. Two 551-lb (250-kg) depth charges were carried for attack and a single rear-firing 7.7-mm (0.303-in) machine-gun for defence, and there was provision for the installation of nose-mounted 20-mm cannon.

Flight tests that followed completion of the first prototype in September 1943 proceeded with few problems, and the navy had no hesitation in ordering the type into production in early 1944 under the official designation Navy Patrol Plane Tokai (eastern sea) Model 11. Only 153 were built by Kyushu before the end of World War II, the total including a small number designated Q1W2 Tokai Model 21, which introduced a wooden rear fuselage, and one Q1W1-K Tokai Ren (eastern sea trainer) prototype which was a four-seat version of all-wood construction that had been intended to serve as a trainer for operations for electronic equipment.

Entering service during 1944, and allocated the Allied codename 'Lorna', the Tokai proved far from effective in operational use because of its inadequate

speed and defensive armament, making the type an easy target for Allied fighter aircraft.

Specification
Kyushu Q1W1
Type: anti-submarine patrol aircraft
Powerplant: two 610-hp (459-kW) Hitachi GK2C Amakaze 31 9-cylinder radial piston engines
Performance: maximum speed 199 mph (320 km/h) at 4,395 ft (1340 m); cruising speed 149 mph (240 km/h) at 3,280 ft (1000 m); service ceiling 14,765 ft (4500 m); range 833 miles (1340 km)
Weight: empty 6,834 lb (3100 kg); maximum take-off 11,718 lb (5315 kg)
Dimensions: span 52 ft 6 in (16.00 m); length 39 ft 8 in (12.09 m); height 13 ft 6 in (4.12 m); wing area 411.19 sq ft (38.20 m²)
Armament: one rear-firing 7.7-mm (0.303-in) machine-gun, plus two 551-lb (250-kg) depth charges or bombs; one or two 20-mm cannon in fuselage nose optional
Operator: Japanese Navy

Carrying two depth charges under its fuselage, the Kyushu Q1W1 Tokai was too slow for it to be fully successful, and proved easy pickings for Allied fighters.

Letov Š 328

Letov Š 328 of the Slovakian insurgent air arm, Tri Duby, near Zvolen during the Slovak National uprising in September 1944

History and notes

The Czech Letov company began in 1932 the design of a general-purpose biplane for service with the Finnish air force. An equal-span single-bay biplane with fixed tailwheel landing gear and conventional braced tail unit, this Letov Š 328 had accommodation for a pilot and observer/gunner in separate open cockpits in tandem. The Š 328 F prototype for Finland was completed during 1933, its powerplant a 580-hp (433-kW) Bristol Pegasus IIM-2 radial engine. Armament comprised two 7.7-mm (0.303-in) forward-firing machine-guns in the upper wing, and two more weapons of the same calibre on a flexible mounting in the rear cockpit. However, no production aircraft were ordered by Finland, though political changes and growing tension in Europe caused the Czech air ministry to order the type into production during 1934 for use by its own air force in the role of a bomber/reconnaissance aircraft. A total of 445 was built under the designation Š 328, and most of these were impressed for service with the Luftwaffe or the new Slovak air force when Bohemia-Moravia was occupied by German forces in March 1939, but a small number were later supplied to Bulgaria. When production ended a total of 470 had been built, and included 13 examples of a night-fighter variant designated Š 328 N which was armed with four fixed forward-firing and two trainably-mounted machine-guns, and four Š 328 V target-tug aircraft in which the wheel landing gear was replaced by twin floats. Letov had plans to produce developed versions, one Š 428 prototype resulting from the conversion of an Š 328 production aircraft by replacing the standard powerplant with a 650-hp (485-kW) Avia Vr-36 (licence-built Hispano-Suiza 12Nbr) and with armament of four forward-firing machine-guns. Subsequently, six Š 528 aircraft were built and differed primarily from the standard Š 328 by the installation of 800-hp (597-kW) Gnome-Rhône Mistral Major engines in NACA-type cowlings.

Slovak Š 328 aircraft took part in the campaign against Poland in 1940 and were operating on the Eastern Front in 1941, but by 1944 there came a reversal of loyalties, many Slovak pilots defecting to the USSR in their Š 328s to take part in operations against the German forces on Soviet territory.

Specification
Letov Š 328

Type: two-seat bomber/reconnaissance aircraft
Powerplant: one 635-hp (474-kW) Walter-built Bristol

Widely used on the Eastern Front by Slovak and Luftwaffe pilots, the Š 328 was operated in the battlefield reconnaissance and light bomber roles.

Letov Š 328

Pegasus IIM-2 9-cylinder radial piston engine
Performance: maximum speed 174 mph (280 km/h) at 5,905 ft (1800 m); service ceiling 23,620 ft (7200 m); range 435 miles (700 km)
Weight: empty 3,704 lb (1680 kg); maximum take-off 5,897 lb (2675 kg)
Dimensions: span 44 ft 11¼ in (13.70 m); length 34 ft 1½ in (10.40 m); height 11 ft 1¾ in (3.40 m); wing area 722.28 sq ft (67.10 m²)
Armament: four 7.7-mm (0.303-in) machine-guns, two in upper wing and two on flexible mount in rear cockpit, plus up to 1,102 lb (500 kg) of bombs
Operators: Slovakia, Bulgaria, Germany, USSR

Macchi MC.200 Saetta

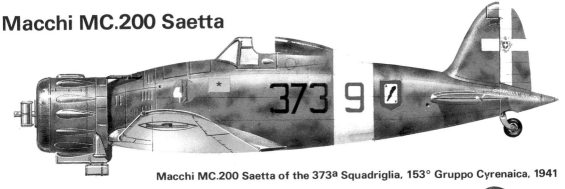

Macchi MC.200 Saetta of the 373ª Squadriglia, 153° Gruppo Cyrenaica, 1941

Macchi MC.200 Saetta of the 86ª Squadriglia, 7° Gruppo, 54° Stormo, Palermo, 1942

History and notes

It is unlikely that in the mid-1930s there was anyone in Italy better experienced to create a new single-seat fighter than Dr Mario Castoldi, chief designer of the Aeronautica Macchi company. Like R.J. Mitchell in the UK, Castoldi had adequately demonstrated his originality and attention to detail in the series of racing seaplanes developed by Macchi to compete in the Schneider Trophy contests. His MC.72, prevented by problems with its Fiat AS.6 engine from contending in the final contest in 1931, twice captured the world absolute speed record for seaplanes during 1934. The speed of 440.68 mph (709.209 km/h) established on 23 October of that year remained unbeaten in 1984.

Following the end of Italy's military campaigns in East Africa a programme was initiated to re-equip the Regia Aeronautica, the Macchi MC.200 Saetta (lightning) being designed by Mario Castoldi to meet the requirement for a new single-seat fighter. The resulting prototype (MM 336) was flown for the first time on 24 December 1937 as a cantilever low-wing monoplane of all-metal construction, except for fabric-covered tail control surfaces, with retractable tailwheel landing gear and an enclosed cockpit. Castoldi's advanced design for the wing resulted in a completely hinged trailing edge, the hydraulically-actuated flaps being interconnected with the ailerons so that when the flaps were lowered the ailerons were drooped simultaneously. Power was provided by a Fiat A.74 RC.38 radial engine, an interesting change after the Fiat inline success in the Schneider Trophy contests. Italian engine manufacturers had now been instructed to concentrate on the development of radial engines. Castoldi would dearly have liked to power the MC.200 by a high-performance inline engine, for he was concerned that the bulky radial would limit the performance of the new fighter, but he was to find a solution to this problem for the later MC.202.

Flight testing of the two MC.200 prototypes was successful, one of them attaining a speed of 500 mph (805 km/h) in a dive, and during 1938 the MC.200 won the fighter contest and was ordered into production with an initial contract for 99 aircraft, a total of more than 1,100 being constructed eventually, about 400 being built by Macchi and the remainder by Breda and SAI-Ambrosini. Numbered among them were sub-

Macchi MC.200 Saetta

Macchi MC.200 Saetta of the 371ª Squadriglia, 22° Gruppo, based at Ciampino, June 1940

variants that included the MC.200AS which was equipped for tropical operation, and the MC.200CB fighter-bomber with provision to carry a maximum 705-lb (320-kg) bombload or, when deployed as an escort-fighter, two underwing auxiliary fuel tanks. The single prototype of a developed version was built under the designation MC.201, introducing a revised fuselage. It was designed to be powered by the 1,000-hp (746-kW) Fiat A.76 RC.40 radial engine, but had been flown only with the Fiat A.74 RC.38 of the standard MC.200 when its development was abandoned in favour of the MC.202.

The type began to enter service in October 1939, by which time the MC.200 had been given the name Saetta, and when Italy entered World War II in June 1940 about 150 had been delivered to the Regia Aeronautica. The first combat missions were flown as escorts for bombers/fighter-bombers attacking Malta in the autumn of 1940, and the type served subsequently in actions over Greece and Yugoslavia. The MC.200 saw extensive use in North Africa and a number were involved in operations on the Eastern Front during 1941-2. Following the Italian armistice with the Allies in September 1943, 23 of the Saettas were flown to Allied airfields in southern Italy, to be flown shortly afterwards by pilots of the Italian Co-Belligerent Air Force.

Specification
Macchi MC.200

Type: single-seat interceptor fighter
Powerplant: one 870-hp (649-kW) Fiat A.74 RC.38 14-cylinder radial piston engine
Performance: maximum speed 312 mph (502 km/h) at 14,765 ft (4500 m); cruising speed 283 mph (455 km/h); service ceiling 29,200 ft (8900 m); range with auxiliary fuel 540 miles (870 km)
Weight: empty 4,178 lb (1895 kg); maximum take-off 5,710 lb (2590 kg)
Dimensions: span 34 ft 8½ in (10.58 m); length 26 ft 10¼ in (8.19 m); height 11 ft 5¾ in (3.50 m); wing area 180.84 sq ft (16.80 m²)
Armament: two 12.7-mm (0.5-in) Breda-SAFAT machine-guns in upper cowling; some later aircraft had two additional 7.7-mm (0.303-in) Breda-SAFAT machine-guns mounted in the wings
Operators: Italian Regia Aeronautica, Aeronautica Cobelligerante del Sud, and Aeronautica Nazionale Repubblicana

Showing the prevalent Italian design philosophy of using radial engines, the MC.200 Saetta was never a match for the inline-engined Hurricanes, Spitfires, Mustangs and Kittyhawks it encountered over the North African desert.

Macchi MC.202 Folgore

Macchi MC.202 Serie III Folgore of 378ª Squadriglia, 155° Gruppo, 51° Stormo

History and notes

Mario Castoldi had been convinced from the earliest days of MC.200 flight testing that full potential of the design would be achieved only by the installation of an inline engine. This opinion was confirmed during August 1940 when the prototype Macchi MC.202 (MM 445) was tested with an imported Daimler-Benz DB 601A-1 engine. The prototype was first flown on 10 August 1940, and its initial trials were so impressive that it was ordered into production without delay.

Generally similar in overall configuration to the MC.200, the MC.202 Folgore (thunderbolt) introduced a new fuselage structure with an enclosed cockpit, similar wings, but retained the tail unit and landing gear of its predecessor. However, the single MC.202 prototype, which was basically a re-engined MC.200 airframe, was flown with a retractable tailwheel. Because of the degree of commonality there was little delay in starting production, the first deliveries being made in the spring of 1941. Built alongside the MC.200 by Macchi, Breda and SAI-Ambrosini, early series aircraft were powered by imported DB 601A-1 engines until such time as Alfa Romeo had a licence-built version in production as the RA.1000 RC.41-1 Monsone (monsoon). However, it was limited manufacture of this engine which restricted the number of MC.202s to a total of about 1,500 when production ended in 1943, and so the MC.200 continued to be manufactured simultaneously, instead of being supplanted completely by the Folgore. Like its predecessor, the MC.202 was built in generally similar MC.202AS and MC.202CB tropicalised and fighter-bomber variants respectively, plus a single MC.202D experimental aircraft which introduced a revised radiator for the engine cooling system.

Undoubtedly the best wartime fighter to serve in large numbers with the Regia Aeronautica, initial deliveries of production aircraft were made in November 1941 to units operating in Libya. The Folgore also took part in actions against Malta and Allied convoys in the Mediterranean and, in September 1942, was deployed in some numbers on the Eastern Front. They played a significant role in the defence of Sicily and southern Italy against bombing attacks launched by the USAF, but by the time of the Allied invasion of Sicily they were less effective as attrition had reduced the total number available.

Specification
Macchi MC.202

Type: single-seat interceptor fighter
Powerplant: one 1,175-hp (876-kW) Alfa Romeo RA.1000 RC.41-I Monsone 12-cylinder inverted-Vee piston engine
Performance: maximum speed 370 mph (595 km/h) at 16,405 ft (5000 m); service ceiling 37,730 ft (11500 m); range 475 miles (765 km)
Weight: empty 5,181 lb (2350 kg); maximum take-off 6,636 lb (3010 kg)
Dimensions: span 34 ft 8½ in (10.58 m); length 29 ft 0½ in (8.85 m); height 9 ft 11½ in (3.04 m); wing area 180.84 sq ft (16.80 m²)
Armament: initially two 12.7-mm (0.5-in) Breda-SAFAT machine-guns in upper engine cowling, but later series added two wing-mounted 7.7-mm (0.303-in) Breda-SAFAT guns; one production batch introduced a 20-mm cannon beneath each wing
Operators: Luftwaffe (small number ex-Italian), Italian Regia Aeronautica, Aeronautica Cobelligerante del Sud, and Aeronautica Nazionale Repubblicana

By fitting a Daimler-Benz DB 601A engine into the MC.200 airframe, Castoldi produced the finest Italian fighter to see large scale service, the Macchi MC.202 Folgore. However, it suffered from lack of armament.

Macchi MC.202 Folgore

Identified by the Spauracchio (sparrow) device on the fuselage as belonging to 22° Gruppo, and by the numerals as belonging to 369a Squadriglia, this mid-series MC.202 was based at Capodichino, Naples as part of 53° Stormo.

Macchi MC.205V Veltro

Macchi MC.205V Veltro of 351ª Squadriglia, 155° Gruppo, 51° Stormo, Monserrato, June 1943

Macchi MC.205V 1ª Serie, 79ª Squadriglia, 6° Gruppo, 1° Stormo

History and notes

Fundamentally a developed version of the MC.202, the Macchi MC.205V prototype comprised a production MC.202 airframe with an imported Daimler-Benz DB 605A engine of 1,475 hp (1100 kW). Flown for the first time on 19 April 1942, it was put into production immediately, but some delay resulted before Fiat's licence-built version of the Daimler-Benz engine, the RA.1050 RC.58 Tifone (typhoon), became available in significant numbers. As a result the production MC.205V Veltro (greyhound) did not become operational until mid-1943, its first known action occurring in early July when the type was deployed in support of torpedo-bombers attacking Allied naval forces off Sicily. Just two months later, when the Italian government headed by Marshal Badoglio made peace with the Allies, the Regia Aeronautica had a total of 66 Veltros. Of this total only six gained Allied airfields to serve with the

Developed from the MC.202 using a DB 605A engine, the Macchi MC.205V Veltro was a fine fighter but only small numbers were built.

Macchi MC.205V Veltro

Macchi MC.205V of 1ª Squadriglia, 1° Gruppo, Aeronautica Nazionale Repubblicana, late 1943

Macchi MC.205V 155° Gruppo, 51° Stormo of the Co-Belligerent Air Force at Lecce-Galatina, autumn 1944

Italian Co-belligerent Air Force, the remainder being used by the Republican Socialist Italian air force.

Production continued on a limited scale after the armistice and ultimately a total of 265 had been built. In addition to the production MC.205V, single prototypes had been built of an MC.205N-1 high-altitude interceptor with an increased-span wing and armament comprising one engine-mounted 20-mm cannon and four fuselage-mounted 12.7-mm (0.5-in) machine-guns, and an alternative MC.205N-2 which differed only in having an armament of three 20-mm cannon and two 12.7-mm (0.5-in) machine-guns. The construction of prototypes of an MC.206 with increased wing span and armament as for the MC.205N-1, and a similar MC.207 which differed by having four wing-mounted 20-mm cannon, was not completed.

Regarded as the best Italian fighter aircraft of World War II, the Veltro was capable of meeting on equal terms such renowned fighters as the North American P-51D Mustang, a capability which encouraged the Luftwaffe to use a number of these aircraft to equip one *Gruppe*.

Specification
Macchi MC.205V Veltro
Type: single-seat interceptor fighter/fighter-bomber
Powerplant: one 1,475-hp (1100-kW) Fiat RA.1050 RC.58 Tifone 12-cylinder inverted Vee piston engine

A further development of the Macchi MC.200 series was the MC.205N Orione high altitude fighter but this did not see service.

Macchi MC.205V Veltro

Performance: maximum speed 399 mph (642 km/h) at 23,620 ft (7200 m); maximum cruising speed 310 mph (500 km/h); service ceiling 37,090 ft (16370 m); range 646 miles (1040 km)
Weight: empty 5,691 lb (2581 kg); maximum take-off 7,514 lb (3408 kg)
Dimensions: span 34 ft 8½ in (10.58 m); length 29 ft 0½ in (8.58 m); height 9 ft 11½ in (3.04 m); wing area 180.84 sq ft (16.80 m²)
Armament: two 12.7-mm (0.5-in) machine-guns in upper engine cowling, and two wing-mounted 7.7-mm (0.303-in) guns; late series had the wing-mounted guns replaced by two 20-mm cannon
Operators: Luftwaffe, Italian Regia Aeronautica, Aeronautica Cobelligerante del Sud, and Aeronautica Nazionale Repubblicana

Meridionali Ro.37bis

History and notes
Meridionali, then named Officine Ferroviarie Meridionali, first became involved in the Italian aircraft industry in 1923, beginning manufacturing activities two years later by licence-construction of Fokker designs. Subsequently, after two years under the name Romeo, the title Industrie Meccaniche e Aeronautiche Meridionali (IMAM) was adopted in 1936.

In 1934 the company had started design and production of a two-seat fighter/reconnaissance biplane under the designation Romeo Ro.37. This was an unequal-span single-bay biplane of mixed wood and metal construction. Its design included fixed tailwheel landing gear, all three wheels being provided with speed fairings; a braced tail unit incorporating a variable-incidence tailplane; and accommodation for two in tandem enclosed cockpits. Power was provided by a 700-hp (522-kW) Fiat A.30RA Vee engine. An improved Ro.37bis was developed subsequently, and this introduced an optional radial powerplant comprising either the Piaggio P.IX or P.X supercharged engine. Both models proved popular for their day, with production of the Ro.37 and Ro.37bis exceeding 160 and 475 respectively, and export orders were received from Afghanistan, Hungary and from countries in Central and South America.

Ro.37 and Ro.37bis aircraft were involved in the Spanish Civil War from October 1936 and were used extensively by the Regia Aeronautica during Mussolini's invasion of Abyssinia between October 1935 and May 1936 and during the Italian occupation of that country until 1941. Some 275 Ro.37bis aircraft were in service with the Regia Aeronautica when Italy became involved in World War II, and these saw first-line service in the East and North African campaigns and in the Balkans. After withdrawal from first-line service they found a variety of uses, but all had been retired before Italy's armistice with the Allies on 8 September 1943.

Small numbers of Meridionali Ro.37s were used by the Regia Aeronautica during the war, but they saw their heyday during the Spanish Civil War, including this example here, pictured in Nationalist markings.

Specification
Meridionali Ro.37bis
Type: two-seat fighter/reconnaissance aircraft
Powerplant: one 560-hp (418-kW) Piaggio P.IX RC.40 9-cylinder radial piston engine
Performance: maximum speed 205 mph (330 km/h) at 16,405 ft (5000 m); cruising speed 155 mph (250 km/h); service ceiling 23,620 ft (7200 m); maximum range 696 miles (1120 km)
Weight: empty 3,494 lb (1585 kg); maximum take-off 5,335 lb (2420 kg)
Dimensions: span 36 ft 4¼ in (11.08 m); length 28 ft 1 in (8.56 m); height 10 ft 4 in (3.15 m); wing area 337.46 sq ft (31.35 m²)
Armament: two fixed forward-firing 7.7-mm (0.303 in) machine-guns and one gun of same calibre on trainable mount in rear cockpit, plus up to 397 lb (180 kg) of bombs on underfuselage racks
Operators: Italian Regia Aeronautica, Hungary

Meridionali Ro.43/Ro.44

History and notes
Contemporary with the Ro.37/37bis, the Meridionali Ro.43 was designed and developed as an attractive-looking two-seat fighter/reconnaissance floatplane for ship-based service. It was an unequal-span single-bay biplane with foldable wings, the upper and lower wing

centre-sections being built integrally with the fuselage. Basic structure was of mixed steel-tube and wood, with light alloy and fabric covering, and the landing gear consisted of a large single-step central float of wood, with small stabilising floats mounted beneath each wingtip. Tandem cockpits were provided for the pilot and observer/gunner, and power was provided by a Piaggio P.XR radial engine.

When Italy entered the war in June 1940, the Ro.43 was the Italian navy's standard ship-based catapult-launched floatplane, approximately 100 being in service; about half of these were still on strength at the time of the armistice in September 1943. Some 40 generally similar aircraft were built as Ro.44 single-seat fighters, these having the observer's position faired over and his armament and equipment removed, while two forward-firing machine-guns replaced the standard single gun of the Ro.43. A number of Ro.43s and Ro.44s were used for shore-based defence of the Aegean islands, and a small number of Ro.43s supplied to neutral Spain were used for air/sea rescue operations throughout World War II.

Used as the Italian navy's standard shipboard general purpose floatplane, the Ro.43 also saw limited land-based service in the Aegean.

Specification
Meridionali Ro.43

Type: ship-based reconnaissance/fighter floatplane
Powerplant: one 700-hp (522-kW) Piaggio P.XR 9-cylinder radial piston engine
Performance: maximum speed 186 mph (300 km/h) at 8,200 ft (2500 m); cruising speed 155 mph (250 km/h); service ceiling 21,655 ft (6600 m); range 932 miles (1500 km)
Weight: empty 3,924 lb (1780 kg); maximum take-off 5,291 lb (2400 kg)
Dimensions: span 38 ft 0¾ in (11.60 m); length 31 ft 9¾ in (9.70 m); height 11 ft 5¾ in (3.50 m); wing area 359.10 sq ft (33.36 m²)
Armament: one fixed forward-firing 7.7-mm (0.303-in) machine-gun and one gun of the same calibre on trainable mount in rear cockpit
Operators: Italian and Spanish naval air arms

Messerschmitt Bf 108

History and notes

Flown in prototype form in June 1934, the Messerschmitt Bf 108 four-seat cabin monoplane with retractable landing gear was a considerable advance on contemporary touring aircraft. It originated with a contract awarded to Bayerische Flugzeugwerke AG (BFM) for an aircraft to compete in the Fourth Challenge de Tourisme International of 1934, and six were built with 225-hp (168-kW) Hirth HM8U engines to fulfil this contract. A seventh Bf 108A, as the first series was designated, had a 220-hp (164-kW) Argus As 17B engine.

While training for the contest one of the Bf 108As crashed, and pressure by the German team manager almost caused the type's withdrawal. However, four did compete, but unsuccessfully, since their all-metal construction made them considerably heavier than their wood and fabric competitors.

In 1935 the Bf 108B appeared with a 240-hp (179-kW) Argus As 10 engine, with modifications to the fin and rudder, removal of upper external tailplane bracing and the substitution of a tail wheel for the skid. A 160-hp (119-kW) Siemens Sh 14A radial engine was tried experimentally but proved unsuitable.

The high performance of the Bf 108 led to a number of record flights and some contest success. A German woman pilot, Elly Beinhorn, made a return flight from Berlin to Constantinople in one day during 1935 using a Bf 108A named *Taifun* (typhoon), a name which was adopted subsequently for the type. Bf 108s competed

Messerschmitt Bf 108

in aviation rallies held during the 1936 Olympic Games, and in the following year Elly Beinhorn was in the news again when she flew from Berlin to Capetown and back.

The obvious sterling qualities of the Bf 108 were not overlooked by the Luftwaffe, and the type was adopted as a communications aircraft. Others were exported to various countries and two former German embassy aircraft were impressed into RAF service during the war, while a few others served with the RAF for a short time after the end of the war.

Early production aircraft had been built at Augsburg in the BFW factory (hence the Bf of the designation) but this became Messerschmitt AG in July 1938. By that time, production had been moved to a new factory at Regensburg, and more than 500 had been built by 1942 when another move was made, this time to the SNCAN factory at Les Mureaux, near Paris.

Although several further variants of the design were proposed, only one was built before the end of the war. This was the Me 208, which had retractable tricycle landing gear but was otherwise very similar in appearance to its predecessor. Of the two prototypes built one was destroyed in an air raid, but the design lived on after the war, developed as the Nord 1101 Noralpha. The Bf 108 also received a new lease of life, entering production at Les Mureaux after the war as the Nord 1000 Pingouin (penguin) series. The Nord

Willy Messerschmitt's award-winning Bf 108 Taifun was taken up by the Luftwaffe as its main communications aircraft, proving fast and reliable.

1001 had a 240-hp (179-kW) Renault 60-10 engine, while the Nord 1002 had a Renault 60-11. Other projected developments were not built.

By the end of the war, Bf 108 production in Germany and France totalled 885, and some 285 were built post-war in France. A few original Bf 108s and some Nord-built examples are still flying.

Specification
Messerschmitt Bf 108B

Type: four-seat communications monoplane
Powerplant: one 240-hp (179-kW) Argus As 10C 8-cylinder inverted-Vee piston engine
Performance: maximum speed 186 mph (300 km/h) at 5,005 ft (1525 m); cruising speed 161 mph (260 km/h) at 8,005 ft (2440 m); service ceiling 19,685 ft (6000 m); range 621 miles (1000 km)
Weight: empty 1,941 lb (880 kg); maximum take-off 2,987 lb (1355 kg)
Dimensions: span 34 ft 10 in (10.62 m); length 27 ft 2½ in (8.29 m); height 7 ft 6½ in (2.30 m); wing area 176.53 sq ft (16.40 m²)
Operators: Luftwaffe, Bulgaria, France, Hungary, Romania, UK, Yugoslavia

Messerschmitt Bf 109

History and notes

In the mid-1930s the build-up of the Luftwaffe provided the necessary impetus for considerable updating of both fighter and bomber concepts. German fighter aircraft were then, like those in most other countries, of biplane configuration, but Willy Messerschmitt was

already well forward with the design of the Bf 108 touring monoplane, an extremely advanced aircraft for its time. Before it flew, he had also begun to design a single-seat fighter to meet the military requirement, and prototypes of this, the Messerschmitt Bf 109, were ordered to compete with other designs by Arado,

Messerschmitt Bf 109

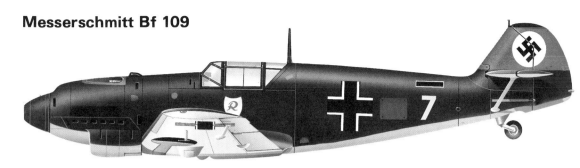

Messerschmitt Bf 109 of 6./JG 132 at Juterbog-Damm, autumn 1937

Messerschmitt Bf 109B of Luftwaffeschule of Luftkreiskommando II, Berlin, 1939

Focke-Wulf and Heinkel. Only the Heinkel He 112 provided any serious competition in trials carried out during October 1935, resulting in orders being placed for 10 prototypes of the He 112 and Bf 109.

It is ironic that the first prototype Bf 109 and final production version (those built in Spain) were powered by Rolls-Royce engines. The prototype flew at Augsburg in September 1935 with a 695-hp (518-kW) Rolls-Royce Kestrel engine, but the second which followed four months later had the 610-hp (455-kW) Junkers Jumo 210A for which the aircraft had been designed. The prototypes had various combinations of armament and the first three became Bf 109A aircraft, while later models were prototypes for the Bf 109B, basically similar to the first small batch of aircraft which was delivered to the Luftwaffe in the spring of 1937. Already subvariants were beginning to appear, the Bf 109B-1 having a 635-hp (474-kW) Jumo 210D engine and the Bf 109B-2 a 640-hp (477-kW) Jumo 210E with licence-built Hamilton variable-pitch metal propeller. The latter engine soon gave way to the 670-hp (500-kW) Jumo 210G.

Production 190B-1s began to be delivered to the

Luftwaffe's top fighter unit, JG 132 Richthofen, in early 1937 and, like several other German types, the Bf 109 was blooded in the Spanish Civil War when the Legion Condor received a batch in the spring of 1937 to replace Heinkel He 51 biplanes. The Messerschmitts acquitted themselves well, but the German propaganda ministry did not wish to publicise their involvement with Spain. Instead, five Bf 109s were sent to an international flying meeting at Zurich in the summer of 1937. Competing in the various events the Bf 109s scored resounding successes, winning the international circuit of the Alps contest, a team race, speed event, and a climb and dive competition. Not one of the Bf 109s was standard, two being fitted with 950-hp (708-kW) Daimler-Benz engines which were then in the development stage and conferred a considerably higher performance. One of the Bf 109s was destroyed in a forced landing following engine failure during the meeting, fortunately without injury to the pilot Ernst Udet.

In July 1938 Messerschmitt was appointed chairman and managing director of the Bayerische Flugzeugwerke and the company name was changed to Messerschmitt

Messerschmitt Bf 109C-2 of 1./JG 137, Bernburg, summer 1938

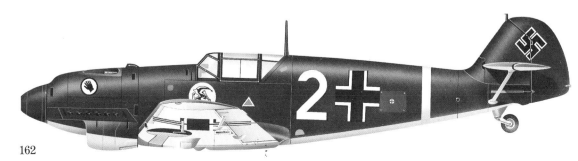

Messerschmitt Bf 109

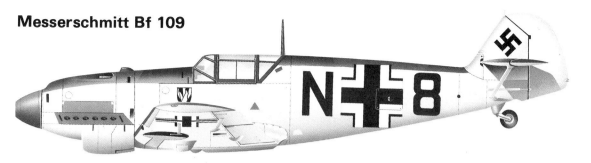

Messerschmitt Bf 109C of 10.(Nacht)/JG 77, Aalborg, July 1940

Meserschmitt Bf 109D of Jagdfliegerschule 1, Werneuchen, 1940

Messerschmitt Bf 109D of Flugzeugführerschule A/B 123 (Kroat.) at Agram, Zagreb, March 1943

Messerschmitt Bf 109E-1 of 7./JG 51 'Molders' at Bönninghardt, April 1940

Messerschmitt Bf 109E-3 of III/JG 2 'Richthofen', France, June 1940

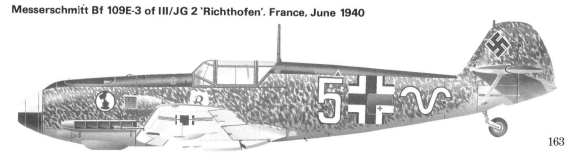

Messerschmitt Bf 109

Messerschmitt Bf 109E-1 of II/JG 26 'Schlageter', Dusseldorf, August 1939

AG; new designs undertaken from that point had Me instead of Bf designations. The first of these was the Me 209, which bore no relationship to the Bf 109 but was built purely to establish a new world air speed record, which it did in April 1939 at 469.22 mph (755.13 km/h). One of the prototype Bf 109s had previously raised the landplane record in November 1937 to 379.38 mph (610.55 km/h) using a boosted DB 601 engine giving 1,650 hp (1230 kW).

Meanwhile, production deliveries of Bf 109Bs con-

A *schwarm* of Bf 109s fly up the French coast in 1940. It was this tactical formation which caused such a surprise to the RAF when it encountered the Bf 109.

A line-up of Messerschmitt Bf 109Es prepare for flight. The Bf 109 fought from day one of the war to the very last, albeit in a variety of marks.

Messerschmitt Bf 109

Messerschmitt Bf 109E-3 of 9./JG 26, Caftiers, August 1940

Messerschmitt Bf 109E-3 of II/JG 77, Aalborg, July 1940

Messerschmitt Bf 109E-3 of 2./JG 3 'Udet', 1940

tinued, gradually being supplanted by Bf 109C-1 aircraft with the 700-hp (522-kW) Jumo 210 Ga engine and two extra wing-mounted machine-guns. Output was being stepped up, and the fighters were also being built by Arado, Erla, Focke-Wulf and Fieseler. By September 1938, almost 600 aircraft had been built (including the Bf 109C-2 with engine-mounted machine-gun), although deliveries of the Bf 109D series with the Daimler-Benz powerplant were delayed by a hold-up in the supply of engines, which necessitated keeping the earlier Jumo-powered models in production. First export customer was Switzerland, which received 10 Bf 109Cs between December 1938 and January 1939. The Bf 109D turned out to be a stop-gap model, since its DB 600 engine was not particularly reliable, and Daimler-Benz production was switched to the DB 601 which gave 1,050-hp (783-kW) for take off. In this form the Messerschmitt fighter entered large scale production in 1939 as the Bf 109E, the variant which was to see action in large numbers during the Battle of Britain as the Luftwaffe's only single-engine fighter engaged in the conflict. The new engine offered one considerable advantage over the DB 600: it had a fuel injection system which kept a constant fuel flow under conditions

of negative-g, enabling pilots to break off combat if they chose and dive away faster than their opponents with float carburettors; this feature was to prove crucial in the forthcoming battle.

Production Bf 109Es were coming off the assembly lines in early 1939, by which time Arado and Focke-Wulf had been transferred to other programmes, leaving the bulk of production to Erla and Fieseler who built nearly 1,400 in 1939; Messerschmitt's own production line had meanwhile been transferred from Augsburg to Regensburg, and the changeover meant that less than 150 aircraft were completed during 1939. Nevertheless, rapid production by the two sub-contractors had been possible since a number of airframes had been available, merely awaiting new engines.

A delivery of the Bf 109E-1 variant (two wing-mounted MG FF cannon and two fuselage-mounted MG 17 machine-guns) was made to Spain in February 1939 for service with the Legion Condor and these, together with the survivors of earlier marks, were transferred to Spanish ownership following the end of the civil war. Swiss contracts for 80 aircraft were met between April 1939 and April 1940.

When World War II began on 1 September 1939,

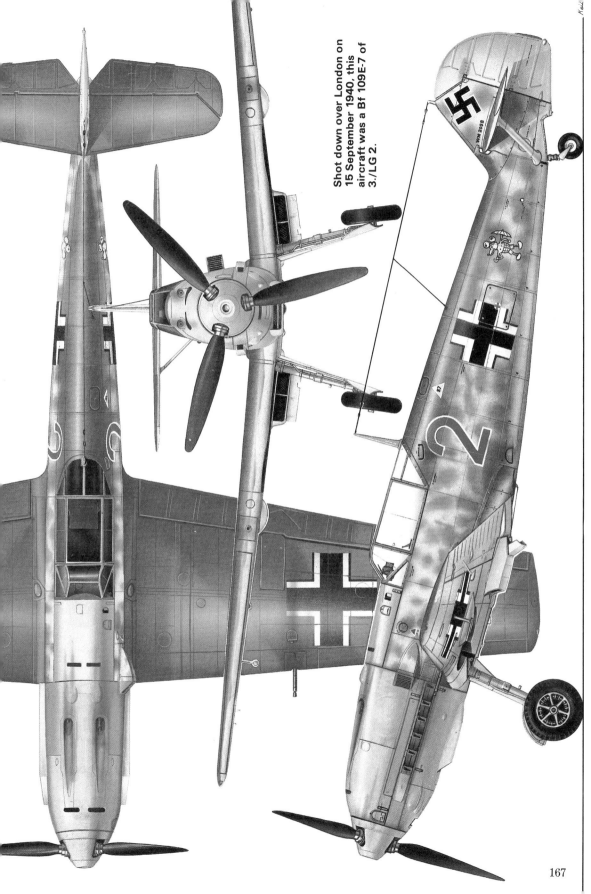

Shot down over London on 15 September 1940, this aircraft was a Bf 109E-7 of 3./LG 2.

Messerschmitt Bf 109

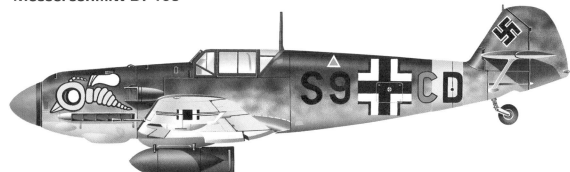

Messerschmitt Bf 109E-4/B of Zerstörergeschwader 1 (Wespen-Geschwader)

with the German attack on Poland, the Luftwaffe had more than 1,000 Bf 109s and the production rate was nearly 140 per month although, surprisingly, this declined by almost 10 per cent over the remaining months of the year. Average monthly production in 1940 increased slightly to around 156 aircraft; since the German considered that the war was virtually over when France collapsed little was done to improve fighter production.

Various combinations of armament had been tried on the Bf 109 since its inception, and the hollow propeller shaft of the Bf 109D series had been designed

A Messerschmitt Bf 109E flies low over the desert, highlighting the excellent camouflage developed for the Luftwaffe in this theatre.

Messerschmitt Bf 109

Messerschmitt Bf 109E-4/B of III/SKG 210 based at El Daba in October 1942

Messerschmitt Bf 109F-4/Trop of II/JG 27, Sanyet, September 1942

Messerschmitt Bf 109F-2/Trop of III/JG 27, Qasaba, autumn 1942

A pair of Bf 109Es over the desert, where they played a great part in the successes of the Luftwaffe, providing much-needed top cover for the Ju 88s attacking the British forces.

Messerschmitt Bf 109

Messerschmitt Bf 109G-2 of 4./JG 54 at Siverskaya, summer 1942, on the northern sector of the Eastern Front

Messerschmitt Bf 109G-6 of IV/JG 5, Petsamo, Soviet Union, winter 1943-4

to take a 20-mm cannon. Tests showed vibration problems and in most cases the engine-mounted cannon was not fitted; similar tests with the Bf 109E showed that the problem still existed and the standard armament of this series was two 20-mm wing cannon and two 7.92-mm (0.31-in) machine-guns in the fuselage above the engine, firing through the propeller arc.

A number of sub-variants entered service, including some tropical versions for the North African campaign, while others included modifications to enable around 551 lb (250 kg) of bombs to be carried. Perhaps the most unusual variant was the Bf 109T, the result of a proposal for a version to be operated from the aircraft-carrier *Graf Zeppelin* which was under construction. In the event the carrier was never completed, and the 60 Bf 109Ts built by Fieseler had their carrier equipment removed. An increase in wing area made this variant particularly suitable for operation from short strips and they served ultimately in Norway and later from Heligoland.

A major airframe redesign led in late 1940 to the appearance of the Bf 109F-1. Four prototypes and 10 pre-production aircraft were built with the 1,350-hp (1007-kW) DB 601E engine in mind, but supplies of this were at least a year late and the first batches of Bf 109Fs to be completed used the DB 601N. It was decided to abandon wing guns in favour of a combination of the two fuselage-mounted 7.92-mm (0.31-in) MG 17 machine-guns and a Mauser cannon firing through the propeller shaft. Earlier vibration problems with this had been cleared, and the first variant to mount the Mauser was the Bf 109F-2 which had a 15-mm cannon; the Bf 109F-3 was similarly fitted while having the DB 601E engine, but the Bf 109F-4 had a 20-mm Mauser. The Bf 109F-5 and Bf 109F-6 were armed and unarmed

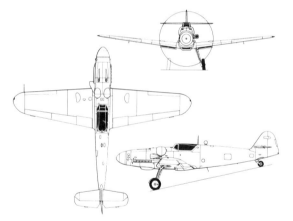

Messerschmitt Bf 109G-14

reconnaissance variants.

By 1941 the Messerschmitt had a rival; the Focke-Wulf Fw 190 was in production not only by its parent company but also by Arado and Ago, both of whom had previously built Bf 109s. Fieseler had also left the programme, leaving only Messerschmitt, Erla and WNF (Austria) building Bf 109s. As development of the Bf 109F series continued, so the weight went up. Many variants and sub-variants appeared before production of the Bf 109F ceased after more than 2,000 had been built, and the final major production model was the Bf 109G, deliveries of which began in 1942.

Powered by a 1,475-hp (1100-kW) DB 605A engine, the Bf 109G-1 had a pressurized cabin, while the Bf 109G-2 was similar but unpressurized. The former had a GM-1 nitrous oxide injection system which gave a considerable boost to its power at high altitude, but

Messerschmitt Bf 109

Messerschmitt Bf 109G of the Luftwaffe, operating in the Mediterranean, 1943

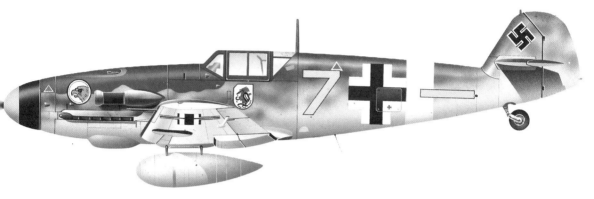

Messerschmitt Bf 109G-2/Trop of II/JG 51 at Casa Zeppera, Sardinia, summer 1943

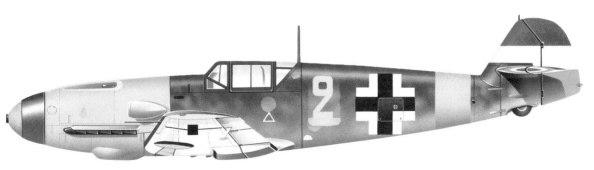

Messerschmitt Bf 109G of a Hungarian Squadron on the Eastern Front

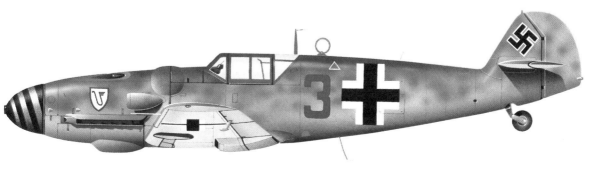

Messerschmitt Bf 109G-10 of I/JG 3 during Operation 'Bodenplatte', Belgium, January 1945

Messerschmitt Bf 109

Messerschmitt Bf 109G-14 of IV/JG 53 during the defence of Germany, 1945

generally this was considered inferior to supercharging.

Various combinations of armament were carried by the different variants; for instance, the Bf 109G-1/Trop used in North Africa had two 13-mm (0.51-in) machine-guns firing through the propeller arc plus the engine-mounted 20-mm cannon, but some of the Bf 109G-6 had a 30-mm Rheinmetall-Borsig MK 108 motor cannon, a lethal weapon with 60 rounds of ammunition —one round was said to be enough to destroy a fighter.

Messerschmitt Bf 109 production in 1942 reached almost 2,700, and manufacture was undertaken in Hungary from 1943, around 600 being built. Experiments were undertaken with Bf 109G-6s in the night-fighter role, but winter conditions made the operations extremely hazardous. In spite of heavy Allied bombing, Bf 109 production in Germany in 1944 reached almost 14,000, and although no complete figures exist on total production it is estimated that some 35,000 were built, a figure second only to the Ilyushin Ir-2/Ir-10 series, which are reported to have reached 42,330. While the Bf 109G was the most prolific version, a few later models should be mentioned.

The Bf 109H was a high-altitude fighter which had a pressurized cockpit, and a DB 605A engine with GM-1 power boosting which gave a ceiling of 47,505 ft (14480 m). Enlarged wing and tail surfaces were fitted and several aircraft were built for evaluation but the type did not enter series production. The designation Bf 109J had been allocated to a licence-built version of the Bf 109G-2 which it was proposed should be built in Spain by Hispano, but this did not fly until 1947. The Bf 109K was the final German production version, being basically improved models of the Bf 109G series from which they differed in detail. The powerplant was the 2,000-hp (1492-kW) DB 605, and variants were as extensive as the ultimate Bf 109K-14 designation would indicate.

Specification
Messerschmitt Bf 109G-6

Type: single-seat fighter

Powerplant: one 1,475-hp (1100-kW) Daimler-Benz DB 605 AM 12-cylinder inverted Vee piston engine

Performance: maximum speed 385 mph (620 km/h) at 22,640 ft (6900 m) or 379 mph (610 km/h) at 13,125 ft (4000 m); service ceiling 37,895 ft (11550 m); range 373 miles (600 km) or 621 miles (1000 km) with 66-Imp gal (300-litre) drop tank

Weight: empty 5,952 lb (2700 kg); maximum take-off 7,055 lb (3200 kg)

Dimensions: span 32 ft 6½ in (9.92 m); length 29 ft 7 in (9.02 m); height 8 ft 6 in (2.59 m); wing area 174.38 sq ft (16.20 m²)

Armament: one 30-mm MK 108 or 20-mm MG 151 cannon firing through propeller shaft and two 0.51-in (13-mm) MG 131 machine-guns above engine, firing through the propeller disc; for special roles some were equipped to carry also two 30-mm or 20-mm cannon beneath the wings

Operators: Luftwaffe, Bulgaria, Croatia, Finland, Hungary, Italy, Romania, Slovakia, Spain, Switzerland

The Bf 109G-12 was a two-seat trainer version modified from earlier G-models.

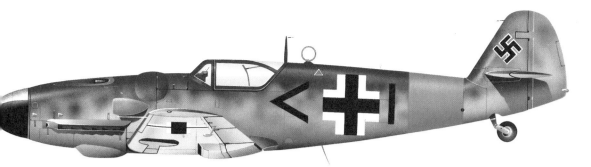

Messerschmitt Bf 109G-14/R2 of III/JG 27, Defence of the Reich

Messerschmitt Bf 109G-10/U4 of the Kroat. Jagdstaffel, Eichwalde, November 1944

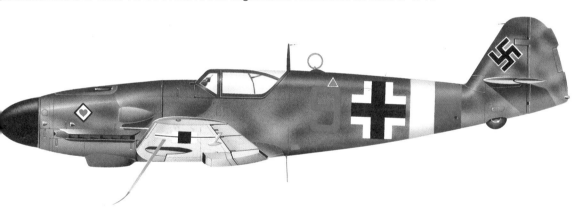

Messerschmitt Bf 109K-4 of II/JG 77 at Bönninghardt, December 1944

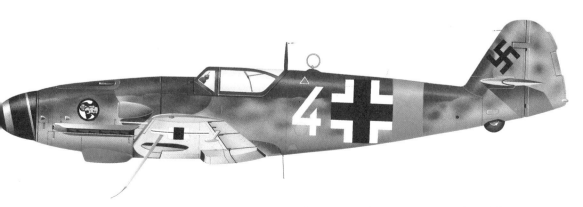

Messerschmitt Bf 109K-4 of I/JG 27, Rheine, December 1944

Messerschmitt Bf 110

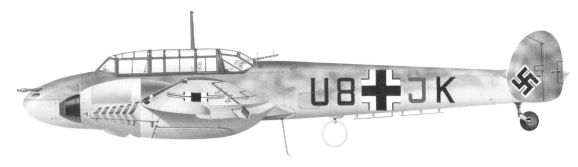

Messerschmitt Bf 110 of 2./ZG 26 'Horst Wessel' summer 1940

History and notes

In the mid-1930s the Luftwaffe was building up its strength with a number of new warplanes, and the Messerschmitt Bf 110 was the company's submission for a twin-engine fighter for which Focke-Wulf and Henschel also prepared designs. They were to be initially heavy fighters, but with the capability of being deployed as high-speed bombers. Changes in requirements for the fighter resulted in Messerschmitt being the only candidate and three prototypes were built, the first flying on 12 May 1936.

The two 910-hp (679-kW) Daimler-Benz DB 600A engines were very unreliable; nevertheless, a speed of 314 mph (505 km/h) was recorded during tests and the general performance was considered reasonable, although swing during take-off and landing gave problems. Engine unreliability plagued the three prototypes, and the pre-production series of Bf 110A-0 aircraft had 680-hp (507-kW) Junkers Jumo 210Da engines which produced a considerable performance penalty, but Messerschmitt was still awaiting the new DB 601A with fuel injection and other improvements. This engine's gestation period stretched even longer, with consequent delays to the Bf 110 programme, and after the fourth pre-production aircraft had been completed in March 1938 the company switched to the Bf 110B, a cleaned-up version with provision for two 20-mm FF cannon in the nose, supplementing the four machine-guns carried by the Bf 110A-0. A total of 45 Bf 110Bs was built, all with Jumo engines: most were Bf 110B-1 aircraft, but some Bf 110B-2 machines had their cannon removed and cameras installed, while the few Bf 110B-3 examples were earlier aircraft modified subsequently for use as trainers.

DB 601A at last became available, resulting in the Bf 110C with some minor airframe changes, including squarer-cut wingtips and new radiators. Ten Bf 110C-0 pre-production aircraft were delivered for evaluation in January 1939, followed closely by Bf 110C-1 production fighters. As production built up, Focke-Wulf and Gotha joined the programme and by the end of August 1939 159 Bf 110Cs had been delivered at a production rate of 30 per month. By the end of the year deliveries had reached 315.

The new fighter proved its abilities in the Polish campaign, and in December 1939 succeeded in destroying

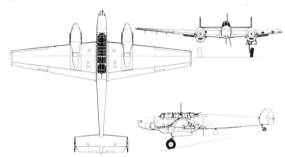

Messerschmitt Bf 110C-3

nine out of 24 Vickers Wellingtons on a mission over the Heligoland Bight. Three other Wellingtons failed to return from this operation and the 50 per cent loss to Bomber Command was a severe blow, but it enhanced the prestige of the Bf 110 as a bomber destroyer.

The high priority afforded to Bf 110 production is reflected in the monthly average of more than 102 aircraft in 1940, but it was in this year, when the Bf 110s began to encounter single-engine fighter opposition, that its shortcomings became apparent, an ominous foretaste of things to come later in the year. While its ability as a day fighter may have been doubted, even in the improved Bf 110C-2 and Bf 110C-3 versions, there were plenty of other roles where it could perform useful tasks.

The Bf 110C-4 with armour for the crew and uprated 1,200-hp (895-kW) DB 601N engines was used as a fighter-bomber and could carry two 551-lb (250-kg) bombs beneath the centre section; in this role it became the Bf 110C-4/B and operated against British shipping in the English Channel in the summer of 1940 with success. The Bf 110C-7 was an improved fighter-bomber with up to 2,205 lb (1000 kg) of bombs, while the Bf 110C-5 was a reconnaissance machine.

A few aircraft were converted as Bf 110D-1/R-1 and Bf 110D-1/R2 aircraft to fly long-range escort missions from Norway with extra jettisonable tanks. However, on their only mission to northern England they were

Right: A Messerschmitt Bf 110 sweeps over the Channel. The type tried to emulate its success over the Low Countries, but it came up against the RAF's Spitfires and Hurricanes—and lost.

Messerschmitt Bf 110

Messerschmitt Bf 110C-2 of I/ZG 52 operating from Charleville, France, June 1940

severely mauled by Supermarine Spitfires and lost seven of their number, some through inability to jettison their tanks, which made them easy prey for the fighters.

As the Battle of Britain began in July 1940, the Bf 110 units were committed to a policy of bringing the RAF fighters to combat, leaving the German bombers to arrive over England while the RAF were refuelling and re-arming. The scheme was a dismal failure, since the Messerschmitts could not match the manoeuvrability of the Hurricanes and Spitfires and were unable to defend themselves sufficiently with only one rear-firing machine-gun. In the resulting battles, the Messerschmitt units suffered very heavy losses (120 in August alone) but such was the shortage of German single-engine fighters that the Bf 110s were kept in service, although switching to fighter-bomber and reconnaissance roles.

As the winter of 1940 drew in, so the Bf 110 was to find itself in a more suitable role, as a night-fighter, although at first the Bf 110Cs had no specialised equipment and had to rely on the crew's eyesight to intercept bombers. An early short-range aid was an infra-red sensor fitted in the nose of the Bf 110D-1/U-1. Systems gradually improved with the setting up of ground control radar stations in mid-1941, but the supposedly much improved Me 210 was expected to be available shortly and production of the Bf 110 was

After the debacle in Britain, the Bf 110 was switched to other theatres where its heavy armament offset its vulnerability to single-engined fighters. These are pictured in the Mediterranean.

Another theatre where the Bf 110 enjoyed some success was North Africa, where the type's good weapons load was put to good use against British forces.

Messerschmitt Bf 110

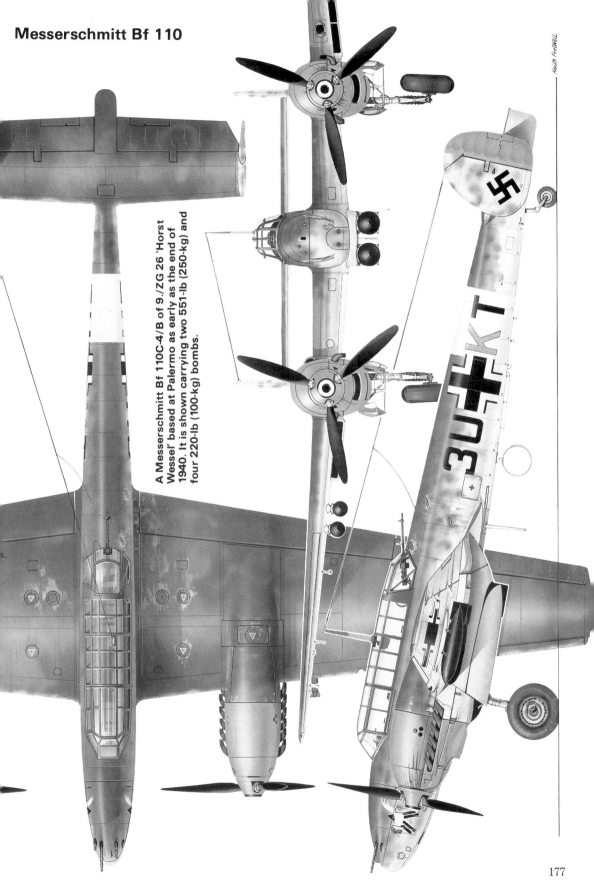

A Messerschmitt Bf 110C-4/B of 9./ZG 26 'Horst Wessel' based at Palermo as early as the end of 1940. It is shown carrying two 551-lb (250-kg) and four 220-lb (100-kg) bombs.

Keith Fretwell

Messerschmitt Bf 110

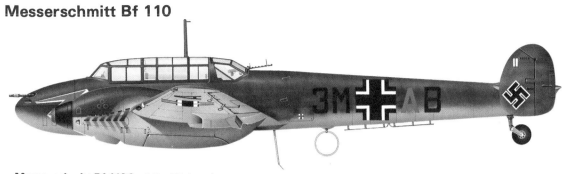

Messerschmitt Bf 110C of the Stabsschwarm (staff flight) I/ZG 2, Amiens, July 1940

considerably cut back. It was an ironic twist of fate that in fact the Me 210 and its developed version the Me 410 were failures, and the Bf 110 continued in production after they were abandoned.

With the phasing out of production of the Bf 110C series in spring 1941, the next series was the Bf 110D, including the Bf 110D-2 long-range fighter-bomber based on the Bf 110D-1/R2, and the Bf 110D-3 convoy escort with special overwater provision and extra fuel. This variant evolved into the Bf 110E-0 pre-production and Bf 110E-1 production aircraft with a bombload of 2,645 lb (1200 kg) and 4,409 lb (2000 kg) respectively, the Bf 110E-2 fighter-bomber and the Bf 110E-3 long-range reconnaissance version with two rearward-firing MG 17 fixed machine-guns.

With the next major sub-type, the Bf 110F, a more powerful engine than the DB 601A or DB 601N of earlier models became available, in the form of the DB 601F which gave 1,350 hp (1007 kW). Extra armour

was installed and a variety of bombs could be carried beneath the wings and fuselage, but the Bf 110F had only been in production for a short time when the type was phased out in favour of the Me 210 in October 1941 only to be phased back in again in the following February, initially as a stop-gap until the Me 210 could be redesigned. New rocket shells which could be used against ground and air targets were tested on a Bf 110F-2; two rocket-launching tubes were mounted beneath each outer wing panel and the weapons were intended to be fired into bomber formations. Also tested was the RZ65 rocket shell, fired from a battery of twelve 73-mm tubes mounted beneath the fuselage but this proved unsatisfactory and was abandoned.

The German authorities were convinced by the *Zerstörer* concept, and the Bf 110 was built in large numbers for the Luftwaffe. The concept proved healthy, but often needed fighter cover.

Messerschmitt Bf 110

Messerschmitt Bf 110C-4/B of 5./ZG 1, Caucasus, October 1942

Messerschmitt Bf 110D-3 of 4./ZG 76 flying from Raschid in support of Iraqi insurgent forces in May 1941

Messerschmitt Bf 110D of I/NJG 3 Catania, Sicily, February 1941

Messerschmitt Bf 110E-1 of an operational conversion unit (Ergänzungszerstörergruppe) based at Deblin-Irena, Poland, summer 1942

Messerschmitt Bf 110

Messerschmitt Bf 110E of 8./ZG 26 at Berca, North Africa in September 1942 armed with MK 101 30-mm cannon

Messerschmitt Bf 110G-2 of 12./NJG 3 based at Stavanger, Norway in the spring of 1945

Final Bf 110F variant was the Bf 110F-4a, which carried a cumbersome array of Lichtenstein intercept radar aerials in the nose and so lost much in performance.

Failure of the Me 210 meant that further development of the elderly Bf 110 had to continue, and the next production model was the Bf 110G-1, a heavy day fighter with 1,475-hp (1100-kW) DB 605B-1 engines. The Bf 110G series went through a mass of subvariants, far too many to describe in detail. The Bf 110G-2/R-1 had a 37-mm cannon in place of the under fuselage bomb racks, and had its two forward firing 20-mm MG 151 cannon removed; one round from the 37-mm cannon could knock out a bomber. The Bf 110G-2/R3 had two 30-mm MK 108 cannon in place of the four 7.92-mm (0.31-in) nose machine-guns, and the Bf 110G-3 was a long-range reconnaissance fighter with cameras replacing its cannon. The final variant was the Bf 110H which was produced in parallel with the Bf 110G from which it differed only in detail, including a strengthened rear fuselage and landing gear.

Total production of the Bf 110 series amounted to about 6,050 aircraft, the last, a Bf 110G, being completed in March 1945. Whatever its faults as a day fighter, it had undoubtedly been a major contributor to Germany's night-fighter defences and outlasted some of its intended replacements such as the He 219.

Specification
Messerschmitt Bf 110G-4/R3
Type: three-seat night fighter
Powerplant: two 1,475-hp (1100-kW) Daimler-Benz DB 601B-1 12-cylinder inverted Vee piston engines
Performance: maximum speed 342 mph (550 km/h) at 22,900 ft (6980 m); cruising speed 317 mph (510 km/h) at 19,685 ft (6000 m); service ceiling 26,245 ft (6780 m); maximum range with drop tanks 1,305 miles (2100 km)
Weight: empty 11,222 lb (5090 kg); maximum take-off weight 21,805 lb (9890 kg)
Dimensions: span 53 ft 3¾ in (16.25 m); length 42 ft

Messerschmitt Bf 110G-4b/R3 of 7 Staffel, III/NJG 4, based in northern Germany in 1944

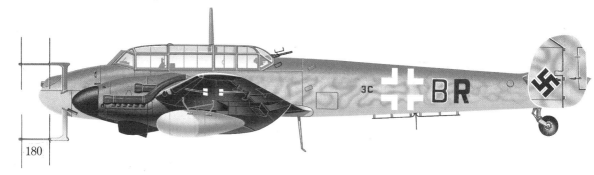

Messerschmitt Bf 110

9¾ in (13.05 m); height 13 ft 8½ in (4.18 m); wing area 413.35 sq ft (38.40 m²)
Armament: two 30-mm MK108 cannon and two 20- mm MG 151 cannon in nose, and two 7.92-mm (0.31-in) MG 81 machine-guns on mounting in rear cockpit
Operators: Luftwaffe, Hungary, Italy, Romania

Messerschmitt Me 163 Komet

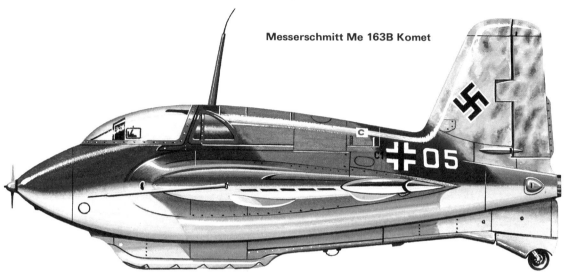

Messerschmitt Me 163B Komet

History and notes

There can be little doubt that if the Messerschmitt Me 163 rocket-powered fighter had been available to the Luftwaffe in quantity a year earlier, the Allied daylight bombing programme would have proved even costlier than it was. With an extra year of development behind it, the Me 163's problems, particularly those concerned with handling its unstable mixture of rocket fuels, might well have been solved, but the whole programme was at the edge of a new technology range, and time was not on Germany's side.

Research had been proceeding in Germany into the possibility of rocket-powered aircraft since the 1920s and Dr Alexander Lippisch, who had been working on tailless sailplane designs, produced the DFS 194 glider in a basic layout which was to be developed into the Me 163. Lippisch and his team joined Messerschmitt in January 1939 and began work on adapting the DFS 194 airframe to take an 882-lb (400-kg) thrust Walter rocket motor. This motor had already flown in the experimental rocket-powered He 176, but that programme had been unsatisfactory. The DFS 194, on the other hand, reached a speed of 342 mph (550 km/h) during tests and this led to increased momentum in the programme, Messerschmitt receiving an order for six prototypes designated Me 163A.

The first prototype was tested originally as a glider, towed behind a Messerschmitt Bf 110, and its flying qualities were good, the few problems being easily ironed out. In the summer of 1941 two of the prototypes were taken to Peenemünde for powered

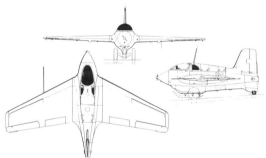

Messerschmitt Me 163B Komet

trials with the new Walter HWK RII-203b rocket motor, which gave 1,653-lb (750-kg) thrust, and the Me 163 was soon attaining speeds of up to 550 mph (885 km/h). Since only a small amount of rocket fuel could be carried there was a danger of running out before higher speeds could be attained but on one occasion, after being towed to a height of 13,125 ft (4000 m), test pilot Heini Dittmar cast off, fired the engine and accelerated to reach the remarkable speed of 623.85 mph (1003.9 km/h) before suffering a loss of stability as a result of compressibility effects. This phenomenon was to become well known later as aircraft approached the speed of sound. Dittmar corrected the situation but a redesign of the wing was undertaken to combat this fault.

There was, in fact, more danger at this stage of the programme in the instability of the fuel, which was a

Messerschmitt Me 163 Komet

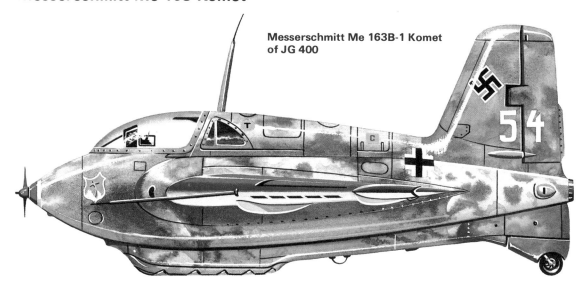

Messerschmitt Me 163B-1 Komet of JG 400

mixture of 80 per cent hydrogen peroxide with oxyquinoline or phosphate (T-Stoff) and an aqueous solution of calcium permanganate (Z-Stoff). An imbalance of these fuels in the combustion chamber could cause an explosion and occasionally did; a replacement for Z-Stoff using a different catalyst (30 per cent hydrazine hydrate solution in methanol) was called C-Stoff and was developed for use in the Walter RII-211 which, in its production form for the later Me 163B was the HWK 109-509A.

Since the Me 163 had to be as light as possible, in order to get the maximum performance from its very limited fuel load, the weight penalty of retractable landing gear was not acceptable. Thus, the take-off was made using a jettisonable two-wheel dolly, the aircraft landing on a retractable skid beneath the forward fuselage plus the tailwheel. The method caused problems, since take-offs had to be made directly into wind; if a concrete runway was to be used and there was a crosswind it was impossible to get airborne as the aircraft would not keep straight below the speed at which the rudder became operative. A subsequent modification to couple rudder control to rocket ignition partially cured this.

Following the six Me 163A prototypes, a pre-production series of 10 Me 163A-0 aircraft was built by Wolf Hirth, the sailplane company, and these were used as training gliders. However, considerable redesign took place before the operational Me 163B Komet (comet) flew. Six prototypes and 70 production models were ordered, but troubles with the new rocket motor held up the programme, and fuel consumption was almost double the calculated figure. Production was subcontracted to a number of component manufacturers and the parts were assembled in a Black Forest factory under the supervision of Klemm Technik GmbH, although this company had many problems since the sub-contractors were not accustomed to close-tolerance work.

First production deliveries of Me 163B-1a interceptors began in May 1944, and the type saw action for the first time on 28 July, when five Me 163s from 1./JG 400, the first operational unit, ineffectively attacked a formation of Boeing B-17s near Merseburg. Their difficulties can be appreciated when it was realised that approaching the target at around 559 mph (900 km/h) when the bombers were travelling at 250 mph (402 km/h), the closing speed allowed the attacker only a three-second burst from a slow-firing cannon before he had to break away. Because of the poor results with the MK 108 cannon an alternative weapon had to be found.

One answer was certainly unusual; the SG 500 Jagdfaust consisted of five vertically mounted firing tubes in each wing root, each containing a 50-mm shell. The system fired in a salvo and was activated by the shadow of the target passing over a light cell (unfortunate if it happened to be your wingman) and the Me 163 merely had to fly at high speed beneath the bomber formation, when the armament was activated automatically. The Jagdfaust system was fitted to 12 Me 163Bs but, although these were not issued for operations, this unlikely weapon destroyed a B-17 on one occasion.

In 1944, to help convert the dwindling supply of pilots to the Me 163, a tandem trainer variant designated Me 163S was developed, an adaptation of the Me 163B with ammunition, T-Stoff tanks and other items removed to make way for the extra seat. The Me 163S was flown only as a glider and few were converted.

Production of the Me 163B-1a ended in February 1945 after almost 400 of all variants had been built. Projected developments included the Me 163C and Me 163D; the former was a modification of the Me 163B with an auxiliary cruising chamber to improve endurance, a new centre-section and a more streamlined fuselage with a blister canopy. Three Me 163C-1a aircraft were built, but only one was flown. The Me 163D was further refined and had retractable tricycle landing gear. One prototype was built and, since Junkers had been

Messerschmitt Me 163 Komet

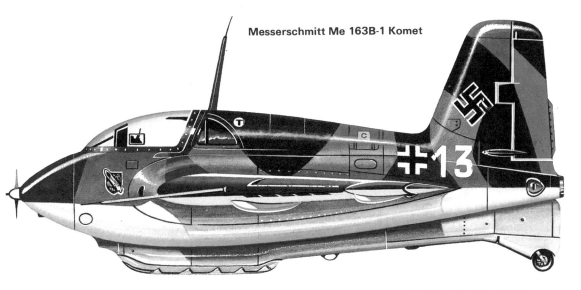

Messerschmitt Me 163B-1 Komet

tasked with development and series production of this model, it was for a while known as the Ju 248 before reverting to a Messerschmitt designation as the Me 263. It did not enter production, the prototype being captured by the Russians who fitted it with new straight wings and modified tail surfaces, flying it in 1946 as the I-270(ZH), but it was soon abandoned.

Mention should be made of a licence-built version of the Me 163B, the Mitsubishi Ki-200 (J8M1), which was to be built in Japan with Mitsubishi and Yokosuka building the HWK 509A motor. Loss of the pattern aircraft on a ship en route to Japan left the Japanese with only an instruction manual, and it is to their credit that they began design of an airframe based on the Me

163B. The first aircraft flew in July 1945 but was destroyed when the motor failed. Several others were built but the programme was terminated by the end of the war.

Specification
Messerschmitt Me 163B-1
Type: single-seat interceptor fighter
Powerplant: one 3,750-lb (1700-kg) thrust Walter HWK 509A-2 bi-fuel rocket motor

The diminutive Me 163 Komet did not alter the war's history, but was an imaginative idea. Principal drawback to the concept was the dangerous fuel.

Messerschmitt Me 163 Komet

Performance: maximum speed 596 mph (960 km/h) at 32,810 ft (10000 m); service ceiling 39,700 ft (12100 m); time to ceiling 3 minutes 30 seconds; maximum powered endurance 7 minutes 30 seconds
Weights: empty 4,200 lb (1905 kg); maximum loaded 9,061 lb (4110 kg)

Dimensions: span 30 ft 7 in (9.32 m); length 19 ft 2 in (5.84 m); height 9 ft 1 in (2.77 m); wing area 199.14 sq ft (18.50 m²)
Armament: two 20-mm MG 151 cannon or two 30-mm MK 108 cannon in wing roots
Operator: Luftwaffe

Messerschmitt Me 210/410

History and notes

Confidence in the original Bf 110 long-range fighter and bomber-destroyer concept led at the beginning of 1938 to Messerschmitt being asked to design an eventual successor. The result was the Messerschmitt Me 210 which first flew on 5 September 1939, powered by two 1,050-hp (783-kW) Daimler-Benz DB 601A engines; it proved to be extremely unsatisfactory, being difficult to handle and suffering from extreme instability.

The prototype had twin fins and rudders, and these were replaced by a single unit, the aircraft flying on 23 September. A slight improvement was apparent, but in spite of a number of modifications carried out on the two prototypes they continued to display poor handling characteristics, being prone to stalling and spinning. In view of these problems it is difficult to understand why production was allowed to begin, but by mid-1940 a first batch of airframes was in final assembly.

The first 15 Me 210s were earmarked as test aircraft and on 5 September 1940 the programme suffered the first of a number of crashes when the second prototype broke up during diving trials; fortunately the pilot escaped. Such were the problems encountered that eight pre-production Me 210A-0 and 13 production Me 210A-1 aircraft were added to the test programme, but in spite of this very little improvement was evident, and it was obvious that only major design changes would have any chance of correcting the faults. At this stage such a move would have caused an unacceptable delay in the production programme, so deliveries began and 64 were supplied during 1941 in two variants, the Me 210A-1 destroyer-bomber which was armed with two 20-mm MG 151/20 cannon and two 7.92-mm (0.31-in) MG 17 machine-guns, and the Me 210A-2 fighter-bomber which had a maximum bombload of 4,409 lb (2000 kg). However, on 14 April 1942, after about 200 Me 210s had been delivered (this number including two Me 210B-0 pre-production and two Me 210B-1 production reconnaissance aircraft), construction was halted in favour of a resumption of manufacture of the Bf 110 to give time to try to resolve some of the Me 210's shortcomings. The stability problem was solved finally by introducing automatic wing leading-edge slots and redesign of the rear fuselage, which was lengthened by 3 ft 1½ in (0.95 m) and made deeper. The improvements were tested and the design was submitted with the proposal that the 1,750-hp (1305-kW) Daimler-

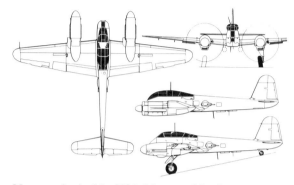

Messerschmitt Me 410A-1 (upper side view:

Benz DB 603A engine should be used to provide better performance. This appealed to the RLM, as a solution of this kind would allow a number of unfinished Me 210 airframes to be used, and Messerschmitt was given the go-ahead and the designation 410 assigned to the revised design.

Before describing the Me 410, mention should be made of the Me 210C, a version of the earlier model which was built in Hungary by the Danube Aircraft Factory. Messerschmitt had supplied jigs and tools, and a new factory had been built for production when the German decision to stop its own Me 210 programme was made. The Hungarians nevertheless decided to proceed and one of the pre-production Me 210A-0s had been fitted with 1,475-hp (1100-kW) DB 605B engines as a prototype for the Me 210C; the engines were licence-built by Manfred Weiss.

The Me 210C had the wing slots and new rear fuselage, and production deliveries from the Hungarian factory started at the beginning of 1943. They were split on the basis of one-third to the Royal Hungarian air force and two-thirds to the Luftwaffe. Production was slow to develop, but by early 1944 the first Hungarian units had been formed. Production ended in Hungary in March 1944, by which time 267 Me 210Cs had been built in two variants, the Me 210C-1 reconnaissance/bomber-destroyer aircraft, and the Me 210Ca-1 bomber-destroyer/dive-bomber. In contrast with the Luftwaffe, Hungarian pilots liked the Me 210 and used it as a close-support aircraft and dive-bomber.

The Me 410 prototype was a converted Me 210A-0, and several other Me 210As were generally brought

Messerschmitt Me 210/410

Messerschmitt Me 410A Hornisse of 9./ZG 1, flown from Gerbini in 1943

up to Me 410 standard but with DB 601F engines. Improvements in handling characteristics made the Me 410 far more acceptable to the Luftwaffe which received the first five Me 410A-1 light bombers in January 1943, this version being armed with two MG 151/20 cannon, two MG 17 machine-guns, and two 13-mm (0.51-in) MG 131 machine-guns mounted one each side of the fuselage in an electrically-powered barbette; maximum internal bombload was 4,409 lb (2000 kg). Demand for these more effective aircraft built up rapidly, with the result that Messerschmitt's Augsburg production line was supplemented by a second line when Dornier entered the programme in early 1944. As Me 410A production expanded a number of sub-variants entered service, including the photoreconnaissance Me 410A-1/U1, Me 410A-1/U2 heavy-fighter, and the Me 410A-1/U4 specialised bomber-destroyer, its armament including a 50-mm BK 5 gun mounted beneath the fuselage. The Me 410A-1 was followed into service by the Me 410A-2 heavy fighter which included two 30-mm cannon in its armament, and also built in sub-variants, including the Me 410A-2/U1 which was similar to the Me 410A-1/U1, the Me 410A-2/U2 radar-carrying night-fighter, and an Me 410A-2/U4 bomber-destroyer similar to the Me 410A-1/U4, and the last of the A-series, the Me 410A-3 reconnaissance aircraft equipped with three cameras.

In April 1944 the first of the improved B-series were delivered, introducing the 1,900-hp (1417-kW) DB 603G engine, and produced in Me 410B-1 and Me 410B-2 sub-variants that were basically similar to those of the A-series. The Me 410B-3 was a reconnaissance version similar to the Me 410A-3, the Me 410B-5 a torpedo and anti-shipping bomber that was in the test stage when the war ended, and the Me 410B-6 a specialised anti-shipping variant, built in small numbers, which was equipped with FuG 200 Hohentwiel search radar, and had armament comprising two 20-mm Mg 151/20 cannon, two 30-mm MK 103 cannon, and two 13-mm (0.51-in) MG 131 machine-guns. Other projects failed to materialize.

As the Allies stepped up the daylight bombing offensive in 1944 the Me 410s were engaged increasingly in home defence and accounted for a number of heavy bombers, although they also suffered heavily at the hands of the escorting fighters. Production was finally phased out in September 1944 after 1,160 Me 410s had been built, and although the type had not achieved the successes hoped for it had been a vast improvement on the disastrous Me 210.

Messerschmitt Me 410s were used for high-speed reconnaissance as well as for heavy fighter/ *Zerstörer* missions.

Messerschmitt Me 210/410

Specification
Messerschmitt Me 410A-1/U2
Type: two-seat heavy fighter
Powerplant: two 1,850-hp (1380-kW) Daimler-Benz DB 603A 12-cylinder inverted Vee piston engines
Performance: maximum speed 388 mph (625 km/h) at 21,980 ft (6700 m); cruising speed 364 mph (585 km/h); service ceiling 32,810 ft (10000 m); maximum range 1,050 miles (1690 km)
Weights: empty equipped 16,574 lb (7518 kg); loaded

21,276 lb (9650 kg)
Dimensions: span 53 ft 7¾ in (16.35 m); length 40 ft 11½ in (12.48 m); height 14 ft 0½ in (4.28 m); wing area 389.67 sq ft (36.20 m²)
Armament: four 20-mm MG 151 cannon and two 7.92-mm (0.31-in) MG 17 machine-guns firing forward, plus two 13-mm (0.51-in) MG 131 machine-guns in remotely-controlled rear-firing barbettes
Operators: Luftwaffe, Hungary

Messerschmitt Me 262

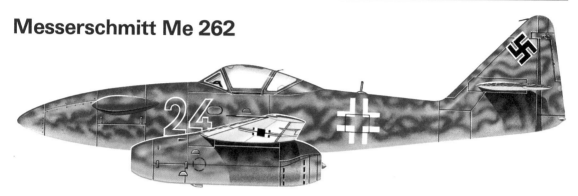

Messerschmitt Me 262A-1A/U3 of Einsatzkommando Braunegg, northern Italy, March 1945

History and notes
As the world's first jet fighter to enter combat, the Messerschmitt Me 262 earned itself a place in history, being the most advanced aircraft of its period to fly and to achieve operational status. That it did not make a bigger impact was not due to any airframe short-comings, but to engine problems, interference from government departments and, in the later stages, from Hitler himself.

In autumn 1938 Messerschmitt was given a contract to design an airframe around the axial-flow turbojets which BMW was developing. At that time the engines were expected to be ready by December 1939, each developing some 1,323-lb (600-kg) thrust.

Messerschmitt's submission, designated originally P.1065, envisaged engines in the wing roots (they were later fitted beneath the wings) and tailwheel landing gear; a speed of 599 mph (900 km/h) was expected and the company received an order for three prototypes plus a static test airframe under the designation Me 262. At the same time the Heinkel company was working independently on a twin-jet fighter, the He 280.

BMW was having problems with its engine, which on bench tests was only giving 573-lb (260-kg) thrust; the rival Junkers Jumo 004 engine also had problems, so the prototype Me 262 flew on 18 April 1941 with a single Jumo 210G piston engine in the nose. Although acceleration was poor, general handling was good and testing continued in this form to prove various systems before the first BMW 003 turbojets were delivered in

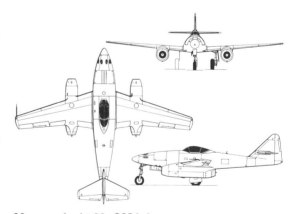

Messerschmitt Me 262A-1a

November 1941. These were installed in the Me 262 prototype but the Jumo piston engine was retained, fortunately as it turned out since both turbojets failed just after take-off and the pilot managed to keep the aircraft airborne only long enough to complete a circuit and land.

The compressor blade failures which had caused the engines to seize necessitated a complete redesign, but the Me 262 could not wait and, since Junkers had overcome most of their problems, the Jumo 004A was chosen as the powerplant. As this engine was heavier and larger than the BMW engine the Me 262 airframe had to be modified, and the third prototype flew with

Messerschmitt Me 262

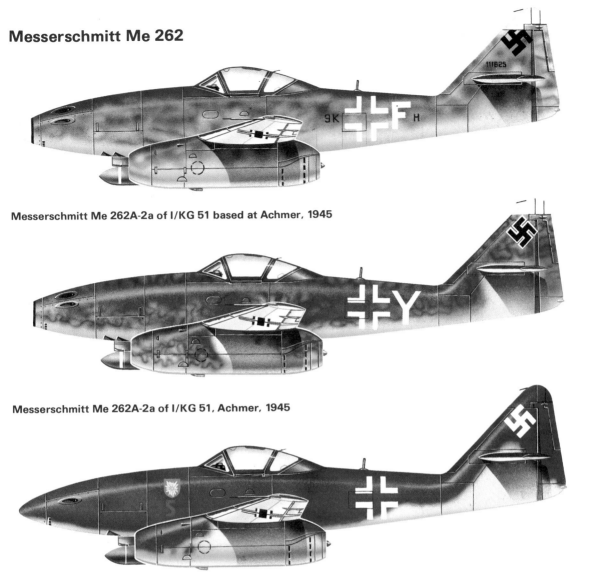

Messerschmitt Me 262A-2a of I/KG 51 based at Achmer, 1945

Messerschmitt Me 262A-2a of I/KG 51, Achmer, 1945

Messerschmitt Me 262A-2a/U1, Erprobungskommando (test detachment) Schenk in the autumn of 1944

two 1,852-lb (840-kg) thrust Jumo 004As on 18 July 1942.

Test flying continued, although there was a knack in getting airborne, because with the tailwheel landing gear the elevators were ineffective in the tail-down position. It was necessary during the take-off run to touch the brakes lightly, which brought the tail up and so made the elevators effective. This was obviously unacceptable in service, and tricycle landing gear with a non-retracting nose unit was designed and fitted to the fifth prototype, by which time two further prototypes and 15 Me 262A-0 pre-production aircraft had been ordered. The landing gear proved satisfactory, and a fully retractable system was introduced on the sixth prototype, which also had 1,984-lb (900-kg) thrust Jumo 0048-1 engines in redesigned nacelles.

Following a demonstration before Hitler in November 1943 the Me 262 was given a top-priority production status, but a number of problems both with the airframe and engine still had to be resolved using 12 prototypes and test aircraft. A hold-up in the supply of engines, which were also being built for the Arado Ar 234 bomber, meant that pre-production Me 262A-0 airframes had to be stockpiled, but 16 of these were delivered in April 1944, followed by a further seven in the following month.

Hitler's early interest in the Me 262 envisaged it as a fighter-bomber after he had been told that it could carry bombs although the necessary equipment had not been fitted. Messerschmitt was not keen to divert research in this direction but was given little choice in the matter, being told to go ahead with adapting the aircraft as a 'super-speed bomber'.

Various bomb racks were tried with combinations of loads up to 2,205 lb (1000 kg); there was even a bomb with a wooden wing, towed at the end of a 20 ft (6.10 m)

Messerschmitt Me 262

tube beneath the aircraft's tail, taking off on a jettison-able dolly. The intention was to dive towards the target and release the bomb and its towbar, the latter being jettisoned along with the bomb's wings. Tests were not promising and the concept was abandoned.

First production Me 262A-1a fighters began to enter service in July 1944 and were basically similar to the late pre-production aircraft. Later sub-variants included the Me 262A-1a/U1 which differed by having two MK 103, two MK 108 and two MG 151/20 cannon in the nose; Me 262A-1a/U2 bad-weather fighter in which the standard radio was supplemented by the FuG 125; and Me 262A-1a/U3 unarmed reconnaissance aircraft with two Rb 50/30 cameras. The subsequent Me 262A-2a production bomber version was virtually identical except for having bomb racks to carry one 1,102-lb (500-kg) or two 551-lb (250-kg) bombs. Variants included the Me 262A-3a with extra armour protection and Me 262A-5a armed reconnaissance aircraft with two MK 108 cannon and two drop tanks.

While the Me 262A series had all been single-seaters, there was an obvious requirement for a two-seat conversion trainer, and this was met by the Me 262B-1a. The second seat replaced the rear main fuel tank, so auxiliary tanks were fitted below the forward fuselage; 15 were built before the obvious potential of the type as a night-fighter brought the conversion of 262B-1a aircraft on the production line to Me 262B-1a/U1 standard. A few were built, fitted with radar and homing equipment, but they proved so effective that they were succeeded by the Me 262B-2a, designed from the outset as a night-fighter. This version, which had a larger fuselage permitting extra fuel to be carried, began flight trials in March 1945, but the end of hostilities came before it could be developed.

This version of the Messerschmitt Me 262 was the Me 262B-1a/U1 night fighter, equipped with SN-2 Lichtenstein radar and the addition of a second seat for the radar operator.

The Me 262C was an experimental variant flown in February 1945 using auxiliary rocket boosting, but it was not developed beyond three prototypes.

Total production of the Me 262 amounted to about 1,430, and there is no doubt that if the type had not been held back through engine and political problems it could well have tipped the scales in Germany's favour by breaking up the Allied day bombing programme. Me 262s using a salvo of 24 R4M missiles against a bomber formation and following these up with 30-mm cannon fire could be lethal, but although the Me 262s were considerably faster than the Allied fighters, a number were destroyed in combat by the superior manoeuvrability of Allied piston-engine aircraft.

Specification
Messerschmitt Me 262A-1a
Type: single-seat interceptor fighter
Powerplant: two 1,984-lb (900-kg) thrust Jumo 004B turbojet engines
Performance: maximum speed 540 mph (870 km/h) at 19,685 ft (6000 m); service ceiling 37,565 ft (11450 m); range on internal fuel 652 miles (1050 km)
Weights: empty 8,378 lb (3800 kg); loaded 14,110 lb (6400 kg)
Dimensions: span 40 ft 11½ in (12.48 m); length 34 ft 9½ in (10.60 m); height 12 ft 7 in (3.84 m); wing area 233.58 sq ft (21.70 m²)
Armament: four 30-mm MK 108 cannon in nose
Operator: Luftwaffe

Messerschmitt Me 262

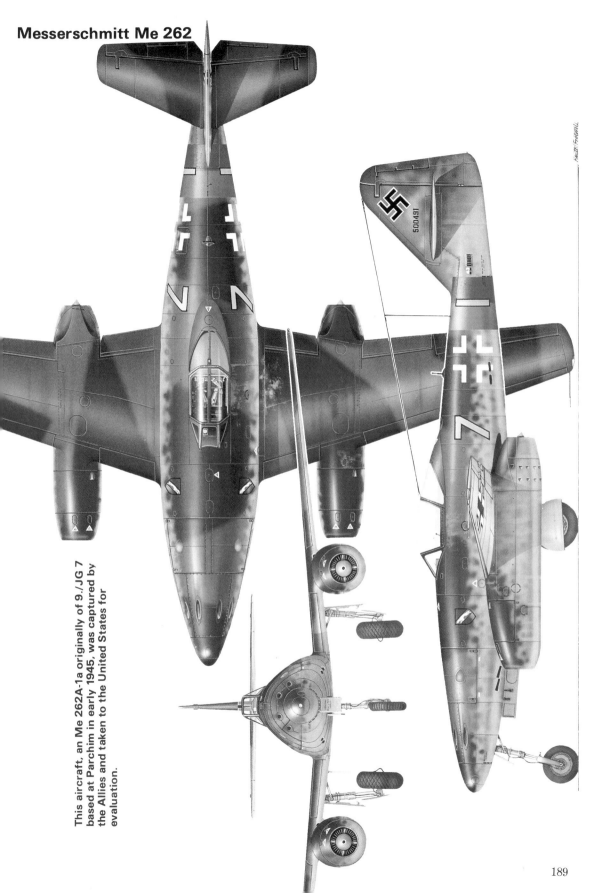

This aircraft, an Me 262A-1a originally of 9./JG 7 based at Parchim in early 1945, was captured by the Allies and taken to the United States for evaluation.

Messerschmitt Me 321/323

History and notes

The giant Messerschmitt Me 321 transport glider and its powered derivative, the Me 323, must be considered as one of Germany's most unusual designs during World War II. The basic type had its origin in the plan to invade the UK, following the fall of France, when the English Channel seemed to provide the only serious obstacle to an invasion. Since the RAF had proved that strenuous opposition would be mounted against any operation of this nature, speed in getting equipment across the Channel was of paramount importance, and a scheme was drawn up for the use of giant gliders to carry tanks, guns and men.

Although Operation 'Sealion', as the planned invasion was codenamed, had been postponed by Hitler in October 1940, in favour of an all-out attack on the USSR, there was still an urgent need to continue design of the glider. In less than a week a broad specification was drawn up, following which Messerschmitt and Junkers were given a mere 14 days for initial design studies to be submitted, each manufacturer also being instructed to acquire materials for the construction of 100 gliders.

It says much for the capability of the design teams that both met the deadline and were then instructed to double the initial order. The Junkers project, the Ju 322, was built only in prototype form and had such poor handling qualities that it was scrapped. However, Messerschmitt's design, the Me 321, was rolled out in 14 weeks from the programme go-ahead; at the time it was the world's second largest aircraft with a span of 180 ft 5¼ in (55.00 m). The cargo hold had a capacity of 3,814 cu ft (108.00 m³) and was 36 ft 1 in (11.00 m) long, 10 ft 10 in (3.30 m) high and 10 ft 4 in (3.15 m) wide. It had a capacity for loads of up to 44,092 lb (20000 kg), almost double its empty weight, and could carry an estimated 200 troops.

A jettisonable take-off dolly was used for flight testing, with the aircraft landing on sprung skids. Up to eight 1,102-lb (500-kg) thrust hydrogen peroxide rockets, giving 30 seconds of power, could be attached to assist the take-off.

A Junkers Ju 90 was used as tug for the first flight on 25 February 1941, when the Me 321 was found to handle satisfactorily although, not surprisingly, the controls were heavy. The tow plane proved barely capable of hauling the glider, through a lack of power, and the twin-fuselage Heinkel He 111Z conversion then being undertaken had not been completed. Further tests were carried out using a triple tow by three Bf 110s, an extremely complex and dangerous operation which resulted in a number of accidents. The worst of these occurred during trials with 120 troops on board, when the booster rockets beneath one wing of the glider failed to ignite; the Me 321 swerved, causing the three Bf 110s to collide and the whole group to crash with the loss of 129 lives.

By late summer 1941 the Messerschmitt plants had delivered the first 100 Me 321A-1 gliders and had begun

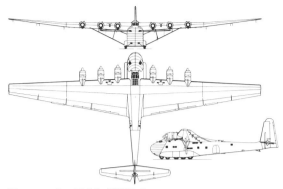

Messerschmitt Me 323D-1

deliveries of the Me 321B-1 with a wider flight deck to accommodate a pilot and co-pilot (the earlier versions had been for single pilot operation). As the gliders were delivered, units were formed, still with trios of Bf 110s, and moved to the Eastern Front where they performed several missions with varying success. It soon became apparent that a powered transport was required and Messerschmitt was therefore tasked with investigating this possibility. Meanwhile, the last of 200 Me 321s was delivered in early 1942, by which time the first He 111Z tugs had flown and proved satisfactory.

Messerschmitt converted the two prototype Me 321s as prototypes for the powered version, the Me 323C with four second-hand Gnome-Rhône radial engines and the Me 323D with six similar engines. The intention was that the Me 323C would be towed off the ground by a trio of Bf 110s and would then be able to cruise under its own power, whereas the Me 323D would not require tug assistance. Because of towing accidents, the Me 323D was chosen for production, and modifications were made to the design before manufacture began of a pre-series batch of 10 Me 323D-0 aircraft. Rocket-assisted take-off was still available and the production Me 323D-1 and Me 323D-2, which differed only in detail, could each carry a 21,495-lb (9750-kg) cargo load over 621 miles (1000 km). As a troop transport each type could carry 120 with full equipment, and a detachable floor could be removed to accommodate 60 stretcher patients with medical attendants. What was considered to be heavy and adequate defensive armament comprised five 7.92-mm (0.31-in) MG 15 machine-guns in the nose and upper fuselage, with up to 10 MG 34 infantry machine-guns of similar calibre in the fuselage sides.

Production deliveries began in August 1942, and two months later two Ju 52/3m groups were re-equipped with these giant transports. In November the Me 323s began Mediterranean operations in support of the Axis forces in North Africa, and the first aircraft were lost shortly afterwards to British fighters. Operating in groups of up to 100 transports (together with the Ju 52/3m aircraft) and with fighter escort, the Me 323s at first enjoyed immunity from attacks, but gradually the Allied aircraft began to take their toll and in mid-April

Messerschmitt Me 321/323

Messerschmitt Me 323E of I/TG5 serving behind the southern sector of the Eastern Front in late 1943

1943 a formation of 16 Me 323s was attacked by RAF fighters and lost 14 of its number. The low speed of these giant transports and their inability to adopt evasive manoeuvres when attacked meant it was essential to increase defensive armament, and the Me 323D-6 began this trend by uprating the five MG 15s to five 13-mm (0.51-in) MG 131 machine-guns. It was followed by the Me 323E-1 which introduced two HDL 151 gun turrets with a 20-mm MG 151/20 cannon in each, with an increase of two crew members to operate them; and the Me 323E-2 with the same armament, but which housed the MG 151/20s in low-drag EDL 151 gun turrets. However, these increases in armament proved to be ineffective, and attempts were then made to increase performance, a number of Me 323E-2s being given six 1,350-hp (1007-kW) Junkers Jumo 211R engines, with the resulting conversion redesignated Me 323F-1. This also failed to reduce the vulnerability of these transports to any worthwhile degree, and plans to develop the Me 323E-2/WT with an armament of 11 cannon and four machine-guns, and the redesigned Gnome-Rhône-powered Me 323G were abandoned. Me 323s were withdrawn from the Mediterranean theatre where losses were unacceptably high and transferred for use on the Eastern Front. Production ended in April 1944, after a total of 198 had been built, and it

would seem that their operational deployment ended at about the same time or very shortly afterwards.

Specification
Messerschmitt Me 323E-2

Type: heavy general-purpose transport
Powerplant: six 1,140-hp (850-kW) Gnome-Rhône 14N 14-cylinder piston engines
Performance: maximum speed 149 mph (240 km/h) at 4,920 ft (1500 m); cruising speed 140 mph (225 km/h) at sea level; service ceiling 14,760 ft (4500 m); maximum range 808 miles (1300 km)
Weights: empty equipped 64,066lb (29060 kg); maximum take-off 99,210 lb (45000 kg)
Dimensions: span 180 ft 5½ in (55.00 m); length 93 ft 6in (28.50 m); height 31 ft 6 in (9.60 m); wing area (28.50 m); height 31 ft 6 in (9.60 m); wing area 3,229.28 sq ft (300.00 m²)
Armament: two 20-mm MG 151 cannon in turrets on wings, two 13-mm (0.51-in) MG 131 machine-guns in nose doors and five more rear-firing from beam positions and rear of flight deck
Operator: Luftwaffe

Developed from the Me 321 glider, the Me 323 featured six radial engines. The type was easy meat for fighters, and so operated behind the front line.

Mitsubishi A5M

History and notes

In February 1934 the Imperial Japanese Navy drew up its specification for a new single-seat fighter, the requirements including a challenging maximum speed of 217 mph (350 km/h) and a rate of climb that would take it to 16,405 ft (5000 m) in only 6 minutes 30 seconds. Mitsubishi took up this challenge with a design team headed by Jiro Horikoshi, later to gain his place in aviation history for the remarkable A6M Zero, working against difficult odds to gain what was seen by Mitsubishi to be a potentially important contract. All single-seat fighters then in service with the navy were of biplane configuration so the team's monoplane layout was seen as something of a gamble, especially as an earlier monoplane design from Mitsubishi had failed to gain the navy's approval. Horikoshi's design for the prototype united an inverted gull wing to a narrow-section fuselage, the gull wing being chosen to combine a large-diameter propeller with main landing gear units that would be as short as possible. The tail unit was conventional, the powerplant was a 550-hp (410-kW) Nakajima Kotobuki (congratulation) 5 radial engine, and the pilot was accommodated in an open cockpit directly over the wing. Designated Mitsubishi Ka-14, it was flown for the first time on 4 February 1935 and demonstrated very quickly that it was more than capable of meeting the navy's requirements. In early tests a maximum speed of 280 mph (450 km/h) was recorded, and the climb to 16,405 ft (5000 m) was achieved in only 5 minutes 54 seconds. There were, however, aerodynamic shortcomings and so the second prototype was given a conventional cantilever low-wing with split trailing-edge flaps; at the same time a 560-hp (418-kW) Kotobuki 3 engine was installed. Four

other prototoypes were completed with varying powerplants, and it was with the low-wing configuration of the second prototype combined with a 585-hp (436-kW) Kotobuki 2 KAI-1 engine that the Mitsubishi A5M1 was ordered into production as the Navy Type 96 Carrier Fighter Model 1.

The A5M1 of 1936 was the Japanese navy's first monoplane fighter, the basic model being armed with two forward-firing 7.7-mm (0.303-in) machine-guns, but the A5M1a variant carried two 20-mm Oerlikon FF cannon. The A5M2 of 1937 was regarded as the most important fighter aircraft in the navy's inventory during the Sino-Japanese War, the performance of the initial A5M2a being improved, by comparison with the A5M1, by installation of the 610-hp (455-kW) Kotobuki 2-KAI-3 engine; the ensuing generally similar A5M2b differed primarily by the introduction of more power, in the shape of the 640-hp (477-kW) Kotobuki 3, and early production aircraft had an enclosed cockpit. This did not prove popular with its pilots, and late-production A5M2b fighters reverted to open cockpit configuration. Under the designation A5M3 two experimental aircraft were built and these, similar to earlier open-cockpit production aircraft, each had a 610-hp (455-kW) Hispano-Suiza 12Xcrs 'moteur canon' engine installed, with a 20-mm cannon firing through the propeller hub. Final production version was the A5M4 with the uprated Kotobuki 41 radial engine, and under the designation A5M4-K a total of 103 was completed as tandem two-

This Mitsubishi A5M4b clearly shows the elliptical wing which gave it good performance for its day. This 1930s type saw service during World War II, especially as a fighter-trainer.

Mitsubishi A5M

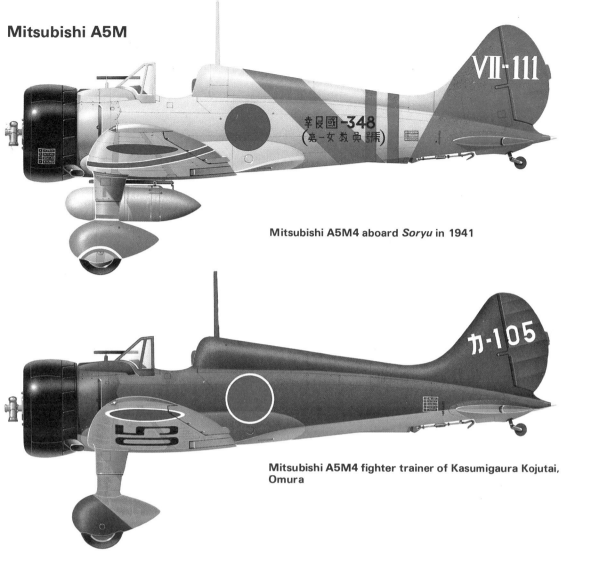

Mitsubishi A5M4 aboard *Soryu* in 1941

Mitsubishi A5M4 fighter trainer of Kasumigaura Kojutai, Omura

seat trainers. At the outbreak of war in the Pacific the A5M4 was then the navy's standard fighter, but this situation was of only short duration for, when confronted by Allied fighter aircraft, the A5M's performance was soon found to be inadequate; by the summer of 1942 the type had been relegated to second-line duties.

The A5M had also come very close to being procured by the Japanese army, for the remarkable performance of the second prototype had resulted in a smilar prototype being evaluated by the army under the designation Ki-18. Flown in competitive evaluation against the Kawasaki Ki-10-I biplane then entering service it was found to be considerably faster but inferior in manoeuvrability. Two modified and re-engined Ki-18s were submitted for further testing under the designation Ki-33, but still lacking in manoeuvrability failed to gain an army contract.

Production of all versions of the A5M, which was allocated the Allied codename 'Claude', reached a total of 1,094, built by Mitsubishi (791), the Omura Naval Air Arsenal (264) and Watanabe (39). In the final stages of the Pacific war A5M4s and A5M4-Ks were used in a *kamikaze* role against Allied shipping operating off Japan's coastal waters.

Specification
Mitsubishi A5M4

Type: single-seat ship-based fighter
Powerplant: one 710-hp (529-kW) Nakajima Kotobuki 41 9-cylinder radial piston engine
Performance: maximum speed 273 mph (440 km/h) at 9,840 ft (3000 m); service ceiling 32,150 ft (9800 m); maximum range 746 miles (1200 km)
Weights: empty 2,681 lb (1216 kg); maximum take-off 3,759 lb (1705 kg)
Dimensions: span 36 ft 1 in (11.00 m); length 24 ft 9¼ in (7.55 m); height 10 ft 6 in (3.20 m); wing area 191.60 sq ft (17.80 m²)
Armament: two fixed forward-firing 7.7-mm (0.303-in) machine-guns, and two 66-lb (30-kg) bombs
Operator: Japanese Navy

Mitsubishi A6M Zero-Sen

Mitsubishi A6M2 of the 12th Combined Kokutai, Hankow region of China, winter 1940-1

History and notes

Without doubt the most famous Japanese single-seat fighter aircraft of World War II, the Mitsubishi Zero (Type 0 Fighter) was designed by Jiro Horikoshi to meet an Imperial Japanese Navy requirement for an A5M replacement. A cantilever low-wing monoplane of all-metal construction, except for fabric-covered tail control surfaces, the aircraft had retractable tailwheel landing gear, an enclosed cockpit directly over the wing, and in prototype form was powered by a 780-hp (582-kW) Mitsubishi MK2 Zuisei (auspicious star) radial engine. In this form it was flown for the first time on 1 April 1939 and flight testing showed that this A6M1, and a similarly-powered second prototype flown in October 1939, more than satisfied the requirements of the navy's specification except in terms of maximum speed. To overcome this shortcoming the navy requested that the design should be modified to incorporate as powerplant the 925-hp (690-kW) Nakajima NK1C Sakae (prosperity) 12 radial engine and, although somewhat larger and heavier, this was installed successfully in a third prototype which had the company designation A6M2. First flown on 18 January 1940 this combination proved so successful that, following service trials of this and a similar fourth prototype, the navy arranged with Mitsubishi on 21 July 1940 to supply 15 pre-production A6M2s for operational evaluation in China. Then, on the last day of the month, the type was ordered into production with the official designation Navy Type 0 Carrier Fighter Model 11.

The pre-production A6M2s used operationally in China proved almost unbelievably successful for, despite their small numbers, they were used extensively and as the first production aircraft became available they were reinforced. Large numbers of enemy aircraft were destroyed with only a handful of A6M2s lost to defensive fire from the ground. So devastating was the apparent potential of these aircraft that the American Claire Chennault, who as early as 1937 had been an adviser to the Chinese air force, sent a report on their capability to USAAF headquarters. It can only be assumed that this was ignored completely, for at the outbreak of the Pacific war the performance of the A6M came as a complete surprise to the Allies, unaware that the Japanese nation was so advanced in aircraft design and construction.

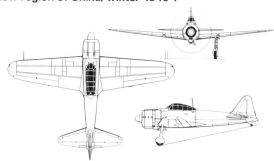

Mitsubishi A6M2 Zero-Sen

Mitsubishi's manufacture of A6M2s was supplemented by that of Nakajima, a production line being established at the company's Koizuma factory, and by the time of the attack on Pearl Harbor on 7 December 1941 more than 400 aircraft had been delivered to the navy; these comprised the initial production A6M2 Model II with Nakajima NK1C Sakae 12 powerplant and armament comprising two 7.7-mm (0.303-in) machine-guns in the fuselage and two wing-mounted 20-mm Type 99 cannon; and the A6M2 Model 21 which differed by having manually-folding wingtips to simplify carrier stowage. Six months before the Pacific war started, Mitsubishi had flown an improved version, the A6M3 which introduced the 1,130-hp (843-kW) Nakajima Sakae 21 engine with a two-stage supercharger, and had clipped wings to avoid the production complication of the folding wingtips introduced on the A6M2. This was duly ordered into production as the Navy Type 0 Fighter Model 32, and was followed in early 1942 by the A6M2-K two-seat trainer based on the A6M2. Operational experience showed that the A6M3 Model 32 had inferior range capability compared with its predecessor, resulting in a reversion to the full span wing and restoration of the manually folding wingtips in the A6M3 Model 22.

Allocated the Allied codename 'Zeke', during 1941 and early 1942 this amazing fighter seemed to fill the skies over the Pacific, but after the Battle of Midway in June 1942 Allied fighters began gradually to regain the initiative; by 1943 it was essential to improve the Zero's capabilities, leading to the major production version, the A6M5. It had been preceded by two A6M4 prototypes which were conversions from A6M2s, intro-

Mitsubishi A6M Zero-Sen

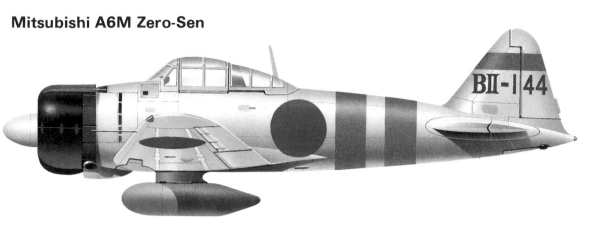

Mitsubishi A6M2 of the fighter complement aboard Hiryu, during the attack on Pearl Harbor, December 1941

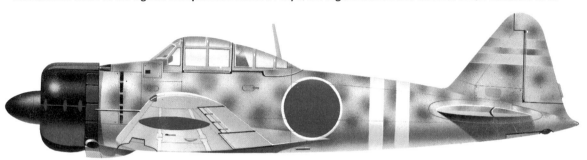

Mitsubishi A6M2 of the 6th Kokutai, Rabaul, New Britain, November 1942

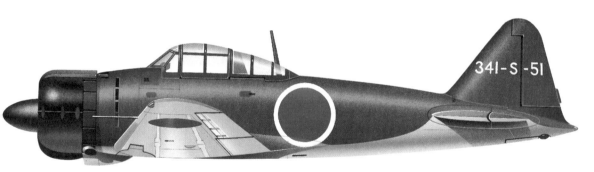

Mitsubishi A6M2 of 402nd Chutai, 341st Kokutai, Clark Field, Manila, Philippines, winter 1944

ducing an experimental turbocharged Sakae engine to give better performance at altitude, but problems with development of this engine compelled Mitsubishi to retain the Sakae 21 for the A6M5, ordered into production under the designation Navy Type 0 Carrier Fighter Model 52. This version had a redesigned clipped non-folding wing with rounded wingtips, introduced individual exhaust ejectors on the Sakae 21 to provide some thrust augmentation, and was armed by two 20-mm Type 99 cannon and two 7.7-mm (0.303-in) machine-guns. Sub-variants included the A6M5a with a modified wing to accept belt-fed (instead of magazine-fed) cannon; the similar A6M5b which had one 7.7-mm (0.303-in) machine-gun replaced by one of 13.2-mm (0.52-in) calibre and introduced armoured glass in the

cockpit canopy: the A6M5c with three 13.2-mm (0.52-in) machine-guns and two 20-mm cannon; the A6M5d-S night-fighter conversion of the A6M5 with a 20-mm cannon mounted obliquely in the rear fuselage: plus a small number of A6M5-K two-seat trainers.

Development continued with the conversion of an A6M5 airframe to A6M6 standard by the installation of a Sakae 31 engine with water-methanol injection, making possible a maximum speed of 345 mph (555 km/h); production A6M6c aircraft, which began to enter service in late 1944, also introduced self-sealing fuel tanks. Operational units carried out field conversions of many aircraft to carry a 551-lb (250-kg) bomb on the drop tank-mounting, enabling them to be used as fighter-bombers, and the final production A6M7 which

Mitsubishi A6M Zero-Sen

Symbolic of the fierce air war fought over the islands of the Pacific, this A6M lies wrecked after having been brought down by American forces.

entered service in mid-1945 was modified specifically for this role. In addition to the installation of a special bomb rack, it had a reinforced tailplane and underwing attachments for two drop tanks. The A6M8c represented a final attempt to extend the life and capability of the Zero, two prototypes converted from A6M7 airframes having a redesigned and strengthened forward fuselage for installation of the 1,560-hp (1163-kW) Mitsubishi MK8P Kinsei 62 radial engine. Service testing showed this to be a formidable fighter and some 6,300 were ordered, but none was completed before the end of the war.

Production of A6Ms continued until the chaotic conditions in Japan virtually brought everything to a halt, but even then the type was still being deployed in large numbers in the last desperate struggles against the Allies, many of the early versions then being used in a *kamikaze* role. When the production lines finally came to a halt a total of 10,449 A6Ms had been built by Mitsubishi (3,879) and Nakajima (6,570).

Specification
Mitsubishi A6M6c Model 53c

Type: single-seat interceptor fighter/fighter-bomber
Powerplant: one 1,130-hp (843-kW) Nakajima Sakae 31 14-cylinder radial piston engine
Performance: maximum speed 346 mph (557 km/h) at 19,685 ft (6000 m); cruising speed 201 mph (323 km/h); service ceiling 35,105 ft (10700 m); maximum range 1,118 miles (1800 km)
Weights: empty 4,175 lb (1894 kg); maximum take-off 6,504 lb (2950 kg)
Dimensions: span 36 ft 1 in (11.00 m); length 29 ft 9 in (9.07 m); height 11 ft 5¾ in (3.50 m); wing area 229.28 sq ft (21.30 m²)
Armament: three 13.2-mm (0.52-in) machine-guns (one in the upper fuselage decking and two wing-mounted) and two wing-mounted 20-mm Type 99 cannon, plus underwing launch rails for eight 22-lb (10-kg) or two 132-lb (60-kg) air-to-air rockets
Operators: China (a small number of captured aircraft), Japanese Navy

Known to the Allies as 'Zeke', but to pilots by the more usual name of 'Zero', the A6M was a feared aircraft due to its high manoeuvrability.

Mitsubishi A6M Zero-Sen

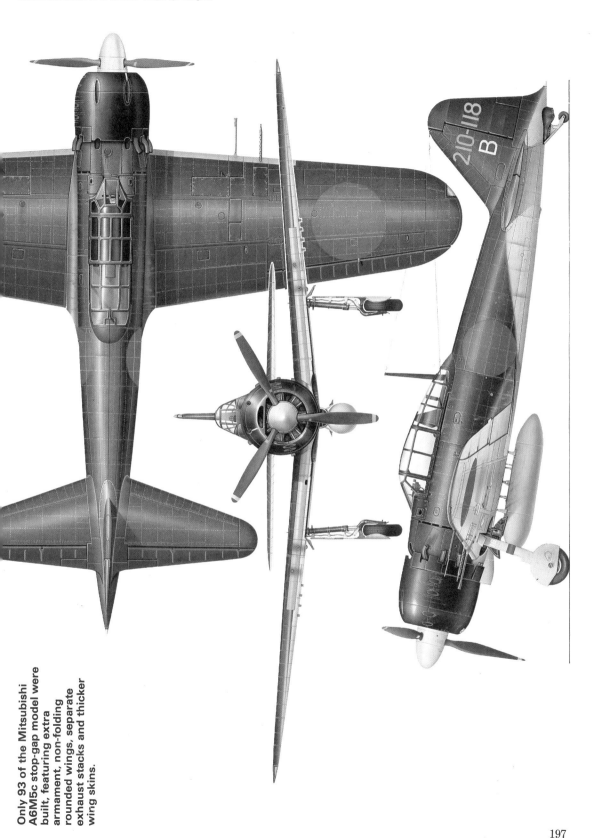

Only 93 of the Mitsubishi A6M5c stop-gap model were built, featuring extra armament, non-folding rounded wings, separate exhaust stacks and thicker wing skins.

Mitsubishi F1M

History and notes

Under the designation Mitsubishi Ka-17 the company designed during 1935 a two-seat aircraft to meet an Imperial Japanese Navy requirement for a catapult-launched short-range observation floatplane. A very clean equal-span single-bay biplane, the Ka-17 had a large central float and strut-mounted stabilising floats beneath the lower wings, adjacent to the wingtips. The fuselage accommodated the crew of two in tandem open cockpits, the pilot seated forward beneath a large cut-out in the trailing edge of the upper wing. Powerplant of the first prototype, flown during June 1936, was an 820-hp (611-kW) Nakajima Hikari (splendour) 1 radial engine, but early tests showed that performance on the water left much to be desired. After four F1M1 prototypes had been completed a number of changes were introduced to eradicate the shortcomings revealed in flight testing, including redesigned wings and increased vertical tail surface area, plus installation of the more powerful Mitsubishi Zuisei (holy star) 13 radial engine. Subsequent company testing showed that the remedial action had been successful, and service trials led to the type being ordered into production as the Navy Type 0 Observation Seaplane Model 11, Mitsubishi designation F1M2. A total of 1,118 was built by Mitsubishi (528) and the Sasebo Naval Air Arsenal (590), and in addition to the standard production aircraft, a small number was converted to serve as two-seat trainers under the designation F1M2-K.

Allocated the Allied codename 'Pete', and used extensively from both ships and shore bases, because of their excellent performance F1M2s found employment in the unexpected roles of fighter and dive-bomber, as well as their intended use for coastal patrol, convoy escort and reconnaissance. In addition to those delivered to the Japanese navy, a small number was supplied to Thailand for use on coastal patrol duties.

Specification
Mitsubishi F1M2

Type: two-seat patrol/reconnaissance floatplane
Powerplant: one 875-hp (652-kW) Mitsubishi Zuisei 13 14-cylinder radial piston engine
Performance: maximum speed 230 mph (370 km/h) at 11,285 ft (3440 m); service ceiling 30,970 ft (9440 m); range 460 miles (740 km)
Weights: empty 4,251 lb (1928 kg); maximum take-off 5,622 lb (2550 kg)
Dimensions: span 36 ft 1 in (11.00 m); length 31 ft 2 in (9.50 m); height 13 ft 1½ in (4.00 m); wing area 317.89 sq ft (29.54 m²)
Armament: two fixed forward-firing 7.7-mm (0.303-in) machine-guns and one gun of same calibre on trainable mounting in rear cockpit, plus two 132-lb (60-kg) bombs
Operators: Japanese Navy, Thailand

Due to its excellent performance, the Mitsubishi F1M found itself performing bombing and even fighter missions from both ship and shore.

Mitsubishi G3M

Mitsubishi G3M3 of the Takao Kokutai, 21st Koku Sentai, operating from Hanoi in March 1941

History and notes

Successful demonstration by Mitsubishi of its Ka-9 twin-engine long-range reconnaissance aircraft during 1934 led to the company designing and developing a twin-engine bomber/transport under the initial company designation Mitsubishi Ka-15. A cantilever mid-wing monoplane with wings tapering in thickness and chord from wing root to wingtip, a tail unit incorporating twin fins and rudders, retractable tailwheel landing gear and two 750-hp (559-kW) Hiro Type 91 engines, the prototype was flown for the first time during July 1935. A total of 21 prototypes was built (eight with an unglazed nose) and several engine/propeller combinations were evaluated. Service trials left little doubt that Mitsubishi had developed an excellent aircraft with exceptional range capability, and in June 1936 the type entered production with the official designation Navy Type 96 Attack Bomber Model 11, Mitsubishi designation G3M1. This first production version was powered by two 910-hp (679-kW) Mitsubishi Kinsei 3 radial engines and had a defensive armament of three 7.7-mm (0.303-in) machine-guns, one each in two dorsal and one ventral turret, all three turrets being retractable. However, only 34 G3M1 production aircraft were built before availability of 1,075-hp (802-kW) Kinsei 41 or 42 radials gave the promise of even better performance. The resulting G3M2 Model 21 differed from the early production version by the installation of these engines and by having increased fuel capacity. They soon

demonstrated their capability, on 14 August 1937, when a force of G3M2s based on Taipei, Taiwan, attacked targets 1,250 miles (2010 km) distant in China, recording simultaneously the world's first trans-oceanic air attack.

Subsequent production, which eventually totalled 1,048 aircraft built by Mitsubishi (636) and Nakajima (412), included the G3M2 Model 22 in which the five-men crew of all earlier versions was increased to seven to provide additional gunners to cope with armament that comprised one 20-mm cannon and four 7.7-mm (0.303-in) machine-guns; and the generally similar G3M2 Model 23 which introduced Kinsei 51 engines and increased fuel capacity. A number of G3M1s were converted for service as military transport aircraft under the designation G3M1-L, being provided with two 1,075-hp (802-kW) Kinsei 45 engines, and from 1938 about 24 G3M2s were converted for transport use by civil operators, these being designated Mitsubishi Twin-Engined Transport. Two other transport models were produced later in the war, when the First Naval Air Arsenal at Kasumigaura converted a number of G3M1s and G3M2s to L3Y1 Model 11 and L3Y2 Model 12 Navy Type 96 Transports respectively. Both incorporated cabin windows, a door on the port side

The Mitsubishi G3M, known as 'Nell' in the bomber version, proved highly successful during the early war in the Pacific.

Mitsubishi G3M

and were armed by a single 7.7-mm (0.303-in) machine-gun. When deployed throughout the war zone they were allocated the Allied codename 'Tina', and all bomber versions had the codename 'Nell'.

Mitsubishi G3Ms are remembered for their part in a number of important engagements, but almost certainly best known was the attack made on the British battleship HMS *Prince of Wales* and battle-cruiser HMS *Repulse* on 10 December 1941, just three days after the initial attack on Pearl Harbor. The British vessels were steaming off Malaya, believing they were out of range of shore-based aircraft, when they were caught by a force of G3Ms with a smaller number of G4Ms and sunk. The type remained in service until the end of the Pacific war, but by 1943 most were being used in second-line roles.

Specification
Mitsubishi G3M3 Model 23

Type: twin-engine long-range bomber
Powerplant: two 1,300-hp (969-kW) Mitsubishi Kinsei 51 14-cylinder radial piston engines
Performance: maximum speed 258 mph (415 km/h) at 19,360 ft (5900 m); cruising speed 183 mph (295 km/h) at 13,125 ft (4000 m); service ceiling 33,725 ft (10280 m); maximum range 3,871 miles (6230 km)
Weights: empty 11,552 lb (5240 kg); maximum take-off 17,637 lb (8000 kg)
Dimensions: span 82 ft 0¼ in (25.00 m); length 53 ft 11¾ in (16.45 m); height 12 ft 1¼ in (3.69 m); wing area 807.32 sq ft (75.00 m²)
Armament: one 20-mm Type 99 cannon in a dorsal turret and four 7.7-mm (0.303-in) machine-guns (one each in a dorsal turret, lateral side blisters, and one fired through the cockpit windows), plus one 1,764-lb (800-kg) torpedo or an equivalent weight of bombs carried beneath the fuselage
Operator: Japanese Navy

Mitsubishi G4M

History and notes
In September 1937 Mitsubishi received from the Imperial Japanese Navy a specification for a new land-based bomber. This presented more than the average challenge, demanding speed and range performance better than that of the G3M1, which had entered service in the previous year, and which was then regarded as probably the world's best land-based naval bomber. The achievement of such performance required high-powered engines and a clean low-drag design of minimum structural weight, and these factors contributed to what were later considered to be the shortcomings of the Mitsubishi G4M, which was otherwise an outstanding design.

A cantilever mid-wing monoplane with conventional tail unit and retractable tailwheel landing gear, the G4M had a fuselage of basically circular cross-section. This was of sufficient diameter to accommodate an uncluttered bomb bay beneath the wing centre-section, and was intended also to make it easy for the crew to move around or interchange in flight. With range being vital the wings were designed to provide integral tanks, but as weight saving was also vital these had no armour or self-sealing protection. For the same reason there was no armour protection for the crew, and defensive weapons and ammunition for them were kept to a minimum. Ironically, by late 1942 when the Allies began pushing the Japanese back towards their homeland, the range capability of the G4M was progressively less important and the type became easy prey for Allied fighters, so easily converted from a potent bomber into a useless flaming torch. It was not until it was virtually too late that production versions were delivered for service with armour protection, self-sealing fuel tanks and more effective defensive

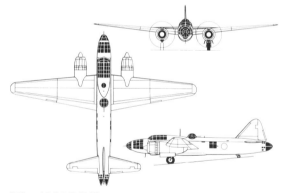

Mitsubishi G4M2

armament.

The first of two prototypes of the G4M1 was flown initially on 23 October 1939 on the power of two 1,530-hp (1141-kW) Mitsubishi Kasei 11 radials, and as a result of subsequent flight testing only minor modifications were required. Service trials progressed equally well, and production was authorised during 1940 under the official designation Navy Type 1 Attack Bomber Model 11, the first operational deployment of the type being made during the summer of 1941. The G4M1 Model 12 which followed on the production lines retained the same defensive armament of four 7.7-mm (0.303-in) machine-guns and one 20-mm cannon, but introduced the MK4E Kasei 15 engine which, with the same take-off output as the Kasei 11, had a higher performance rating at altitude. An important new version was flown in late 1942, the G4M2 Model 22 incorporating several modifications to improve performance and capability, including a laminar-flow wing,

Mitsubishi G4M

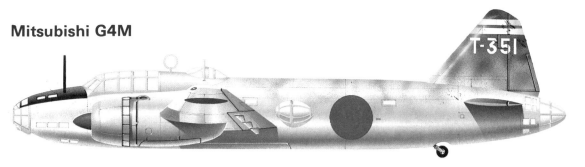

Mitsubishi G4M1 of Takao Kokutai at Rabaul, October 1942

Mitsubishi G4M1 of 705th Kokutai, Rabaul, 1943

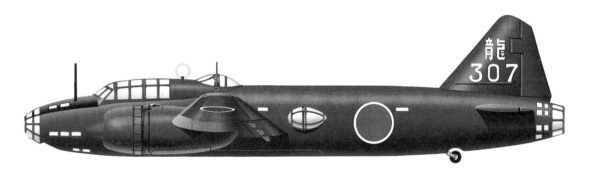

Mitsubishi G4M1 of 761st Kokutai, Kanoya, 1943

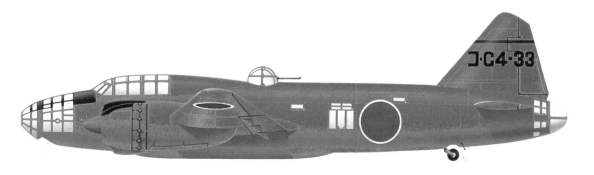

Mitsubishi G4M2a of Koku Gijitsu Sho (Air Technical Arsenal) for research duties

Mitsubishi G4M

enlarged tailplane, increased nose glazing, and the installation of 1,800-hp (1342-kW) Mitsubishi MK4P Kasei 21 engines. By comparision with the G4M1, armament of the initial G4M2 differed by the addition of a second 20-mm cannon, but variants included the G4M2 Model 22A with two 7.7-mm (0.303-in) machine-guns and four 20-mm cannon, and the generally similar G4M2 Model 22B which differed only in the type of cannon installed. The G4M2a Model 24 was a revised version of the Model 22, introducing 1,825-hp (1361-kW) Mitsubishi MK4T Kasei 25 engines and bulged bomb bay doors; the G4M2a Model 24A and Model 24B were variants that were armed similarly to the Model 22A and Model 22B respectively, and the Model 24C carried the same armament as the Model 24B, plus an additional 13-mm (0.51-in) machine-gun in the nose.

In attempts to give the G4M better performance a number of experimental variants were built with different powerplant: they included the single G4M2b Model 25 with 1,795-hp (1339-kW) Mitsubishi MK4V Kasei 27 engines, two G4M2c Model 26s with turbo-charged 1,825-hp (1361-kW) MK4T-B Ru Kasei 25b Ru engines, and one G4M2d Model 27 which had two 1,825-hp (1361-kW) MK4T-B Kasei 25b radials. The designation G4M2e Model 24J was applied to a fairly large number of G4M2a Model 24B and Model 24C aircraft modified by the removal of their bomb bay doors to carry an MXY7 Ohka piloted missile but, slow and heavy when carrying this weapon, the G4M2e was an easy target for Allied fighter aircraft. On 21 March 1945, when acting as carriers on the first Ohka sortie, 16 were shot down before they could launch their missiles.

During the last months of the war, G4Ms were modified to carry the Yokosuka MXY7 Ohka piloted bomb over the American fleets.

The final attempt to make the G4M more combat-worthy resulted in the G4M3 Model 34, the first of three prototypes being completed in January 1944. This introduced a revised wing structure to incorporate self-sealing tanks, armour protection for the crew and a revised tail unit, but retained the powerplant, armament and bomb bay doors of the G4M2a Model 24. Limited production of this version began in November 1944, but only 60 had been completed when the war ended. Variants of the G4M3 included an ASW/transport G4M3a Model 34a which was not built, and two experimental G4M3 Model 36 aircraft which had the turbocharged powerplant of the G4M2c Model 26.

In the early development stage of the G4M the Japanese navy had an urgent requirement for a heavily-armed escort fighter, and Mitsubishi accordingly devised such an aircraft from the basic G4M. Designated G6M1 it preceded the G4M into production, but when operational use showed it to be unsuitable for its escort task construction ended after only 30 had been built. They were converted subsequently for use as G6M1-K trainers and G6M1-L2 transports. Including prototypes, Mitsubishi built a total of 2,416 G4Ms, plus the 30 generally similar G6Ms.

Allocated the Allied codename 'Betty', the type served the Japanese navy from the beginning to the end of the Pacific war and was involved in momentous events. Just three days after Pearl Harbor G4M1s

Mitsubishi G4M

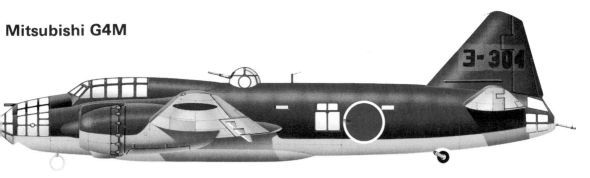

Mitsubishi G4M3 of the Yokosuka Kokutai based at Atsugi in September 1945

had been a component of the force which sank the British battleship HMS *Prince of Wales* and battle-cruiser HMS *Repulse*; they took part in the first air raid on Darwin, Australia; two carried Admiral Isoroku Yamamoto and his staff, the man who had foreseen the requirement for such an aircraft, when they were intercepted and destroyed by Lockheed P-38 Lightnings over Bougainville on 18 April 1943; they were modified as carriers for the MXY7 Ohka piloted missile; and, on 19 August 1945 two more G4M1s carried the Japanese surrender delegation to Ie-Shima, en route to discuss the final requirements for their nation's unconditional surrender.

Specification
Mitsubishi G4M3 Model 34
Type: twin-engine long-range bomber
Powerplant: two 1,825-hp (1361-kW) Mitsubishi

MK4T Kasei 25 14-cylinder radial piston engines
Performance: maximum speed 292 mph (470 km/h) at 16,895 ft (5150 m); cruising speed 195 mph (315 km/h) at 13,125 ft (4000 m); service ceiling 30,250 ft (9220 m); maximum range 2,694 miles (4335 km)
Weights: empty 18,409 lb (8350 kg); maximum take-off 27,558 lb (12500 kg)
Dimensions: span 82 ft 0¼ in (25.00 m); length 63 ft 11¾ in (19.50 m); height 19 ft 8¼ in (6.00 m); wing area 841.01 sq ft (78.13 m²)
Armament: four 7.7-mm (0.303-in) machine-guns (two in the nose and two in beam positions) and two 20-mm Type 99 cannon (one each in dorsal and tail turrets), plus one 1,764-lb (800-kg) torpedo or up to 2,205 lb (1000 kg) of bombs
Operator: Japanese Navy

Mitsubishi J2M Raiden

History and notes
Although a product of the same design team, headed by Jiro Horikoshi, that had given the Imperial Japanese Navy its important A6M Zero, the Mitsubishi J2M was not to enjoy the same degree of success. The very different purpose for which its specification was written probably had some bearing on this, for the J2M was the first single-seat fighter to be procured by the navy for the specific role of interception. The specification was drawn up at a time when Japan was anxious to establish the so-called Greater East Asia Co-Prosperity Sphere and there may well have been a realisation that captured territory would need quick-response active defence. Consequently, the new fighter was required to climb to 19,685 ft (6000 m) for an interception in about 5 minutes and to have a speed of some 373 mph (600 km/h) at that altitude. The resulting J2M1 proto-types were of cantilever low-wing monoplane configu-ration with a conventional tail unit and retractable tailwheel landing gear. Construction was all-metal, with fabric-covered control surfaces, but the high performance requirement meant that a powerful engine was essential. Because of demands on engine production choice was limited, and selection of the large-diameter 1,430-hp (1066-kW) Mitsubishi Kasei (Mars) 13 radial

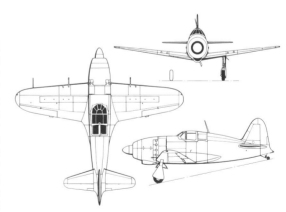

Mitsubishi J2M3 Raiden

engine meant that extra effort was needed to keep fuselage drag as low as possible. This factor explains the unusual installation of the engine, with an extension shaft between it and the reduction gear so that the nose entry could be of minimum diameter.

The first of the prototypes was flown on 20 March 1942, but although testing showed that the aircraft handled easily there were problems with the landing gear mechanism and pilots complained that the low-

Mitsubishi J2M Raiden

drag curved windscreen distorted the view. As testing continued it was found that the J2M could not meet the climb and high speed requirements. To gain the required performance improvement the fourth airframe was modified to accept the more powerful MK4R-A Kasei 23a engine and, at the same time, the windscreen was modified to incorporate optically flat panels. In this form the aircraft was designated J2M2 and it was this version that was accepted for production by the navy in October 1942 under the official designation Navy Interceptor Fighter Raiden Model 11. But despite the improvements the development and production of this fighter continued to be dogged by problems; it was not until December 1943 that the type began to enter service. By then the J2M3 version was beginning to come off the production line, and this was the most extensively built, about 260 being completed. It differed from the J2M2 by detail improvements to rectify some of the shortcomings, but particularly in revision of the armament, with the fuselage-mounted machine-guns removed and the cannon supplemented by two extra and faster-firing wing-mounted 20-mm cannon; a later variant, designated J2M3a, had all four of the wing-mounted cannon of the Mk 2 faster-firing type. The urgent need to improve high-altitude performance led first to the construction of two J2M4 Model 34 prototypes which introduced the turbocharged 1,820-hp (1357-kW) Mitsubishi MK4R-C Kasei 23c engine, and testing showed that this version was capable of a speed of 362 mph (583 km/h) at 30,185 ft (9200 m), but unreliability of the turbochargers led to development of this version being abandoned. Instead, work was concentrated on the J2M5 which had basically the same airframe as the J2M4, but which was powered by a 1,820-hp (1357-kW) MK4U-4 Kasei 26a radial which incorporated a mechanically-driven three-stage supercharger. This was shown to be reliable, and the J2M5 demonstrated a maximum speed of 382 mph (615 km/h) at 22,310 ft (6800 m) during official tests. Ordered into production with a redesigned cockpit canopy and the same armament as the J2M3, the J2M5, and J2M5a which had the same armament as the J2M3a, were the last production versions of the Raiden. A single experimental J2M6 was flown, this being a conversion of a J2M3 airframe with a wider cockpit, J2M3 armament and the redesigned canopy of the J2M5, but the projected J2M6a, J2M7 and J2M7a which would have introduced armament and engine changes were not built.

When production ended, Mitsubishi had built a total of 476 J2Ms of all versions, these being supplemented by a small, but unknown, number of J2M5s which had been manufactured by the Naval Air Arsenal at Koza. Allocated the Allied codename 'Jack', the J2M first saw operational use during 1944 and continued in service until the end of the Pacific War, playing a more conspicuous and vital role as the defensive perimeter became little more than Japan's home islands. In the closing stages J2Ms gained notable success against Allied bombers, and it was either unfortunate for the Japanese or lucky for the Allies that the J2M was not more reliable and available in greater numbers.

Specification
Mitsubishi J2M3 Raiden

Type: single-seat interceptor fighter
Powerplant: one 1,820-hp (1357-kW) Mitsubishi MK4R-A Kasei 23a 14-cylinder radial piston engine
Performance: maximum speed 371 mph (597 km/h) at 19,360 ft (5900 m); cruising speed 219 mph (352 km/h) at 9,840 ft (3000 m); service ceiling 38,385 ft (11700 m); maximum range 655 miles (1055 km)

Gaining many successes over American bombers during the closing stages of the war, the J2M was a useful fighter. This example is a J2M3 Raiden pictured at Kasumigaura in 1945.

Mitsubishi J2M Raiden

Mitsubishi J2M Raiden during the mainland defence, 1945

Weights: empty 5,423 lb (2460 kg); maximum take-off 8,695 lb (3945 kg)
Dimensions: span 35 ft 5¼ in (10.80 m); length 32 ft 7¾ in (9.95 m); height 12 ft 11½ in (3.95 m); wing area 215.82 sq ft (20.05 m²)

Armament: four-wing mounted 20-mm cannon (comprising two Type 99 Model 1 and two Type 99 Model 2), plus two 132-lb (60-kg) bombs or two 44-Imp gal (200-litre) drop tanks on external racks
Operator: Japanese Navy

Mitsubishi Ki-15

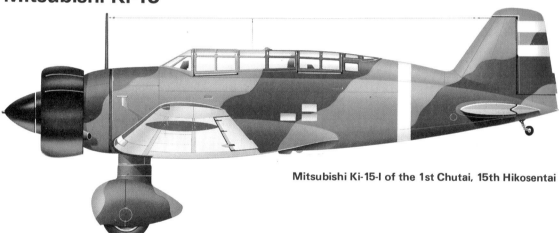

Mitsubishi Ki-15-I of the 1st Chutai, 15th Hikosentai

History and notes

In July 1935 the Imperial Japanese Army drew up its specification for a new two-seat reconnaissance aircraft and Mitsubishi responded with a cantilever low-wing monoplane of clean design. Two prototypes were built, one civil and one military, and the first was flown during May 1936. Powered by a Nakajima Ha-8 radial engine, the Mitsubishi Ki-15 could be recognised easily by the considerable dihedral on its outer wing panels and by the wide-track fixed and spatted tailwheel landing gear. Service testing was completed without difficulty and the type was ordered into production under the official designation Army Type 97 Command Reconnaissance Plane Model 1. In May 1937, a year after the first flight, delivery of production aircraft to the army began.

Just before that, however, military observers in the west should have gained some premonition of Japan's growing capability in aircraft design when the second (civil) prototype was used to establish a new record flight time between Japan and England: to celebrate the coronation of HM King George VI in Britain, the prototype named *kamikaze* (divine wind) and registered J-BAAI was flown from Tachikawa to London between 6 and 9 April 1937 at an average speed of 101.2 mph (162.9 km/h). Following this achievement a small number of Ki-15s was to be used by civil operators in Japan.

The army's Ki-15-I had been received in time to make a significant impact at the beginning of the war with China, the type's high speed giving it freedom of the skies until China introduced the Russian Polikarpov I-16. However, plans had already been made to upgrade performance of the Ki-15-I, this being achieved by installing the 900-hp (671-kW), smaller-diameter Mitsubishi Ha-26-I engine, its incorporation providing an opportunity to overcome what had been the major shortcoming of the type, a poor forward field of view

Mitsubishi Ki-15

past the large-diameter Nakajima engine. The improved version entered production for the army in September 1939 as the Ki-15-II, but before that the Japanese navy, impressed by the performance of this aircraft, ordered 20 examples of the Ki-15-II under the official designation Navy Type 98 Reconnaissance Plane Model 1, Mitsubishi designation C5M1. The navy acquired subsequently 30 C5M2 aircraft that were generally similar except for installation of the more powerful 950-hp (708-kW) Nakajima Sakae (prosperity) 12 engine. At a later date the army was also looking for higher performance, two Ki-15-III prototypes being built with the 1,050-hp (783-kW) Mitsubishi 102 radial engine, but this version failed to gain production status as more advanced aircraft were already under development. When production ended almost 500 of all versions had been built, the majority being in first-line service when the Pacific war started. Given the Allied codename 'Babs', the type was relegated to second-line roles in early 1943, but many survived to be used in *kamikaze* attacks at the war's end.

This example of the Mitsubishi Ki-15 was flown by the Japanese newspaper 'Asakaze', demonstrating the type's good performance for its day.

Specification
Mitsubishi Ki-15-I
Type: two-seat reconnaissance aircraft
Powerplant: one 640-hp (477-kW) Nakajima Ha-8 9-cylinder radial piston engine
Performance: maximum speed 298 mph (480 km/h) at 13,125 ft (4000 m); cruising speed 199 mph (320 km/h) at 16,405 ft (5000 m); service ceiling 37,400 ft (11400 m); range 1,491 miles (2400 km)
Weights: empty 3,086 lb (1400 kg); maximum take-off 5,071 lb (2300 kg)
Dimensions: span 39 ft 4½ in (12.00 m); length 28 ft 6½ in (8.70 m); height 11 ft 0 in (3.35 m); wing area 219.16 sq ft (20.36 m²)
Armament: all versions had one 7.7-mm (0.303-in) machine-gun on a trainable mount in the rear cockpit
Operators: Japanese Army and Navy

Mitsubishi Ki-21

History and notes
Winning a production order in November 1937, following competition with Nakajima's Ki-19 prototype, the Mitsubishi Ki-21 was designed and built to meet an Imperial Japanese Army requirement of early 1936 for a four-seat bomber that would have a maximum speed of at least 249 mph (400 km/h) and an endurance of more than 5 hours. Few twin-engine bombers anywhere in the world could exceed such performance at that time and, not surprisingly, the Ki-21 was later recognised as the best bomber in Japanese service during World War II. A cantilever mid-wing monoplane of all-metal construction, the design incorporated retractable tailwheel landing gear, a ventral bomb bay and two

radial engines, one mounted in a nacelle at the leading edge of each wing. As first flown, on 18 December 1936, the Ki-21 had 825-hp (615-kW) Mitsubishi Ha-6 radial engines, but competitive evaluation against the Nakajima Ki-19 powered by that company's Ha-5 engine led the army to instruct Mitsubishi to introduce similar engines on the Ki-21. When the aircraft had been tested again with revised vertical tail surfaces and these more powerful engines, the army had no hesitation in ordering the aircraft into production under the designation Army Type 97 Heavy Bomber Model 1A, company designation Mitsubishi Ki-21-Ia. The first of the production aircraft began to enter service in the summer of 1938 but, when used

Mitsubishi Ki-21

Mitsubishi Ki-21-IIb in 1944

operationally in China later that year, they were soon found to be lacking in defensive armament and self-sealing fuel tanks.

Improved versions were developed to overcome these and other shortcomings, the Ki-21-Ib introducing revised horizontal tail surfaces, larger-area trailing-edge flaps, an enlarged bomb bay and armament increased to a total of five 7.7-mm (0.303-in) machine-guns; the generally similar Ki-21-Ic differed by having increased fuel capacity and the addition of one more 7.7-mm (0.31-in) gun. To increase performance four improved Ki-21-Ics were given more powerful Mitsubishi Ha-101 engines and these, redesignated Ki-21-II, were used for service trials. Ordered into production as the Army Type 97 Heavy Bomber Model 2A (Mitsubishi Ki-21-IIa), this version was operated by most of the army's heavy bomber groups at the beginning of the Pacific war. These aircraft played a significant role in the opening phase of the war, but as Allied resistance began to increase and bomber crews found themselves confronted by fighter aircraft of increased quality and in greater quantity, Ki-21 losses began to rise steeply. Further revisions of defensive armament were made, the Ki-21-IIb replacing the dorsal gun position by a manually-operated gun turret containing one 12.7-mm (0.5-in) machine-gun, and this version also introduced redesigned cockpit canopies and individual engine exhaust stacks to give some thrust augmentation. However, it soon became clear that the Ki-21 was

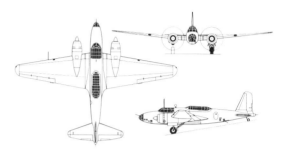

Mitsubishi Ki-21-IIa

gradually becoming obsolescent, and during the last year of the war the majority were relegated to second-line duties. Allocated the Allied codename 'Sally', the Ki-21 was built to a total of 2,064 by Mitsubishi (1,713) and Nakajima (351). From this total a number of Ki-21-Ia aircraft were modified to serve as freight transports for use by Greater Japan Air Lines. Designated MC-21, these aircraft had all armament and military equipment removed and could, if required, be fitted with nine troop seats.

Designated by the Japanese authorities as a heavy bomber, the Mitsubishi Ki-21 was a valuable asset during the opening rounds of the war in the East, but soon ran foul of the increasingly superior Allied fighters.

Mitsubishi Ki-21

Specification
Mitsubishi Ki-21-IIb
Type: five/seven-seat heavy bomber
Powerplant: two 1,500-hp (1119-kW) Mitsubishi Ha-101 14-cylinder radial piston engines
Performance: maximum speed 301 mph (485 km/h) at 15,485 ft (4720 m); cruising speed 236 mph (380 km/h) at 16,405 ft (5000 m); service ceiling 32,810 ft (10000 m); range 1,678 miles (2700 km)
Weights: empty 13,382 lb (6070 kg); maximum take-off 23,391 lb (10610 kg)
Dimensions: span 73 ft 9¾ in (22.50 m); length 52 ft 6 in (16.00 m); height 15 ft 11 in (4.85 m); wing area 749.19 sq ft (69.60 m²)
Armament: five 7.7-mm (0.303-in) Type 89 machine-guns (in nose, ventral, tail, and port and starboard beam positions) and one 12.7-mm (0.5-in) Type 1 machine-gun in dorsal turret, plus up to 2,205-lb (1000 kg) of bombs
Operators: Japanese Army, Thailand

Mitsubishi Ki-30

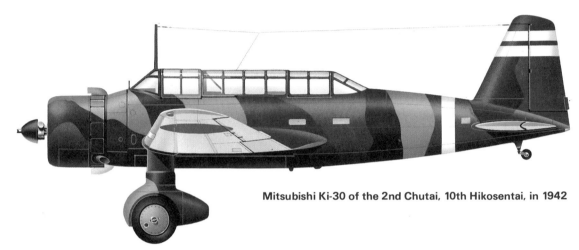

Mitsubishi Ki-30 of the 2nd Chutai, 10th Hikosentai, in 1942

History and notes
In May 1936 the Imperial Japanese Army issued its specification for a light bomber required to supersede the Mitsubishi Ki-2 and Kawasaki Ki-3 then in service. The Mitsubishi Ki-30 prototype that resulted was of cantilever mid-wing monoplane configuration with fixed tailwheel landing gear, the main units faired and spatted, and powered by an 825-hp (615-kW) Mitsubishi Ha-6 radial engine. Flown for the first time on 28 February 1937 this aircraft performed well, but it was decided to fly a second prototype with the more powerful Nakajima Ha-5 KAI radial engine. This aircraft showed some slight improvement in performance but, in any case, exceeded the army's original specification, so there was no hesitation in ordering 16 service trials aircraft. These were delivered in January 1938 and, two months later, the Ki-30 was ordered into production as the Army Type 97 Light Bomber.

First used operationally in China during 1938, the Ki-30s proved to be most effective, for in that theatre they had the benefit of fighter escort. The situation was very much the same at the beginning of the Pacific war, but as soon as the Allies were in a position to confront unescorted Ki-30s with fighter aircraft they immediately began to suffer heavy losses and were soon relegated to second-line use. The Allied codename 'Ann' was allocated to the Ki-30, but few were seen operationally after the opening phases of the war. A total of 704 had been built when production ended in 1941, 68 manufactured by the First Army Air Arsenal at Tachikawa, and many of these ended their days in a *kamikaze* role during the closing stages of the war.

Specification
Type: two-seat light bomber
Powerplant: one 950-hp (708-kW) Nakajima Ha-5 KAI 14-cylinder radial piston engine
Performance: maximum speed 263 mph (423 km/h) at 13,125 ft (4000 m); cruising speed 236 mph (380 km/h); service ceiling 28,115 ft (8570 m); range 1,056 miles (1700 km)
Weights: empty 4,916 lb (2230 kg); maximum take-off 7,099 lb (3220 kg)
Dimensions: span 47 ft 8¾ in (14.55 m); length 33 ft 11½ in (10.35 m); height 11 ft 11¾ in (3.65 m); wing area 329.17 sq ft (30.58 m²)
Armament: one wing-mounted 7.7-mm (0.303-in) machine-gun and one gun of the same calibre on trainable mount in rear cockpit, plus a maximum bombload of 882 lb (400 kg)
Operators: Japanese Army, Thailand

Mitsubishi Ki-46

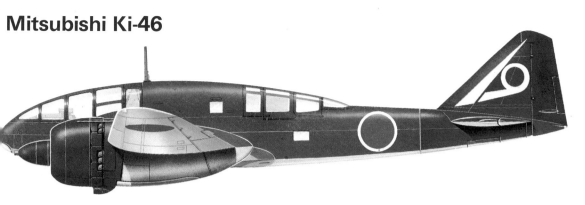

Mitsubishi Ki-46-III based in Japan during 1944-5

History and notes

The Mitsubishi Ki-15, which entered service in 1937, confirmed very quickly the value of high-speed reconnaissance aircraft. Used operationally in the Sino-Japanese conflict, it provided the Imperial Japanese Army with invaluable intelligence of enemy concentrations and movements. Impressed by the capability of the Ki-15, and considering its requirements when the moment came for the expansion of the Japanese empire, the army drew up the specification of a higher-performance long-range aircraft of this category. This would be essential considering the vast area over which operations might develop, and early and accurate knowledge of enemy countermoves would be vital if quick and effective response was to be made.

At the end of 1937 Mitsubishi received the army's specification, which made speed and range paramount to any other consideration, leaving the company free to adopt any configuration/powerplant combination that would achieve the desired performance. The resulting aircraft, first flown in prototype form in late November 1939, was a cantilever low-wing monoplane, its thin-section wings incorporating considerable dihedral. A slender fuselage mounted a conventional tail unit, landing gear was of retractable tailwheel type and power was provided by two 900-hp (671-kW) Mitsubishi Ha-26-I radial engines which were wing-mounted in very clean nacelles. In fact, considerable efforts had been made to keep drag to a minimum and the Mitsubishi Ki-46, as the type was designated, was undoubtedly one of the best-looking aircraft of World War II.

Flight testing went well, but a maximum speed some 10 per cent below that specified caused some concern. However, as the Ki-46 was faster than the most recent army and navy fighters to enter service, it was ordered into production under the official designation Army Type 100 Command Reconnaissance Plane Model 1, this version being identified by Mitsubishi as the Ki-46-I. Early production aircraft, which began to enter service in early 1940, were found to have a number of teething problems. While these took considerable time to rectify, at no time was production status in doubt and the development of an improved Ki-46-II was soon under way. This introduced the 1,080-hp (805-kW) Mitsubishi Ha-102 engine with two-stage supercharger,

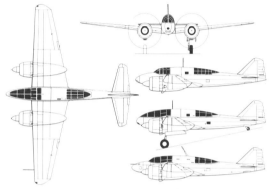

Mitsubishi Ki-46-III (upper view: Ki-46-II, lower view: Ki-46-III KAI)

and when tested in early 1941 this new version was found just able to exceed the originally specified maximum speed of 373 mph (600 km/h). Production Ki-46-IIs were delivered to operational units as quickly as production would allow, and by the beginning of the Pacific war units with small numbers of these aircraft were dispersed throughout the entire area of intended operations.

Initially the high speed of the Ki-46-IIs at their optimum altitude made them immune from interception by Allied fighters, which were then operating without the benefits of ground control radar. However, as soon as US and British forces re-established themselves and began to introduce new-generation fighters, Ki-46-II losses began to mount rapidly. Such a situation had been foreseen by the army, and by the time that it arose the Ki-46-III with more powerful Mitsubishi Ha-112-II engines was almost ready to enter service. This new reconnaissance aircraft, which supplemented rather than replaced the Ki-46-IIs, was to be virtually free from interception until the closing stages of the Pacific war. In fact, its performance was such that a fighter interceptor version was produced in small numbers under the designation Ki-46-III KAI, these being conversions from standard Ki-46-III production aircraft. They carried an armament of two nose-mounted 20-mm cannon plus an obliquely-mounted 37-mm cannon in the upper fuselage, but they were not particularly successful and not many conversions were made. A

Mitsubishi Ki-46

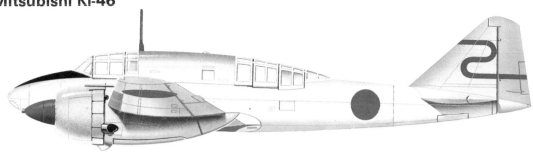

Mitsubishi Ki-46-II of the 76th Dokuritsu Dai Shijugo Chutai (Independent Squadron), East Indies, 1943

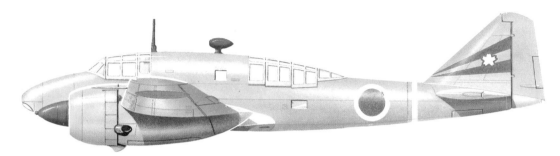

Mitsubishi Ki-46-II of the 51st Dokuritsu Dai Shijugo Chutai, China, late 1941

small number of ground-attack aircraft was also produced by conversions of Ki-46-IIIs and these, designated Ki-46-IIIb, were armed with only nose-mounted 20-mm cannon. An improved Ki-46-IV was planned in both reconnaissance and fighter versions, but did not progress beyond the prototype stage by the war's end. Allocated the Allied codename 'Dinah', the Ki-46 was in service from the beginning to end of the Pacific war, and its significance to the Japanese army can be judged by a production total no smaller than 1,742 of all versions.

Specification
Mitsubishi Ki-46-III
Powerplant: two 1,500-hp (1119-kW) Mitsubishi Ha-112-II 14-cylinder radial piston engines

Performance: maximum speed 391 mph (630 km/h) at 19,685 ft (6000 m); service ceiling 34,450 ft (10500 m); range 2,485 miles (4000 km)
Weights: empty 8,444 lb (3,830 kg); maximum take-off 14,330 lb (6500 kg)
Dimensions: span 48 ft 2¾ in (14.70 m); length 36 ft 1 in (11.00 m); height 12 ft 8¾ in (3.88 m); wing area 344.46 sq ft (32.00 m²)
Armament: none, but some Ki-46-I and Ki-46-II aircraft carried a single 7.7-mm (0.303-in) Type 89 machine-gun on a trainable mount in the rear cockpit
Operators: Japanese Army, plus a small number used by the Japanese Navy

Flying as a high altitude reconnaissance aircraft, the Ki-46-II was initially immune from interception, but new fighter types soon became equal to it.

Mitsubishi Ki-46

Mitsubishi Ki-46-II of the 82nd Sentai operating in Manchuria, 1944

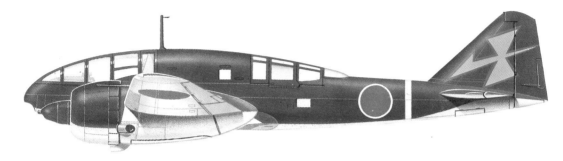

Mitsubishi Ki-46-III of the 3rd Chutai, 81st Sentai, Java, 1944

Mitsubishi Ki-46-III KAI of the 17th Dokuritsu Dai Shijugo Chutai, Japan, 1944-5

Mitsubishi Ki-51

History and notes

To meet an Imperial Japanese Army specification of December 1937 for a ground-attack aircraft, which it was suggested could be a development of the Ki-30 light bomber, Mitsubishi produced two prototypes under the designation Mitsubishi Ki-51. Of similar external appearance to the Ki-30, the new design was generally of smaller dimensions, had a revised and simplified cockpit that put the two-man crew more closely together and, because the bomb bay was not required, the monoplane wing was moved from a mid- to low-wing configuration. Powerplant chosen was the Mitsubishi Ha-26-II radial engine.

Tested during the summer of 1939, the two prototypes were followed by 11 service trials aircraft, these being completed before the end of the year. They differed from the prototypes by incorporating a number of modifications, but most important were the introduction of fixed leading-edge slots to improve slow-speed handling and armour plate beneath the engine and crew positions. Ordered into production in this form as the Army Type 99 Assault Plane, the Ki-51 began a production run that totalled 2,385 aircraft, built by Mitsubishi (1,472) and by the First Army Air Arsenal at Tachikawa (913), before production ended in July 1945. In addition to the standard production aircraft,

Mitsubishi Ki-51

there were attempts to develop dedicated reconnaissance versions, initially by the conversion of one Ki-51 service trials aircraft which had the rear cockpit redesigned to accommodate reconnaissance cameras. Test and evaluation of this aircraft, redesignated Ki51a, brought a realisation that the standard Ki-51 could be modified to have provisions for the installation of reconnaissance cameras, and this change was made on the production line. Subsequently, three Ki-71 tactical reconnaissance prototypes were developed from the Ki-51, introducing the 1,500-hp (1119-kW) Mitsubishi Ha-112-II engine, retractable landing gear, two wing-mounted 20-mm cannon and other refinements, but no production examples were built.

Allocated the Allied codename 'Sonia', the Ki-51 was used initially in operations against China, and was deployed against the Allies until the end of the Pacific war. In more intensely contested areas the fairly slow Ki-51s were easy prey for Allied fighters, but in secondary theatres, where an ability to operate from rough and short fields was valuable, these aircraft gave essential close support in countless operations. In the closing stages of the war they were used in *kamikaze* attacks.

When able to operate in remote areas away from the attentions of Allied fighters, the rough-field capabilities of the Ki-51 made it a useful weapon.

Specification
Mitsubishi Ki-51

Type: two-seat ground attack/reconnaissance aircraft
Powerplant: one 940-hp (701-kW) Mitsubishi Ha-26-II 14-cylinder radial piston engine
Performance: maximum speed 264 mph (425 km/h) at 9,845 ft (3000 m); service ceiling 27,130 ft (8270 m); range 659 miles (1060 km)
Weights: empty 4,129 lb (1873 kg); maximum take-off 6,437 lb (2920 kg)
Dimensions: span 39 ft 8¼ in (12.10 m); length 30 ft 2¼ in (9.20 m); height 8 ft 11½ in (2.73 m); wing area 258.56 sq ft (24.02 m²)
Armament: two wing-mounted 7.7-mm (0.303-in) machine-guns (early production) or two wing-mounted 12.7-mm (0.5-in) guns (late production), and one 7.7-mm (0.303-in) gun on trainable mount in rear cockpit, plus a bombload of 441 lb (200 kg) increasing to 551 lb (250 kg) in *kamikaze* role
Operator: Japanese Army

Mitsubishi Ki-57

History and notes
When in 1938 the Mitsubishi Ki-21 heavy bomber began to enter service with the Imperial Japanese Army, its capability attracted the attention of Japan Air Lines. In consequence a civil version was developed and this, generally similar to the Ki-21-I and retaining its powerplant of two 950-hp (708-kW) Nakajima Ha-5 KAI radial engines, differed primarily by having the

same wings transferred from mid- to low-wing configuration and the incorporation of a new fuselage to provide accommodation for up to 11 passengers. This transport version appealed also the the navy, and following the flight of a prototype in August 1940 and subsequent testing, the type was ordered into production for both civil and military use. This initial production Mitsubishi Ki-57-I had the civil and military designations of MC-

Mitsubishi Ki-57

20-I and Army Type 100 Transport Model 1 respectively. A total of 100 production Ki-57-Is had been built by early 1942, and small numbers of them were transferred for use by the Japanese navy in a transport role, then becoming redesignated L4M1. After the last of the Ki-51s had been delivered production was switched to an improved Ki-57-II, which introduced more powerful Mitsubishi Ha-102 radial engines installed in redesigned nacelles and, at the same time, incorporated a number of detail refinements and minor equipment changes. Civil and military designations of this version were the MC-20-II and Army Type 100 Transport Model 2 respectively, and 406 were built before production ended in January 1945. Both versions were covered by the Allied codename 'Topsy'.

Specification
Mitsubishi Ki-57-II
Type: twin-engine personnel transport

Developed as a civil version of the Mitsubishi Ki-21 bomber, the Ki-57 was used by the military forces as a staff transport. The navy operated the type under the designation L4M and it was known to the Allies as 'Topsy'. 406 were built and the aircraft was unarmed.

Powerplant: two 1,080-hp (805-kW) Mitsubishi Ha-102 14-cylinder radial piston engines
Performance: maximum speed 292 mph (470 km/h) at 19,030 ft (5800 m); service ceiling 26,245 ft (8000 m); range 1,864 miles (3000 km)
Weights: empty 12,313 lb (5585 kg); maximum take-off 20,106 lb (9120 kg)
Dimensions: span 74 ft 1¾ in (22.60 m); length 52 ft 9¾ in (16.10 m); height 15 ft 11 in (4.85 m); wing area 754.36 sq ft (70.08 m²)
Armament: none
Operators: Japanese Army, Japanese Navy

Mitsubishi Ki-67 Hiryu

History and notes
Following a series of incidents on the Manchukuo-Siberia border in the mid-1930s, the Imperial Japanese Army could foresee the possibility of war with the USSR. As a result it began to draw up the specification for a tactical heavy bomber, and in February 1941 instructed Mitsubishi to design and build three prototypes to the requirement. The first of the prototypes was flown on 27 December 1942 as a cantilever mid-wing monoplane with wings and tail unit resembling those of the navy's G4M bomber, retractable tailwheel landing gear, and power provided by two wing-mounted Mitsubishi Ha-104 fan-cooled radial engines. The fuselage provided accommodation for a crew of six to eight and incorporated a bomb bay able to accept a maximum

load of up to 1,764 lb (800 kg). Before the first Ki-67 prototype had flown an additional 16 prototype and service test aircraft had been ordered; the first two of these, together with the initial prototype, were armed with three 7.92-mm (0.31-in) and two 12.7-mm (0.5-in) machine-guns; the remaining prototypes and pre-production aircraft substituted one 20-mm cannon for one of the three 7.92-mm (0.31-in) machine-guns. The test programme of these aircraft was highly successful, in fact almost too successful, for the army began to think in terms of several different variants, which at one time almost threatened its entry into production. Finally, on 2 December 1943, the manufacture of a single version was authorised as the Army Type 4 Heavy Bomber Model 1 Hiryu (flying dragon), company

Mitsubishi Ki-67 Hiryu

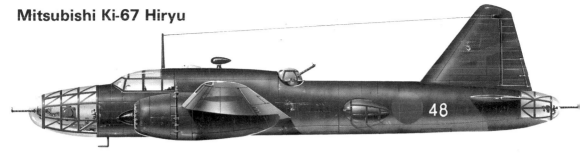

Mitsubishi Ki-67-I Hiryu of the Imperial Japanese Air Force

designation Mitsubishi Ki-67-I. There were only two variants the designation Ki-67-KAI being allocated to conversions of production aircraft for use in a three-seat *kamikaze* role, and the Ki-109 being a heavy fighter version which introduced a solid nose and armament of one forward-firing 75-mm cannon and one 12.7-mm (0.5-in) machine-gun in a tail turret, but only 22 of these were built. Projected versions, none of them built, included the Ki-67-II powered by two 2,400-hp (1790-kW) Mitsubishi Ha-214 engines (this powerplant was tested in two pre-production Ki-67s), Ki-69 escort fighter, Ki-97 transport version, and Ki-112 multi-seat fighter. One unexpected addition to the standard bomber version was the provision of torpedo racks on all aircraft subsequent to production number 160, following highly successful tests of one prototype as a torpedo-bomber. In fact, it was in the torpedo attack role that the Ki-67 was used operationally for the first time in October 1944. In its designated role of heavy bomber the type saw considerable action in the final months of the Pacific war in operations against Iwo Jima, the Marianas and Okinawa.

Allocated the Allied codename 'Peggy', the Ki-67 was undoubtedly Japan's best bomber in operation during the Pacific war, and the army must have looked back on the time-wasting year of indecision to December 1943 with great regret. Because of the delay in starting production and the growing effectiveness of Allied attacks on Japanese production sources only 698 Ki-67s were built: by Mitsubishi (606), Kawasaki (91) and the Army Air Arsenal at Tachikawa (1). Nippon also assembled 29 Mitsubishi-built aircraft, which accounts for the erroneous production figure of 727 quoted in some reference books.

Specification
Mitsubishi Ki-67-I
Type: heavy bomber/torpedo-bomber

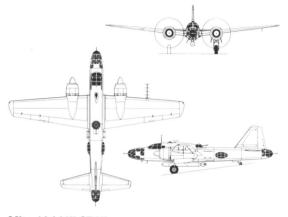

Mitsubishi Ki-67 Hiryu

Powerplant: two 1,900-hp (1417-kW) Mitsubishi Ha-104 18-cylinder radial piston engines
Performance: maximum speed 334 mph (537 km/h) at 19,980 ft (6090 m); cruising speed 249 mph (400 km/h) at 26,245 ft (8000 m); service ceiling 31,070 ft (9470 m); maximum range 2,361 miles (3800 km)
Weights: empty 19,070 lb (8650 kg); maximum take-off 30,347 lb (13765 kg)
Dimensions: span 73 ft 9¾ in (22.50 m); length 61 ft 4¼ in (18.70 m); height 25 ft 3¼ in (7.70 m); wing area 708.83 sq ft (65.85 m²)
Armament: (late production) three 12.7-mm (0.5-in) machine-guns (one each in nose and port and starboard beam positions) twin machine-guns of the same calibre in the tail turret, and one 20-mm Ho-5 cannon in the dorsal turret, plus a maximum bombload of 1,764 lb (800 kg) or one 1,764-lb (800-kg) or 2,359-lb (1070-kg) torpedo
Operators: Japanese Army, Japanese Navy

Nakajima A6M2-N

History and notes

When, in late 1940, the Imperial Japanese Navy realised that the Kawanishi N1K1 Kyofu would not be available in time to meet operational requirements, Nakajima was instructed to proceed with rapid development of a floatplane version of the Mitsubishi

A6M2. Nakajima began work on this project in early 1941 and its AS-1 prototype was flown for the first time on 7 December of that year. Basically a floatplane version of the A6M2 Zero, it had a large central float which also contained an auxiliary fuel tank, stabilising floats beneath the wing and vertical tail surfaces of

Nakajima A6M2-N

increased area. Very shortly after the prototype's first flight the type entered production as the Navy Type 2 Floatplane Fighter Model 11, company designation Nakajima A6M2-N, and a total of 326 production aircraft had been built when production ended in September 1943. Allocated the Allied codename 'Rufe', the A6M2-N proved to be an effective defensive fighter when deployed where it was not opposed by Allied land-based fighters.

Specification

Type: single-seat floatplane fighter
Powerplant: one 940-hp (701-kW) Nakajima NK1C Sakae 12 14-cylinder radial piston engine
Performance: maximum speed 271 mph (436 km/h) at 16,405 ft (5000 m); cruising speed 184 mph

Allocated the codename 'Rufe', the A6M2-N was a floatplane version of the Mitsubishi A6M2 Zero-Sen. Carrying extra fuel in the central float, the type proved successful only away from Allied fighters.

(296 km/h); service ceiling 32,810 ft (10000 m); maximum range 1,106 miles (1780 km)
Weights: empty 4,215 lb (1912 kg); maximum take-off 6,349 lb (2880 kg)
Dimensions: span 39 ft 4½ in (12.00 m); length 33 ft 1¾ in (10.10 m); height 14 ft 1¼ in (4.30 m); wing area 241.55 sq ft (22.44 m²)
Armament: two fuselage-mounted 7.7-mm (0.303-in) machine-guns and two wing-mounted 20-mm cannon, plus external racks for two 132-lb (60-kg) bombs
Operator: Japanese Navy

Nakajima B5N

History and notes

Nakajima's Type K prototype, first flown during January 1937, had been designed to meet an Imperial Japanese Navy requirement of 1935 for a single-engine carrier-based attack bomber. A cantilever low-wing monoplane with retractable tailwheel landing gear, the prototype accommodated a crew of three (pilot, radio operator and observer/bomb-aimer) all enclosed beneath a long 'greenhouse' canopy. To meet the requirement for carrier operations, this first prototype, powered by a 700-hp (522-kW) Nakajima Hikari 2 radial engine, had a large-area wing incorporating Fowler-type trailing-

edge flaps and hydraulic folding, but fears that this might prove difficult to maintain at sea resulted in a second prototype with plain flaps and a manually-folded wing. It was this latter prototype, powered by a Nakajima Hikari 3 radial engine, that was ordered into production in November 1937 as the Navy Type 97 Carrier Attack Bomber Model 1, company designation Nakajima B5N1. Introduced into operational use during the Sino-Japanese War, the B5N1 was found to be an effective tactical bomber providing support for ground operations. However, its limited defensive armament of a single 7.7-mm (0.303-in) machine-gun meant that it

Nakajima B5N

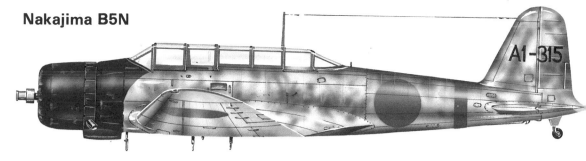

Nakajima B5N of the Imperial Japanese Navy

could only be operated with fighter escort. This was not of great importance when it was confronted by the standard fighters then equipping the Chinese air force. When, however, more effective fighters became available to the Chinese from Soviet sources, the B5N1 ceased to be a viable weapon and the development of a more effective version was initiated in 1939. When they were replaced in service by this 'improved' aircraft, the B5N1s were converted for use in the advanced trainer role under the designation B5N1-K.

Nakajima's developed B5N2, first flown in December 1939, was little more than a version with a far more powerful Nakajima Sakae engine, one which failed to have any significant effect on maximum speed. Nevertheless, the B5N2s which spearheaded the Japanese attack at Pearl Harbor provided adequate evidence of their capability, and it was not until they were confronted by more advanced Allied fighters that their losses became unacceptable. Allocated the Allied codename 'Kate', the type soldiered along in first-line use until early 1944, then being transferred to serve effectively in maritime reconnaissance and anti-submarine roles. Some operated with ASV radar, and a few ASW aircraft were equipped with an early form of magnetic anomaly detection (MAD) gear. When production ended in 1943 a total of 1,149 had been built by Nakajima (669), Aichi (200) and the Navy's Hiro Air Arsenal (280).

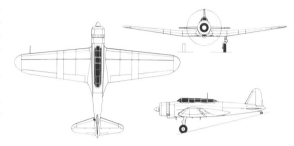

Nakajima B5N2

Specification
Nakajima B5N2
Type: carrier-based torpedo-bomber
Powerplant: one 1,000-hp (746-kW) Nakajima NK1B Sakae 11 14-cylinder radial piston engine
Performance: maximum speed 235 mph (378 km/h) at 11,810 ft (3600 m); cruising speed 161 mph (259 km/h) at 9840 ft (3000 m); service ceiling 27,100 ft (8260 m); maximum range 1,237 miles (1990 km)
Weights: empty 5,024 lb (2279 kg); maximum take-off

A Nakajima B5N1 carrying three bombs on its underfuselage racks. This early version was only a viable weapon when fighter cover was provided.

Nakajima B5N

9,039 lb (4100 kg)
Dimensions: span 50 ft 11 in (15.52 m); length 33 ft 9½ in (10.30 m); height 12 ft 1½ in (3.70 m); wing area 405.81 sq ft (37.70 m²)
Armament: one 7.7-mm (0.303-in) machine-gun on a trainable mount in rear cockpit, plus a bombload of

Two late-production B5N2s fly over the 60,000-ton battleship *Yamato*.

up to 1,764 lb (800 kg) or one torpedo of equivalent weight
Operator: Japanese Navy

Nakajima B6N Tenzan

History and notes

In 1939 the Imperial Japanese Navy drew up its specification for a carrier-based torpedo-bomber to supersede the Nakajima B5N, and to meet the requirement Nakajima decided to use an airframe very similar to that of the earlier aircraft, differing primarily in its vertical tail surfaces. The navy had specified use of the Mitsubishi Kasei radial engine, but Nakajima decided to use instead its own Mamoru 11 radial engine of similar output. The first of two prototypes was flown in early 1941, but flight testing revealed a number of problems, requiring revised vertical tail surfaces and strengthened arrester gear, and it was not until 1943 that the type entered production as the Navy Carrier Attack Bomber Tenzan Model 11, company designation Nakajima B6N1, incorporating a number of refinements as a result of extended flight testing. However, after only 135 production Tenzan (heavenly cloud) aircraft had been delivered a new crisis arose when Nakajima was ordered to terminate

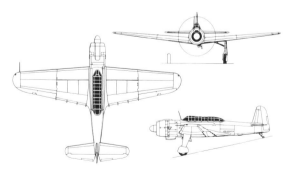

Nakajima B6N2 Tenzan

manufacture of the Mamoru engine, a step taken to allow greater emphasis to be placed on production of the widely-used Nakajima Homare and Sakae engines. The company was now compelled to use the engine which the navy had specified originally, the Mitsubishi Kasei, but fortunately the adaptation of the B6N

Nakajima B6N Tenzan

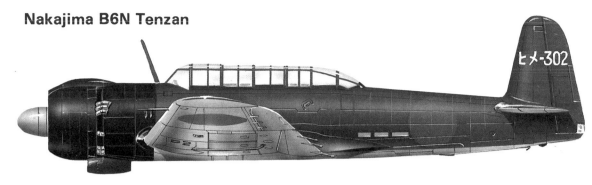

Nakajima B6N2 Tenzan of the Imperial Japanese Navy

airframe to accept this powerplant presented no major difficulties. The resulting aircraft, which was also the major production version, had the designation B6N2 and differed only from the B6N1 by installation of the Mitsubishi Kasei 25 engine; the B6N2a variant had the rear-firing 7.7-mm (0.303-in) machine-gun replaced by one of 13-mm (0.51-in) calibre. When production ended, Nakajima had built a total of 1,268 B6Ns of all versions, this number including two modified B6N2 airframes which had served as prototypes for a proposed land-based B6N3 Model 13; powerplant had been the Mitsubishi MK4T-C 25c version of the Kasei engine and the strengthened landing gear had larger wheels for operation from unprepared runways, but production did not start before the war ended. Allocated the Allied codename 'Jill', the B6Ns saw intensive use during the last two years of the war for conventional carrier operations and, in the latter stages, in *kamikaze* roles.

Specification
Nakajima B6N2

Type: carrier-based torpedo-bomber
Powerplant: one 1,850-hp (1380-kW) Mitsubishi MK4T Kasei 25 14-cylinder radial piston engine
Performance: maximum speed 298 mph (480 km/h) at 16,075 ft (4900 m); cruising speed 208 mph (335 km/h) at 13,125 ft (4000 m); service ceiling 29,660 ft (9040 m); maximum range 1,892 miles (3045 km)
Weights: empty 6,636 lb (3010 kg); maximum take-off 12,456 lb (5650 kg)
Dimensions: span 48 ft 10½ in (14.90 m); length 35 ft 8 in (10.87 m); height 12 ft 5½ in (3.80 m); wing area 400.43 sq ft (37.20 m²)
Armament: two 7.7-mm (0.303-in) machine-guns (one on a trainable mount in the rear cockpit and one firing through a ventral tunnel), plus a 1,764-lb (800-kg) torpedo, or a bombload of equivalent weight
Operator: Japanese Navy

Nakajima C6N Saiun

History and notes

Identifying the need for a long-range carrier-based reconnaissance aircraft, as a result of early experience in the Pacific war, the Imperial Japanese Navy drew up a specification which it issued to Nakajima in early 1942 for an aircraft to meet this requirement. The combination of high-speed, long-range and carrier compatibility presented considerable problems which Nakajima resolved by adopting its own efficient 1,820-hp (1358-kW) NK9B Homare 11 engine and incorporating in the wing design leading-edge slats and a combination of Fowler-type and split trailing-edge flaps. Appearing similar in external configuration to the company's B6N, the Nakajima C6N had a fuselage also accommodating a crew of three, but the lower surfaces and sides of the structure incorporated camera ports and observation windows.

The first C6N1 prototype made its maiden flight on 15 May 1943, but disappointing performance of the Homare 11 engine led to 18 more prototypes/pre-production aircraft, some tested with the more powerful

Homare 21, before the type was ordered into production in early 1944 as the Navy Carrier Reconnaissance Plane Saiun (painted cloud) which had the company designation Nakajima C6N1. Entering service in the summer of 1944, these aircraft soon demonstrated their long-range capability in keeping a watchful eye on the US fleet, and their speed was good enough to give them almost complete immunity from interception by Allied fighters. The type played a significant role in the closing stages of the war and a total of 463 had been built by Nakajima when production ended in August 1945. Allocated the Allied codename 'Myrt', the total included a small number of C6N1-S two-seat night-fighter conversions from C6N1s, armed with two 20-mm cannon mounted to fire obliquely forward and upward, and one C6N2 which was flown with a prototype installation of a 1,980-hp (1476-kW) Homare 24 turbocharged engine. Projected, but not built, were the C6N1-B carrier-based attack bomber and the C6N3 night-fighter powered by the Homare 24 engine.

Nakajima C6N Saiun

Specification
Nakajima C6N1

Type: carrier-based reconnaissance aircraft
Powerplant: one 1,990-hp (1484-kW) Nakajima
NK9H Homare 21 18-cylinder radial piston engine
Performance: maximum speed 379 mph (610 km/h)
at 20,015 ft (6100 m); cruising speed 242 mph
(390 km/h); service ceiling 35,235 ft (10740 m);
maximum range with auxiliary fuel 3,299 miles
(5310 km)
Weights: empty 6,543 lb (2968 kg); maximum take-off
11,596 lb (5260 kg)

Employed as long-range carrierborne reconnaissance aircraft, the Nakajima C6N Saiun proved highly successful in this role, being able to outrun fighters. It provided much useful material for the Japanese on American fleet movements.

Dimensions: span 41 ft 0 in (12.50 m); length 36 ft 1 in
(11.00 m); height 12 ft 11½ in (3.95 m); wing area
274.49 sq ft (25.50 m²)
Armament: one rear-firing 7.92-mm (0.31-in)
machine-gun on trainable mounting
Operator: Japanese Navy

Nakajima J1N Gekko

History and notes

The lack of a long-range fighter to protect its bombers making attacks deep in Chinese territory prompted the Imperial Japanese Navy to draw up the specification for an aircraft of this category. The requirement was issued to Mitsubishi and Nakajima, and the response of the latter company was a cantilever low-wing monoplane with retractable tailwheel landing gear. Power was provided by two wing-mounted 1,130-hp (843-kW) Nakajima Sakae 21 and 22 engines, these being counter-rotating to avoid the effect of propeller torque, and accommodation was provided for a crew of three. The first of two Nakajima J1N1 Gekko (moonlight) prototypes made its maiden flight during May 1941, but flight testing soon revealed the aircraft to be quite unsuited for the fighter role and it was decided instead to continue its development as a long-range reconnaissance aircraft. The handed Sakae engines were replaced by two Sakae 21s, crew accommodation was revised,

and weight saving was accomplished by reducing the armament of the J1N1 (which comprised one 20-mm cannon and six 7.7-mm (0.303-in) machine-guns) to a single rear-firing 13-mm (0.51-in) machine-gun and by reducing internal fuel capacity; to retain long-range capability provision was made for external drop tanks. In this form, and redesignated J1N1-C, the type completed its service trials successfully and was ordered into production as the Navy Type 2 Reconnaissance Plane. Some of these production aircraft had the rear-firing machine-gun replaced subsequently by a 20-mm cannon in a dorsal turret, then being redesignated J1N1-F.

In early 1943 it was suggested that the J1N1 might be suitable for deployment as a night-fighter, leading first to the conversion of some J1N1-C production aircraft by the installation of four obliquely-mounted 20-mm cannon, two downward- and two upward-firing; aircraft so converted were redesignated J1N1-C KAI.

Nakajima J1N Gekko

Complete with oblique mounted cannon in the rear cockpit, the J1N was a useful night fighter.

Successful deployment of these aircraft brought development of a specialised night-fighter version which, as the J1N1-S Gekko Model 11, entered production in August 1943. These had the same armament as the J1N1-C KAI and some carried AI radar or a small searchlight in the nose. Late production aircraft, which had the designation J1N1-Sa, had the downward-firing cannon removed as these had been shown to be ineffective, and most carried AI radar. When neither radar nor a searchlight was installed, many J1N1-Sa night-fighters carried a nose-mounted 20-mm Type 99 Model 2 cannon.

In its night-fighter role the Gekko enjoyed some early success, especially when deployed against the Consolidated B-24 Liberator, but confrontation with the Boeing B-29 Superfortress was for less conclusive. Allocated the Allied codename 'Irving', the J1N was built to the extent of 479 examples of all versions by the time production ended in December 1944. Many were deployed in *kamikaze* attacks in the closing stages of the Pacific war.

Specification
Nakajima J1N1-S
Type: two-seat night-fighter
Powerplant: two 1,130-hp (843-kW) Nakajima Sakae 21 14-cylinder radial piston engines
Performance: maximum speed 315 mph (507 km/h) at 19,030 ft (5800 m); cruising speed 207 mph (333 km/h) at 13,125 ft (4000 m); service ceiling 30,580 ft (9320 m); maximum range 2,348 miles (3780 km)
Weights: empty 10,692 lb (4850 kg); maximum take-off 18,045 lb (8185 kg)
Dimensions: span 55 ft 8½ in (16.98 m); length 41 ft 10¾ in (12.77 m); height 13 ft 1½ in (3.99 m); wing area 430.57 sq ft (40.00 m²)
Armament: four 20-mm Type 99 cannon, obliquely mounted to provide two downward-firing and two upward-firing
Operator: Japanese Navy

Nakajima Ki-27

History and notes
When in mid-1935 Kawasaki, Mitsubishi and Nakajima were instructed by the Imperial Japanese Army to build competitive prototypes of advanced fighter aircraft, Nakajima responded with a single-seat monoplane fighter derived from the company's Type P.E., which it had started to develop as a private venture. A cantilever low-wing monoplane of all-metal construction, except for fabric-covered control surfaces, the aircraft had a conventional tail unit, fixed tailskid landing gear and power provided by a 650-hp (485-kW) Nakajima Ha-1a radial engine. First flown during July 1936, this aircraft was followed three months later by the first

Nakajima Ki-27 prototype which incorporated minor modifications and refinements that resulted from the early tests of the Type P.E. Service trials proved the Kawasaki Ki-28 to be fastest of the three contenders, but Nakajima's Ki-27 was by far the most manoeuvrable and, on that basis, 10 pre-production examples were ordered for further service evaluation. They differed from the prototype by having wings of increased span and area, and the cockpit enclosed by a sliding canopy. Following further testing in late 1937 the type was ordered into production as the Army Type 97 Fighter Model A (Mitsubishi Ki-27a). Late production aircraft which introduced some refinements, including a further

Nakajima Ki-27

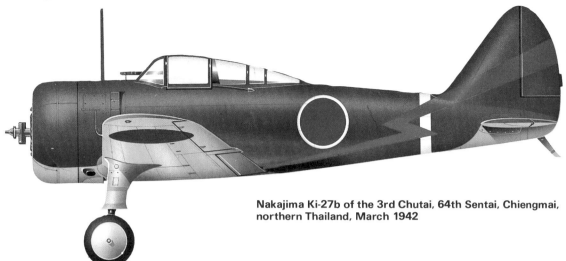

Nakajima Ki-27b of the 3rd Chutai, 64th Sentai, Chiengmai, northern Thailand, March 1942

improved cockpit canopy, had the designation Ki-27b. Subsequently two Ki-27 KAI experimental aircraft were built, introducing a lighter-weight structure to improve performance, but no production examples followed.

Nakajima could not have guessed that 3,999 aircraft would be built, by Nakajima (2,020) and Mansyu (1,379), before production came to a halt at the end of 1942, but the type's entry into service over northern China in March 1938 gave an immediate appreciation of its capability, the Ki-27s becoming masters of the airspace until confronted later by the faster Soviet Polikarpov I-16 fighters. At the beginning of the Pacific war the Ki-27s took part in the invasion of Burma, Malaya, the Netherlands East Indies and the Philippines. Allocated the Allied codename 'Nate' (initially 'Abdul' in the China-Burma-India theatre), the Ki-27 had considerable success against the Allies in the initial stages before more modern fighters became

Almost 4,000 Ki-27s were built, and the type saw much service as, initially, a fighter and fighter-trainer and eventually as a kamikaze aircraft.

available. When this occurred they were transferred for air defence of the home islands, remaining deployed in this capacity until 1943 when they became used increasingly as advanced trainers. As with many Japanese aircraft, their final use was in a *kamikaze* role.

Specification
Nakajima Ki-27a
Type: single-seat fighter
Powerplant: one 710-hp (529-kW) Nakajima Ha-1b 9-cylinder radial piston engine
Performance: maximum speed 292 mph (470 km/h) at 11,485 ft (3500 m); cruising speed 217 mph (350 km/h) at 11,485 ft (3500 m); range 389 miles (625 km)
Weights: empty 2,447 lb (1110 kg); maximum take-off 3,946 lb (1790 kg)
Dimensions: span 37 ft 1½ in (11.31 m); length 24 ft 8½ in (7.53 m); height 10 ft 8 in (3.25 m); wing area 199.68 sq ft (18.55 m²)
Armament: two forward-firing 7.7-mm (0.303-in) machine-guns
Operators: Japanese Army, Thailand

Nakajima Ki-43 Hayabusa

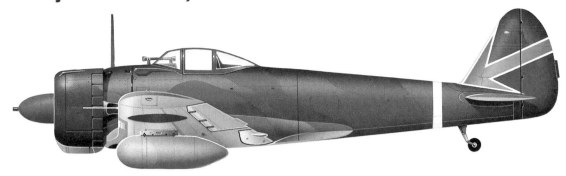

Nakajima Ki-43-Ic of HQ Chutai, 64th Sentai, Chiengmai,
northern Thailand in March 1942

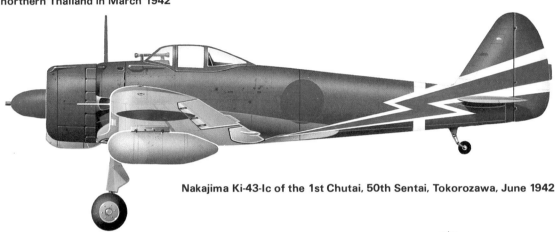

Nakajima Ki-43-Ic of the 1st Chutai, 50th Sentai, Tokorozawa, June 1942

History and notes

In December 1939 Nakajima was instructed by the
Imperial Japanese Army to initiate development of a
more advanced fighter to supersede the company's
own Ki-27, the first of three prototypes making its
maiden flight during January 1939. A cantilever low-
wing monoplane, this Kawasaki Ki-43 had retractable
tailwheel landing gear, seated its pilot in an enclosed
cockpit and was powered by Nakajima's new supercharged Ha-25 Sakae radial engine with a take-off
rating of 975 hp (727-kW). Service testing of the
prototypes showed that the type met the specification,
but manoeuvrability was so poor that, at one time, it
seemed the new fighter was unlikely to be accepted by
the army. However, 10 pre-production aircraft were
ordered and in attempts to improve manoeuvrability,
modifications were introduced. These included increased
wing area, weight reduction and, finally, the incorporation
of manoeuvring or so-called 'combat' flaps. This proved
to be the answer to the problem, to the extent that the
type was ordered into production as the Army Type 1
Fighter Model 1A Hayabusa (peregrine falcon), company
designation Ki-43-1a. This version was armed with two
7.7-mm (0.303-in) machine-guns and carried two 33-lb
(15-kg) bombs on external racks, but two sub-variants
differed in armament, the Ki-43-1b having one 7.7-mm
(0.303-in) and one 12.7-mm (0.5-in) and the Ki-43-1C two
12.7-mm (0.5-in) machine-guns. Production started in

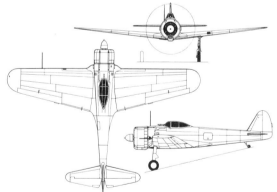

Nakajima Ki-43-Ia Hayabusa

March 1941, and when the Ki-43 began to reach
operational units it proved to be by far the most
manoeuvrable fighter in the army's inventory, enjoying
considerable success in the early stages of the Pacific
war. With the advent of more effective Allied fighters,
however, the Ki-43's shortcomings became apparent,
leading first to the construction of five Ki-43-II prototypes
for evaluation. These introduced the more powerful
Nakajima Ha-115 engine, some armour protection for
the pilot, and an early form of self-sealing fuel tank.
Satisfactory testing brought construction of the initial
Ki-43-IIa production version which had reduced wing

Tachikawa-built Ki-43-III-Ko of the 48th Sentai operating in Manchuria during the summer of 1945. Despite its looks, the Ki-43 was severely outdated, carrying only two machine-guns in the upper fuselage decking.

Nakajima Ki-43 Hayabusa

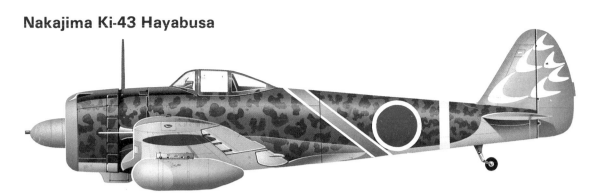

Nakajima Ki-43-IIb of HQ Chutai, 77th Sentai, Burma, 1943-4

span, a modified canopy, machine-gun armament as for the Ki-43-Ic, and two underwing racks each able to carry a 551-lb (250-kg) bomb; late series aircraft, designated Ki-43-IIb, were generally similar but for some equipment changes, and the final production Ki-43-II KAI incorporated the progressive modifications introduced on Ki-43-IIa and Ki-43-IIb aircraft. Further development followed with the construction of 10 Ki-43-IIIa prototypes, which were similar to the Ki-43-II KAI except for introducing the 1,150-hp (858-kW) Nakajima Ha-115-II engine to give improved performance at rated altitude, and two Ki-43-IIIb interceptor prototypes with the 1,300-hp (969-kW) Mitsubishi Ha-112 engine and forward-firing armament of two 20-mm cannon, but neither of these versions entered production before the Pacific war ended.

Allocated the Allied codename 'Oscar', the Hayabusa remained in service from beginning to end of the Pacific war, taking an active part in operations for the defence of Tokyo, and by use in a *kamikaze* role. Production had totalled 5,919, built by Nakajima (3,239), Tachikawa (2,631) and the Army Air Arsenal at Tachikawa (49).

Specification
Nakajima Ki-43-IIb
Type: single-seat fighter/fighter-bomber
Powerplant: one 1,150-hp (858-kW) Nakajima Ha-115

A Nakajima Ki-43-Ib of the 47th Independent Fighter Chutai at rest on a Japanese airfield. The type was widely used in all theatres of the Pacific war.

14-cylinder radial piston engine
Performance: maximum speed 329 mph (530 km/h) at 13,125 ft (4000 km); cruising speed 273 mph (440 km/h); service ceiling 36,745 ft (11200 m); maximum range 1,988 miles (3200 km)
Weights: empty 4,211 lb (1910 kg); maximum take-off 5,710 lb (2590 kg)
Dimensions: span 35 ft 6¾ in (10.84 m); length 29 ft 3¼ in (8.92 m); height 10 ft 8¾ in (3.27 m); wing area 230.36 sq ft (21.40 m²)
Armament: two 12.7-mm (0.5-in) forward-firing machine-guns, plus two bombs up to 551-lb (250-kg) in weight on underwing racks
Operators: Japanese Army, Thailand

Nakajima Ki-44 Shoki

History and notes
Very soon after design of the Ki-43 Hayabusa had been started by Nakajima, the company received instruction from the Imperial Japanese Army to initiate the design of a new interceptor fighter. In this case, however, manoeuvrability was required to give precedence to overall speed and rate of climb, and the company's design team selected the 1,250-hp (932-kW) Nakajima Ha-41 as the powerplant for this new project. Of similar general configuration to the Ki-43, the new Nakajima Ki-44 prototypes also incorporated the manoeuvring flaps that had been introduced on that aircraft, and carried an armament of two 7.7-mm

(0.303-in) and two 12.7-mm (0.5-in) machine-guns. First flown on August 1940, the Ki-44 was involved in a series of comparative trials against Kawasaki's Ki-60 prototype, based on use of the Daimler-Benz DB 601 engine, and an imported Messerschmitt Bf 109E. The result of this evaluation, and extensive service trials, showed the Ki-44 to be good enough to enter production, and it was ordered under the designation Army Type 2 Single-seat Fighter Model 1A Shoki (demon), company designation Ki-44-Ia, which carried the same armament as the prototypes. A total of only 40 Ki-44-I aircraft was produced, including small numbers of the Ki-44-Ib armed with four 12.7-mm (0.5-in) machine-guns, and

Nakajima Ki-44 Shoki

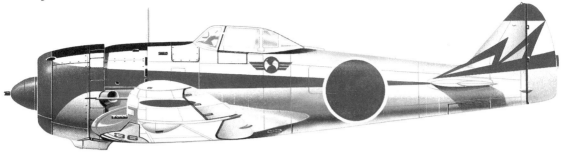

Nakajima Ki-44-IIb of Shinten (air superiority) unit of the 47th Sentai, Narimasu, Tokyo, summer 1944

Nakajima Ki-44-IIb of the 23rd Sentai for home island defence in 1944

Nakajima Ki-44-IIb of the 2nd Chutai, 87th Sentai, Eastern Defence Sector, Japan, early 1945

the similar Ki-44-Ic with some minor refinements.

When introduced into service the high landing speeds and limited manoeuvrability of the Shoki made it unpopular with pilots, and very soon the Ki-44-II with a more powerful Nakajima Ha-109 engine was put into production. Only small numbers of the Ki-44-IIa similarly armed to the Ki-44-Ia, were built, the variant being followed by the major production Ki-44-IIb which, apart from the different engine, was identical to the Ki-44-Ic. The Ki-44-IIc introduced much heavier armament, comprising four 20-mm cannon or, alternatively two 12.7-mm (0.5-in) machine-guns and two 40-mm cannon, and these proved to be very effective when deployed against Allied heavy bombers attacking Japan. However, the increased power had done nothing to eliminate the reasons for its unpopularity with the pilots and, in fact, the higher wing-loading of this version meant that it had some violent reactions to high-speed manoeuvres; however, it later gained their

respect because of its capability as an interceptor. Final production version was the Ki-44-III with a 2,000-hp (1491-kW) Nakajima Ha-145 radial engine, an increase in wing area and enlarged vertical tail surfaces, but comparatively few were built before production ended in late 1944. They included the Ki-44-IIIa and similar Ki-44-IIIb, armed with four 20-mm cannon, and two 20-mm and two 37-mm cannon respectively.

Nakajima had built a total of 1,225 Ki-44s of all versions, including prototypes, and these were allocated the Allied codename 'Tojo'. They were deployed primarily in Japan, but were used also to provide an effective force of interceptors to protect vital targets, as in Sumatra where they defended the oil fields at Palembang.

Specification
Nakajima Ki-44-IIb

Type: single-seat interceptor fighter

Nakajima Ki-44 Shoki

A Nakajima Ki-44-IIb showing its neatly cowled Ha-109 14 cylinder radial engine.

Powerplant: one 1,520-hp (1133-kW) Nakajima Ha-109 14-cylinder radial piston engine
Performance: maximum speed 376 mph (605 km/h) at 17,060 ft (5200 m); cruising speed 249 mph (400 km/h) at 13,125 ft (4000 m); service ceiling 36,745 ft (11200 m); maximum range 1,056 miles (1700 km)
Weights: empty 4,641 lb (2105 kg); maximum take-off 6,598 lb (2993 kg)
Dimensions: span 31 ft 0 in (9.45 m); length 28 ft 10 in (8.79 m); height 10 ft 8 in (3.25 m); wing area 161.46 sq ft (15.00 m²)
Armament: two fuselage-mounted and two wing-mounted 12.7-mm (0.5-in) machine-guns
Operator: Japanese Army

Nakajima Ki-49 Donryu

Nakajima Ki-49-I of Hamamatsu Army Flying School, late 1943

History and notes

When the Mitsubishi Ki-21 began to enter service in August 1938, the Imperial Japanese Army was already drawing up a specification for the aircraft that would supersede it. Appreciating from service trials that the Ki-21, however advanced at that time, would in due course be unable to operate without fighter escort, the army required that its new heavy bomber should have a combination of speed and defensive armament that would enable it to operate independently.

The Nakajima Ki-49 prototype, first flown during August 1939, was a cantilever mid-wing monoplane of all-metal construction with retractable tailwheel landing gear, its fuselage providing accommodation for a crew of eight and a maximum bombload of 2,205 lb (1000 kg). Powerplant comprised two 950-hp (708-kW) Nakajima Ha-5 KAI radial engines, but the second and third prototypes had the 1,250-hp (932-kW) Nakajima Ha-41 engines intended for production aircraft. Seven basically similar pre-production aircraft followed and these, together with the second and third prototoypes, completed an extensive test programme during which a number of minor developmental modifications were incorporated before, in March 1941, the type was, ordered into production as the Army Type 100 Heavy Bomber Model 1, or Ki-49-I Donryu (storm dragon).

Production Ki-49-Is began to enter service in the autumn of 1941 and these, like the prototypes, carried an armament of five 7.7-mm (0.303-in) machine-guns and one 20-mm cannon. Following initial deployment in

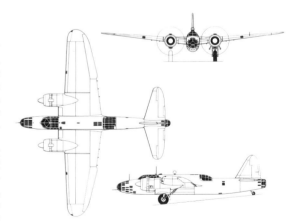

Nakajima Ki-49-II Donryu

China the type became involved in the Pacific war in the New Guinea area and in attacks on Australia. Such actions confirmed that the Ki-49 was underpowered, with bombload or speed suffering as a result. In the spring of 1942 it was decided to introduce a new version with more powerful Nakajima Ha-109 engines, and the two resulting Ki-49-II prototypes also incorporated improved armour and self-sealing tanks. Service testing led to this new version being ordered into production as the Army Type 100 Heavy Bomber Model 2A, the initial Nakajima Ki-49-IIa having the same armament as the Ki-49-I, but the Ki-49-IIb

Nakajima Ki-49 Donryu

Nakajima Ki-49-I with segment-type camouflage, China, early 1944

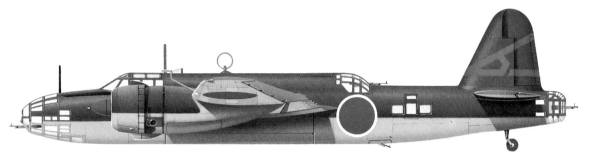

Nakajima Ki-49-IIa of the 3rd Chutai, 61st Sentai

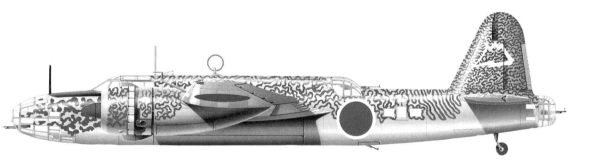

Nakajima Ki-49-IIa of the 1st Chutai, 7th Sentai, 1943

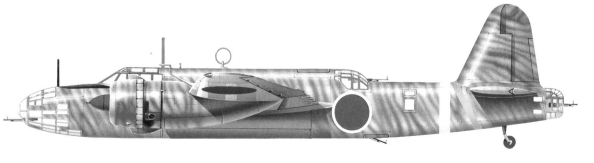

Nakajima Ki-49-IIa of the 3rd Chutai, 95th Sentai, north east China, March-September 1944

Nakajima Ki-49 Donryu

The improvement in Allied fighters meant that the Ki-49 had to find employment in other fields than bombing. Such roles included ASW, transport and kamikaze.

introduced revised armament in which three of the 7.7-mm (0.303-in) machine-guns were replaced by three of 12.7-mm (0.5-in) calibre. Although performance was improved, it was insufficient to provide an adequate margin of superiority over Allied fighters, and as the capability of the latter improved the losses of Ki-49s began to mount. A final attempt to resolve the situation was made in early 1943 with the installation of two 2,420-hp (1805-kW) Nakajima Ha-117 engines, but the teething problems of this new powerplant were such that only six Ki-49-III prototypes were built. Under the designation Ki-58, Nakajima also built three prototypes of an escort fighter version, with Nakajima Ha-109 engines and armament of three 12.7-mm (0.5-in) machine-guns and five 20-mm cannon, but no production resulted. There were also two Ki-80 prototypes for use as formation lead aircraft, or pathfinders, but the project was cancelled and the aircraft were used instead as test-beds for Nakajima Ha-117 engines.

The vulnerability of the Ki-49 in its intended role meant that in the later stages of the Pacific war the type was deployed in a variety of roles, including ASW patrol, troop transport and, of course, *kamikaze* attacks. A total of 819 had been built, 50 by Tachikawa, when production ended in December 1944. The type was allocated the Allied codename 'Helen'.

Specification
Nakajima Ki-49-IIa
Type: heavy bomber
Powerplant: two 1,500-hp (1119-kW) Nakajima Ha-109 14-cylinder radial piston engines
Performance: maximum speed 306 mph (492 km/h) at 16,405 ft (5000 m); cruising speed 217 mph (350 km/h) at 9,840 ft (3000 m); service ceiling 30,510 ft (9300 m); maximum range 1,833 miles (2950 km)
Weights: empty 14,396 lb (6530 kg); maximum take-off 25,133 lb (11400 kg)
Dimensions: span 67 ft 0 in (20.42 m); length 54 ft 1½ in (16.50 m); height 13 ft 11¼ in (4.25 m); wing area 743.27 sq ft (69.05 m²)
Armament: one 20-mm cannon (in the dorsal turret) and five 7.7-mm (0.303-in) machine-guns (in nose, ventral, port and starboard beam and tail positions) plus a bombload of up to 2,205 lb (1000 kg)
Operator: Japanese Army

Nakajima Ki-84 Hayate

History and notes
In the summer of 1944 the Imperial Japanese Army introduced into operational service a new single-seat interceptor fighter/fighter-bomber, the Nakajima Ki-84 Hayate (gale). With better manoeuvrability and climb rate than the redoubtable North American P-51H Mustang and Republic P-47N Thunderbolt operating in the Pacific zone, it was encountered in all operational theatres and was effective at all altitudes. Allocated the Allied codename 'Frank', the Ki-84 would have

posed considerable problems for the USAF had it appeared earlier and in larger numbers. In the event, Allied numerical superiority meant that the Japanese army overworked its Ki-84s, bringing unserviceability and maintenance problems that would not have arisen with more moderate usage.

Design of this new fighter began in early 1942 and the first prototype was flown in April 1943, its early testing progressing so well that a first service trials batch of 83 aircraft was ordered into production only

Nakajima Ki-84 Hayate

Nakajima Ki-48-Ia of the 1st Chutai, 73rd Sentai, Philippines, December 1944

Nakajima Ki-84-Ia of the 1st Chutai, 102nd Sentai, Kyushu, April 1945

Nakajima Ki-84-Ia of the HQ Chutai, 29th Sentai, Formosa, 1945

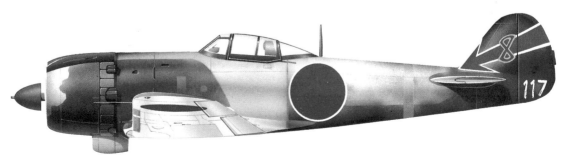

Nakajima Ki-84-Ia of the 183rd Shimbutai (Special Attack Group) at Tatebayashi, Japan, August 1945

Nakajima Ki-84 Hayate

Nakajima Ki-84-Ia of the 1st Chutai, 47th Sentai, Narumatsu, Japan, August 1945

four months later. A cantilever low-wing monoplane of all-metal construction, except for fabric-covered control surfaces, the Ki-84 had retractable tailwheel landing gear, a Nakajima Ha-45 radial engine, and armament comprising two fuselage-mounted 12.7-mm (0.5-in) machine-guns and two wing-mounted 20-mm cannon. Service trials under operational conditions were convincing enough for the Ki-84 to be ordered into full-scale production in late 1943 under the designation Army Type 4 Fighter Model 1A Hayate (Nakajima Ki-84-Ia), and later sub-variants included the Ki-84-Ib armed with four 20-mm cannon, and the Ki-84-Ic with two 20-mm and two 30-mm cannon.

The type's first major operational involvement was in the battle of Leyte at the end of 1944, and from that moment until the end of the Pacific war the Ki-84 was found wherever the action was intense. It was used as a fighter to attack and repel the Americans as they approached the home islands, as a dive-bomber to harass enemy landings on the island stepping-stones to Japan, in fighter-bomber attacks against the US bases on Okinawa and, finally, as an interceptor in the air defence of Tokyo. In attempts to conserve light alloys three versions of the Hayate appeared with alternative construction. Only the first entered production, the Ki-84-II, which introduced wooden wingtips and rear fuselage; built in two variants, these differed only by having armament similar to either the Ki-84-Ib or Ki-84-Ic. The other two aircraft in this category were the three Ki-106 prototypes of all-wood construction, and the single Ki-113 which used a maximum content of steel for the same alloy-saving purpose. Only one other prototype was built and flown, the experimental Ki-116 which, converted from a Ki-84-Ia, had a lighter-weight 1,500-hp (1119-kW) Mitsubishi Ha-33 radial engine. When production ended in August 1945, a total of 3,514 Ki-84s and derivatives had been built by Nakajima (3,416), Mansyu (95) and Tachikawa (3), a

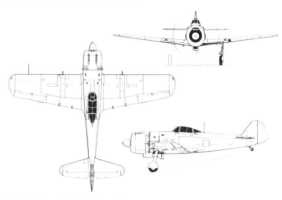

Nakajima Ki-84 Hayate

remarkable short-term achievement resulting from a programme that gave the Hayate utmost priority.

Specification
Nakajima Ki-84-Ia
Type: single-seat interceptor fighter/fighter-bomber
Powerplant: one 1,900-hp (1416-kW) Nakajima Ha-45 18-cylinder radial piston engine
Performance: maximum speed 392 mph (631 km/h) at 20,080 ft (6120 m); crusing speed 277 mph (445 km/h); service ceiling 34,350 ft (10500 m); maximum range 1,347 miles (2168 km)
Weights: empty 5,864 ft (2660 kg); maximum take-off 8,576 lb (3890 kg)
Dimensions: span 36 ft 10½ in (11.24 m); length 32 ft 6½ in (9.92 m); height 11 ft 1½ in (3.39 m); wing area 226.05 sq ft (21.00 m²)
Armament: two fuselage-mounted 12.7-mm (0.5-in) Type 1 machine-guns and two wing-mounted 20-mm Ho-5 cannon, plus two 551-lb (250-kg) bombs or two 44-Imp gal (200-litre) drop tanks on external racks
Operator: Japanese Army

Nakajima Ki-115 Tsurugi

History and notes
Design and development of the Nakajima Ki-115 Tsurugi (sabre) marked the realisation by Japan's army

that an Allied invasion of the home islands was daily becoming more certain, and that desperate measures would be needed if victory was to be snatched from the

Nakajima Ki-115 Tsurugi

disaster that was overtaking the country. *Kamikaze* attacks represented an important aspect of the desperate measures, and the Ki-115 was intended to provide a cheap, easy to build aircraft that could carry a bomb of up to 1,764-lb (800-kg) weight in such attacks. Nakajima was instructed by the Imperial Japanese Army in January 1945 to design and develop such a machine with all speed, a purposely very limited specification requiring the main units of the non-retractable tailskid landing gear to be jettisoned immediately the aircraft was airborne, a maximum speed of 320 mph (515 km/h) and an engine mounting designed to accept any radial engine available in the 800-to 1,300-hp (597-to 969-kW) class.

The resulting Ki-115a prototype was a cantilever low-wing monoplane with an all-metal wing, the fuselage and tail unit being of mixed construction, and the main landing gear units of welded steel tube without any form of shock absorption. Flight testing, which began in March 1945, showed a number of deficiencies, which was not surprising considering the speed of design and construction. Quite unacceptable was the ground handling with rigid main landing gear units, leading to refined main gear with simple shock-absorbers. In this form the aircraft was ordered into production, a total

The crudeness of the Ki-115 belied its intended role as a suicide bomber, able to carry a bomb to its target in the most expedient way possible.

of 104 being built by the end of the war, but none of them was used operationally. A version with larger-area wings of wooden construction had been projected under the designation Ki-115b, but no examples were built.

Specification
Type: single-seat suicide attack aircraft
Powerplant: one 1,130-hp (843-kW) Nakajima Ha-35 14-cylinder radial piston engine
Performance: maximum speed 342 mph (550 km/h) at 9,185 ft (2800 m); range 746 miles (1200 km)
Weights: empty 3,616 lb (1640 kg); maximum take-off 6,439 lb (2880 kg)
Dimensions: span 28 ft 2½ in (8.60 m); length 28 ft 0½ in (8.55 m); height 10 ft 10 in (3.30 m); wing area 133.48 sq ft (12.40 m²)
Armament: one bomb of up to 1,764-lb (800-kg) weight semi-recessed beneath fuselage
Operators: (intended) Japanese Army and Japanese Navy

Piaggio P.108

History and notes
The only four-engine heavy bomber to see operation with Italian forces during World War II, the Piaggio P.108 was an interesting design. Long established in Italy as engineers and shipbuilders, Piaggio had entered aviation during World War I, producing some aircraft and components under subcontract. Developed from an earlier P.50-II design for a four-engine bomber, the P.108 was a cantilever low-wing monoplane of all metal construction, with retractable tailwheel landing gear and power provided by four Piaggio P.XII RC.35 radial engines, two on each wing, in nacelles at the wing

leading edges. Four versions were planned, but only the P.108 Bombardiere, which was first flown in prototype form during 1939, was built in any quantity. The variants, built only as prototypes or in small numbers, comprised first the single P.108A Artiglieri anti-shipping aircraft which, converted from the P.108 prototype, had its standard armament supplemented by the installation of a 102-mm cannon. Captured by German forces at the time of the Allied-Italian armistice, it was impressed for service with the Luftwaffe. The P.108C Civile was a civil transport version with increased wing span and a redesigned fuselage to

Piaggio P.108

The Piaggio P.108 was the only Italian four-engined bomber of the war, and did not measure up in any way to the British or American designs.

accommodate 32 passengers. A total of 16 was built, including one prototype, but these were modified for use as military transports accommodating 56 troops, and about 24 P.108Bs were also converted to this configuration. One P.108T (Trasporto) military transport prototype was built as a conversion from a P.108C, from which it differed primarily by incorporating side loading doors and a ventral hatch. Proposed variants included the P.108M (Modificato), a development of the P.108B with the single machine-gun in the nose turret replaced by four guns and a 20-mm cannon; and the P.133, an advanced version of the P.108B with uprated engines and an increased bombload.

The P.108B was first deployed in night attacks on Gibraltar during early 1942, and the type saw service subsequently in the Mediterranean, North African and Russian theatres of operation. A total of 163 was built, but heavy losses meant that less than five per cent

survived to serve with the Republican Socialist air force after the armistice with the Allies.

Specification
Piaggio P.108B
Type: four-engine heavy bomber
Powerplant: four 1,500-hp (1119-kW) Piaggio P.XII RC.35 18-cylinder radial piston engines
Performance: maximum speed 267 mph (430 km/h) at 13,780 ft (4200 m); cruising speed 199 mph (320 km/h); service ceiling 27,885 ft (8500 m); maximum range 2,187 miles (3520 km)
Weights: empty 38,195 lb (17,325 kg); maximum take-off 65,885 lb (29885 kg)
Dimensions: span 104 ft 11¾ in (32.00 m); length 73 ft 2 in (22.30 m); height 19 ft 8¼ in (6.00 m); wing area 1,453.18 sq ft (135.00 m²)
Armament: eight 12.7-mm (0.5-in) machine-guns, plus a bombload of up to 7,716 lb (3500 kg)
Operators: Italian Regia Aeronautica and Aeronautica Nazionale Repubblicana, and Germany

Reggiane Re.2000 series

History and notes
Officine Meccaniche Reggiane SA was a subsidiary of the Caproni company, for which it built aircraft during World War I, but it had no direct association with the aircraft industry from the end of that war until resuming design and manufacture in the mid-1930s. In 1937 the company began development of a single-seat fighter which was based very closely on the US Seversky Aircraft Corporation's P-35 designed by Alexander Kartveli. A cantilever low-wing monoplane with retractable tailwheel landing gear, the Reggiane Re.2000 Falco I prototype, powered by an 870-hp (649-kW) Piaggio P.XI RC.40 radial engine, was flown for the first time during 1938. Competitive evaluation against the Macchi MC.200 resulted in this latter aircraft being ordered into production for the Regia Aeronautica, although the Re.2000 had shown itself to be superior in manoeuvrability, even when flown

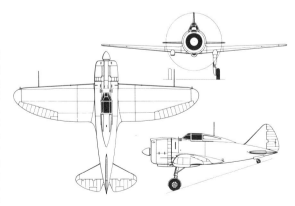

Reggiane Re.2000

against the Messerschmitt Bf 109E. However, the Re.2000's deficiencies (primarily structural) did not

Reggiane Re.2000 series

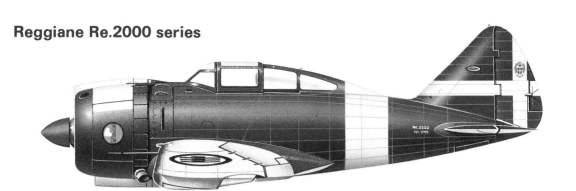

Reggiane Re.2000 of the Regia Aeronautica

Reggiane Re.2000 of the 1st Division, Flygflottilj Ängelholm, Sweden 1945

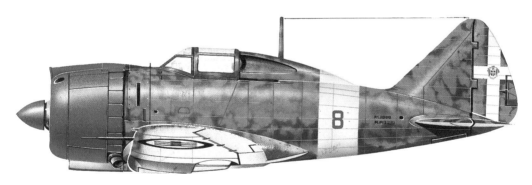

Reggiane Re.2000GA Serie IIIa of 377ª Squadriglia Autonoma, Palermo-Boccadifalco, March 1942

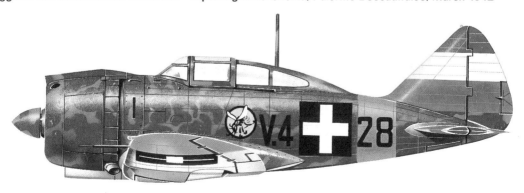

Reggiane Re.2000 Heja I of 1./1 Szazad, Önálló Vadász Ostály (Independent Fighter Group) attached to the Hungarian army in Russia in 1942

Reggiane Re.2000 series

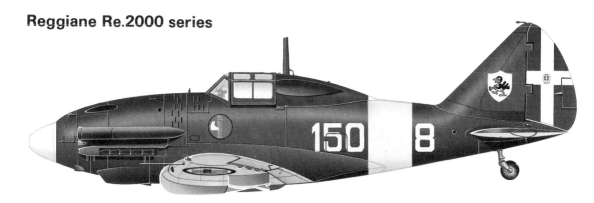

Reggiane Re.2001 of 150ª Squadriglia, 2° Gruppo, 6° Stormo at Pantellaria, August 1942

Reggiane Re.2001 of the 362ª Squadriglia, 22° Gruppo, 52° Stormo at Capodichino, May 1943

deter export customers and the type was built for the Hungarian government, which also acquired a manufacturing licence; the type was operated by the Hungarian air force as the Hejja (hawk). Re.2000s were supplied also to Sweden, being operated until 1945 by the Flygvapen under the designation J 20. And though the type had been rejected by the Regia Aeronautica, the Italian navy acquired 12 Re.2000 Serie II fighters especially strengthened for catapult launching, followed by 24 Re.2000 Serie III aircraft with increased fuel capacity for deployment as long-range fighters.

Belief that performance would benefit by installation of the Daimler-Benz DB 601A-1 inline led to the Re.2001 Falco II, first used operationally by the Regia Aeronautica over Malta in 1942. Luftwaffe priorities for DB 601 engines meant that the Re.2001 had to be powered by a licence-built version of this engine, the Alfa Romeo RA.1000 RC.41-1a Monsonie, but with the Macchi MC.202 having first call on production of these engines the manufacture of Re.2001s was to be limited to only 252. This number included 100 Re.2001 Serie I, Serie II and Serie III fighters with armament variations, the Re.2001 Serie IV fighter-bomber, and 150 Re.2001 CN night-fighters. Experimental conversions included a tandem two-seat trainer, tank-buster, torpedo-fighter and one with an Isotta Fraschini Delta IV engine.

About 50 Re.2002 Ariete (ram) fighter-bombers followed for service with the Regia Aeronautica, these being powered by the 1,175-hp (876-kWk) Piaggio P.XIX RC.45 radial engine mounted in a slightly lengthened and strengthened fuselage. The type first saw operational service in 1942, suffering heavy losses while contesting the Allied landings on Sicily. Last of this related family of fighters, and almost certainly the best produced in Italy during World War II, the Re.2005 Sagittario (archer) had the same general configuration as its predecessors. However, its design incorporated considerable structural redesign, and refined landing gear, and the type reverted to the inline engine. First flown in September 1942 with a Daimler-Benz DB 605A-1, the Re.2005 led to a production model, of which deliveries began in 1943, with a licence-built version of this engine, the Fiat RA.1050 RC.58 Tifone. Only 48 had been delivered before finalisation of the armistice with the Allies, these aircraft fighting in the defence of Naples, Rome and Sicily, the survivors battling above the crumbling ruins of Berlin.

Specification
Reggiane Re.2005 Sagittario
Type: single-seat fighter/fighter-bomber
Powerplant: one 1,475-hp (1100-kW) Fiat RA.1050 RC.58 Tifone 12-cylinder inverted Vee piston engine
Performance: maximum speed 391 mph (630 km/h) at 22,800 ft (6950 m); service ceiling 40,000 ft (12,190 m); range 786 miles (1265 km)
Weights: empty 5,732 lb (2600 kg); maximum take-off

Reggiane Re.2000 series

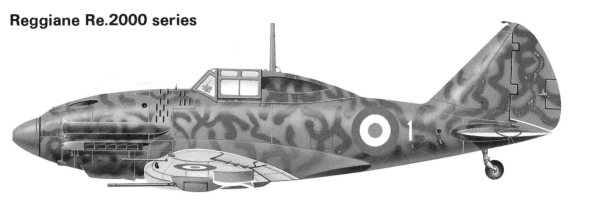

Reggiane Re.2001 of the 82ª Squadriglia, 21° Gruppo, 51° Stormo, Co-Belligerent Air Force, Puglia, late 1943

7,848 lb (3560 kg)
Dimensions: span 36 ft 1 in (11.00 m); length 28 ft 7¾ in (8.73 m); height 10 ft 4 in (3.15 m); wing area 219.59 sq ft (20.40 m²)
Armament: three 20-mm cannon and two 12.7-mm (0.5-in) machine-guns, all forward-firing, plus up to 1,390 lb (630 kg) of bombs when operated as a

fighter-bomber
Operators: Italian Regia Aeronautica and Aeronautica Nazionale Repubblicana, and Germany

Closely modelled on the Seversky P-35, the Re.2000 suffered structural problems, but this did not prevent its sale to Hungary and Sweden.

Repülögpégyàr Levente II

History and notes
In October 1940 Repülögpégyàr flew the prototype of a parasol-wing two-seat primary trainer which it designated Repülögpégyàr Levente I. This was modified subsequently to serve as the prototype of an improved Levente II which entered service with the Hungarian air force during 1943. By then, Hungary had allied itself with Germany and had participated in the invasion of the USSR. The result was that the 100 Levente IIs built to serve with the air force as primary

trainers were, in fact, deployed with operational squadrons where they were used in communications/liaison roles until the end of the war.

Specification
Repülögpégyàr Levente II
Type: two-seat liaison/training aircraft
Powerplant: one licence-built 105-hp (78-kW) Hirth HM 504A-2 4-cylinder inverted inline piston engine
Performance: maximum speed 112 mph (180 km/h);

Repülögpégyàr Levente II

cruising speed 99 mph (160 km/h); service ceiling 14,765 ft (4500 m); range 404 miles (650 km)
Weights: empty 1,036 lb (470 kg); maximum take-off 1,653 lb (750 kg)
Dimensions: span 31 ft 0 in (9.45 m); length 19 ft 11¼ in (6.08 m); height 8 ft 3½ in (2.53 m); wing area

The Levente II was used on the Eastern Front as a communications/liaison aircraft by the Hungarian air force allied to Germany.

145.32 sq ft (13.50 m²)
Operator: Hungary

Savoia-Marchetti S.M.79 Sparviero

History and notes

Designed originally as a three-engine civil transport with accommodation for eight passengers, the prototype Savoia-Marchetti S.M.79 (I-MAGO) was flown for the first time in late 1934. It was soon realised that the design could be adapted easily for service as a bomber/reconnaissance aircraft, resulting in one of the most successful Italian bomber aircraft of World War II, some 1,300 of all versions being built. A cantilever low-wing monoplane, the S.M.79 Sparviero (sparrowhawk) was structurally a mixture of light alloy, steel and wood, with fabric, light alloy and plywood being used for covering. Accommodating a crew of four or five, the type incorporated retractable tailwheel landing gear, and power for the bomber prototype was provided by three 780-hp (582-kW) Alfa Romeo 126 RC.34 radial engines. Successful testing led to a first production order for the type as the S.M.79-I, which differed from the initial prototype by having a revised cockpit and a ventral gondola beneath the fuselage, just to the rear of the wing trailing edge. This version saw service with the Aviazione Legionaria during the Spanish Civil War, and good reports of its capability and reliability led Yugoslavia to order 45 generally similar aircraft in

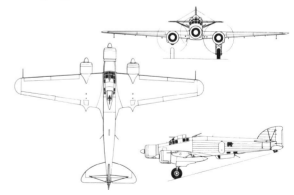

Savoia-Marchetti SM.79-II Sparviero

1938, these being designated S.M.79T.

Earlier, in 1937, the S.M.79 was evaluated for use in a torpedo-bomber role, resulting in the S.M.79-II equipped to carry two 450-mm (17.7-in) torpedoes, the majority of the type being powered by 1,000-hp (746-kW) Piaggio P.XI RC.40 radial engines. Almost 600 S.M.79-I and S.M.79-II aircraft were in service when Italy entered World War II, they and subsequent

Savoia-Marchetti S.M.79 Sparviero

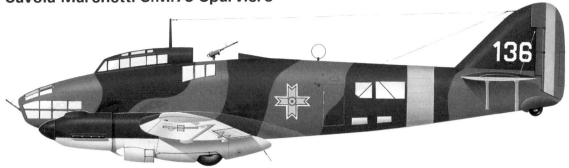

Savoia-Marchetti SM.79-JR of 3rd Air Corps, Romanian air force in 1943 on the Eastern Front

Savoia-Marchetti SM.79B flown by the Iraqi air force during the war

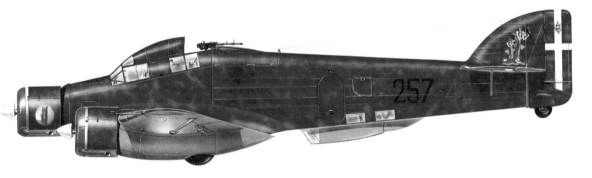

Savoia-Marchetti SM.79 of the 257ª Squadriglia, 108° Gruppo, 36° Stormo, Sicily, early 1941

Savoia-Marchetti SM.79 of 193ª Squadriglia, 87° Gruppo, 30° Stormo, Sicily, 1941

Savoia-Marchetti S.M.79 Sparviero

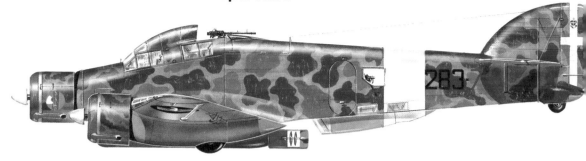

Savoia-Marchetti SM.79 of the 283ª Squadriglia, 130° Gruppo Autonomo operating in the Mediterranean in 1942

production aircraft being deployed in every theatre where Italian forces were operating.

Attempts had also been made to gain large-scale export orders, but only three countries finalised contracts, twin-engine S.M.79B aircraft being supplied to Brazil (3 with 930-hp/694-kW Alfa Romeo 128 RC.18 engines), Iraq (4 with 1,030-hp/768-kW Fiat A.80 RC.14s), and Romania (24 with 1,000-hp/746-kW Gnome-Rhône Mistral Major 14Ks). This last country later acquired an additional 24 aircraft, designated S.M.79JR, and then built another 16 under licence. A long-range variant with increased fuel capacity and Alfa Romeo 126 RC.34 engines was built under the designation S.M.79T. In addition to wide-scale deployment with Italian forces in its intended bomber or torpedo-bomber role, the S.M.79 was used also for close support, reconnaissance and transport missions. In fact, the type's use as a transport continued after the war, some remaining in service with Italy's post-war

Aeronautica Militare Italiana until the early 1950s. Transports included the S.M.79C VIP version with 1,000-hp (746-kW) Piaggio P.XI RC.40 engines and dorsal and ventral gun positions deleted, these being conversions from S.M.79-Is, and S.M.83, S.M.83A and S.M.83T civil transport versions of the S.M.79 with Alfa Romeo 126 RC.34 engines, in 10-passenger or six-passenger plus mail configurations.

When the Italians surrendered to the Allies a small number of S.M.79-I and S.M.79-II aircraft entered service with the Aeronautica Cobelligerante del Sud, and the S.M.79-III, which was an improved version of the S.M.79-II with the ventral gondola deleted and armament revised, proved of great value to the Aeronautica Nazionale Repubblicana.

Two S.M. 79 Sparviero bombers fly over the desert, displaying their rear-cockpit mounted machine-guns. The type was still in service at the end of the war.

Savoia-Marchetti S.M.79 Sparviero

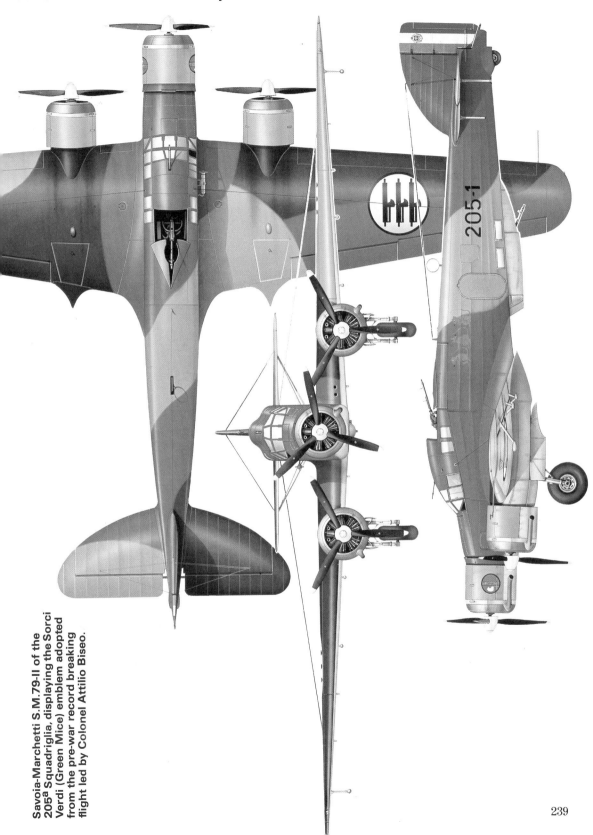

Savoia-Marchetti S.M.79-II of the 205ª Squadriglia, displaying the Sorci Verdi (Green Mice) emblem adopted from the pre-war record breaking flight led by Colonel Attilio Biseo.

Savoia-Marchetti S.M.79 Sparviero

Savoia-Marchetti SM.79 of the Gruppo Aerosiluranti 'Buscaglia' of the Aviazione Nazionale Repubblicana at Gorizia in March 1941

Specification
Savoia-Marchetti S.M.79-I

Type: medium bomber

Powerplant: three 780-hp (582-kW) Alfa Romeo 126 RC.34 9-cylinder radial piston engines

Performance: maximum speed 267 mph (430 km/h) at 13,125 ft (4000 m); cruising speed 233 mph (375 km/h); service ceiling 21,325 ft (6500 m); range 1,181 miles (1900 km)

Weights: empty 14,991 lb (6800 kg); maximum take-off 23,104 lb (10480 kg)

Dimensions: span 69 ft 6¾ in (21.20 m); length 51 ft 10 in (15.80 m); height 14 ft 1¼ in (4.30 m); wing area 664.16 sq ft (61.70 m²)

Armament: three 12.7-mm (0.5-in) machine-guns and one 7.7-mm (0.303-in) machine-gun, plus a bombload of up to 2,756 lb (1250 kg) carried internally

Operators: Italian Regia Aeronautica, Aeronautica Cobelligerante del Sud and Aeronautica Nazionale Repubblicana, Brazil, Croatia, Germany, Iraq, Romania, Spain, Yugoslavia

---

Savoia-Marchetti S.M.81 Pipistrello

History and notes

The Savoia-Marchetti S.M.81 Pipistrello (bat) was a development of the Savoia-Marchetti S.M.73 18-passenger airliner which had first flown in prototype form on 4 June 1934. Like the airliner from which it was derived, the S.M.81 was a three-engine cantilever low-wing monoplane with fixed tailwheel landing gear. First flown in early 1935, it was available in some numbers by the time that Italy invaded Abyssinia (Ethiopia) on 3 October 1935. Here, in addition to its dedicated bomber role, it was used also for reconnaissance and transport. The next operational use of the type came during the Spanish Civil War, S.M.81s being among the first aircraft provided in support of General Franco, and others served in Spain a little later as components of the Aviazione Legionaria. By the time Italy became involved in World War II about 100 remained in service with the Regia Aeronautica, but although it was already completely outdated the S.M.81 was to be found wherever Italian forces were fighting. Because of its low speed and vulnerability to attack, it was used primarily for second-line duties, but with the protection of darkness many found important use as night bombers, particularly in North Africa. Some remained in service at the time of the Italian surrender, continuing in operation with the Aeronautica Cobelligerante del Sud, and a few survived the war to serve for five or six years with the post-war Aeronautica Militare Italiana. A total of approximately 535 S.M.81s had been built

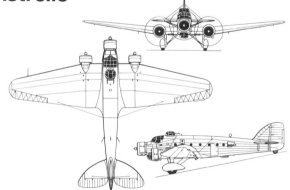

Savoia-Marchetti S.M.81

and flown with a variety of powerplants including the 650-hp (485-kW) Gnome-Rhône 14K or similarly powered Alfa Romeo 125 RC.35, the 900-hp (671-kW) Alfa Romeo 126 RC.34, and the 700-hp (522-kW) Piaggio P.X RC.35. Under the designation S.M.81B a single experimental twin-engine prototype had been flown on the power of two 840-hp (626-kW) Isotta Fraschini Asso XI RC engines, but no production examples followed.

Specification
Savoia-Marchetti S.M.81 Pipistrello

Type: bomber/transport

Savoia-Marchetti S.M.81 Pipistrello

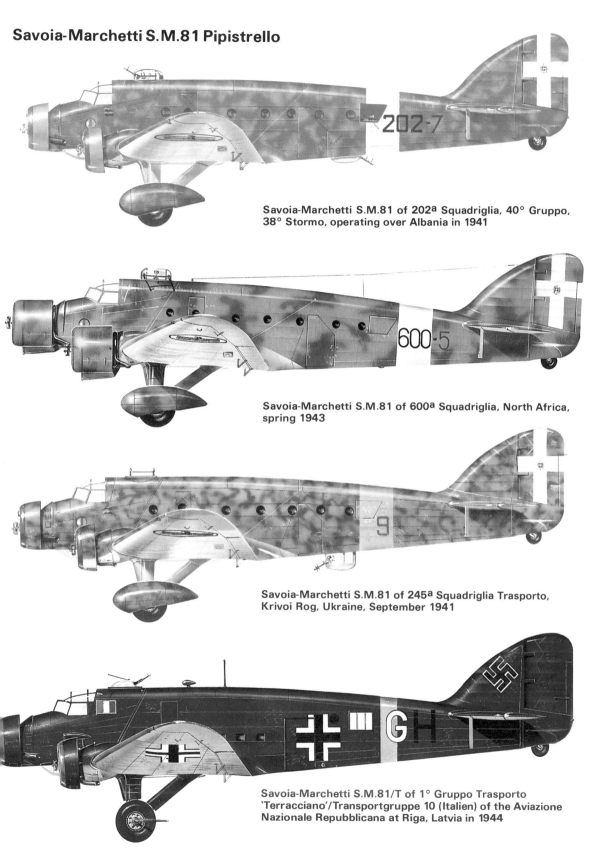

Savoia-Marchetti S.M.81 of 202ª Squadriglia, 40° Gruppo, 38° Stormo, operating over Albania in 1941

Savoia-Marchetti S.M.81 of 600ª Squadriglia, North Africa, spring 1943

Savoia-Marchetti S.M.81 of 245ª Squadriglia Trasporto, Krivoi Rog, Ukraine, September 1941

Savoia-Marchetti S.M.81/T of 1° Gruppo Trasporto 'Terracciano'/Transportgruppe 10 (Italien) of the Aviazione Nazionale Repubblicana at Riga, Latvia in 1944

Savoia-Marchetti S.M.81 Pipistrello

Powerplant: three 700-hp (522-kW) Piaggio P.X RC.35 9-cylinder radial piston engines
Performance: maximum speed 211 mph (340 km/h) at 3,280 ft (1000 m); service ceiling 22,965 ft (7000 m); range 1,243 miles (2000 km)
Weights: empty 13,889 lb (6300 kg); maximum take-off 20,503 lb (9300 kg)
Dimensions: span 78 ft 9 in (24.00 m); length 58 ft 4¾ in (17.80 m); height 14 ft 7¼ in (4.45 m); wing area 1,001.08 sq ft (93.00 m²)

Due to its vulnerability, the S.M.81 Pipistrello was used as a bomber mainly during the hours of darkness. It was also used widely as a transport.

Armament: usually five 7.7-mm (0.303-in) machine-guns, plus a bombload of up to 2,205 lb (1000 kg) carried internally
Operators: Italian Regia Aeronautica, Aeronautica Cobelligerante del Sud and Aeronautica Nazionale Repubblicana

---

Savoia-Marchetti S.M.82 Canguru

History and notes
First flown during 1939, the Savoia-Marchetti S.M.82 Canguru (kangaroo) was developed from the earlier S.M.75 Marsupiale (marsupial) civil transport, of which a number were impressed into service with the Regia Aeronautica in June 1940: a militarised version designated S.M.75bis was also built for the air force. The S.M.82 prototype was basically an enlarged version of its predecessor with a fuselage that was both longer and deeper, in configuration a cantilever mid-wing monoplane with retractable tailwheel landing gear and the three-engine powerplant that was a feature of the Savoia-Marchetti bomber/transport designs of this era. Despite being underpowered, the S.M.82 cargo/troop transport saw wide-scale use with the Regia Aeronautica, and several were used in similar roles by the Luftwaffe. Specially equipped for the cargo role, it even included handling gear to simplify the loading and unloading of items such as aero engines, and its cabin volume enabled it to transport a dismantled Fiat CR.42 biplane without difficulty. In the troop transport role it had folding seats to provide standard accommodation for 40 and their equipment, but many more than this number were carried in emergency. About 400 were

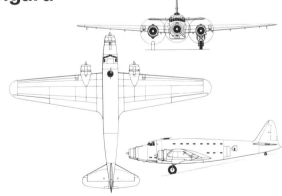

Savoia-Marchetti S.M.82

built, the first of them entering service in 1941, but although able to operate as a bomber with a maximum bombload of up to 8,818 lb (4000 kg), the S.M.82 saw very limited use in this role. Following the armistice between Italy and the Allies the type continued to operate in the transport role, about 50 with the Aeronautica Nazionale Repubblicana and 30 with the Aeronautica Cobelligerante del Sud. Post-war some 30

Savoia-Marchetti S.M.82 Canguru

continued in service with the Aeronautica Militare Italiana, many remaining in use until the early 1960s.

Designed as a bomber, the S.M.82 Canguru was more widely used as a transport and was operated as such by both Germans and Italians.

Specification

Type: heavy bomber/transport
Powerplant: three 950-hp (708-kW) Alfa Romeo 128 RC.21 9-cylinder radial piston engines
Performance: maximum speed 230 mph (370 km/h); cruising speed 186 mph (300 km/h); service ceiling 19,685 ft (6000 m); range 1,864 miles (3000 km)
Weights: empty 23,259 lb (10550 kg); maximum take-off 39,727 lb (18020 kg)
Dimensions: span 97 ft 4½ in (29.68 m); length 75 ft 1½ in (22.90 m); height 19 ft 8¼ in (6.00 m); wing area 1,276.64 sq ft (118.60 m²)
Armament: (bomber) one 12.7-mm (0.5-in) and four 7.7-mm (0.303-in) machine-guns, plus up to 8,818 lb (4000 kg) of bombs
Operators: Italian Regia Aeronautica, Aeronautica Nazionale Repubblicana and Aeronautica Cobelligerante del Sud, Germany

Siebel Fh 104/Si 204

History and notes

The Siebel factory at Halle was set up originally by Hans Klemm Flugzeugbau as Flugzeugbau Halle GmbH and used initially for licence production of the Focke-Wulf Fw 44 Stieglitz and, later, of the Heinkel He 46 and Dornier Do 17. In 1937, however, the prototype Flugzeugbau Halle Fh 104 Hallore made its first flight, a five-seat cabin monoplane with light alloy fuselage and tail surfaces, and a plywood-covered wooden wing. Power was supplied by two 270-hp (201-kW) Hirth HM 508C engines, which were used also for the second prototype; the latter differed by having revised main

landing gear legs and modified windscreen. The Hallore made a number of noteworthy flights, winning the Littorio Rally in Italy, covering 3,853 miles (6200 km) across 12 countries during the 1938 Europa Rundflug and, in March 1939, flying a 24,840-mile (39975-km) tour of Africa. Some 46 production Fh 104s were built between 1938 and 1942, powered by 280-hp (209-kW) Hirth HM 508D engines driving variable-pitch propellers, and most of them saw Luftwaffe service in the communications and liaison roles.

In 1941 Siebel flew the prototype of another twin, the larger and heavier Si 204 which appeared originally

Siebel Fh 104/Si 204

Siebel Si 204E of 2./NSchGr 4 at Malacky, Slovakia in November 1944

Siebel Si 204D-1 of Stab, III/KG 200 at Fürsterwalde, May 1944, on communications duties

with a conventional stepped cockpit and a powerplant of two 360-hp (268-kW) Argus As 410 engines. The Si 204D appeared in 1942, with its characteristic glazed nose and cockpit and with two 600-hp (447-kW) As 411 engines. The Si 204A was essentially a transport and communications aircraft, with a crew of two and eight passengers, while the Si 204D was used for radio, navigation and instrument flying training. The Forhambault and Bourges factories of SNCAC in France

were charged with production for the Luftwaffe, and after the Liberation 350 were built for the French armed forces as the NC 702 (Si 204A) and NC 701 (Si 204D) Martinet, powered by 590-hp (440-kW) Renault 12S-00 engines. Manufacture was also undertaken at

A general-purpose type operated in a number of roles including communications and crew training, the Si 204 was powered by two Argus As 411 engines developing 600-hp (447-kW) each.

Siebel Fh 104/Si 204

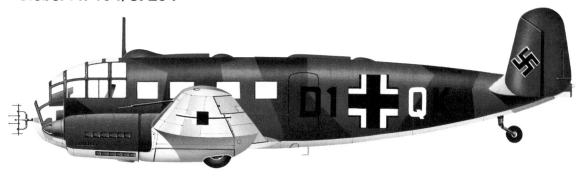

Siebel Si 204D-1 of 2./SAGr 126 in 1945. The aircraft carries Hohentwiel search radar

the Aero factory in Czechoslovakia as the military C-3 and the civil C-103.

Specification
Siebel Si 204D

Type: light transport/crew trainer
Powerplant: two 600-hp (447-kW) Argus As 411 12-cylinder inverted Vee piston engines
Performance: maximum speed 226 mph (364 km/h)

at 9,840 ft (3000 m); cruising speed 211 mph (340 km/h); service ceiling 24,605 ft (7500 m); range 1,118 miles (1800 km)
Weights: empty 8,708 lb (3950 kg); maximum take-off 12,346 lb (5600 kg)
Dimensions: span 69 ft 11¾ in (21.33 m); length 39 ft 2½ in (11.95 m); height 13 ft 9½ in (4.20 m); wing area 495.16 sq ft (46.00 m²)
Operator: Luftwaffe, Czechoslovakia, France

Tachikawa Ki-36/Ki-55

History and notes

The Tachikawa Aeroplane Company, established at Tachikawa in 1924, was regarded as a comparatively small organisation before the beginning of the Pacific war. However, in 1937 it began the design of a two-seat

army co-operation aircraft that was to change the company image. First flown in prototype form on 20

The Tachikawa Ki-36 was used as an army co-operation aircraft, but was also used as a trainer.

Tachikawa Ki-36/Ki-55

April 1938, the Tachikawa Ki-36 was a cantilever low-wing monoplane of all-metal basic structure, covered by a mix of light alloy and fabric. Landing gear was of fixed tailwheel type, the main units enclosed in speed fairings, and power was provided by a 450-hp (336-kW) Hitachi Ha-13 radial engine. The two-man crew was enclosed by a long 'greenhouse' canopy and both men had good fields of view, that of the observer being improved by clear-view panels in the floor. Flown in competitive trials against the Mitsubishi Ki-35, Tachikawa's design proved to be the more effective and the type was ordered into production in November 1938 as the Army Type 98 Direct Co-Operation Plane, company designation Ki-36; generally similar to the prototypes, they were armed with two 7.7-mm (0.303-in) machine-guns and introduced the more powerful Hitachi Ha-13a engine. When construction ended in January 1944, a total of 1,334 had been built by Tachikawa (862) and Kawasaki (472). An advanced version of the Ki-36 was proposed under the designation Ki-72, gaining improved performance by installation of the 600-hp (447-kW) Hitachi Ha-38 engine and retractable landing gear, but no examples were built.

The handling characteristics and reliability of the Ki-36 made the army realise that it was ideal for use as an advanced trainer, resulting in development of the Ki-55, intended specifically for this role, and having armament reduced to a single forward-firing machine-gun. Following the testing of a prototype in September 1939, the army ordered this aircraft as the Army Type 99 Advanced Trainer; when production was terminated

in December 1943 a total of 1,389 had been built by Tachikawa (1,078) and Kawasaki (311).

Both versions were allocated the Allied codename 'Ida', and the Ki-36 was first deployed with considerable success in China. However, when confronted by Allied fighters at the beginning of the Pacific war it was found to be too vulnerable, being re-deployed in China where it was less likely to be confronted by such aircraft. It was also considered suitable for *kamikaze* use in the closing stages of the war, being modified to carry internally a bomb of up to 1,102 lb (500 kg).

Specification
Tachikawa Ki-36

Powerplant: one 510-hp (380-kW) Hitachi Ha-13a 9-cylinder radial piston engine
Performance: maximum speed 216 mph (348 km/h) at 5,905 ft (1800 m); cruising speed 146 mph (235 km/h); service ceiling 26,740 ft (8150 m); range 767 miles (1235 km)
Weights: empty 2,749 lb (1247 kg); maximum take-off 3,660 lb (1660 kg)
Dimensions: span 38 ft 8½ in (11.80 m); length 25 ft 3 in (8.00 m); height 11 ft 11¼ in (3.64 m); wing area 215.29 sq ft (20.00 m²)
Armament: two 7.7-mm (0.303-in) machine-guns (one forward-firing and one on a trainable mounting in the rear cockpit), plus an external bombload of up to 331 lb (150 kg)
Operators: Japanese Army, Thailand

Tachikawa Ki-54

History and notes
The Tachikawa Ki-54 was designed to meet an Imperial Japanese Army requirement for a twin-engine advanced trainer that would be suitable for a variety of training roles but, in particular, to enable a potential bomber crew to work together as a team for operational training. First flown during the summer of 1940, the prototype was a cantilever low-wing monoplane with

Incorporating two gun turrets in the dorsal position, the Ki-54 was used by the Japanese army as a bomber crew trainer. Some were built for the anti-submarine role but were little used.

retractable tailwheel landing gear and power provided by two Hitachi Ha-13a radial engines nacelle-mounted at the wing leading edges. Manufacturer's and service testing of this prototype, which was intended primarily for pilot training, resulted in only minor modifications, and the Ki-54 was ordered into production during 1941 as the Army Type 1 Advanced Trainer Model A, company designation Ki-54a. It was followed after comparatively few had been built by the major production variant, the Ki-54b, which had the full crew training capability that had been planned from the beginning, with armament of four 7.7-mm (0.303-in) machine-guns and external racks for practice bombs. A number of Ki-54c light transport aircraft were also built, providing seats for eight passengers and, in addition, a small number were built for civil use under the designation Y-59. Under the designation Ki-54d several aircraft were built for use in an ASW role, carrying eight 132-lb (60-kg) depth charges, but were little used. A single prototype of a version of the Ki-54c of all-wood construction had the designation Ki-110, but was destroyed in an Allied air raid before being flown, and plans for a fuel tanker version of the Ki-56c of

Tachikawa Ki-54

conventional construction (Ki-111) and all-wood construction (Ki-114) did not mature and none were built. The Ki-54b and Ki-54c proved to be both successful and popular. Allocated the Allied codename 'Hickory', irrespective of role, 1,368 Ki-54s of all versions were built by Tachikawa before production was terminated by the end of the Pacific war.

Specification
Tachikawa Ki-54b
Type: twin-engine crew trainer
Powerplant: two 510-hp (380-kW) Hitachi Ha-13a 9-cylinder radial piston engine
Performance: maximum speed 233 mph (375 km/h) at 6,560 ft (2000 m); cruising speed 149 mph (240 km/h); service ceiling 23,555 ft (7180 m); range 597 miles (960 km)
Weights: empty 6,512 lb (2954 kg); maximum take-off 8,591 lb (3897 kg)
Dimensions: span 58 ft 8¾ in (17.90 m); length 39 ft 2 in (11.94 m); height 11 ft 9 in (3.58 m); wing area 430.57 sq ft (40.00 m²)
Armament: four 7.7-mm (0.303-in) machine-guns plus practice bombs
Operator: Japanese Army

Weiss WM 21 Sólyom

History and notes
Manfreid Weiss Flugzeug und Motorenfabrik was the name given to the aviation division of one of Hungary's largest industrial organisations. Established at Budapest in 1928, the company began aircraft production by building the Fokker F.VIII and C.V under licence. In 1935 the company initiated the design of a two-seat biplane intended for use in a reconnaissance role. This was clearly derived from the radial-engined Fokker C.V-D and the company's own WM 16 which was a refined version of the C.V. An unequal-span biplane of mixed construction, its configuration included a braced tail unit, fixed tailskid landing gear and accommodation for two in tandem open cockpits. Power was provided by one of the company's WM K-14 radial engines.

Successful testing of the WM 21 prototype led to an order for production aircraft to serve with the Hungarian air force, which named the type Sólyom (falcon), and initial deliveries began in 1938. A total of 128 was built, these equipping several reconnaissance squadrons when, on 27 June 1941, Hungary joined forces with Germany in its five-day-old invasion of the USSR. Within six months the WM 21's vulnerability to enemy fighters brought redeployment in Hungary for roles such as communications and training, and these second-line duties came to an end when the Sólyoms were retired during 1943.

Specification
Type: two-seat reconnaissance aircraft

A refined version of the Fokker C.V, the Weiss WM 21 Sólyom was flown by the Hungarians on light reconnaissance duties.

Powerplant: one 870-hp (649-kW) Weiss WM K-14 radial piston engine
Performance: maximum speed 199 mph (320 km/h); cruising speed 171 mph (275 km/h); service ceiling 26,245 ft (8000 m); range 373 miles (600 km)
Weights: empty 5,401 lb (2450 kg); maximum take-off 7,606 lb (3450 kg)
Dimensions: span 42 ft 4 in (12.90 m); length 31 ft 8 in (9.65 m); height 11 ft 5¾ in (3.50 m); wing area 352.53 sq ft (32.75 m²)
Armament: two 7.92-mm (0.31-in) forward-firing machine-guns and one similar gun on flexible mount in rear cockpit, plus provision for light bombs on underwing racks
Operator: Hungary

Yokosuka D4Y Suisei

History and notes
In late 1938 the Imperial Japanese Navy's Air Technical Arsenal at Yokosuka was instructed to design a single-engine bomber, a carrier-based aircraft in this category being required urgently by the navy. The resulting Yokosuka D4Y1 prototype was a low/mid-wing cantilever monoplane of all-metal construction with retractable tailwheel landing gear and accommodating a crew of two in tandem beneath a continuous transparent canopy. Features of the design to make it suitable for carrier operation included short-span wings that precluded the need for wing-folding, with Fowler-type

Yokosuka D4Y Suisei

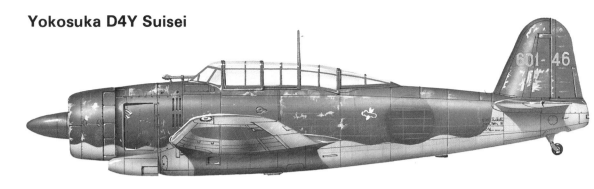

Yokosuka D4Y3 Model 33 of the 601st Kokutai

flaps and three underwing dive brakes on each wing; landing gear mainwheels with hydraulic braking system; and a retractable arrester hook mounted in the rear fuselage. An internal bomb bay was also incorporated in the fuselage structure, having the volume to accommodate a single bomb of up to 1,102 lb (500 kg), and defensive armament comprised two 7.7-mm (0.303-in) forward-firing machine-guns and one rear-firing gun of 7.92-mm (0.31-in) calibre. Intended powerplant was a licence-built version of the Daimler-Benz DB 601A, but as the Japanese-built Aichi Atsuta was not available in time an imported DB 600G of 960 hp (716 kW) was installed in each of the early prototypes. Although the DB 600G had an output some 20 per cent below the expected rating of the Atsuta, the performance of the D4Y1 prototypes exceeded all expectations, but service trials with these, and pre-production aircraft powered by the 1,200-hp (895-kW) Aichi AE1A Atsuta 32 engine, revealed weakness in the wing structure. As a result of this the first production version was the Navy Type 2 Carrier Reconnaissance Plane Model 11 Suisei (comet), manufacturer's designation D4Y1-C, with wing structural requirements far less demanding than a dive-bomber, and initial production deliveries were made in the autumn of 1942.

Wing reinforcement and improved dive brakes led to production of the Navy Suisei Carrier Bomber Model 11 (D4Y1) in March 1943, and within a year some 500 had entered service. This total included a number of D4Y1 KAI aircraft which were identical to the D4Y1 Suisei except that they were equipped for catapult launching. Deployed in June 1944 against allied amphibious attacks on the Mariana group of islands, the force of Suiseis operating from the Japanese carriers was mauled severely by Allied fighters, a lack of armour protection and self-sealing tanks making it 'easy meat' for even small calibre machine-gun fire. The 'improved' D4Y2 that followed was still without such protection and differed primarily by having a more powerful Aichi AE1P Atsuta 32 engine. It was produced in a number of sub-variants, including a reconnaissance D4Y2-C, or D4Y2 KAI when equipped for catapult launching; the D4Y2a which introduced the first armament change, the rear-mounted 7.92-mm (0.31-in) machine-gun of all earlier models replaced by one of 13-mm (0.51-in) calibre, was available also as the

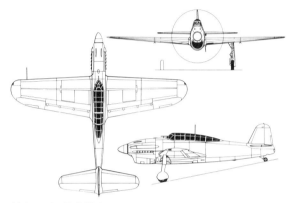

Yokosuka D4Y2 Suisei

D4Y2a-C or D4Y2a KAI when equipped for reconnaissance or catapult launching respectively. However, no significant effort had been made to make the D4Y any less vulnerable to Allied fighters and this version, too, was 'shot out of the skies' when deployed in defence of the Philippines.

Still ignoring crew protection, the D4Y3 was evolved to overcome maintenance problems with the Atsuta engine, introducing a reliable 1,560-hp (1163-kW) Mitsubishi MK8P Kinsei 62 radial, and a D4Y3a variant was also available, this having the armament of the D4Y2a. Some late production D4Y3s were equipped for rocket-assisted take-off, enabling them to operate from small carriers with maximum weapon loads. Final production version was the single-seat D4Y4 which, intended for *kamikaze* attacks, was able to carry a 1,764-lb (800-kg) bomb semi-recessed under the fuselage.

In addition to new production aircraft, several D4Y2s were converted by the Naval Air Arsenal at Hiro to serve as night-fighters, redesignated D4Y2-S; the type's primary armament in this role was an obliquely-mounted 20-mm cannon, firing upward and forward. Such night-fighters gained some limited success against Boeing B-29s attacking Japanese cities during the closing stages of the Pacific war.

Allocated the Allied codename 'Judy', a total of 2,038 D4Ys was built by the First Naval Air Technical Arsenal at Yokosuka (5 prototypes), Aichi (1,818) and the 11th Naval Air Arsenal at Hiro (215). For the Japanese navy it was little short of a tragedy that the

Yokosuka D4Y Suisei

full potential of this important dive-bomber was never realised, its vulnerability to enemy weapons preventing the majority from pressing home their attack.

Specification
Yokosuka D4Y2
Type: single-seat carrier-based dive bomber
Powerplant: one 1,400-hp (1044-kW) Aichi Atsuta 32 12-cylinder inverted-Vee piston engine
Performance: maximum speed 342 mph (550 km/h) at 15,585 ft (4750 m); cruising speed 264 mph (425 km/h) at 9,840 ft (3000 m); service ceiling 35,105 ft (10700 m); range 910 miles (1465 km)
Weights: empty 5,379 lb (2440 kg); maximum take-off 9,370 lb (4250 kg)
Dimensions: span 37 ft 8¾ in (11.50 m); length 33 ft 6¼ in (10.22 m); height 12 ft 3¼ in (3.74 m); wing area 254.04 sq ft (23.60 m²)

Easily shot out of the sky, the full potential of the D4Y was never realised by the Japanese navy.

Armament: two forward-firing 7.7-mm (0.303-in) Type 97 machine-guns and one 7.92-mm (0.31-in) gun on a trainable mount in the rear cockpit, plus up to 1,235 lb (560 kg) of bombs
Operator: Japanese Navy

Yokosuka K5Y

History and notes
Designed by the naval Air Technical Arsenal at Yokosuka, and developed as a collaboration between the Yokosuka Arsenal and Kawanishi, the Yokosuka K5Y1 was first flown in prototype form during December 1933. Early flight tests and service trials proceeded without any serious problems, the type entering production in January 1934 under the official designation Navy Type 93 Intermediate Trainer. Most extensively-built of all Japanese navy training aircraft, 5,770 K5Ys were built by Fuji (896), Hitachi (1,393), Kawanishi (60), Mitsubishi (60), Nakajima (24), Nippon (2,733), Watanabe (556) and the 1st Naval Air Arsenal at Kasumigaura (75), their production extending from 1934 until the end of the Pacific war. The initial K5Y1 had wheel landing gear, but alternative twin-float versions were available as the K5Y2 with a Hitachi Amakaze 11 engine or K5Y3 with a 515-hp (384-kW) Hitachi Amakaze 21 radial engine. Projected but not built were two land-based versions, the K5Y4 with a 480-hp (358-kW) Amakaze 21A engine, and K5Y5 with the 515-hp (384-kW) Amakaze 15.

An unequal-span biplane with fixed tailskid landing gear as standard, all were powered by radial engines and had two separate open cockpits in tandem. Allocated the Allied codename 'Willow', these trainers saw extensive use throughout the whole of their production period.

Specification
Yokosuka K5Y1
Type: two-seat land-based intermediate trainer
Powerplant: one 340-hp (254-kW) Hitachi Amakaze 11 9-cylinder radial piston engine
Performance: maximum speed 132 mph (212 km/h) at sea level; cruising speed 86 mph (138 km/h) at 3,280 ft (1000 m); service ceiling 18,700 ft (5700 m); range 634 miles (1020 km)
Weights: empty 2,205 lb (1000 kg); maximum take-off 3,307 lb (1500 kg)
Dimensions: span 36 ft 1 in (11.00 m); length 26 ft 5 in (8.05 m); height 10 ft 6 in (3.20 m); wing area 298.17 sq ft (27.70 m²)
Armament: (all versions) one fixed forward-firing 7.7-mm (0.303-in) machine-gun and one gun of same calibre on trainable mount in rear cockpit, plus up to 220 lb (100 kg) of bombs on external racks
Operator: Japanese Navy

With Mount Fuji in the background, these K5Ys are seen on a formation-flying training exercise, a function which the aircraft performed well. Floats were available for this type.

Yokosuka MXY7 Ohka

History and notes

The Yokosuka MXY7 Ohka (cherry blossom) epitomises, perhaps more than any other weapon of World War II, the desperate measures that, given the time and opportunity, a nation will take in an attempt to defend its homeland. The MXY7 Ohka was intended primarily for this purpose, being envisaged as a rocket-propelled piloted aircraft with a large high-explosive warhead in the nose. To be carried and launched from a 'mother' aircraft, the Ohka would then glide as far as possible before making a final high-speed approach under rocket-power to impact on its target. Design emphasis was to make the aircraft simple to build, using non-strategic materials, and very easy to fly.

Early unpowered prototypes were available for testing in October 1944, the first powered flight being made during the following month, but even before these trials had been made the MXY7 had entered production as the Navy Suicide Attacker Ohka Model 11. A total of 755 was built by March 1945, and this version was the only one to see operational service. The type's initial deployment, carried into action by Mitsubishi G4M2e aircraft, was little short of disastrous, all the 'mother' aircraft being destroyed by Allied fighters and their Ohkas being released uselessly short of their intended targets. Limited success came later when, for example, the American destroyer USS *Mannert L. Abele* was sunk by a direct hit on 12 April 1945. By then, however, production of the Ohka Model 11 had been terminated, for it was realised that the launch vehicle was too slow and vulnerable. An unpowered water-ballasted version known as the Ohka K-1 (45 built) was developed for training purposes, the water being jettisoned to reduce landing speed.

Subsequent attempts to give the weapon greater capability resulted in the very interesting Ohka Model 22 with reduced span and a lighter warhead, necessitated by the intention to launch it from the much faster Yokosuka P1Y1 Ginga. The Model 22 dispensed with the rocket power of the earlier version, a TSU-11 jet engine with a 100-hp (75-kW) four-cylinder piston-engine compressor being used in its stead, but testing showed the variant to be underpowered. Only one other version was built, the Ohka Model 43 K-1 KAI two-seat trainer, which had flaps and extendable skids for landing and a single rocket to give some experience under power.

Planned variants that were not built included the Ohka Model 33 to be powered by a 1,047-lb (475-kg) thrust Ne-20 turbojet engine and incorporate a 1,764-lb (800-kg) warhead; the similarly-powered and armed Ohka Model 43A and Model 43B, both with folding wings and catapult-launch equipment for use from a submarine and shore base respectively; and the Ohka Model 53 with Ne-20 turbojet powerplant which was to be towed off the ground and released as near as possible to its target. Allied seamen who were witnesses and/or survivors of *kamikaze* attacks believed that if there had been sufficient time for the Japanese navy to develop the Ohka to potent accuracy it would have been a very formidable weapon.

Specification
Yokosuka MXY7 Model 11

Type: single-seat suicide attack aircraft
Powerplant: three Type 4 MK 1 solid-propellant rockets with a combined thrust of 1,764 lb (800 kg)
Performance: maximum speed 404 mph (650 km/h); range 23 miles (37 km)
Weights: empty 970 lb (440 kg); maximum launch 4,718 lb (2140 kg)
Dimensions: span 16 ft 9½ in (5.12 m); length 19 ft 11 in (6.07 m); height 3 ft 9¾ in (1.16 m); wing area 64.59 sq ft (6.00 m²)
Operator: Japanese Navy

The Ohka was not a very pleasant aircraft to fly, as the canopy was sealed before the flight, leaving the pilot only one choice: to ensure his aircraft hit its desired target.

Yokosuka P1Y Ginga

History and notes

Requiring a fast medium-bomber that would be suitable for deployment in dive-bombing, low-altitude or torpedo attacks, the Imperial Japanese Navy instructed the Yokosuka Naval Air Arsenal in 1940 to proceed with the design and development of such an aircraft. The first Yokosuka P1Y prototype, flown during August 1943, was a cantilever mid-wing monoplane of all-metal construction, incorporating retractable tailwheel landing gear, powered by two Nakajima NK9B Homare 11 radial engines in wing-mounted nacelles, and armed with one 7.7-mm (0.303-in) machine-gun in the nose and one rear-firing 20-mm cannon. Flight testing showed that performance in the air was more than satisfactory, but the P1Y suffered serious maintenance problems that plagued this aircraft throughout its service life. Attempts to remedy the shortcomings were unsuccessful, with the result that it was not until early 1945 that the P1Y, designated officially as the Navy Bomber Ginga Model 11, or P1Y1, was introduced into operational service, rather as an act of desperation. In addition to the initial production version, in which the nose-mounted machine-gun was replaced by a 20-mm cannon, the Ginga (milky way) was built as the P1Y1a with 1,825-hp (1361-kW) Nakajima NK9C Homare 12 engines, a 20-mm cannon in the nose and a 13-mm (0.51-in) rear-firing machine-gun; the similar P1Y1b which introduced twin 13-mm (0.51-in) rear-firing machine-guns; the P1Y1c with one forward-firing and two rear-firing 13-mm (0.51-in) machine-guns; and the P1Y1-S night-fighter conversions of P1Y1 production aircraft, which were armed with four obliquely-mounted 20-mm cannon firing forward and upward plus one rear-firing 13-mm (0.51-in) machine-gun. A P1Y2-S production night-fighter was introduced later, powered by two 1,850-hp (1380-kW) Mitsubishi MK4T-A Kasei 25a radial engines and armed with three 20-mm cannon, two obliquely-mounted and one rear-firing. The same Kasei 25a engine served as powerplant for the 96 P1Y2 bombers that were built before production came to halt at the end of the war, in P1Y2, P1Y2a, P1Y2b and P1Y2c sub-

A potentially formidable aircraft in a variety of roles, the P1Y Ginga was plagued by maintenance problems and played little part in the defence of the homeland.

variants that were armed similarly to the corresponding P1Y1 sub-variants.

Provided that it could be serviced adequately before each operational sortie the P1Y proved to be a formidable aircraft, and it was a disaster for the Japanese navy that at this critical time, when large-scale sorties were required and skilled man-power was at a premium, the Ginga should be so unreliable. Some appreciation of the size of the maintenance problems caused by this aircraft can be gained from the small total of 1,098 built by Nakajima (1,002) and Kawanishi (96). Allocated the Allied codename 'Frances', the P1Y was tried in alternative roles but proved equally disappointing, and the type's brief operational life of only six months was terminated by the end of the Pacific war.

Specification
Yokosuka P1Y1 Ginga

Type: twin-engine medium bomber
Powerplant: two 1,820-hp (1357-kW) Nakajima NK9B Homare 11 18-cylinder radial piston engines
Performance: maximum speed 340 mph (547 km/h) at 19,355 ft (5900 m); cruising speed 230 mph (370 km/h) at 13,125 ft (4000 m); service ceiling 30,840 ft (9400 m); maximum range 3,337 miles (5370 km)
Weights: empty 16,017 lb (7265 kg); maximum take-off 29,762 lb (13500 kg)
Dimensions: span 65 ft 7½ in (20.00 m); length 49 ft 2½ in (15.00 m); height 14 ft 1¼ in (4.30 m); wing area 592.03 sq ft (55.00 m²)
Armament: two 20-mm cannon (one forward-firing and one rear-firing), plus a bombload of up to 2,205 lb (1000 kg) or one 1,764-lb (800-kg) torpedo
Operator: Japanese Navy

INDEX

NOTE: codenames allocated to Japanese aircraft in the Pacific theatre are listed alphabetically under the heading 'Allied Codenames'

A

A5M (Mitsubishi) **192-193, 194**
A6M (Mitsubishi Zero-Sen) **192, 194-197, 203, 214**
A6M2-N (Nakajima) **214-215**
A 44 (Focke-Wulf) **64**
AB-6 (Aichi) **133**
AM-22 (Aichi) **11**
AM-23 (Aichi) **8**
Ar see Arado
AS-1 see Nakajima
AS.14 see Fiat
Aero C-3 **245**
Aero C-4 **28**
Aero C-103 **245**
Aichi AB-6 **133**
Aichi AM-22 **11**
Aichi AM-23 **8**
Aichi B7A Ryusei **8**
Aichi D1A **9**
Aichi D3A **9-10**
Aichi E12A **10**
Aichi E13A **10-11**
Aichi E16A1 Zuiun **11**
Alcione see CRDA
Allied Codenames:
  'Abdul' **221**
  'Alf' **134**
  'Ann' **208**
  'Babs' **206**
  'Betty' **202**
  'Claude' **193**
  'Dinah' **210**
  'Emily' **136**
  'Frances' **251**
  'Frank' **228**
  'George' **138**
  'Grace' **8**
  'Helen' **228**
  'Hickory' **247**
  'Ida' **246**
  'Irving' **220**
  'Jack' **204**
  'Jake' **10-11**
  'Jill' **18**
  'Judy' **248**
  'Kate' **216**
  'Lily' **143**
  'Lorna' **151**
  'Mary' **141**
  'Mavis' **135**
  'Myrt' **218**
  'Nate' **221**
  'Nell' **200**
  'Nick' **142**
  'Oscar' **224**
  'Paul' **11**
  'Peggy' **214**
  'Perry' **140**
  'Pete' **198**
  'Randy' **148**
  'Rex' **138**
  'Rufe' **215**
  'Sally' **207**
  'Sonia' **212**
  'Tillie' **135**
  'Tina' **200**
  'Tojo' **225**
  'Tony' **144**
  'Topsy' **213**
  'Val' **9-10**
  'Willow' **247**
  'Zeke' **194**
Arado Ar 65 **12**
Arado Ar 66 **12**
Arado Ar 67 **12**
Arado Ar 68 **12-14, 17**
Arado Ar 76 **65**
Arado Ar 81 **111**
Arado Ar 96 **14**
Arado Ar 196 **15-16**
Arado Ar 197 **17**
Arado Ar 232 **17-18**
Arado Ar 234 Blitz **18-20, 187**
Ariete (Reggiane Re.2002) **234**
Army Type 1 Advanced Trainer **246**
Army Type 1 Fighter Hayabusa **222**
Army Type 2 Single-seat Fighter Shoki **224**
Army Type 2 Two-seat Fighter Toryu **142**
Army Type 3 Fighter **144**
Army Type 4 Assault Plane **148**
Army Type 4 Fighter Hayate **230**
Army Type 4 Heavy Bomber Hiryu **213**
Army Type 4 Primary Trainer **28**
Army Type 5 Fighter **147**
Army Type 93 Single-engined Bomber **141**
Army Type 95 Fighter **140**
Army Type 97 Command Reconnaissance Plane **205**
Army Type 97 Fighter **220**
Army Type 97 Heavy Bomber **206-207**
Army Type 97 Light bomber **208**
Army Type 98 Direct Co-Operation Plane **246**
Army Type 98 Single-engined Light Bomber **141**
Army Type 99 Advanced Trainer **246**
Army Type 99 Assault Plane **211**
Army Type 99 Twin-engined Light Bomber **143-144**
Army Type 100 Command Reconnaissance Plane **209**
Army Type 100 Heavy Bomber Donryu **226**
Army Type 100 Transport Aircraft **213**
Avia B.34/2 **20**
Avia B.534 **20-22**
Avia B.634 **21**
Avia Bk.534 **21**
Avia C.2B **14**
Avro Lancaster **97**

B

B5N see Nakajima
B6N see Nakajima
B7A see Aichi
B-17 see Boeing
B-24 see Boeing
B-29 see Boeing
B.34/2 see Avia
B.534 see Avia
B.634 see Avia
Ba.65 see Breda
Ba.88 see Breda
Bf 108 see Messerschmitt
Bf 109 see Messerschmitt
Bf 110 see Messerschmitt
Bk.534 see Avia
BR.20 see Fiat
Bü 131 see Bücker
Bü 133 see Bücker
Bü 180 see Bücker
Bü 181 see Bücker
Bv 138 see Blohm and Voss
Bv 222 see Blohm und Voss
Baby see Porte
Bestmann see Bücker
Blitz see Arado
Blohm und Voss Bv 138 **22-23, 45**
Blohm und Voss Bv 22 Wiking **24-25**
Boeing B-17 **182**
Boeing B-29 Superfortress **147, 220, 248**
Borea see Caproni
Breda Ba.65 **25-26**
Breda Ba.88 Lince **27-28**
Bristol Scout **128**
Bücker Bü 131 Jungmann **28-29**
Bücker Bü 133 Jungmeister **29**
Bücker Bü 180 **29**
Bücker Bü 181 Bestmann **28, 29-30**

C

C.2B see Avia
C-3 see Aero
C-4 see Aero
C.V see Fokker
C5M see Mitsubishi
C.6 see Zlin
C6N see Nakajima
C-103 see Aero
C.106 see Zlin
Ca see Caproni
CR see Fiat
Canguru see Savoia-Marchetti
Cap see Mraz
Caproni Ca 100 **34**
Caproni Ca 101 **34**
Caproni Ca 133 **34-35**
Caproni Ca 148 **34-35**
Caproni Bergamaschi Ca 135 **35-36**
Caproni Bergamaschi Ca 306 Borea **36-37**
Caproni Bergamaschi Ca 309 Ghibli **36-37**
Caproni Bergamaschi Ca 310 Libeccio **37-38**
Caproni Bergamaschi Ca 311 **37-38**
Caproni Bergamaschi Ca 312 **37-38**
Caproni Bergamaschi Ca 313 **37-38**
Caproni Bergamaschi Ca 314 **37-38**
CASA 2.111 **89**
CASA 352 **108**
CASA 1145-L **76**
Centauro see Fiat
Chirri see Hispano
Cicogna see Fiat
CMASA ICR.42 **58**
Condor see Focke-Wulf
Consolidated B-24 Liberator **21, 142, 220**
CRDA Cant Z.501 Gabbiano **30-31**
CRDA Cant Z.505 **31**
CRDA Cant Z.506 **31-32**
CRDA Cant Z.508 **31-32**
CRDA Cant Z.509 **32**
CRDA Cant Z.1007 Alcione **32-33**
CRDA Cant Z.1015 **32**
Curtiss P-40 **144**
Curtiss Hawk **55**

D

D1A see Aichi
D3A see Aichi
D4Y see Yokosuka
D.520 see Dewoitine
D.H.60 see de Havilland
Do see Dornier
de Havilland D.H.60 Moth **34**

de Havilland Mosquito **96, 97**
Dewoitine D.520 **21**
DFA Do 17K **40**
DFS 194 **181**
DFS 230 **38-39, 77, 108**
Donryu see Nakajima
Dornier Do 11 **104**
Dornier Do 17 **39-44, 48, 106, 243**
Dornier Do 18 **45-46**
Dornier Do 24 **46-48**
Dornier Do 215 **42-44**
Dornier Do 217 **48-51**
Dornier Do 228 **47**
Dornier Do 317 **50**
Dornier Do 318 **48**
Dornier Do 335 Pfeil **51-52**
Dornier Do 435 **52**
Dornier Do 535 **52**
Dornier Do 635 **52**
Dornier Do P.231 **51**
Dornier Wal **46**

E

E5K see Kawanishi
E7K see Kawanishi
E12A see Aichi
E13A see Aichi
E16A1 see Aichi
Edelkadett see Heinkel

F

F1M see Mitsubishi
F.VIII see Fokker
Fh 104 see Flugzeugbau Halle Hallore
Fi see Fieseler
Fw see Focke-Wulf
Falco (CR.42) see Fiat
Falco (Re.2000) see Reggiane
Falco II see Reggiane
Fiat AS.14 **62**
Fiat BR.20 Cicogna **35, 52-54**
Fiat CR.30 **54-55**
Fiat CR.32 **54-56**
Fiat CR.33 **56**
Fiat CR.40 **56, 57**
Fiat CR.41 **56, 57**
Fiat CR.42 Falco **55, 56-57, 242**
Fiat G.50 **57, 59-60**
Fiat G.55 Centauro **60-61**
Fiat G.56 **60**
Fiat RS.14 **61-62**
Fieseler Fi 97 **62**
Fieseler Fi 98 **98**
Fieseler Fi 156 Storch **62-64**
Fieseler Fi 256 **63**
Flugzeugbau Halle Fh 104 Hallore **243-245**
Focke-Wulf A 44 **64**
Focke-Wulf Fw 44 Stieglitz **64, 243**
Focke-Wulf Fw 56 Stösser **65**

Focke-Wulf Fw 62 **15**
Focke-Wulf Fw 189 Uhu **66-67, 100, 101**
Focke-Wulf Fw 190 **17, 64, 68-73, 75, 121, 128, 170**
Focke-Wulf Fw 190/Ta 154 Mistel **70**
Focke-Wulf Fw 200 Condor **73-75**
Focke-Wulf Ta 152 **75-76, 128**
Focke-Wulf Ta 153 **75**
Focke-Wulf Ta 154 **96**
Fokker C.V **247**
Fokker F.VIII **247**
Folgore see Macchi

G

G3M see Mitsubishi
G4M see Mitsubishi
G6M see Mitsubishi
G.50 see Fiat
G.55 see Fiat
G.56 see Fiat
Gö 9 see Göppingen
Go see Gotha
Gabbiano see CRDA
Gekko see Nakajima
Ghibli see Caproni
Gigant (Me 231) see Messerschmitt
Gigant (Me 323) see Messerschmitt
Ginga see Yokosuka
Gomhouria see Heliopolis
Göppingen Gö 9 **51**
Gotha Go 145 **12, 76**
Gotha Go 242 **77-78**
Gotha Go 244 **77-78**
Greif see Heinkel

H

H3K2 see Kawanishi
H6K see Kawanishi
H8K see Kawanishi
HA-132-L Chirri see Hispano
Ha 137 see Hamburger Flugzeugbau
Ha 138 see Hamburger Flugzeugbau
He see Heinkel
Hs see Henschel
Hallore see Flugzeugbau Halle **243-245**
Hamburger Flugzeugbau Ha 137 **111**
Hamburger Flugzeugbau Ha 138 **22**
Hawk see Curtiss
Hawker Hurricane **176**
Hayabusa see Nakajima
Hayate see Nakajima
Heinkel He 45 **78-79, 99, 100**
Heinkel He 46 **79-80, 99, 100, 243**

Heinkel He 49 **80**
Heinkel He 50 **15**
Heinkel He 51 **80-81, 162**
Heinkel He 52 **80**
Heinkel He 59 **81-82, 90**
Heinkel He 60 **82-83**
Heinkel He 61 **78**
Heinkel He 70 **83**
Heinkel He 72 Edelkadett **83**
Heinkel He 72 Kadett **83**
Heinkel He 74 **65**
Heinkel He 111 **77, 83-90, 106,
  109, 110, 190**
Heinkel He 112 **162**
Heinkel He 115 **90-93**
Heinkel He 118 **111**
Heinkel He 162 Salamander
  93-94
Heinkel He 176 **181**
Heinkel He 177 Greif **95,96, 130**
Heinkel He 219 Uhu **96-98, 180**
Heinkel He 280 **186**
Heinkel P.1041 **95**
Heinkel P.1060 **96**
Hejja (Hungary) **234**
Heliopolis Gomhouria **30**
Henschel Hs 122 **99**
Henschel Hs 123, **98-99, 112**
Henschel Hs 126 **99-101**
Henschel Hs 129 **101-103**
Hien see Kawasaki
Hiryu see Mitsubishi
Hispano HA-132-L Chirri **56**
Hurricane see Hawker

I

I-15 see Polikarpov
I-16 see Polikarpov
I-153 see Polikarpov
I-270 (Zh) (MiG) see Mikoyan-
  Gurevich
ICR.42 (CMASA) **58**
Il see Ilyushin
Ilyushin Il-2 **172**
Ilyushin Il-10 **172**

J

J 1 see Junkers
J1N see Nakajima
J2M see Mitsubishi
J8M1 see Mitsubishi
J 20 (Sweden) **234**
Ju see Junkers
Jungmann see Bücker
Jungmeister see Bücker
Junkers J 1 **103**
Junkers Ju 52 **103**
Junkers Ju 52/3m **17, 103-109,
  190**
Junkers Ju 86 **109-111**
Junkers Ju 87 Stuka **65, 99,
  111-118**
Junkers Ju 88 **50, 89, 118-127,**

128, 129, 131
Junkers Ju 88 Mistel composites
  128
Junkers Ju 89 **130**
Junkers Ju 90 **130, 131, 190**
Junkers Ju 188 **128-130, 132**
Junkers Ju 248 **182**
Junkers Ju 252 **108**
Junkers Ju 288 **128, 131, 132**
Junkers Ju 290 **130-131**
Junkers Ju 322 **190**
Junkers Ju 352 **108**
Junkers Ju 388 **96, 129, 131-132**
Junkers Ju 390 **131**
Junkers W34 **132-133**

K

K5Y (Yokosuka) **249**
K9W1 (Watanabe) **28**
K11W (Kyushu Shiragiku)
  150-151
K-65 (Mraz Cap) **64**
Ka-1 (Kayaba) **149**
Ka-2 (Kayaba) **149**
Ka-9 (Mitsubishi) **199**
Ka-14 (Mitsubishi) **192**
Ka-15 (Mitsubishi) **199**
Ka-17 (Mitsubishi) **198**
KB-1 (Bulgaria) **34**
KD-1A (Kellet) **149**
K.F.1 (Short) **134**
Ki-2 (Mitsubishi) **208**
Ki-3 (Kawasaki) **140, 208**
Ki-10 (Kawasaki) **140, 193**
Ki-15 (Mitsubishi) **205-206, 209**
Ki-18 (Mitsubishi) **193**
Ki-19 (Nakajima) **206**
Ki-21 (Mitsubishi) **53, 206-208,
  212, 226**
Ki-27 (Nakajima) **220-221, 222**
Ki-28 (Kawasaki) **220**
Ki-30 (Mitsubishi) **141, 208, 211**
Ki-32 (Kawasaki) **140-141**
Ki-33 (Mitsubishi) **193**
Ki-35 (Mitsubishi) **246**
Ki-36 (Tachikawa) **245-246**
Ki-38 (Kawasaki) **141**
Ki-43 (Nakajima Hayabusa)
  222-224
Ki-44 (Nakajima Shoki) **224-226**
Ki-45 (Kawasaki Toryu) **141-143**
Ki-46 (Mitsubishi) **209-211**
Ki-48 (Kawasaki) **143-144**
Ki-49 (Nakajima Donryu)
  226-228
Ki-51 (Mitsubishi) **211-212**
Ki-54 (Tachikawa) **246-247**
Ki-55 (Tachikawa) **246**
Ki-57 (Mitsubishi) **212, 213**
Ki-58 (Nakajima) **228**
Ki-60 (Kawasaki) **144, 224**
Ki-61 (Kawasaki Hien) **144-146,**

147
Ki-67 (Mitsubishi Hiryu) **213-214**
Ki-69 (Mitsubishi) **214**
Ki-71 (Mitsubishi) **212**
Ki-72 (Tachikawa) **246**
Ki-84 (Nakajima Hayate) **228-230**
Ki-96 (Kawasaki) **142, 148**
Ki-97 (Mitsubishi) **214**
Ki-100 (Kawasaki) **147-148**
Ki-102 (Kawasaki) **148**
Ki-106 (Nakajima) **230**
Ki-109 (Mitsubishi) **214**
Ki-110 (Tachikawa) **246**
Ki-111 (Tachikawa) **247**
Ki-112 (Mitsubishi) **214**
Ki-113 (Nakajima) **230**
Ki-114 (Tachikawa) **247**
Ki-115 (Nakajima Tsurugi)
  230-231
Ki-116 (Nakajima) **230**
Ki-200 (Mitsubishi) **183**
Kl 25 see Klemm
Kadett see Heinkel
Kawanishi E5K **133**
Kawanishi E7K **133-134**
Kawanishi H3K2 **134**
Kawanishi H6K **134-135**
Kawanishi H8K **136-137**
Kawanishi N1K Kyofu
  137-138, 214
Kawanishi N1K1-J Shiden
  138-140
Kawanishi N1K2-J Shiden
  138-140
Kawanishi N1K3-J **138**
Kawanishi N1K4-J **138**
Kawanishi N1K5-J **138**
Kawanishi Type Q **134**
Kawanishi Type R **134**
Kawanishi Type S **134**
Kawasaki Ki-3 **140, 208**
Kawasaki Ki-10 **140, 193**
Kawasaki Ki-28 **220**
Kawasaki Ki-32 **140-141**
Kawasaki Ki-38 **141**
Kawasaki Ki-45 Toryu **141-143**
Kawasaki Ki-48 **143-144**
Kawasaki Ki-60 **144, 224**
Kawasaki Ki-61 Hien **144-146,
  147**
Kawasaki Ki-96 **142, 148**
Kawasaki Ki-100 **147-148**
Kawasaki Ki-102 **148**
Kayaba Ka-1 **149**
Kayaba Ka-2 **149**
Kellet KD 1A **149**
Klemm Kl 35 **149-150**
Klemm L 25 **149**
Komet see Messerschmitt
Kyofu see Kawanishi
Kyushu K11W Shiragiku **150-151**
Kyushu Q1W Tokai **151**

3Y see Mitsubishi
AM see Mitsubishi
L 25 see Klemm
Lancaster see Avro
Letov Š 328 **152-153**
Letov Š 428 **152**
Levente see Repülöpégyàr
Libeccio see Caproni
Liberator see Consolidated
Lightning see Lockheed
Lince see Breda
Lockheed P.38 Lightning **203**

M

MC-20 see Mitsubishi
MC-21 see Mitsubishi
MC.72 see Macchi
MC.200 see Macchi
MC.201 see Macchi
MC.202 see Macchi
MC.205V see Macchi
MC.206 see Macchi
MC.207 see Macchi
Me see Messerschmitt
M.S. see Morane Saulnier
MXY7 see Yokosuka
Macchi MC.72 **153**
Macchi MC.200 Saetta **153-154, 155, 232**
Macchi MC.201 **154**
Macchi MC.202 Folgore **153, 154, 155-156, 157**
Macchi MC.205V Veltro **157-159**
Macchi MC.206 **158**
Macchi MC.207 **158**
Marsupiale see Savoia-Marchetti
Martin 139 **46**
Martinet see SNCAC
Martinet see SNCAC
Meridionali Ro.37bis **159**
Meridionali Ro.43 **159-160**
Meridionali Ro.44 **160**
Messerschitt Bf 108 Taifun **160-161**
Messerschmitt Bf 109 **68, 128, 144, 161-173, 224, 232**
Messerschmitt Bf 110 **50, 124, 141, 174-181, 184, 190**
Messerschmitt Me 163 Komet **181-184**
Messerschmitt Me 208 **161**
Messerschmitt Me 209 **164**
Messerschmitt Me 210 **176, 178, 180, 184-186**
Messerschmitt Me 262 **18, 75, 186-189**
Messerschmitt Me 321 Gigant **88, 190-191**
Messerschmitt Me 323 Gigant **190-191**
Messerschmitt Me 410 **178, 184-186**

Messerschmitt P.1065 **186**
MiG I-270 (Zh) **183**
Mistel composites see Junkers
Mitsubishi A5M **192-193, 194**
Mitsubishi A6M Zero-Sen **192, 194-197, 203, 214**
Mitsubishi C5M **206**
Mitsubishi F1M **198**
Mitsubishi G3M **199-200**
Mitsubishi G4M **200-203, 213**
Mitsubishi G6M **202**
Mitsubishi J2M Raiden **203-205**
Mitsubishi J8M1 **183**
Mitsubishi Ka-9 **199**
Mitsubishi Ka-14 **192**
Mitsubishi Ka-15 **199**
Mitsubishi Ka-17 **198**
Mitsubishi Ki-2 **208**
Mitsubishi Ki-15 **205-206, 209**
Mitsubishi Ki-18 **193**
Mitsubishi Ki-21 **53, 206-208, 212, 226**
Mitsubishi Ki-30 **141, 208, 211**
Mitsubishi Ki-33 **193**
Mitsubishi Ki-35 **246**
Mitsubishi Ki-46 **209-211**
Mitsubishi Ki-51 **211-212**
Mitsubishi Ki-57 **212-213**
Mitsubishi Ki-67 Hiryu **213-214**
Mitsubishi Ki-69 **214**
Mitsubishi Ki-71 **212**
Mitsubishi Ki-97 **214**
Mitsubishi Ki-109 **214**
Mitsubishi Ki-112 **214**
Mitsubishi Ki-200 **183**
Mitsubishi L3Y **199**
Mitsubishi L4M **213**
Mitsubishi MC-20 **212-213**
Mitsubishi MC-21 **207**
Morane-Saulnier M.S.500 **64**
Morane-Saulnier M.S.501 **64**
Morane-Saulnier M.S.502 **64**
Mosquito see de Havilland
Moth see de Havilland
Mraz K-65 Cap **64**
Mustang see North American

N

N1K see Kawanishi Kyofu
N1K1-J see Kawanishi Shiden
N1K2-J see Kawanishi Shiden
N1K3-J see Kawanishi
N1K4-J see Kawanishi
N1K5-J see Kawanishi
NC 701 see SNCAC
NC 702 see SNCAC
Nakajima A6M2-N **214-215**
Nakajima AS-1 **214**
Nakajima B5N **215-217**
Nakajima B6N Tenzan **8, 217-218**
Nakajima C6N Saiun **218-219**
Nakajima J1N Gekko **219-220**

Nakajima Ki-19 **206**
Nakajima Ki-27 **220-221, 222**
Nakajima Ki-43 Hayabusa **222-224**
Nakajima Ki-44 Shoki **224-226**
Nakajima Ki-49 Donryu **226-228**
Nakajima Ki-58 **228**
Nakajima Ki-84 Hayate **228-230**
Nakajima Ki-106 **230**
Nakajima Ki-113 **230**
Nakajima Ki-115 Tsurugi **230-231**
Nakajima Ki-116 **230**
Nakajima Type K **216-216**
Nakajima Type P.E **220**
Navy Bomber Ginga **251**
Navy Carrier Attack Bomber Ryusei **8**
Navy Carrier Attack Bomber Tenzan **217**
Navy Carrier Reconnaissance Plane Saiun **218**
Navy Experimental 16-Shi Carrier Attack Bomber **8**
Navy Fighter Seaplane Kyofu **138**
Navy Interceptor Fighter Raiden **204**
Navy Interceptor Fighter Shiden **138**
Navy Interceptor Fighter Shiden KAI **139**
Navy Operations Trainer Shiragiku **150**
Navy Patrol Plane Tokai **151**
Navy Reconnaissance Seaplane Zuiun **11**
Navy Suicide Attacker Ohka **250**
Navy Suisei Carrier Bomber **248**
Navy Type 0 Carrier Fighter **195**
Navy Type 0 Observation Seaplane **198**
Navy Type 0 Reconnaissance Seaplane **10**
Navy Type 1 Attack Bomber **201**
Navy Type 2 Carrier Reconnaissance Seaplane Suisei **248**
Navy Type 2 Floatplane Fighter **215**
Navy Type 2 Flying-Boat **136**
Navy Type 2 Primary Trainer **28**
Navy Type 2 Reconnaissance Plane **219**
Navy Type 2 Transport Flying-Boat Seiku **136**
Navy Type 90-3 Reconnaissance Seaplane **133**
Navy Type 90-11 Flying-Boat **134**
Navy Type 93 Intermediate Trainer **249**
Navy Type 94 Reconnaissance Seaplane **133**

Navy Type 96 Attack Bomber **199**

Navy Type 96 Carrier Fighter **192**

Navy Type 96 Transport Aircraft **199**

Navy Type 97 Carrier Attack Bomber **215**

Navy Type 97 Flying-Boat **135**

Navy Type 98 Reconnaissance Plane **206**

Navy Type 99 Carrier Bomber **9**

Noralpha see Nord

Nord 1001 Pingouin **161**

Nord 1002 Pingouin **161**

Nord 1101 Noralpha **161**

North American P-51 Mustang **158, 228**

O

Ohka see Yokosuka

P

P1Y see Yokosuka

P-35 see Seversky

P-38 see Lockheed

P-40 see Curtiss

P-47 see Republic

P.50 see Piaggio

P-51 see North American

P.108 see Piaggio

P.133 see Piaggio

P.1041 see Heinkel

P.1060 see Heinkel

P.1065 see Messerschmitt

Po-2 see Polikarpov

Pfeil see Dornier

Piaggio P.50 **231**

Piaggio P.108 **231-232**

Piaggio P.133 **232**

Pingouin (1001) see Nord

Pingouin (1002) see Nord

Pipistrello see Savoia-Marchetti

Polikarpov I-15 **55**

Polikarpov I-16 **55, 205, 221**

Polikarpov I-153 **20**

Polikarpov Po-2 **76**

Porte Baby **128**

Q

Q1W see Kyushu

R

Re. see Reggiane

Ro.37 see Romeo

Ro. see Meridionali

RS.14 see Fiat

Raiden see Mitsubishi

Reggiane Re.2000 Falco **232-235**

Reggiane Re.2001 Falco II **234**

Reggiane Re.2002 Ariete **234**

Reggiane Re.2005 Sagittario **234**

Republic P-47 Thunderbolt **228**

Repülöpégyàr Levente **235-236**

Romeo Ro.37 **159**

Ryusei see Aichi B7A

S

S-42 see Sikorsky

Š 328 see Letov

Š 428 see Letov

SB-2 see Tupolev

Si 204 see Siebel

SK 15 (Sweden) **150**

SK 25 (Sweden) **30**

S.M. see Savoia-Marchetti

Saetta see Macchi

Sagittario see Reggiane

Saiun see Nakajima

Salamander see Heinkel

Savoia-Marchetti S.M.73 **240**

Savoia-Marchetti S.M.75 Marsupiale **242**

Savoia-Marchetti S.M.79 Sparviero **236-240**

Savoia-Marchetti S.M.81 Pipistrello **240-242**

Savoia-Marchetti S.M.82 Canguru **57, 242-243**

Savoia-Marchetti S.M.83 **238**

Scout see Bristol

Seversky P-35 **232**

Shiden see Kawanishi

Shiragiku see Kyushu

Shoki see Nakajima

Short K.F.1 **134**

Short Sunderland **136**

Short-Mayo Composite **128**

Siebel Si 204 **243-246**

Sikorsky S-42 **134**

SNCAC NC 701 Martinet **244**

SNCAC NC 702 Martinet **244**

Sólyom (Weiss WM21) **247**

Sparviero see Savoia-Marchetti

Spitfire see Supermarine

Stieglitz see Focke-Wulf

Storch see Fieseler

Stösser see Focke-Wulf

Stuka see Junkers

Suisei see Yokosuka

Sunderland see Short

Superfortress see Boeing

Supermarine Spitfire **68, 110, 176**

T

Ta see Focke-Wulf

Tachikawa Ki-36 **245-246**

Tachikawa Ki-54 **246-247**

Tachikawa Ki-55 **246**

Tachikawa Ki-72 **246**

Tachikawa Ki-110 **246**

Tachikawa Ki-111 **247**

Tachikawa Ki-114 **247**

Tachikawa Y-59 **246**

Taifun see Messerschmitt

Tenzan see Nakajima

Thunderbolt see Republic

Tokai see Kyushu

Toryu see Kawasaki

Tsurugi see Nakajima

Tupolev SB-2 **142**

Type 2.111 see CASA

Type 139 see Martin

Type 194 see DFS

Type 230 see DFS

Type 352 see CASA

Type 1001 see Nord Pingouin

Type 1002 see Nord Pingouin

Type 1101 see Nord Noralpha

Type 1145-L see CASA

Type K see Nakajima

Type P.E see Nakajima

Type Q see Kawanishi

Type R see Kawanishi

Type S see Kawanishi

U

Uhu (Fw 189) see Focke-Wulf

Uhu (He 219) see Heinkel

V

Veltro see Macchi MC.205V

Vickers Wellington **174**

W

W34 see Junkers

WM21 see Weiss

Wal see Dornier

Watanabe K9W1 **28**

Weiss WM21 Sólyom **247**

Wellington see Vickers

Wiking see Blohm und Voss

Y

Y-59 see Tachikawa

Yokosuka D4Y Suisei **8, 247-249**

Yokosuka K5Y **249**

Yokosuka MXY7 Ohka **202, 203, 250**

Yokosuka P1Y Ginga **250, 251**

Z

Z.281 see Zlin

Z.381 see Zlin

Z.501 see CRDA

Z.505 see CRDA

Z.506 see CRDA

Z.508 see CRDA

Z.509 see CRDA

Z.1007 see CRDA

Z.1015 see CRDA

Zero-Sen see Mitsubishi

Zlin C.6 **30**

Zlin C.106 **30**

Zlin Z.281 **30**

Zlin Z.381 **30**

Zuiun see Aichi